NUMBER TWO HUNDRED

# THE OLD FARMER'S ALMANAC

CALCULATED ON A NEW AND IMPROVED PLAN FOR THE YEAR OF OUR LORD

## 2022

Being the 2nd after Leap Year and (until July 4) 246th year of American Independence

FITTED FOR BOSTON AND THE NEW ENGLAND STATES, WITH SPECIAL CORRECTIONS AND CALCULATIONS TO ANSWER FOR ALL THE UNITED STATES.

Containing, besides the large number of Astronomical Calculations and the Farmer's Calendar for every month in the year, a variety of NEW, USEFUL, & ENTERTAINING MATTER.

### ESTABLISHED IN 1792
### BY ROBERT B. THOMAS (1766–1846)

*There are only two days in the year when nothing can be done. One is called Yesterday and the other is called Tomorrow. Today is the right day to Love, Believe, Do, and mostly Live.*

–His Holiness the 14th Dalai Lama, Tenzin Gyatso, Tibetan Buddhist monk (b. 1935)

Cover design registered U.S. Trademark Office

Copyright © 2021 by Yankee Publishing Incorporated, An Employee-Owned Company
ISSN 0078-4516

Library of Congress Card No. 56-29681

*Cover illustration by Steven Noble • Original wood engraving (above) by Randy Miller*

The Old Farmer's Almanac • Almanac.com
P.O. Box 520, Dublin, NH 03444 • 603-563-8111

# CONTENTS

## 2022 TRENDS
Facts to Ponder and Forecasts to Watch For   6

74

42

58

# PREVAILING CUSTOMS

*Had it not been the prevailing custom to usher these periodical pieces into the world by a preface, I would have excused myself the trouble of writing, and you of reading one to this: for if it be well executed, a preface will add nothing to its merit; if otherwise, it will be far from supplying its defects.*

So wrote the founder of this Almanac, 26-year-old farmer and teacher Robert Bailey Thomas (the gentleman pictured at right on our cover) on this page of his first edition on the eve of its publication in Sterling, Massachusetts, on September 15, 1792.

He believed that his Almanac—"calculated on a new and improved plan for the year of our Lord, 1793"—needed no introduction.

He offered it as a comprehensive and trustworthy package of "new, useful, and entertaining matter" to an agrarian New England populace eager for exactly that: reliable Moon phase and sunrise/-set times (so important to planting traditions and farm chores), no-nonsense reminders and advisories (e.g., February: "If you neglected cutting timber last month, be sure to cut it now"), timesaving recipes ("a new method of making butter"), home remedies (for ailments afflicting people and animals), court dates, distances between places, math challenges, ac-counts of remarkable events (e.g., in 1571, England's Marcley Hill continuously moved for 2 days, carrying with it trees, hedges, and cattle), and more—all in a mere 46-page booklet.

Thomas's first edition was indeed well executed and without defect. Fulfilling his lifelong goal, it sold out, thus launching him on a career that would last another 53 years (edition years for which he wrote prefaces, later dubbed "To Patrons" in appreciation of readers' patronage) and setting the title—*The [Old] Farmer's Almanac*—on a course that would eventually establish the book as the oldest continuously published periodical in North America.

This is how the Almanac that you hold in your hands began and the reason why its execution—accuracy, relevance, usefulness, and entertainment—continues, we hope, to meet (or exceed!) the expectations of readers—*patrons*—like you. Thank you for your patronage!

–J. S., JUNE 2021

*However, it is by our works and not our words that we would be judged. These, we hope, will sustain us in the humble though proud station we have so long held in the name of*

*Your obedient servant,*

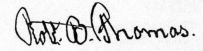

# 2022 TRENDS

## ON THE FARM

*"Municipal and national policies are advancing urban agriculture."*
*–Michael Levenston, executive director, City Farmer, Vancouver, B.C.*

### FORWARD-THINKING FARMERS AND RANCHERS ARE:

- renting out livestock to families to teach children responsibility or to other farmers to try before buying
- using Web sites to accept nutritional assistance programs and arrange food pickup or delivery
- inviting volunteers to do farm chores for increased fitness

**BUZZWORD**
**Farmfluencer:** a farmer who promotes the farming lifestyle

### CONSUMER-CONSCIOUS FARMERS ARE:

- getting the word out on their environmentally friendly practices:

"More farmers are using programs that offer traceability through the supply chain."
*–Gary Joiner, Texas Farm Bureau*

- getting food to people who order directly from the farm:

"Farmers are trying to obtain an economically feasible solution to selling online, with delivery or safe central pickup."
*–Phil Blalock, executive director, National Association of Farmers' Market Nutrition Programs*

**FOLLOW US:**

## ECO-CONSCIOUS FARMERS ARE:

- leaving grasslands undisturbed to leave carbon in the soil, in exchange for carbon credits (which companies buy to offset their own emissions)
- joining neighbors to convert a portion of their land to bee habitat

## TECH TOOLS

In-demand software features for U.S. and Canadian farmers . . .

- yield mapping
- crop-input record-keeping
- imagery (satellite, plane, or drone)
- weather data

## PATIENCE, PLEASE!

"Order-to-grow will emerge as a new way to reduce food waste."
*–Cecelia Girr, director of cultural strategy, TBWA Worldwide*

## THE FUTURE OF FARMING

- Vertical farms, hydroponics, aquaponics, and greenhouses are surging.

"More controlled-environment agriculture projects will be launched."
*–Sylvain Charlebois, director, Dalhousie University's Agri-Food Analytics Lab, Halifax, N.S.*

## COMING SOON

Apps that track who is growing our food and its maturity stage
*(continued)*

## BY THE NUMBERS

**$580:** 6 months' rent for two egg-laying hens and a chicken coop

**$4,100:** average cost of U.S. cropland per acre

**2.76 million:** square footage of the world's largest greenhouse (in Morehead, Ky.)

**More bees, please:**

**82.9 million:** pounds of honey produced annually by Canada's honeybees

**$1.5 billion:** value that wild bee pollination contributes to seven U.S. crops (apples, highbush blueberries, sweet and tart cherries, almonds, watermelons, pumpkins)

**20%:** increase in yield if almond trees are bee-pollinated

# IN THE GARDEN

"Gardeners are planting in stripes—
one row vegetables, one row flowers."

*–C. L. Fornari, author,* The Cocktail Hour Garden *(St. Lynn's Press, 2016)*

### GARDENER GARB

- pants with wraparound hip pockets and/or reinforced knees
- kimono-style jackets
- field shirts with extra pockets

### NEW VEGGIE VARIETIES

- 'Hampton' one-cut lettuce
- 'Prospera' Italian large leaf (4-inch) DMR basil
- disease-resistant 'Marciano' red butterhead lettuce
*–Johnny's Selected Seeds*

- sweet 'Bitesize' hybrid brussels sprouts

- 'Blue Prince' hybrid pumpkin
- 'Depurple' hybrid cauliflower
*–Jung Seed*

- compact 'Hasta La Pasta' winter squash
- 'Veranda Red' cherry tomato (a windowsill houseplant)

'DEPURPLE' CAULIFLOWER

- early-ripening 'Midnight Moon' hybrid eggplant
*–W. Atlee Burpee & Company*

### HARVEST HACKS

- Backyard growers are saving seeds to grow and/or swap— thus saving money and getting rare varieties.

- Companies are installing gardens in yards of people who pay for weeding, tending, and harvesting.

### MADE FOR THE SHADE

"Shade-loving plants are in demand in

*(continued)*

FOLLOW US:

9

urban areas without sunny growing space."
*–Katie Rotella, Ball Horticultural*

● Carnival series 'Cinnamon Stick' and 'Burgundy Blast' compact coral bells *(Heuchera)*

**'CINNAMON STICK' CORAL BELLS**

## NATURAL IS NICE

"Rewilding" gardeners are . . .
● returning a portion or all of their yard to its natural state
● leaving gaps in fences to allow passage by rabbits and other small wildlife

## IN-DEMAND HOUSEPLANTS

● Australian tree fern
● *Calathea orbifolia*
● council tree
● 'Fabian' aralia
● ruffled fan palm
*–Hilton Carter, plant stylist and author of* Wild Creations *(CICO Books, 2021)*

---

**BUZZWORD**
**Plantrepreneur:** someone who makes a living promoting plants—and themselves

## TINY IS TOPS

"As new gardeners learn the ropes, tiny plants that grow faster are all the rage."
*–Katie Dubow, president, Garden Media Group*

*Multiseason smaller solutions:*
● 'Autumn Starburst' and 'Autumn Majesty' dwarf azaleas that

---

**BY THE NUMBERS**

**1.7%** of Canadians grow all of the fruit and vegetables that they eat.

**23.1 million** U.S. adults have converted some lawn to a natural or wildflower landscape.

**36.8 million** U.S. adults have bought at least one plant because it was native to their area.

---

flower across three seasons
*–Encore Azalea*

● 'Little Miss Figgy', which bears figs in spring and fall
*–Southern Living Plant Collection*

## SMALL-SPACE GARDENERS ARE . . .

*Hanging in baskets:*
● 'Midnight Cascade' blueberries with white, bell-shape flowers
*–Bushel and Berry*

**'MIDNIGHT CASCADE' BLUEBERRIES**

*Planting in small pots:*
● 'Red Velvet' and 'Cocoa' tomatoes
*–PanAmerican Seed*

## NO FLOWERS? NO WORRIES!

"The no-flower 'boom without the bloom' foliage look is trending."
*–Katie Rotella*

● Indoor/outdoor varieties include 'Shangri La' philodendron and 'Gryphon' begonia
*(continued)*

---

FOLLOW US:

## GOOD EATS

"Consumers will balance their desire for plant-based alternatives with actual plants to maximize nutritional benefits and watch their wallets."

*–Melanie Bartelme, global food analyst, Mintel Food & Drink*

### GOOD FOR THE GLOBE

"There's more prominence and appreciation of regional ingredients from parts of the world that are often overlooked."

*–Denise Purcell, Specialty Food Association*

- from Cambodia: chile pastes

- from Senegal: fonio (an ancient grain)

- from Nigeria: cassava grits

### HERE NOW

- grocery stores that sell only plant-based products

- peel-and-stick patches that keep takeout food from getting soggy

- "upcycled" food products using *(continued)*

### BY THE NUMBERS

**Food stats, for Canada:**

**80%** of consumers will pay extra for produce that's locally grown.

**$12,667:** amount that households spend on food, annually

**600,000:** the vegan population

**$1,766:** value of food waste, per household

**20%** of consumers never eat food past its expiration date.

**Snack stats, for the U.S.:**

**7%** of consumers snack all day rather than consume meals.

**2.7:** number of food and beverage items consumed each time people snack

**530:** number of between-meal snacks, per capita, annually, in 2020

FOLLOW US:

ingredients or by-products that would have been wasted

## GOOD FOR YOU

Health-conscious shoppers are buying more legumes and other veggies, plus other whole foods—for example:

- chickpea flour
- meat-free "jerky"
- nut butters made with powdered mushrooms

"Carts and food trucks will collaborate with grocery and hardware stores to create shopping events."
*–Dana McCauley, director of new venture creation, Research Innovation Office, University of Guelph, Ont.*

## SERVING UP SUCCESS

Restaurant chefs are meeting customers' needs . . .

### BUZZWORD
**Restaurmart:** eatery selling its own packaged food onsite for takeout
*–Phil Lempert, Supermarket Guru.com*

- *offsite:* by setting up curbside pop-ups in high-traffic locations
- *virtually:* by teaching how to make favorite dishes online
- *at home:* by providing music playlists and plating instructions for takeout meals to replicate the ambiance of the restaurant where they were made
*–Dana McCauley*

## FLAVORS WE'RE CRAVING

- maple syrup with edible glitter
- flash-frozen cups of coffee (as is or to be reconstituted with hot water)
- oat milk powder (after oats are pressed for milk)
- vacuum-fried salmon skins (left over after the fish are filleted)
*–Denise Purcell*

## FOOD ON THE MOVE

- Mobile grocery stores in trucks visit neighborhoods, and shoppers stroll through trailer "aisles." Trucks are then restocked before heading to the next location.
- Groceries in temperature-controlled boxes are delivered to homes at any time, without worry about food spoilage.
- Restaurant kitchens built for takeout orders are occupying former retail spaces and parking lots.

## VAUNTED VENDING

The most tempting vending machines . . .

- offer fresh, healthy food, restocked daily
- cook pizza, quiche, and croissants on demand
- grind coffee beans to order    *(continued)*

FOLLOW US:  f  P  (twitter)  (instagram)

# OUR ANIMAL FRIENDS

"The ability to interface directly with veterinarians will become a new standard for pet wearables."
*–Daniel Granderson, Packaged Facts*

## CATS AND DOGS ARE DINING ON . . .

- pet food with insect-based protein (fly larvae that are fed food waste; crickets)
- ancient grains (quinoa, millet, buckwheat)
- plant-based ingredients (kale, blueberries, spinach)

## FLYING OFF SHELVES

- breed-specific subscription pet food services

### BY THE NUMBERS

**84.9 million** U.S. households have at least one pet.

**14%** of current pet owners got a dog in 2020.

**12%** of current pet owners got a cat in 2020.

**47%** of pet owners are buying lower-cost store brands of pet food more frequently.

- pet bowls that automatically reorder food
- toys, leashes, and collars made from recycled materials

## HEALTHY PETS ARE HAPPY PETS

"There is increasing demand for products touting mental health benefits for pets."
*–Daniel Granderson*

- supplements to calm pets during noisy times or travel

*(continued)*

FOLLOW US:

- dog pillows shaped for a more comfortable head position and calmer sleep
- crates that play soothing music

## NATURAL, NATURALLY

"Consumers are interested in pet food labels. They're looking for natural ingredients and nothing artificial."
*–Glenn A. Polyn, editor in chief, Pet Age*

## PET TECH

In-demand devices monitor a pet's activities, vital signs, body functions, and location.
*–Daniel Granderson*

## FELINE FRENZY

"Cats are an underserved demographic in the pet food and pet durables market. We'll see more and better products and services

and more marketing attention for cats."
*–David Lummis, lead pet analyst, Packaged Facts*

## HEY, SPORT!

More than ever, we're working out alongside our pets . . .

- *kayaking* with canine life vests featuring top-mounted handles for owners to grab in case of emergency

- *running* with leashes that cinch around waists for hands-free exercise

- *hiking* with boots on dogs that protect paws and provide traction

- *camping* with sleeping bags made to fit dogs

## PET PERKS

"Pet products are focusing more on environmental friendliness and the use of quality, human-grade items and ingredients."
*–Jamie Baxter, American Pet Products Association*

*Pet-centric homes feature . . .*
- end tables that double as pet beds
- litter-box planters
- pet-size Murphy beds
- in-ground dog waste composting units

## TALK TO ME!

- Collars can identify a dog's mood based on the sound of its bark.
- Owners are training pets to use push-button audio devices to "speak." *(continued)*

# YOUR HEALTH OUTLOOK

"The 'food as medicine' approach will topple our reliance on pharmaceuticals. Doctor and farmer collaborations will have us trading pills for produce."

*–Skyler Hubler, cultural strategist, TBWA Worldwide*

## FOR SAVVIER SHUT-EYE

- Practice "Circadian eating": Eat in daylight, stop after dark.
- Wear blue light–blocking glasses at night.
- Don sleepwear that adjusts its temperature.
- Use kill switches to shut off all lights and Wi-fi in a room.
- Use lights that automatically go from bright blue-light in daytime to warmer hues at night to boost melatonin levels.

### BY THE NUMBERS

**51%** of consumers are very or extremely likely to tell their doctors when they disagree with them.

**50%** of people who use fitness- and health-tracking devices share the data with their doctors.

## MANDATORY MENTAL HEALTH DAYS

Companies are offering extra "holidays" and requiring that stressed-out employees take them.

## IN DEVELOPMENT

- technology to reprogram cells to speed up healing

## FOOD TO HELP YOU FEEL BETTER

- Community health programs are connecting low-income residents with local produce.
- Doctors are writing prescriptions for produce redeemable at farmers' markets.

*(continued)*

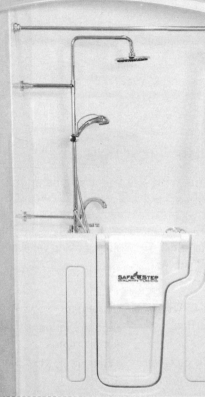

## AROUND THE HOUSE

*"We're seeing sleek, minimal rooms with statement furnishings."*
–Ana Cummings, president, Alberta chapter, Decorators and Designers Association of Canada

### SPACING OUT

"We are utilizing all of our available spaces in our home. Rooms that are adaptable, ergonomic, and private are important as we connect our health with our physical spaces."
–Kelly DeVore, chair, interior architecture & design, Columbus College of Art & Design

### DOUBLE DUTY

- Underutilized walk-in closets are being converted to workout spaces, offices, or guest rooms.
- Greenhouses are becoming dining rooms.
- Tables with adjustable heights are used as desks or dining tables.

### HOME OFFICE OPTIONS

- refitted garden sheds
- leased pods on lawns
- free-standing buildings, with French doors and covered porches

### COLORS FOR HOMES

- kitchens: green marble countertops and bright blue cabinets
- bedrooms: cobalt blues; beige with black accents
- bathrooms: pale blues; golden yellows
- living rooms: teals; light grays

### IN DEMAND

- multifunction, flexible rooms
- electric car docking stations

–American Institute of Architects Home Design Trends Survey

### IN DEVELOPMENT

- windows of transparent wood, which is safer during extreme winds—being nonshattering—and more efficient than glass

*(continued)*

# FIREWOOD ALERT!

## You have the power to protect forests and trees!

# BUY IT WHERE YOU BURN IT.

Pests like the invasive emerald ash borer can hitchhike in your firewood. You can prevent the spread of these damaging insects and diseases by following these firewood tips:

▶ Buy locally harvested firewood at or near your destination.

▶ Buy certified heat-treated firewood ahead of time, if available.

▶ Gather firewood on site when permitted.

## What might be in your firewood?

**GYPSY MOTH** is a devastating pest of oaks and other trees. Female moths lay tan patches of eggs on firewood, campers, vehicles, patio furniture — anything outside! When these items are moved to new areas, this pest gets a free ride.

**SPOTTED LANTERNFLY** sucks sap from dozens of tree and plant species. This pest loves tree-of-heaven but will feed on black walnut, white oak, sycamore, and grape. Like the gypsy moth, this pest lays clusters of eggs on just about any dry surface, from landscaping stone to firewood!

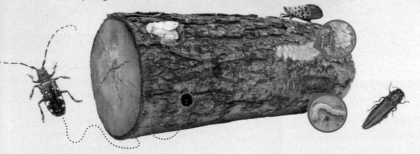

**ASIAN LONGHORNED BEETLE** will tunnel through, and destroy, over 20 species of trees — especially maple trees. The larvae of this beetle bore into tree branches and trunks, making it an easy pest to accidentally transport in firewood.

**EMERALD ASH BORER** — the infamous killer of ash trees — is found in forests and city trees across much of the eastern and central United States. This insect is notoriously good at hitching rides in infested firewood. Don't give this tree-killing bug a ride to a new forest, or a new state!

**DONTMOVE FIREWOOD.org**

This graphic is for illustrative purposes only. Many of these pests will only infest certain types of trees, making it very unlikely for a single log to contain all species as shown.

Visit dontmovefirewood.org for more information.

## NODS TO NATURE

"Biophilic design is the future. Ideas that help to merge indoor and outdoor are extremely vital."

*We'll see . . .*

- terrarium lamps
- plants in hammocks over beds
- plants replacing chandeliers

*–Hilton Carter*

## INTERIOR WISH LISTS

- *On walls:* 3D artwork in trapezoidal and rhombus shapes
- *In bedrooms:* dressers with carved scalloped or fluted edges; walls covered in upholstered fabric
- *In bathrooms:* full marble, from walls to molding to counter and sink—all in the same color

*–Ana Cummings*

## MONEY MATTERS

"U.S. consumers are specifically shopping for products that are made in the USA, even if this means paying a little more."

*–Gabrielle Pastorek, retail analyst, Finder.com*

### PEOPLE ARE TALKING ABOUT . . .

- realtors selling houses with pets included
- financial therapists helping with both money problems and emotions

*(continued)*

### BY THE NUMBERS

**10%** of people have a credit card that they keep secret from their partner.

**70%** of employees say that they got a raise after asking for one.

**35%** of parents admit to trying to "keep up with the Joneses."

**$8.75:** average amount of pocket money parents give kids each week

**21:** number of U.S. states that require a personal finance course for high school graduation

**$120,230:** the maximum amount of debt that women will accept while still continuing a romantic relationship

**$109,127:** the amount of similar debt that a man will accept

# Choose Life
# Grow Young with HGH

From the landmark book Grow Young with HGH comes the most powerful, over-the-counter health supplement in the history of man. Human growth hormone was first discovered in 1920 and has long been thought by the medical community to be necessary only to stimulate the body to full adult size and therefore unnecessary past the age of 20. Recent studies, however, have overturned this notion completely, discovering instead that the natural decline of Human Growth Hormone (HGH), from ages 21 to 61 (the average age at which there is only a trace left in the body) and is the main reason why the body ages and fails to regenerate itself to its 25 year-old biological age.

Like a picked flower cut from the source,

we gradually wilt physically and mentally and become vulnerable to a host of degenerative diseases, that we simply weren't susceptible to in our early adult years.

Modern medical science now regards aging as a disease that is treatable and preventable and that "aging", the disease, is actually a compilation of various diseases and pathologies, from everything, like a rise in blood glucose and pressure to diabetes, skin wrinkling and so on. All of these aging symptoms can be stopped and rolled back by maintaining Growth Hormone levels in the blood at the same levels HGH existed in the blood when we were 25 years old.

There is a receptor site in almost every

cell in the human body for HGH, so its regenerative and healing effects are very comprehensive.

Growth Hormone, first synthesized in 1985 under the Reagan Orphan drug act, to treat dwarfism, was quickly recognized to stop aging in its tracks and reverse it to a remarkable degree. Since then, only the lucky and the rich have had access to it at the cost of $10,000 US per year.

The next big breakthrough was to come in 1997 when a group of doctors and scientists, developed an all-natural source product which would cause your own natural HGH to be released again and do all the remarkable things it did for you in your 20's. Now available to every adult for about the price of a coffee and donut a day.

GHR is now available in America, just in time for the aging Baby Boomers and everyone else from age 30 to 90 who doesn't want to age rapidly but would rather stay young, beautiful and healthy all of the time.

The new HGH releasers are winning converts from the synthetic HGH users as well, since GHR is just as effective, is oral instead of self-injectable and is very affordable.

GHR is a natural releaser, has no known side effects, unlike the synthetic version and has no known drug interactions. Progressive doctors admit that this is the direction medicine is seeking to go, to get the body to heal itself instead of employing drugs. GHR is truly a revolutionary paradigm shift in medicine and, like any modern leap frog advance, many others will be left in the dust holding their limited, or useless drugs and remedies.

It is now thought that HGH is so comprehensive in its healing and regenerative powers that it is today, where the computer industry was twenty years ago, that it will displace so many prescription and non-prescription drugs and health remedies that it is staggering to think of.

The president of BIE Health Products stated in a recent interview, "I've been waiting for these products since the 70's. We knew they would come, if only we could stay healthy and live long enough to see them! If you want to stay on top of your game, physically and mentally as you age, this product is a boon, especially for the highly skilled professionals who have made large investments in their education, and experience. Also with the failure of Congress to honor our seniors with pharmaceutical coverage policy, it's more important than ever to take pro-active steps to safeguard your health. Continued use of GHR will make a radical difference in your health, HGH is particularly helpful to the elderly who, given a choice, would rather stay independent in their own home, strong, healthy and alert enough to manage their own affairs, exercise and stay involved in their communities. Frank, age 85, walks two miles a day, plays golf, belongs to a dance club for seniors, had a girl friend again and doesn't need Viagra, passed his driver's test and is hardly ever home when we call - GHR delivers."

HGH is known to relieve symptoms of Asthma, Angina, Chronic Fatigue, Constipation, Lower back pain and Sciatica, Cataracts and Macular Degeneration, Menopause, Fibromyalgia, Regular and Diabetic Neuropathy, Hepatitis, helps Kidney Dialysis and Heart and Stroke recovery.

**For more information or to order call**
**877-849-4777**
**www.biehealth.us**

- laundromats playing soothing music
- "dark sky" locations (with no light pollution) for stargazing

## MORE REUSE NEWS

"We will see more grocery subscription services with items delivered in reusable containers that are picked up at the next delivery."
–Michael G. Luchs, professor, Raymond A. Mason School of Business, College of William & Mary

*(continued)*

## CULTURE

"The fastest-growing industries are artificial intelligence, healthcare, robotics, and travel."
–Daniel Levine, Avant-Guide Institute

### COMING SOON
- artificial intelligence to sort nonrecyclable plastics for reuse as fuels
- roads that alert cars of hazards—e.g., black ice, potholes
- biodegradable "plastics" made from trees

### GROUP EFFORTS
- firms setting up compost hubs where residents can drop off food waste
- companies exchanging collected compost scraps for produce from local farms for a fee

### PEOPLE ARE TALKING ABOUT . . .
- mobile work vans with a desk, chair, and built-in coffee machine
- "random" camping (for free, on public land)
- hotels providing waterproof books for guests to read in pools

### BY THE NUMBERS

**1,000 miles:** maximum distance achieved in 1 day by a hybrid solar/electric car

**45 miles:** maximum distance achieved from one full solar-only charge of such a car

**17%** of U.S. consumers think that self-driving cars will be safer than those with human drivers.

*Train at home to*

# Work at Home

## *Be a Medical Coding & Billing Specialist*

### WORK AT HOME!

✓ Be home for your family
✓ Be your own boss
✓ Choose your own hours

**SAVE MONEY!**

✓ No day care, commute, or office wardrobe/lunches
✓ Possible tax breaks
✓ Tuition discount for eligible military and their spouses
✓ Military education benefits & MyCAA approved

## Train at home in as little as 5 months to earn up to $42,630 a year!*

Now you can train in the comfort of your own home to work in a medical office, or from home as your experience and skills increase.

Make great money…up to $42,630 a year with experience! It's no secret, healthcare providers need Medical Coding & Billing Specialists. **In fact, the U.S. Department of Labor projects 8% growth, 2019 to 2029, for specialists doing coding and billing.

| 10 Years | 8% |
| 5 Years | Increase In Demand!** |

## No previous medical experience required. Compare the money you can make!

Coders earn great money because they make a lot of money for the people they work for. Entering the correct codes on medical claims can mean the difference in thousands of dollars in profits for doctors, hospitals and clinics. Since each and every medical procedure must be coded and billed, there's plenty of work available for well-trained Medical Coding & Billing Specialists.

## Get FREE Facts. Contact Us Today!

 **U.S. Career Institute®**
2001 Lowe St., Dept. FMAB2A91
Fort Collins, CO 80525

# 1-800-388-8765
**Dept. FMAB2A91**
www.uscieducation.com/FMA91

SENT FREE!

**YES!** Rush me my free Medical Coding & Billing information package.

Name _____ Age_____

Address _____ Apt _____

City, State, Zip _____

E-mail _____ Phone _____

*Accredited • Affordable • Approved*
*Celebrating over 35 years of education excellence!*

DEAC
DISTANCE EDUCATION ACCREDITING COMMISSION

BBB
ACCREDITED BUSINESS
A+ Rating

*With experience, https://www.bls.gov/ooh/healthcare/medical-records-and-health-information-technicians.htm, 12/1/20
**https://www.bls.gov/ooh/healthcare/medical-records-and-health-information-technicians.htm, 12/1/20

CB010

# FASHION

"Retailers will offer the best of human and automated services—the beginning of a truly 'bionic' customer experience."

*–Achim Berg, global leader, Apparel, Fashion, & Luxury Group, McKinsey*

## SUSTAINABLE NOTIONS

"Cradle-to-cradle concepts will really start to take off."

*–Kelly DeVore*

*Products will get a second life:*

● Jeans will be transformed into housing insulation.

● Shoes will be made out of soda bottles.

*We'll also see . . .*

● "leather" clothing and shoes made from mushroom roots

● naturally dyed sneakers

● technology that identifies fabric so that it can be recycled before ending up in a landfill

## LET'S FACE IT

"Consumers will see stories and photos of farmers and clothing sewers on hangtags, Web sites, and QR codes, to put a face behind the fashion products that we buy."

*–Andrea Kennedy, faculty, LIM College Fashion Merchandising Dept.*

## "USED" IS MAKING NEWS

"Secondhand apparel retailing will become the fastest growing segment of the Canadian retail apparel market."

*–Randy Harris, president, Trendex North America*

Clothing brands are offering "take back" programs: Customers return items to be cleaned, repaired, and resold, instore or online.

*–Andrea Kennedy* ■

### BY THE NUMBERS

**69%** of consumers want to know how their clothing was manufactured.

**53%** of consumers give unwanted clothes to others for reuse.

FOLLOW US:

# When it's built by *hand,*

## It's connected to the *Heart.*

**For three generations,** the builders, blacksmiths, and craftsmen at Country Carpenters put their hands and their hearts into designing and building the finest New England Style buildings available. Hand-selected materials, hand-forged hardware, all hand-built and hand-finished by real people. You can feel the difference in your heart.

NEW ENGLAND STYLE
**Country Carpenters** INC.
since 1974
POST & BEAM BUILDINGS

Scan to Receive $500 Off Your
Purchase of a Country Barn,
Carriage House or Outbuilding*

**Scan Me**

Use PROMO Code AYOFA22
*Offer Valid with Deposit Paid
before Oct. 1, 2022

**COUNTRY BARNS, CARRIAGE HOUSES, POOL & GARDEN SHEDS, CABINS**
*Visit our models on display! We ship nationwide!*
326 Gilead Street, Hebron, CT 06248 • 860.228.2276 • countrycarpenters.com

# BEYOND
## THE

**Secrets for
success with
fancy cucurbits**

BY SUSAN PEERY

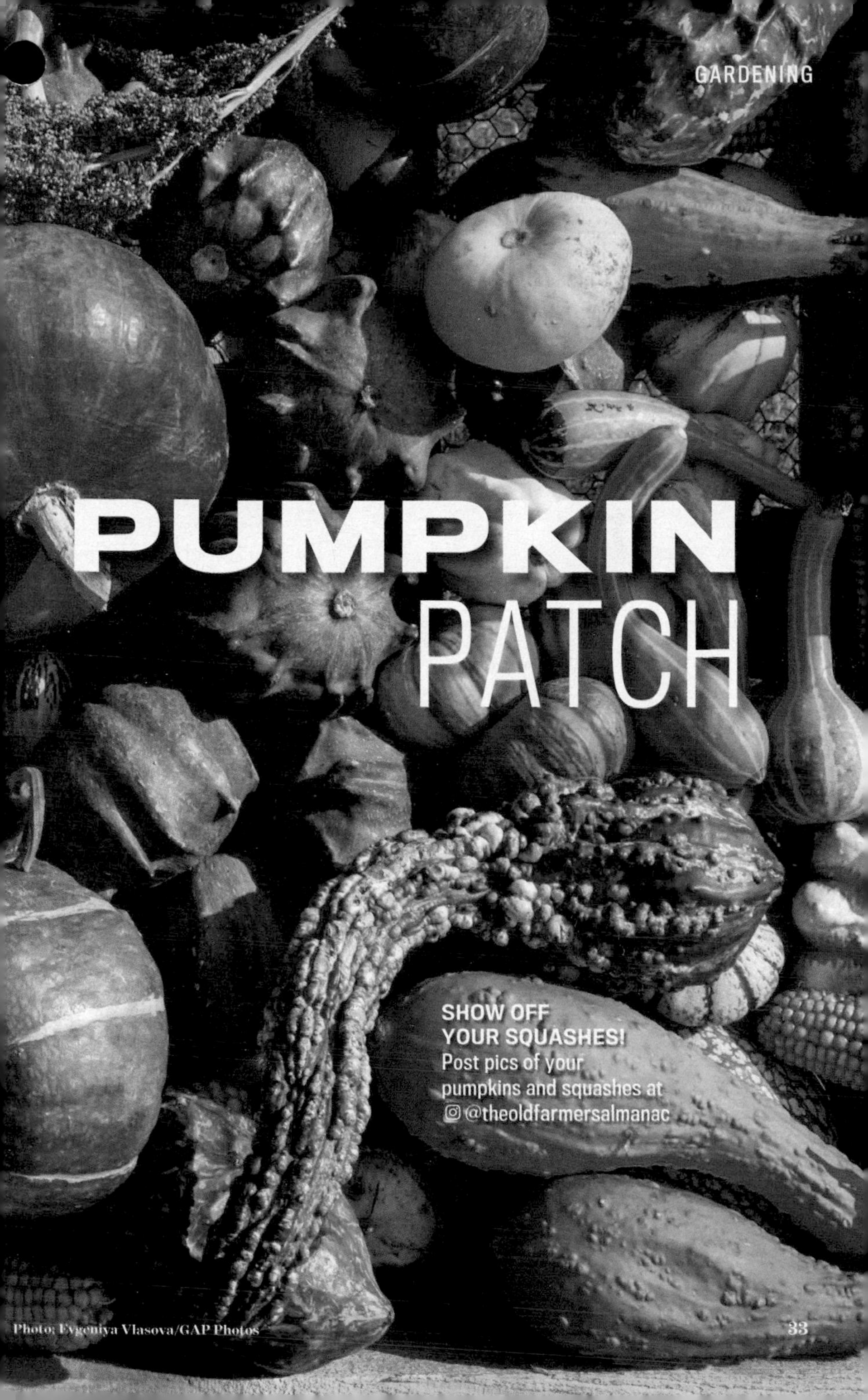

# PUMPKIN PATCH

**SHOW OFF YOUR SQUASHES!**
Post pics of your pumpkins and squashes at @theoldfarmersalmanac

Photo: Evgeniya Vlasova/GAP Photos

'GILL'S BLUE HUBBARD'

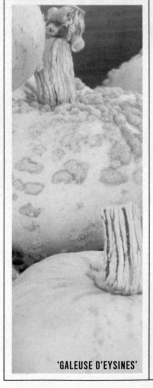

'GALEUSE D'EYSINES'

'CASPER'

**A**utumn brings out the cucurbit beauties. A field of orange pumpkins in October, a pyramid of butternut and acorn squashes at the farmers' market: To a gardener, what could be more inspiring? Only these: a warty 'Galeuse d'Eysines' squash (the bumps are the measure of sweetness) or a smooth white 'Casper' pumpkin (developed in Canada as a container plant, both edible and ornamental); a jade-color 'Gill's Blue Hubbard' (cousin of the Boston Marrow, the quintessential New England pie pumpkin); or a turbaned 'Kindred' (born and raised in Kindred, North Dakota, and as sweet as it is handsome). With care, you can grow these and other fancy fruit.

Pumpkin- and squash-growing is a pleasure and an accomplishment that will make you proud, but it can also be fraught with setbacks. Plant

Photos, clockwise from top: Johnny's Selected Seeds; emer1940/Getty Images; AlpamayoPhoto/Getty Images

scientists at Purdue University say that they get more questions about pumpkin diseases than on any other crop. Blights and rots and spots and wilts are out there, lurking. Striped and spotted cucumber beetles, squash bugs, and squash vine borers can attack without warning. The weather is beyond any gardener's control. But don't despair! Here are a few strategies for pumpkin and squash success. We encourage you to try planting some of the more unusual heirloom varieties listed; this gardening advice applies to all types.

'WHITE ICICLE' RADISHES

## 1. EDGE WITH ICICLE RADISHES

Early in the season, plant a large circle of 'White Icicle' radishes around the perimeter of your pumpkin patch. By the time the radishes go to seed, it will be warm enough to plant the cucurbits. As an additional benefit, the adult clearwing moth, which emerges from last year's squash borer cocoon, dislikes radishes and will not try to lay eggs or overwinter in this spot.

## 2. PLANT PROPITIOUSLY

It can be tempting to be the first in your neighborhood to get the garden planted. But look at a soil thermometer, not the calendar, and do not plant pumpkin or squash seeds until the soil registers 70°F at a depth of 1 to 2 inches. In northern gardening zones, and depending on the weather, this can mean the end of June. This helps the harvest in four ways.

FIRST, male blossoms (the ones with a straight stem) must open first so that their pollen will be

## MEET THE FAMILY

All pumpkins and squashes originated in Central and South America, cultivated first as livestock food. Seeds from the sweetest, least watery specimens were saved and replanted over generations. In eastern North America, Native Americans shared their life-sustaining crop with the early settlers.

Pumpkins, squashes, and some gourds belong to the genus *Cucurbita* and are now grown worldwide for their edible fruit. The three main species of pumpkins and winter squashes are *C. pepo*, which includes acorn squashes and jack-o'-lantern—type pumpkins (notably the classic 'Connecticut Field' pumpkin, an heirloom); *C. moschata* (the butternut squash family); and *C. maxima*, which is soft-stemmed and less fibrous and includes varieties ranging from the celebrated Cinderella pumpkin 'Rouge Vif d'Étampes' (translation from the French: "vivid red from Étampes") and the whole Hubbard squash family to the giant (if inedible) pumpkins grown for competitions.

# Breakthrough
# Joint Pain Discovery

## Doctor's Formula Eases Joint Issues

If you're over 40 or 50, odds are you suffer pain or stiffness in at least one of your body's 230 joints.

In fact, over 21 million Americans suffer from "wear and tear" concerns such as:

- **Joint pain or stiffness**
- **Restricted motion in joints**
- **Grinding, crackling**
- **Mild joint swelling or warmth**
- **Enlargement of joints**

These issues can make it difficult to climb stairs, clean house, do yardwork, enjoy hobbies, or even just keep up with the grandkids.

Many doctors tell you pain is just part of growing older. They say you should learn to "live with it."

### Don't Ignore Joint Pain

Renowned holistic doctor David Brownstein, M.D., decided to search for new natural strategies to help soothe and comfort aching joints.

After seeing so many patients take handfuls of expensive but low-quality joint supplements, Dr. Brownstein formulated **LIMBEX®**.

This advanced joint support formula contains 11 premium ingredients to improve and maintain healthy joints, cartilage, and connective tissue.

### ApresFlex® Starts Helping Joints in as Little as 5 Days!

**LIMBEX** contains ApresFlex, a new next-generation boswellia extract that quickly helps balance the body's inflammatory response. There are 10 more hard-working ingredients in **LIMBEX** that support healthy joints, including bromelain, turmeric, glucosamine, chondroitin, holy basil, green tea, pomegranate, piperine, and vitamins C & E.

These ingredients work to reduce inflammation, block damaging enzymes, and lubricate joints. They improve blood flow to damaged joints while reducing swelling, pain, and stiffness.

### The Simple Solution for Joint Health Support

**LIMBEX** now makes it easy to help support and soothe your joints.

Get back to living your life again with less pain and stiffness. Try **LIMBEX** today, at no cost!

accessible when the female flowers (which have a bulge at the base) appear. Male blossoms are especially sensitive to nighttime temperatures below 65° and are more prolific once it warms up.

**SECOND,** bacterial wilt and squash mosaic virus are carried by the cucumber beetle, a

spotted in the West.)

**THIRD,** downy mildew, a fungus-like organism, germinates from spores in the cool and moist conditions of spring. Waiting until the soil warms up and dries out before planting seeds makes the pathogen less likely to thrive.

**FOURTH,** the squash

waiting until July to plant can shorten your growing season enough that a frost can come before the pumpkins are ready to harvest, if you regularly get frosts in September. Pumpkins and winter squashes usually need a minimum of 100 days from planting to harvest.

MALE BLOSSOM

FEMALE BLOSSOM

SPOTTED CUCUMBER BEETLE

ubiquitous insect that is the bane of all vining plants. Although these beetles chew tender leaves, their role as a disease vector, or transmitter, is the most damaging. This beetle is most active in May and early June and usually dies out by late June. (Cucumber beetles are striped east of the Rocky Mountains and

vine borer, which is the larval stage of a clearwing moth, tunnels into tender vines to eat in late spring and then buries itself in the soil to form a cocoon until the next year. Waiting to plant until later in its life cycle can save your pumpkin vines.

A caveat: In garden Zones 4 and colder,

### 3. SEEDS OR SEEDLINGS?

Most growers agree that planting pumpkin and squash seeds directly into warm soil, either into hills for better drainage (thin to two or three plants once seeds have sprouted) or rows (allow 6 feet in every direction between seeds), will yield the most robust plants.

*(continued)*

Photos, from left: Liudmyla/Getty Images; Subas chandra Mahato/Getty Images; johnandersonphoto/Getty Images

## HEIRLOOM HALL OF FAME

In addition to the varieties already mentioned, consider growing these unusual pumpkins and squashes, all open-pollinated (they will produce true to type).

**'Pennsylvania Dutch Crookneck'** *(C. moschata):* Excellent keeper and best for pies and soups. After harvest, hook the squash over a pole to cure in a warm place. Close relative of the 'Canada Crookneck' and favorite of homesteaders in the 19th century.

**'Marina di Chioggia'** *(C. maxima):* This gorgeous green pumpkin, warts and all, started in South America and was developed in Chioggia, on the Adriatic coast of what is now Italy, in the 1600s.

The bumps are also called "sugar warts" because of the concentration of sugars below the skin. Born to be stuffed into ravioli. Also known as Chioggia sea pumpkin.

**'Blue Banana' and 'Pink Banana'** *(C. maxima):* These oblong pumpkins, introduced in the United States in the 1890s, may have originated in Peru more than 800 years ago. The flesh is intensely sweet. Some say that 'Sibley' (aka 'Pike's Peak'), introduced by Hiram Sibley & Co., of Rochester, New York, in 1887, is the best of this Banana group.

**'Cutchogue Flat Cheese'** *(C. moschata):* Cousin to 'Long Island Cheese' (which is larger) and 'Musquee de Provence' (also larger, with a darker rind, and good flavor). The cheese pumpkin is known strictly for its looks (it resembles a wheel of cheese), not its

taste, and for its longevity. Beautiful on your doorstep long after other pumpkins have turned to glop.

**'Winter Luxury Pie'** *(C. pepo):* Lauded by pumpkin expert and *The Compleat Squash* (Artisan, 2004) author Amy Goldman for making "the smoothest and most velvety pumpkin pie" ever. Introduced in 1893.

Photos: EdenBrothers.com (Blue Banana); Nova Photo Graphik/GAP Photos (Crookneck); Baker Creek Heirloom Seeds (all others)

### 4. USE MULCH AND/OR ROW COVERS

These will conserve soil moisture, warm the soil, and protect young plants from insects and windborne spores. Once vining and flowering begin, be sure to remove row covers during the day

You can even gently vacuum the leaves to remove the eggs. A hand vacuum is perfect for this. Vigilance early in the growing season will really pay off. Wrap aluminum foil around the base of stems as an additional deterrent to squash

stem. They are fragile at this stage and will bruise or nick easily. Bring the plump beauties into a heated space and let them cure for 2 to 3 weeks at temperatures of 60° to 70°. This toughens the skins, lowers the water content, and helps the

ASSORTED *CUCURBITA PEPO*

so that pollinators can do their work. Once pumpkins and squashes form, slip an old shingle or piece of cardboard under them if the soil is soggy.

### 5. BE PICKY

That is, if you spot eggs of squash bugs or cucumber beetles on the top or underside of leaves, pick them off by hand and destroy them.

borers. Plant nasturtiums nearby, as these repel squash bugs.

### 6. DON'T WAIT FOR FROST ON THE PUMPKIN

Cold temperatures (under 50°F) reduce the quality and keeping power of your pumpkins and squashes, and freezing is fatal. Harvest by cutting the fruit from the vine, leaving a few inches of

crop to keep longer. As squashes and pumpkins age, enzymes convert starches to sugars, making them much tastier than when first harvested. Once cured, store them at 50° to 60°. The traditional advice is to put them under a bed in an unheated bedroom. ∎

**Susan Peery** is a regular contributor to Almanac publications.

# THE OLD FARMER'S GUIDE TO
## SEEDS, PLANTS, AND BULBS

41

# Dazzling Dahlias, DARLINGS OF SUMMER

**DAZZLE US WITH YOUR DAHLIAS!**
Post pics at
@theoldfarmersalmanac

THERE IS NOTHING LIKE THE FIRST
HOT DAYS OF SPRING WHEN THE GARDENER
STOPS WONDERING IF IT'S TOO SOON
TO PLANT THE DAHLIAS AND STARTS
WONDERING IF IT'S TOO LATE.

–Henry Mitchell (1923–93), garden columnist
and author of The Essential Earthman
(Indiana University Press, 2003)

POMPONS

*Dahlias have a place in any sunny garden with a growing season that's at least 120 days long.*

**W**ant to grow something spectacular? Plant dahlias. Unlike perennials and flowering shrubs, dahlias go from nothing to big in one season and make a sensational finish. As Scott Kunst, former proprietor of Old House Gardens in Ann Arbor, Michigan, once observed: "Dahlias get more and more charged up. They're like fireworks—they can animate and transform the garden."

Although not well suited to extremely hot and humid climates (as in much of Texas and Florida), dahlias have a place in any sunny garden with a growing season that's at least 120 days long. Resolve to make your garden pop by planting dahlias now, because it may take you a while to choose a few from the amazing array of options—20,000 by one count!

These relatives of daisies and sunflowers brighten up the garden after so many ornamentals begin to wane. More important, there is a size—both in plant height and bloom dimension—to suit almost any situation or imagination.

## COLOR YOUR WORLD

Picking a favorite dahlia is next to impossible for many people, so wildly varied are the blooms in color and form. The American Dahlia Society (ADS) recognizes 15 color categories, but the spectrum of flower colors includes all shades of white,

MIGNONS

# BRECK'S
# Dahlia Lovers

## 34 new varieties for 2022

We offer an extensive selection of outstanding dahlia varieties—all grown in Holland and shipped directly to you. They produce lush, gorgeous, mid- to late-season blooms in a countless combination of colours, forms and sizes.

For a limited time, you can **save up to 75%** on your dahlia order from Breck's and **enjoy free shipping**. To claim this special offer, enter the code **DAHLIA22** at checkout!

*Brecks.com/dahlialovers*

yellow, orange, pink, red, purple, and bronze—plus two-tones and blends of all of these. (Blue dahlias don't exist.) A few dahlias bear a sweet, mellow scent, but most lack fragrance.

There are many classifications of dahlias, including . . .

• flat, daisylike, *single* and smaller (under 2 inches wide) *mignon* blooms, beloved by pollinators as well as planters

• *collarettes,* small to medium-size flowers with a short ruff of inner ("collar") petals, bred for everywhere from bedding to balcony

• *anemones,* prolific multipurpose plants with a wreath of petals evoking a pincushion

• lollipop-style, nearly round, 2-inch *pompons* and slightly larger but flatter *balls* that brighten beds, borders, and bouquets

• fantastically frilly *decoratives* in two bloom styles: *informal,* with generally flat petals in an irregular formation and best suited for borders and containers, and *formal,* with

regularly placed or perfectly packed petals, which make eye-catching arrangements as cut flowers

• *cactuses,* with dense cushions of quilled petals in profusions of blooms from 2 to 12 inches wide on stems up to 6 feet in height, which can play many roles

• the exotically delicate-looking and slightly fragrant *orchid* style, both single- and double-flower, which displays well in the ground, in containers, or in a vase

• *peony* dahlias, which yield multi-petaled blossoms around prominent

ANEMONES

*Collarettes are bred for everywhere from bedding to balcony.*

COLLARETTES

POMPONS

centers that are all the more striking above often blackish stems and foliage

## PREP FOR PERFECTION

Dahlias prefer at least half a day of sun, fertile soil with good drainage, and a bit of protection from wind.

Don't be in a hurry to plant; dahlias will struggle in cold soil. Plant them shortly after tomato plants go in; in Zone 6, this is in early June. (Some gardeners start tubers indoors a month ahead to get a jump on the season.)

Avoid dahlia tubers that appear wrinkled or rotten. A little bit of green growth is a good sign.

Don't break or cut individual dahlia tubers as you would potatoes. Plant them whole, with the growing points, or "eyes," facing up, about 6 to 8 inches deep.

There's no need to water the soil

until the dahlia plants appear; in fact, overwatering can cause tubers to rot.

Dahlias tend to be tall plants that need anchoring. It's a good idea to plant a tuber with a sturdy stake right in the planting hole. Like many large-flower hybrids, the big dahlias may need extra attention before or after rain, when open blooms tend to fill up with water or take a beating from the wind.

## FINDING A FEEDING PATTERN

Dahlias are heavy feeders and, arguably, finicky; it's difficult to generalize about fertilizing requirements from one region to another. Some professional growers advise feeding dahlias a month after they sprout with a low-nitrogen fertilizer, such as bonemeal or any 5-10-10 or 10-20-20 balanced product. Too much nitrogen (represented by the first number in the NPK formula) results in big leaves and stalks but not optimum flowering. A grower on Cape Cod (Mass.) for years noted that his

INFORMAL DECORATIVES

CACTUSES

*In cold climates of North America, dahlias are known as tender perennials: They do not handle frost well.*

dahlias needed more manure than he could conveniently supply, while an avid Maryland dahlia devotee claimed that gardeners who have sandy soil and frequent rain or irrigation need to be sure that they supply enough water-soluble nutrients (primarily potassium and sulfur) during the growing season. Be sure to withhold fertilizer about a month before frost; this will help the tubers to keep better over the winter.

### BED BUG BITES

Dahlias sometimes fall prey to disease, frequently spread by mites and aphids. Pesky mites may appear on plants toward the end of summer; they start on the bottom of the plant, where they cause the leaves to yellow, and work their way up to the top. Leaves chewed by mites have a gritty feel. Remedies include spraying plants with conventional insecticides from mid-August through September or using alternative soap sprays against mites and neem oil on aphids. Unfortunately, deer, slugs, and groundhogs may also discover the joy of a dahlia.

### COLD STORAGE

In cold climates of North America, dahlias are known as tender perennials: They do not handle frost well. In cold regions (generally Zone 7 and northward), if you wish to save your plants, you have to dig up the tubers in early fall and store them over the winter.

To avoid the risk of injury to the tubers from the cold, cut back the foliage and dig up the plants before the first killing frost. Use a spading fork and gently shake the soil off the tubers. Cut rotten or mummified tubers off the clump and discard them. Don't let the tubers dry out too much before packing

SINGLE ORCHIDS

PEONIES

them up in some sort of loose, fluffy material. The possibilities for packing materials are many, including pet-shop animal bedding, coarse vermiculite, wood shavings, and newspaper. (For years, coarse peat moss was recommended, but the impact of its harvest on the environment has caused it to fall out of favor.) The ADS suggests common kitchen plastic wrap (see Dahlia.org for details). Bear in mind that what works in one case may not work in another, so experiment.

For storage over the winter, temperatures in the 40° to 45°F range are ideal, with 35° to 50° acceptable. Warmer conditions tend to cause rot, although shriveling seems to be a more common complaint.

Take out the tubers in the spring, separate them from the parent clump, swap favorites with friends, and begin again. Too much bother? You can skip digging and storing and just start over by buying new tubers in the spring. ■

*–with assistance from Rosalie Davis*

## DAHLIA DIEHARDS GO THE DISTANCE(S)

The many-colored varieties of garden dahlias are hybrids, descendants of wild species with red to yellow single-flower heads that were first cultivated by the Aztecs. Botanical literature from the 16th century shows that they used the stems medicinally. Dahlia seeds were introduced to Europeans in the late 18th century through the Madrid (Spain) Royal Botanical Garden; although such efforts came to naught, it was hoped that the bitter but starchy tubers would serve as a food crop. By the mid-19th century, the acclaim generated by dahlias' ornamental qualities had led to the development of many garden varieties in England as well as continental Europe. This popularity spread back to America, where they remained a staple of flower gardens at least through the 1950s. Amazingly enough, in the early 1980s, horticultural trendsetters began to scoff at bold tropicals like dahlias in favor of more refined perennials and hardy bulbs. Nonetheless, true fans of these exuberant summer flowers have never forsaken them.

# Making Scents
## OF THE SEASONS

With fragrant potpourris, the aromas
of the outdoors are never far away.

**BY BETTY EARL**

**T**he delicate scents of flowers, herbs, and spices in homemade potpourris can fill a room, evoking pleasant memories of a summer garden well beyond the season's end. And did you know? Making them is easier than you think. A potpourri is simply a mixture of dried fragrant flowers, herbs, spices, leaves, and twigs, enhanced with a few drops of essential oil to intensify the scent and orrisroot, a fixative to make the fragrance last.

A potpourri's scent can be flowery, woodsy, fruity, spicy, or musky. Its look can present varying shades of the same color, be tenderly muted or assertively bold, or be immortalized by artistic blends of delicate dried blossoms, leaves, and spices to create a collage of color, texture, and shape.

Although flower petals may have lost their moist blush and heady fragrance, dried blossoms retain the exquisite charm and shadowy perfume of the flowers. Because essential oils produce most of the scent, the possibilities for creating relaxing, refreshing, or even sensual combinations of custom-made potpourris are virtually infinite. *(continued)*

No bought potpourri is so pleasant as
that made from one's own garden, for the
petals of the flowers one has gathered
at home hold the sunshine and memories
of summer, and of past summers only
the sunny days should be remembered.

–*Eleanour Sinclair Rohde (1881–1950), English
gardener, designer, and author of*
The Scented Garden *(Medici Society, 1931)*

# POPULAR POTPOURRIS

## FLORAL

Rose, jasmine, and orange blossom are the primary scents of floral potpourris. They retain their scents when dried and are used for color and texture. Other fragrant favorites include heliotrope, honeysuckle, jonquil, lilac, lily-of-the-valley, mock orange, nicotiana, peony, pinks, dame's rocket, stock, violet, and sweet William. The best flowers for color are black-eyed Susan, borage, cornflower, delphinium, geranium, hydrangea, larkspur, marigold, nasturtium, periwinkle, poppy, and zinnia.

Pick flowers on a sunny day after the dew has evaporated. Use petal colors of yellow, pink, rose, and purple, which retain their colors best when dried. White petals can turn an unsightly brown, and some red flowers become very dark.

## HERBAL

Pungently aromatic and heady, herbs add color, bulk, and texture. Lavender, the most popular herb, is almost a standard addition to most potpourri mixtures. Other good choices include sweet herbs such as the pink flower heads of chives; the leaves of artemisia, bay, lemon verbena, sage, and scented geranium; and the flowers and leaves of chamomile, hyssop, marjoram, monarda, oregano, sweet woodruff, and thyme. Consider also mentholated herbs, including eucalyptus, evergreen, and peppermint (but use these with discretion).

## CITRUS

Peels of lemon, lime, orange, and tangerine are prized for their fresh, clean scents. If you don't have these growing at home, find what you need at the grocery store.

## WOODLAND

Outdoorsy aromas come from ingredients that you can purchase or find in your neighborhood. Allspice berries, cardamom seeds, cinnamon sticks, cloves, coriander, cumin seeds, mace, nutmeg, star anise, and vanilla beans are all effective. Include bits of wood and cones, such as acorns, cedar wood shavings, gingerroot, sandalwood chips, and small cones from alder, larch, and pine. Don't forget colorful elderberries, hawthorn berries, juniper berries, and rose hips.

*(continued)*

54

LAVENDER

HELIOTROPE

SWEET WILLIAM

JAPANESE HONEYSUCKLE

ANNUAL PINK

COMMON THYME

## PLANT A POTPOURRI GARDEN

Make space in a bed or container to grow some of your own ingredients.

**LAVENDER** (*Lavandula angustifolia* 'Hidcote'): This perennial produces gray-green foliage and thick spikes of deep violet-blue blossoms in early summer. Grow it in full sun and average, well-drained, preferably alkaline soil. Give plants a light to medium trimming each spring just as new growth starts.

**HELIOTROPE** (*Heliotropium arborescens* 'Marine'): Producing flowers in a bewitching shade of dark violet-blue, this annual likes full sun and rich, well-drained soil.

**SWEET WILLIAM** (*Dianthus barbatus*): A biennial in the North, sweet William often behaves as a perennial in warmer areas. It's prized for its sweet-scented small flowers and densely packed heads. Plant in full sun and average to rich soil.

**JAPANESE HONEYSUCKLE** (*Lonicera japonica* 'Halliana'): Although this climbing perennial vine can become a rampant pest, its hauntingly fragrant pure white flowers turn soft yellow with age. Provide it with a fence or pergola and plant in sun or shade and rich, well-drained soil.

**ANNUAL PINK** (*Dianthus chinensis* 'Telstar Picotee'): A fast grower, this easy annual produces white-edged red flowers in great profusion. Plant it in full sun and well-drained, alkaline soil and pick the flowers diligently to encourage a long season of bloom.

**COMMON THYME** (*Thymus vulgaris*): Use both the aromatic foliage and rose-purple flowers of this perennial herb. It prefers full sun and well-drained soil.

*(continued on page 196)*

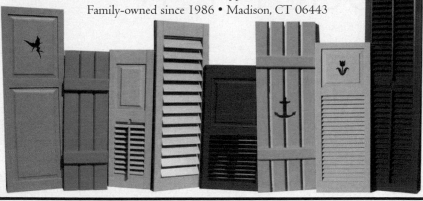

# GROWING
## TOGETHER

By Stacey Kusterbeck
and Karen Davidson

## SU'S FARMING
### SIMCOE, ONTARIO

"If I'm awake, I'm working," says Henry Su, a Canadian-born Chinese farmer. He grew up on his immigrant parents' farm in Simcoe and while a teenager enjoyed a career as a competitive figure skater.

Figure eights behind him, he's continuing the family brand started 30 years ago; today, he nurtures 7 to 10 acres of eggplants (aka aubergines) and several more of zucchini.

Producing eggplants with perfectly glossy purple skin is a summer-long challenge. As Su explains, wind-whipped leaves can easily scratch the fruit's complexion, so about mid-season, the lower leaves are removed by hand to ensure the produce's appeal to the diverse population of the Toronto area.

While Italians seem to favor thick-skin Sicilian varieties of eggplant, Asians prefer the thin, violet-color Chinese long varieties or round, midnight-purple Indian eggplants for their softer flesh. These are also in demand by the green grocers and restaurateurs who buy wholesale at the Ontario Food Terminal—or at least did until the COVID-19 virus struck.

Restaurants closed. Neighborhood stores had little foot traffic. Zucchini and aubergines had no takers. Su was skating on thin ice.

"In 2019, the buyers said, 'We can take all of the zucchini that you can grow.' In 2020, we couldn't give it away," says Su wistfully.

While pandemic economics saw eggplants and zucchini fall out of favor for food businesses, Su continues to hope that consumers will try more adventuresome ingredients in home cooking. Asian eggplant is an appealing option.

"Eggplant is the perfect vessel for flavor,' says Su, who remains determined to carry on.

After all, one bad year is a blip in the history of the eggplant, which has been grown in China since at least the T'ang dynasty—A.D. 618. Undaunted, Su plans to perpetuate its legacy.

*(continued)*

## MUGRAGE HAY & CATTLE
### DELTA JUNCTION, ALASKA

**W**ith experience in the South and Midwest behind him, veteran cattleman Scott Mugrage at first had little interest when in 2013 his son pointed out an ad for a 550-acre farm in Alaska—but he couldn't get the idea out of his mind. Both the challenge and the slower-paced lifestyle sounded appealing. Mugrage traveled to see the place in an uncharacteristically warm late July and was struck by the extraordinary beauty of the site, with mountains on both sides of a valley. "In every direction you look, it's like a photograph on the wall," observes Mugrage.

His operation now boasts the largest private herd of cattle (650 Black Angus and Scottish Highland) in the state and is its only large-scale finisher of beef as well as biggest beef supplier. Most is sold wholesale. The farm produces most of the grain needed to keep the herd fed through 7-month winters, but they buy from local producers, too.

While Mugrage found ways to cope with Alaska's short growing seasons and abundant wildlife, the lack of infrastructure to support agriculture turned out to be more daunting. "All of our input costs are higher, from fuel to fertilizer to parts," he notes. "Most of our equipment is from an era that allows us to still work on it, and we just keep repairing it."

Still, Mugrage sees potential everywhere: He continually tries new crops in order to improve soil quality and eliminate weeds. "There is so much good-quality land and such a diverse variety of crops," he says. "I can see Alaska becoming the breadbasket of the nation."

Experiential agritourism is promising. In the works is a cattle drive across the wilderness. "Riders will travel hundreds of miles and likely never cross privately owned land," he says. "That's something you can't do in the Lower 48." *(continued)*

## KALALA ORGANIC ESTATE WINERY
### WEST KELOWNA, BRITISH COLUMBIA

**K**arnail Sidhu is that rarest of grape growers: He is intolerant of alcohol. "I do taste, but I don't drink," he says, savoring a 2019 award from the British Columbia Grapegrowers' Association as viticulturalist of the year.

Fortunately, Sidhu's aversion to alcohol has not detoured a 30-year career path that started with a post as an electrical engineer in India's Punjab state and has now evolved to include the role of Canadian vineyard/winery owner.

Today, his combined 70-acre organic vineyards, Oliver and Osoyoos, are known for their viticulture practices. One intervention is to hand-pull the lower leaves of the grapevines in mid-June. By this time of year, leafhoppers have laid eggs on the undersides of the leaves. If they are allowed to hatch, the leaves will be sucked dry of nutrients.

While his workers remove the hosts of these voracious pests, Sidhu allows other beneficial insects to thrive in the unmowed grass lanes that burst with spring dandelions. While the vineyards may appear unruly, they are thriving with plant and insect diversity.

"We work with the ecosystem in the vineyards," notes Sidhu. "We deal with whatever comes from nature."

Besides his capable hand at canopy management, Sidhu has a nose for wine—and specifically for the aromas that might signal a fermentation process gone awry. A whiff of wet dog, for example, or rotten eggs will tell him that there may not be enough oxygen for yeast to survive. Early detection of such defects can be fixed by his winemaker.

Since 2008, Kalala Organic Estate Winery has produced a number of acclaimed vintages, including a Chardonnay ice wine. However, it turns out that Sidhu's favorite is Zweigelt, a disease-resistant, medium-body red first cultivated in Austria. "It's our signature sip," he reports. *(continued)*

Photo: Kalala Organic Estate Winery

# The taste rats and house mice just die for!®

Rodents in your barn aren't up to anything good. Put an end to feed contamination and waste, damage to equipment and electrical wiring, and risk of serious disease.

It's time to take action with **Just One Bite®*** II rodent bait made especially for agricultural use to effectively control rodents and help prevent reinfestation.

Reclaim your barn! Visit justonebitebrand.com to find a retail location near you.

## WEST END COMMUNITY GARDEN
### ATLANTA, GEORGIA

**A**fter moving to New York City from Jamaica at age 14, Haylene Green ("The Garden Queen") found her favorite pastime to be breaking off small pieces of plants and putting them into pots to see if they would grow. "I was never taught to farm. I grew up loving to grow things," recalls Green, who comes from a long line of farmers.

During a family reunion in Atlanta, the region's plentiful trees caught her attention. "I assumed that they were for fruit or bark or leaves for eating," says Green. Drawn to the good growing conditions, she moved south, only to find that the trees that she had admired weren't for edibles after all.

Green searched at markets for the tropical produce of her childhood—not just to eat, but also for its seeds. Soon, turmeric, tropical pumpkins, pomegranates, persimmons, ackee, breadfruit, and peach, plum, and pear trees were springing up on her half-acre plot of land.

"I was just growing for fun—people were the ones who turned it into a business," recalls Green. Passersby took note of the fruit; some offered money for them. Green soon set up a small stand to sell her hibiscus sorrel tea—after a free sample and conversation, one customer offered her a grant from the Southern Foodways Alliance. The money allowed her to build a greenhouse and hire some help. With the first harvest, neighbors became customers.

Green now sells fruit and vegetables, the tea, and tropical pumpkin soup at five farmers' markets. Over 300 schoolchildren have visited the farm, where a "garden therapy" program also connects seniors with young people. Green never tires of teaching the joys of growing healthy food. "As long as I am alive," she vows, "I am going to be teaching the young ones how to grow." *(continued)*

# TEES BEES
## TEES, ALBERTA

**H**ome to about 300,000 bee-hives in 2019, the province of Alberta is the largest honey producer in Canada. The COVID-19 crisis threatened this distinction when borders closed, delaying international shipments of queen bees as well as the travel of temporary foreign workers and completely halting imported replacement stock.

The year 2020 was the second bad one in a row for overwintering survival and honey production, says Jeremy Olthof, president of the Alberta

Beekeepers Commission. In 2019, a wet, cool spring delayed the foraging of bees. In 2020, the delay of trained seasonal workers compounded the stress. Of eight Mexican workers booked, only six arrived at Olthof's Tees, Alberta, farm.

Many of these workers have a decade of experience in the care of bee "livestock" (bees are considered food producers). Explains Olthof: "It requires an early, 1:00 A.M. rise to move the hives in the cool of night and drive 3 to 4 hours before even working the bees."

Starting in late June, the men round up nearly a quarter of Olthof's beehives and move them to pollinate hybrid canola fields. Honeybee hives are placed in the dryland corners of irrigated fields at a stocking density of one per acre, depending on whether leafcutting bees (an important native pollinator) are placed throughout the field as well. Then the honeybees fan out to forage among the yellow-petal blooms. From mid-July through September, the workers are busy extracting honey from the hives' frames.

Olthof's goal is 150 pounds of honey per hive. In 2020, he did not expect to meet it: "We'll be lucky to get 120 pounds of honey per hive," he observed that October. This low forecast stung, but there was a balm: higher prices of $1.80 to $2.00 per pound, up from $1.40. Olthof's bottom line was also cushioned by another source of revenue: His bees pollinate commercial hybrid seed canola.

While ups and downs are part of the profession, the beekeeper takes comfort in knowing that canola country will continue to be an annual opportunity for his apiary.

# RESENDIZ BROTHERS PROTEA GROWERS
## FALLBROOK, CALIFORNIA

In his two decades of working on a protea ("sugarbush") farm (eventually becoming manager) after immigrating from Mexico with his three brothers, Ismael "Mel" Resendiz learned to grow—and love—the huge and bright but little-known blooms. In 1999, he started his own operation on a 10-acre parcel. "I never considered doing anything else," says Resendiz. "I love what I am doing."

Sales were slow at first, with just a few local wholesalers as customers. Then Resendiz devised a new marketing strategy: Over a few years, he showed off his own protea varieties (created by cross-pollinating flowers and grafting ones he especially liked onto more vigorous root stock) at trade shows and also began serving as president of both the California and International Protea Associations.

Soon the farm was shipping flowers throughout the state and nationally, as well as to Canada, China, Korea, and Japan. Today, it consists of some 250 acres across 15 parcels; some of the land is very steep, but it has the good drainage that the flowers require. Finding good labor and growing in extreme weather (up to 120°F in summer) are constant challenges. On the hottest days, Resendiz works day and night to irrigate the plants.

During the pandemic, special events slowed to a trickle. Fortunately, online sales boomed, fueled by social media posts of gorgeous protea arrangements. "More people are buying direct, which is better, because they get fresher flowers," Resendiz reports. A typical order was once hundreds of boxes of flowers shipped to a wholesaler—now, it's more often a single bouquet sent to someone's home.

Answering dozens of phone calls from customers each day requires friendliness, patience, and plenty of time. "But you have to go where the business is," says business manager Diana Roy. Their proteas are sold at only one farmers' market currently, but others are knocking at their door. "Our goal is to teach people about proteas," says Roy. "Food feeds the body, but flowers feed the soul." ■

U.S. profiles are by **Stacey Kusterbeck**, a regular contributor to the Almanac. Canadian profiles are by **Karen Davidson**, editor of *The Grower*, a leading Canadian horticultural magazine, and frequent contributor to the Almanac.

# FOUR SEASONS OF GREAT TASTE

### BY SARAH PERREAULT, ALMANAC FOOD EDITOR

Whether fall, winter, spring, or summer, each season brings its own bounty of flavors and benefits. Not only do fresh fruit and vegetables taste better in season, but also they are often more nutritious than produce that has been stored for weeks or even months. Choose and use each season's best with a little help from these recipes. As the year rolls along, be sure to check out additional seasonal recipes by searching for key ingredients at Almanac.com/Cooking.

---

## FALL
## PUMPKIN PICKLES

*Use a "cooking" type of pumpkin—usually called "sugar pumpkins" or "pie pumpkins." They're round and small.*

**4 cups pumpkin, peeled and cut into bite-size cubes**
**1½ cups sugar**
**1½ cups apple cider vinegar**
**10 whole cloves**
**2 sticks cinnamon**

Steam pumpkin until barely tender, about 10 minutes (don't let pumpkin touch the boiling water or it will get mushy). Drain thoroughly and set aside.

In a saucepan, combine sugar, vinegar, cloves, and cinnamon and simmer, covered, for 20 minutes. Add pumpkin, return to a simmer, cover, and cook for 3 minutes more. Remove from heat and leave pumpkin in the syrup; refrigerate for 24 hours.

Heat mixture to simmering and cook for 5 minutes. Remove spices and pack pumpkin into sterilized pint jars, then fill with the syrup. Seal and process for 10 minutes in a boiling water bath.

**Makes about 3 pints.**

*(continued)*

### WHAT'S IN SEASON?

This depends on where you live. Your local farmers' markets and co-ops will always have the best tastes of the season. Also, many grocery stores now have an "in season" area in the produce section.

## FALL
# CREAM OF BRUSSELS SPROUTS SOUP

*Brussels sprouts have more flavor if harvested after a frost or two.*

4 tablespoons (½ stick) butter
2 shallots, chopped
3 tablespoons all-purpose flour
1 cup light cream
½ cup milk
5 cups chicken stock
4 cups chopped cooked brussels sprouts
salt and freshly ground black pepper, to taste
crumbled cooked bacon or bacon bits, for garnish

In a soup pot over medium heat, melt butter. Add shallots and cook until soft. Sprinkle in flour and stir until blended. Slowly add cream and milk and stir until smooth. Add chicken stock and brussels sprouts. Simmer for 10 minutes, uncovered. Do not boil. Taste, then season with salt and pepper. Garnish each serving with bacon.

**Makes 4 to 6 servings.**

## WINTER
# BROILED GRAPEFRUIT

*Ripe citrus, such as grapefruit, should have a smooth, firm skin. If you feel soft spots, the fruit is going bad.*

4 large grapefruit
¼ cup maple or white sugar
¼ cup fresh mint, whole leaves or finely diced

Preheat broiler to high. Line a baking sheet with aluminum foil.

Cut a thin slice of rind (don't cut into fruit) off each end of grapefruit so that halves will lie flat. Cut grapefruit in half.

Place halves, large cut sides up, on prepared baking sheet. Sprinkle with maple sugar. Cook 3 to 4 inches from broiler, until sugar has melted and begins to bubble. Watch it closely, as sugar burns easily. Remove from broiler, top with mint, and serve.

**Makes 8 servings.**

Photos: Samantha Jones/Quinn Brein Communications

# WINTER
# TURNIP SOUFFLÉ

*Turnips can be eaten raw, baked, boiled, roasted, or mashed.*
*Try them as an alternative to potatoes.*

1 pound turnips, peeled and cut into chunks
½ cup heavy cream
2 whole cloves
1 bay leaf
pinch of freshly grated nutmeg
4 tablespoons (½ stick) unsalted butter
3 tablespoons all-purpose flour
pinch of kosher salt
pinch of white pepper (optional)
4 eggs, separated
maple syrup, for serving

Preheat oven to 375°F. Butter six 6-ounce ramekin dishes.

In a pot of boiling salted water, cook turnips for 20 minutes, or until tender. Drain and pat dry. Press through a food mill or ricer. Set aside.

In a saucepan over medium heat, combine cream, cloves, bay leaf, and nutmeg. When cream is scalded, strain it and discard the solids.

In a separate saucepan over medium heat, melt butter. Whisk in flour and cook for 1 minute. Whisk in strained cream, half at a time. Whisk in turnips. Cook, stirring constantly, until mixture thickens. Season with salt and white pepper (if using). Cool to room temperature.

In a bowl, beat egg yolks. Fold in one-third of the turnip mixture. Fold in remaining turnip mixture.

In a chilled bowl, beat egg whites until stiff. Fold egg whites into turnip mixture.

Spoon mixture into prepared dishes and place on a baking sheet. Bake for 18 to 20 minutes, or until soufflés are browned and rise 1 inch or more.

Serve with maple syrup.

**Makes 6 servings.**

*(continued)*

## SPRING
# RISOTTO WITH ASPARAGUS AND SCALLOPS

*Asparagus does not keep for very long after it's picked,*
*so be sure to eat it within 2 to 3 days of harvest.*

1 bunch asparagus, trimmed and cut into 2-inch pieces

½ pound bay or sea scallops

6 to 8 cups chicken broth

3 tablespoons butter

1 onion, chopped

1½ cups arborio rice

2 tablespoons heavy cream

½ cup grated Parmesan cheese

salt and freshly ground black pepper, to taste

Steam asparagus briefly and set aside. For thin asparagus, this will take only 3 to 5 minutes. The pieces should be bright green in color and just slightly tender (not hard).

In a saucepan, bring 3 cups of lightly salted water to a boil. Add scallops and cook (poach) until white and firm. Drain, set aside, and keep warm.

In a separate saucepan, heat chicken broth.

In a skillet over medium heat, melt butter. Add onions and sauté until soft. Add rice to the skillet, reduce heat, and stir for 3 minutes. Add hot broth, half a cup at a time, stirring until liquid is absorbed before adding more. Continue cooking and stirring for about 20 minutes, or until rice is tender. Remove from heat. Add cream, Parmesan, scallops, and asparagus. Season with salt and pepper.

**Makes 8 servings.**          *(continued on page 198)*

73

# RECIPE CONTEST WINNERS

Last year, we asked you for your best recipes using five or fewer ingredients (salt and pepper excluded), and we received a record amount of entries! Our most sincere thanks go out to all of you who took the time to enter.

**STYLING AND PHOTOGRAPHY:**
**SAMANTHA JONES/QUINN BREIN COMMUNICATIONS**

### FIRST PRIZE: $300
## APRICOT SRIRACHA-GLAZED BABY BACK RIBS

4 to 5 pounds baby back pork ribs
2 tablespoons Cajun spice blend
¾ cup apricot preserves
1 tablespoon sriracha sauce
1 tablespoon soy sauce

Remove ribs from packaging and rinse with cold water. Pat dry with paper towels. Rub Cajun spice all over the ribs. Place in a large baking pan and cover tightly with foil. Keep in the refrigerator for 4 hours, or overnight. Bring to room temperature 30 minutes before cooking.

Preheat oven to 325°F.

Leave baking pan covered and bake for 1½ hours.

While ribs are cooking, combine apricot preserves, sriracha, and soy sauce in a saucepan over medium heat. Cook for 3 minutes, stirring frequently, until melted and syrupy.

Remove ribs from the oven and brush with the glaze, reserving about ½ cup. Increase oven temp to 375°F and cook ribs, uncovered, for an additional 30 to 40 minutes, or until meat falls off the bone easily. Brush with the remaining sauce and serve immediately.

**Makes 6 servings.**

–Pamela Gelsomini, Wrentham, Massachusetts
*(continued)*

SECOND PRIZE: $200
# EASY LATTE TRUFFLES

¾ cup white
chocolate
chips
¾ cup heavy
whipping
cream
2 teaspoons
instant coffee
granules
1 cup milk
chocolate
melting
wafers,
divided

Line a standard loaf pan with parchment paper.

Place white chocolate chips in a heatproof bowl.

In a saucepan over medium heat, warm the cream. Add instant coffee and mix well until combined. Once cream starts to bubble, turn off heat and pour over white chocolate chips. Let sit for a few minutes, then stir until the white chocolate chips are melted. Continue stirring until mixture thickens and resembles a very sticky dough.

Transfer truffle mixture to the prepared pan and press with a spatula to even out. Let sit at room temperature for 1 to 2 hours, or until set.

Lift parchment paper out of baking pan and cut truffles into desired shapes.

In the top of a double boiler, melt ½ cup of chocolate wafers. Once they are fully melted, remove from heat and add in remaining ½ cup of chocolate wafers. Stir until melted.

Using a fork or spoon, dip truffles in melted chocolate, then place on parchment paper. If desired, melt more white chocolate chips and decorate the truffles. Let sit at room temperature for 2 to 4 hours, or until set. Store in an airtight container for up to 3 days.

**Makes 16 pieces.**

*–Kiran Upadhyayula, Folsom, California*
*(continued)*

## ENTER THE 2022 RECIPE CONTEST: BANANAS

Got a great recipe using bananas (that's not banana bread!)? Send it in and it could win! See contest rules on page 251.

### THIRD PRIZE: $100
# PESTO RICOTTA WITH ASPARAGUS ON TOAST

1 cup ricotta cheese

¼ cup plus 2 teaspoons basil pesto

salt and freshly ground black pepper, to taste

16 asparagus spears

4 slices hearty white, whole wheat, or Panella bread

4 eggs

In a bowl, combine ricotta, ¼ cup of pesto, and salt and pepper.

Break ends off asparagus. Place spears in a shallow, nonstick pan with a lid. Add enough water to just cover asparagus. Cover and cook over medium-high heat for 6 to 8 minutes, or until crisp tender. Remove asparagus from water and blot with paper towels to dry. Sprinkle with salt and pepper. Drain water from pan and set aside for cooking the eggs.

While asparagus is cooking, toast bread slices in a toaster or under the broiler until golden brown.

Put remaining 2 teaspoons of pesto into the pan and spread out evenly. Over medium-high heat, cook eggs for about 1 to 2 minutes on one side and 30 seconds to 1 minute on the other. (You want the yolk to be runny.)

Spread one-quarter of the ricotta mixture on top of a piece of toast, then add four asparagus spears and top with an egg. Repeat for the rest of the pieces of toast. **Makes 4 servings.**

*–Renee Seaman, Andover, New Jersey*

*(continued on page 200)*

# ROUGH TIMES
# for Ruffed Grouse

## WHY IS THE DRUMMER GROWING QUIET?

by Jeff Helsdon

**ARE YOU A BIRDER?**
Show us your feathered
friends, whether in the wild or
at home. Post pics at
@theoldfarmersalmanac

"Drumming" produces a sound that is created by air filling the vacuum left by a grouse's rapidly flapping wings.

more about the ruffed grouse is the key to understanding its plight.

## A "RUFF" LIFE

The most common upland game bird in North America, the ruffed grouse has a range that stretches from Alaska and the Yukon Territory in the north down across the American Midwest to the Appalachians.

Average ruffed grouse are about 16 to 19 inches in length and weigh 17 to 25 ounces, or about 1 to 1½ pounds. Their main background color can be either gray or reddish brown. "Ruff" refers to the male's darker-color neck feathers, which are puffed out when the bird is displaying to a hen or defending its territory. A darker band is also found on the tail of both sexes, in both color phases.

One unique adaptation that grouse have to survive the winter is small lateral extensions of the scales on their feet that act like snowshoes.

Like the call of the loon, the sound of a ruffed grouse's drumming echoing through woodlots has an almost mystical quality that speaks of wild places. Starting slowly at first, the pace picks up before stopping, beating a rhythm that is eons old.

Drumming is the mating call of the ruffed grouse, intended to attract females and ward off other males. Called (in translation) the "carpenter bird" by some Native Americans because they thought that the bird was beating its wing against the log where drumming takes place, the bird produces a sound that is actually more like a sonic boom created by air filling the vacuum left by its rapidly flapping wings.

While this sound was once a commonplace sign of spring, it is being heard less and less across the ruffed grouse's range. Knowing

*(continued)*

After finding a drumming male and participating in a brief courtship, the hen searches for a nest site. Ruffed grouse are ground-nesting birds, usually making their nests in a hollowed depression in leaves. Nests are usually next to a tree trunk, stump, or a bush pile to allow the hen to watch for approaching predators.

A normal clutch is 8 to 14 buff-colored eggs. A new egg is laid every 36 hours, meaning that laying a complete clutch can take more than 2 weeks. Chicks hatch 24 to 26 days after the last egg is laid.

At hatching, ruffed grouse chicks are about the size of a person's thumb. Chicks leave the nest after they dry off and begin feeding themselves immediately. The young birds eat insects in the first few weeks, before gradually switching to plants and fruit as they become larger. Birds are fully grown by 17 weeks.

In their first fall, young males start looking for a drumming log—ideally, a fallen mature tree—and then claim the surrounding territory. Males spend the remainder of their lives within 300 yards of their drumming log.

## CHALLENGES ABOUND

The ruffed grouse's reaction to humans varies, depending on the remoteness of where it lives with its

"Ruff" refers to the male's darker-color neck feathers, which puff out when it's displaying to a hen or defending its territory.

# GROW BETTER WITH A HAND FROM US!

*Created for aspiring growers, novices, green thumbs, and old hands alike,* The Old Farmer's Almanac *gardening publications and programs always root for your success!*

### Vegetable Gardener's Handbook

"Down-to-earth" guidance on cultivating, harvesting, and storing 30+ veggies, plus advice on soil, water, fertilizer, seed-saving, pests, and more

### Gardening Webinars

*Exclusive:* Experts share techniques and tips for beginning gardens, container plants, attracting pollinators, thwarting pests, hydroponics, and more, both live and recorded for later reference

### Garden Guide

120+ inspiring pages on edibles and ornamentals, landscaping and decorating, and new products and DIY projects, plus recipes and essential reference tables

### EARLY SPRING 2022— Flower Gardener's Handbook

Essential information about growing 30+ blooming plants and shrubs, plus advice on native plants, pollinators, plot-planning, cutting and drying flowers, easy maintenance, and more

### The Gardening Club

*Exclusive (U.S. only):* Members get the annual *Old Farmer's Almanac,* best-selling Gardening Calendar, *Gardening for Everyone* magazine, and *EXTRA!* monthly e-magazine

**PRINT PRODUCTS AVAILABLE WHEREVER BOOKS AND MAGAZINES ARE SOLD. ONLINE, GO TO ALMANAC.COM OR AMAZON. FOR WEBINARS AND CLUB, VISIT ALMANAC.COM.**

Grouse thrive in areas with a comparatively greater number of tree stems per acre of forest. An important component of grouse habitat is a fallen mature tree for drumming.

surroundings. In more populated areas, it will hold perfectly still, hoping that its camouflage will conceal it, before bursting into the air in a heart-stopping flush. The same bird is unafraid of humans in remote areas and can be approached to within feet.

The grouse was an important food source for early settlers and still is in northern areas. Its natural predators include the bobcat, fisher, fox, goshawk, and great horned owl.

Ruffed grouse are a bird of secondary growth or early transitional forest, although they use all forest stages. They thrive in areas with a comparatively greater number of tree stems per acre of forest. An important component of grouse habitat is a fallen mature tree for drumming.

A serious problem is that young forest is disappearing from the United States and southern parts of Canada. This type of forest is caused by clear-cutting, a practice that is often frowned upon, and fire, which is suppressed. As the forest matures, young forest growth diminishes. To have good habitat for grouse as well as other species dependent on early successional (age-diverse) forest, repeated disturbances are needed. However, there is a societal swing toward managing for mature forestland.

*(continued)*

# START EACH DAY WITH A SMILE!

Just like this Almanac, our free **DAILY ALMANAC** newsletter is "useful, with a pleasant degree of humor"!

Written by the editors of this Almanac, this daily email arrival is full of ideas and inspirations that are specific to each day, including verse and timely articles on the topics you love—weather, gardening, nature, astronomy, recipes, natural remedies, humor, and more. The **DAILY ALMANAC**, sent straight to your Inbox first thing in the morning, will get you thinking about, talking, sharing, and doing things that brighten your day.

## PLUS . . .

With the **DAILY ALMANAC**, you'll be the first to know when new Almanac publications and products are available and get details on exclusive special offers—like this one: Sign up now for the **DAILY ALMANAC**, and you will receive our free *Beginner Gardening Guide!*

Make every "Good morning!" even better with Almanac wit and wisdom!

Sign up today! Go to

# ALMANAC.COM/SIGNUP

## A DRUMBEAT OF ALARM

The situation is dire. Grouse are listed as a species of concern in 18 states, and Indiana has recently listed the bird as an endangered species. (Grouse were once found in all of Indiana's counties but can now be found in only a few.) While grouse numbers are healthy in most Canadian provinces, there is concern in southern Ontario and Quebec.

Besides diminishing habitat, there are other factors against ruffed grouse. Grouse survive the winter by snow roosting, a technique whereby the birds literally dive into a snowbank for warmth. One concern is that a changing climate—for example, less snow in mountainous regions of the lower Appalachian states and more freeze-and-thaw cycles in the Great Lakes states, resulting in a crust on the snow—is making survival more challenging for grouse. Research is also pointing to West Nile virus negatively affecting grouse populations, especially in areas of marginal habitat.

What can you do? To learn more about ruffed grouse and/ or their habitat, visit Ruffedgrousesociety .org (in the U.S.), Rgs .ca (in Canada), or Audubon.org.

To hear and see a ruffed grouse drumming, visit Allaboutbirds.org. ∎

---

**Jeff Helsdon** is a freelance writer and photographer based in Ontario. He writes for several publications in the United States and Canada, including *Ontario OUT of DOORS*.

## GROUSE FACTS

- The ruffed grouse's Latin name, *Bonasa umbellus*, literally means "good when roasted" and "sunshade." The latter refers to the ruff on its neck.
- The ruffed grouse is the state bird of Pennsylvania.
- A group of grouse is referred to as a chorus, covey, drumming, grumbling, or leash.
- Ruffed grouse don't mate for life, and males can mate with several females in a season.
- Although ruffed grouse can survive up to 10 years, they rarely live more than a year or two due to predation and disease.
- Ruffed grouse populations in Newfoundland and Nevada were established through introduction by wildlife authorities.
- Ruffed grouse are one of 10 grouse species native to North America.
- A male grouse can be discerned from a female by looking at the feathers on its upper side, in front of the tail. Two or three whitish spots indicate a male. If there are no spots or only one, it is a female.
- The ruffed grouse is known to many Americans and Canadians as a partridge. Many attribute the origin of the term "partridge" to early European settlers, who were familiar with the partridge of their homelands. The two birds are not the same.

# THE #1 GARDEN PLANNER ON EARTH JUST GOT BETTER

## Newly designed to be easier and faster!

## USE THE PLANNER TO CREATE YOUR PERFECT VEGETABLE GARDEN THIS YEAR.

- Quickly find the best plants to grow. You can even select "easy" veggies if you're a beginner.
- Draw beds and move plants around to get the perfect layout on your computer. Have fun creating!
- Our garden planning tool calculates how many plants fit your space to avoid wasting seed.
- We'll also calculate all your planting and harvesting dates—and send along email reminders of when to do what.

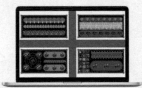

## Grow your future with a well-planned garden!

## LEARN MORE AT ALMANAC.COM/GARDENPLANNER

Versions available for PC and Mac.

### THE OLD
# FARMER'S ALMANAC
### GARDEN PLANNER

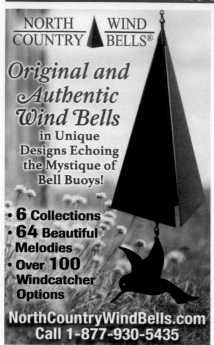
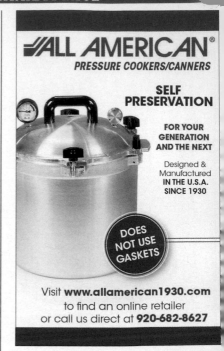
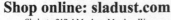
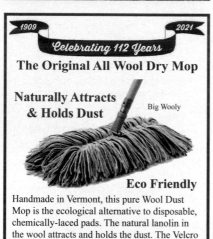

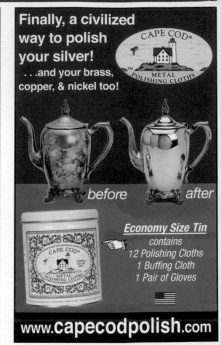

# WINTER 2021–22

MILD, SNOWY

COLD, DRY

COLD, WET

COLD, WET

COLD, SNOWY

COLD, DRY

COLD, DRY

COLD, SNOWY

COLD, DRY

MILD, DRY

MILD, WET

COLD, DRY

MILD, SNOWY

COLD, SNOWY

COLD, WET

MILD, WET

WARM, DRY

COLD, DRY

These weather maps correspond to the winter and summer predictions in the General Weather Forecast (opposite) and on the regional forecast pages, 206–223. To learn more about how we make our forecasts, turn to page 202.

# SUMMER 2022

HOT, DRY

COOL, RAINY

COOL, RAINY

HOT, RAINY

COOL, DRY

HOT, DRY

HOT, DRY

HOT, RAINY

WARM, DRY

WARM, DRY

WARM, RAINY

WARM, DRY

Maps: AccuWeather, Inc

# THE GENERAL WEATHER REPORT AND FORECAST

FOR REGIONAL FORECASTS, SEE PAGES 206-223.

What's shaping the weather? We are currently in the early stages of Solar Cycle 25, which is expected to reach its maximum peak at around July 2025. Cycle 24 was the smallest in more than 100 years, while Cycle 25 is also expected to bring very low solar activity. Low levels of solar activity have historically been associated with cooler temperatures, on average, across Earth, and we believe that most of the U.S. will have a colder-than-normal winter, although summer temperatures will average mostly above normal. Important factors include a weak La Niña, a continued warm phase in the Atlantic Multidecadal Oscillation (AMO), a neutral to positive phase in the North Atlantic Oscillation (NAO), and the Pacific Decadal Oscillation (PDO) in the early stages of its warm cycle.

WEATHER

**WINTER** will be milder than normal from eastern Montana and the western Dakotas southward to the Texas Panhandle, in western areas of the Desert Southwest, and in the Pacific coast regions, Alaska, and Hawaii, while temperatures in other areas will average below normal. Precipitation will be above normal in northern Maine, from north-central Georgia into northern Florida and westward to southeastern New Mexico, and in upper Michigan, most of the High Plains, and southern Alaska and below normal elsewhere. Snowfall will be greater than normal in the northern and central Atlantic Corridor, from Buffalo southward to northwest Georgia and westward through the Ohio Valley and northern Deep South, across much of Missouri and Kansas, in the eastern Desert Southwest, throughout the northern and central High Plains, and in much of Alaska but near or below normal in most other areas that receive snow.

**SPRING** will be warmer than normal in most of the nation, with the only exceptions being Florida and the Pacific Southwest. Rainfall will be above normal in Georgia, southern Florida, southern Texas, Minnesota, the eastern Dakotas, the Intermountain region, the Pacific Northwest, and Hawaii and from Arizona westward into southern California and near or below normal elsewhere.

**SUMMER** will be cooler than normal in the Northeast, Upper Midwest, and eastern Ohio Valley, with above-normal temperatures, on average, elsewhere. Rainfall will be less than normal from southern New England southward to Florida, from the Appalachians westward through the eastern Ohio Valley, from southern Texas westward through the Desert Southwest, and in the northern High Plains, Alaska, and eastern Hawaii and above normal elsewhere.

The best chance for a major **HURRICANE** strike will be in Georgia or the Carolinas in mid-September, with **TROPICAL STORM** threats in Texas in mid- to late June, the Southeast in mid- to late August, and the Deep South in mid- to late July and late October.

**AUTUMN** will be cooler than normal in Maine and the Southeast and from Washington southward into northern California and nearly as warm or warmer than normal elsewhere. Precipitation will be below normal in Georgia, Florida, Texas, Oklahoma, the High Plains, central and southern California, northern Alaska, and Hawaii and near or above normal elsewhere.

TO GET A SUMMARY OF THE RESULTS OF OUR FORECAST FOR LAST WINTER, TURN TO PAGE 204.

### THE OLD
# FARMER'S ALMANAC
#### FOUNDED IN 1792

*Established in 1792 and published every year thereafter*
ROBERT B. THOMAS, *founder* (1766–1846)

### YANKEE PUBLISHING INC.
**EDITORIAL AND PUBLISHING OFFICES**
P.O. Box 520, 1121 Main Street, Dublin, NH 03444
Phone: 603-563-8111 • Fax: 603-563-8252

EDITOR *(13th since 1792):* Janice Stillman
ART DIRECTOR: Colleen Quinnell
MANAGING EDITOR: Jack Burnett
SENIOR EDITORS: Sarah Perreault, Heidi Stonehill
ASSISTANT EDITOR: Benjamin Kilbride
WEATHER GRAPHICS AND CONSULTATION:
AccuWeather, Inc.

V.P., NEW MEDIA AND PRODUCTION:
Paul Belliveau
PRODUCTION DIRECTOR: David Ziarnowski
PRODUCTION MANAGER: Brian Johnson
SENIOR PRODUCTION ARTISTS:
Jennifer Freeman, Rachel Kipka, Janet Selle

**WEB SITE: ALMANAC.COM**
SENIOR DIGITAL EDITOR: Catherine Boeckmann
ASSOCIATE DIGITAL EDITOR: Christopher Burnett
NEW MEDIA DESIGNER: Amy O'Brien
DIGITAL MARKETING SPECIALIST: Holly Sanderson
E-MAIL MARKETING SPECIALIST: Samantha Caveny
E-COMMERCE DIRECTOR: Alan Henning
PROGRAMMING: Peter Rukavina

**CONTACT US**
We welcome your questions and comments about articles in and topics for this Almanac. Mail all editorial correspondence to Editor, The Old Farmer's Almanac, P.O. Box 520, Dublin, NH 03444-0520; fax us at 603-563-8252; or contact us through Almanac.com/Feedback. *The Old Farmer's Almanac* can not accept responsibility for unsolicited manuscripts and will not acknowledge any hard-copy queries or manuscripts that do not include a stamped and addressed return envelope.

All printing inks used in this edition of *The Old Farmer's Almanac* are soy-based. This product is recyclable. Consult local recycling regulations for the right way to do it.

*Thank you for buying this Almanac! We hope that you find it "useful, with a pleasant degree of humor." Thanks, too, to everyone who had a hand in it, including advertisers, distributors, printers, and sales and delivery people.*

## THE OLD
# FARMER'S ALMANAC
### FOUNDED IN 1792

### OUR CONTRIBUTORS

**Bob Berman,** our astronomy editor, leads annual tours to Chilean observatories as well as to view solar eclipses and the northern lights. He is the author of *Earth-Shattering: Violent Supernovas, Galactic Explosions, Biological Mayhem, Nuclear Meltdowns, and Other Hazards to Life in Our Universe* (Little Brown, 2019).

**Julia Shipley,** a journalist and poet, wrote the Farmer's Calendar essays that appear in this edition. She raises animals and vegetables on a small farm in northern Vermont.

**Tim Clark,** a retired English teacher from New Hampshire, has composed the weather doggerel on the Calendar Pages since 1980.

**Bethany E. Cobb,** our astronomer, is an Associate Professor of Honors and Physics at George Washington University. She conducts research on gamma-ray bursts and specializes in teaching astronomy and physics to non–science majoring students. When she is not scanning the sky, she enjoys rock climbing, figure skating, and reading science fiction.

**Celeste Longacre,** our astrologer, often refers to astrology as "a study of timing, and timing is everything." A New Hampshire native, she has been a practicing astrologer for more than 25 years. Her book, *Celeste's Garden Delights* (2015), is available for sale on her Web site, www.celestelongacre.com.

**Michael Steinberg,** our meteorologist, has been forecasting weather for the Almanac since 1996. In addition to college degrees in atmospheric science and meteorology, he brings a lifetime of experience to the task: He began predicting weather when he attended the only high school in the world with weather Teletypes and radar.

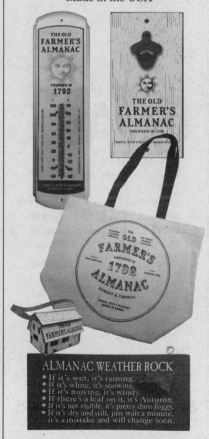
## THE OLD
# FARMER'S ALMANAC

*Established in 1792 and published every year thereafter*
ROBERT B. THOMAS, *founder* (1766–1846)

### YANKEE PUBLISHING INC.
P.O. Box 520, 1121 Main Street, Dublin, NH 03444
Phone: 603-563-8111 • Fax: 603-563-8252

PUBLISHER *(23rd since 1792):* Sherin Pierce
EDITOR IN CHIEF: Judson D. Hale Sr.

**FOR DISPLAY ADVERTISING RATES**
Go to Almanac.com/AdvertisingInfo or
call 800-895-9265, ext. 109

Stephanie Bernbach-Crowe • 914-827-0015
Steve Hall • 800-736-1100, ext. 320

**FOR CLASSIFIED ADVERTISING**
Cindy Levine, RJ Media • 212-986-0016

AD PRODUCTION COORDINATOR:
Janet Selle • 800-895-9265, ext. 168

**PUBLIC RELATIONS**
Quinn Brein • 206-842-8922
Ginger Vaughan • ginger@quinnbrein.com

**CONSUMER ORDERS & INFO**
Call 800-ALMANAC (800-256-2622)
or go to Almanac.com/Shop

**RETAIL SALES**
Stacey Korpi • 800-895-9265, ext. 160
Janice Edson, ext. 126

**DISTRIBUTORS**
NATIONAL: Comag Marketing Group
Smyrna, GA
BOOKSTORE: Houghton Mifflin Harcourt
Boston, MA
NEWSSTAND CONSULTANT: PSCS Consulting
Linda Ruth • 603-924-4407

Old Farmer's Almanac publications are available
for sales promotions or premiums. Contact Beacon
Promotions, info@beaconpromotions.com.

### YANKEE PUBLISHING INCORPORATED
#### AN EMPLOYEE-OWNED COMPANY

Jamie Trowbridge, *President;* Paul Belliveau,
Ernesto Burden, Judson D. Hale Jr.,
Brook Holmberg, Jennie Meister, Sherin Pierce,
*Vice Presidents.*

# Natural Pill Shocker Beats Out Other Powerful Joint Treatments

*2022's first major breakthrough is a new pill that uses the science behind an immune modulating botanical that "drastically reduces joint discomfort"*

A New Discovery is Quietly Helping Millions Maintain Vital Joint Health

From comfort to mobility, the relief users report continues to amaze the millions who seek non-pharma therapies for joint comfort.

The pill, sold as VeraFlex®, contains a concentrated dose of a patented natural flavonoid. Scientific studies show it promotes immune modulation, which supports healthy inflammation response, a key function to prevent further joint deterioration, and improve comfort.

"Our customers say the first thing they notice is within days of using there's greater mobility and comfort around joints. Users may also feel less bloated and experience far less digestive discomfort," explains Dr. Liza Leal, a board-certified pain-management specialist and spokesperson for VeraFlex.

"It's why they love the product. It helps relieve excess discomfort, especially around stiff and degrading joints. It's remarkable."

## An Amazing Breakthrough

Until now, many doctors have overlooked the idea of combining ingredients from different health categories, specifically linking joint health to gut health.

But researchers at the University of Rochester Medical Center provided the first evidence that bacteria in your gut could be the key driving force behind joint discomfort. And VeraFlex is proving it may be the only way going forward.

"Most of today's top treatments are financially out of reach. That's why millions of adults are still in excruciating discomfort most days or willing to accept potentially devastating side effects," explains Dr. Leal.

"VeraFlex is a cost-effective way for virtually anyone looking to improve joint mobility and comfort."

## Support Immune Health and Fight Joint Discomfort

Sufferers across the country are eager to get their hands on the new pill and according to the research, they should be.

This is because the other patented ingredient in VeraFlex is called Maxcell®, a bioenhancer made from a blend of aloe vera (acid buffer), jujube (immune support), black pepper (helps absorption), and licorice root (supports digestive health).

Studies have found that this special blend has the remarkable ability to protect the active ingredient through the digestive system and simultaneously support healthy immune function!

## The Science Behind VeraFlex

Research shows that the joint soreness and discomfort are likely caused by certain enzymes released by the body's immune system.

The featured ingredient in VeraFlex supports a healthy immune response that can inhibit the production of these enzymes. The results can be a dramatic improvment in comfort and mobility.

This immune supporting characteristic is why researchers believe people experience relief so quickly.

VeraFlex users can generally expect to start to see more flexibility in just a few days...and with continued use, a tremendous improvement to overall joint function that may help them move more like they did years prior," explains Dr. Leal. "I recommend this product because it works."

## Rapid Results & Lasting Comfort

The secret behind VeraFlex is its active ingredient UP446 which is protected by 8 patents and is backed by over $2 Million in safety studies. It's also undergone two double blind placebo controlled clinical trials, with 8 different research publications confirming the incredible results.

In the first, 60 participants were randomly placed into four groups.

The data collected by researchers was stunning.

The groups taking the VeraFlex ingredient reported staggering improvements over a 30-, 60-, and 90-day period including flexibility,

improved comfort, and joint mobility.

A second study was conducted to ensure the data was accurate. But this time, the study was done to see how quickly it worked and again the results participants experienced while taking the VeraFlex compound blew away researchers.

Shockingly, both men and women experienced an improvement in flexibility in as little as 3 days, which was 2 days faster than the group using powerful traditional treatments.

The ingredients create a triple play for supporting joint health. First is accelerated action that's clinically shown to improve comfort and mobility...second is lasting comfort... and third is long-term safety without known side effects.

This would explain why so many users are experiencing impressive results so quickly. Because each dose of VeraFlex delivers the same amount of UP446 as the clinical studies, readers can now experience the same affordable comfort with daily use.

"The science and clinical studies are remarkable," explains Dr. Leal. "This product starts working incredibly fast. Users should expect to be highly satisfied with the results."

## How to Claim Three Free Months of VeraFlex

This is the official nationwide release of the new VeraFlex pill. And so, the company is offering our readers up to 3 FREE bottles with their order.

This special give-away is available for only a limited time so don't wait. All you have to do is call toll free **1-800-997-5967** and provide the operator with the Approval Code: VF2104. The company will do the rest.

The company is so confident it will work that each order is backed by our 100% satisfaction guarantee; if you don't love the results, we'll refund the purchase price, no questions asked.

With such an incredible offer this is expected to sell out. Don't wait to call, US operators are standing by.

# ECLIPSES

There will be four eclipses in 2022, two of the Sun and two of the Moon. Solar eclipses are visible only in certain areas and require eye protection to be viewed safely. Lunar eclipses are technically visible from the entire night side of Earth, but during a penumbral eclipse, the dimming of the Moon's illumination is slight. See the **Astronomical Glossary, page 110,** for explanations of the different types of eclipses.

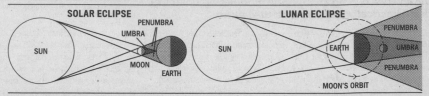

**APRIL 30: PARTIAL ECLIPSE OF THE SUN.** This eclipse is not visible from North America. (The partial solar eclipse is visible from the southeastern Pacific Ocean, the Antarctic Peninsula, and southern South America.)

**MAY 15-16: TOTAL ECLIPSE OF THE MOON.** This eclipse is visible from North America, except in northwestern regions. The Moon will enter the penumbra at 9:31 P.M. EDT on May 15 (6:31 P.M. PDT) and leave it at 2:52 A.M. EDT on May 16 (11:52 P.M. PDT on May 15).

**OCTOBER 25: PARTIAL ECLIPSE OF THE SUN.** This eclipse is not visible from North America. (The partial solar eclipse is visible from Greenland, Iceland, Europe, northeastern Africa, the Middle East, western Asia, India, and western China.)

**NOVEMBER 8: TOTAL ECLIPSE OF THE MOON.** This eclipse is visible from North America, although the Moon will be setting during the eclipse for observers in eastern regions. The Moon will enter the penumbra at 3:01 A.M. EST on November 8 (12:01 A.M. PST) and leave it at 8:58 A.M. EST (5:58 A.M. PST).

**TRANSIT OF MERCURY.** Mercury's proximity to the Sun makes it difficult to observe. The planet can be seen for only a few weeks before and after times of greatest elongation. Near its greatest eastern and western elongations, Mercury is observable during evening twilight and morning twilight, respectively. In 2022, Mercury is best viewed from the Northern Hemisphere just after sunset from mid-April to early May and shortly before sunrise during the first 3 weeks of October. Look for a conjunction between Mercury and Saturn on the morning of March 2 and between Mercury and Jupiter on the morning of March 20.

## THE MOON'S PATH

The Moon's path across the sky changes with the seasons. Full Moons are very high in the sky (at midnight) between November and February and very low in the sky between May and July.

### FULL-MOON DATES (ET)

|      | 2022 | 2023 | 2024 | 2025 | 2026 |
|------|------|------|------|------|------|
| JAN. | 17   | 6    | 25   | 13   | 3    |
| FEB. | 16   | 5    | 24   | 12   | 1    |
| MAR. | 18   | 7    | 25   | 14   | 3    |
| APR. | 16   | 6    | 23   | 12   | 1    |
| MAY  | 16   | 5    | 23   | 12   | 1 & 31 |
| JUNE | 14   | 3    | 21   | 11   | 29   |
| JULY | 13   | 3    | 21   | 10   | 29   |
| AUG. | 11   | 1 & 30 | 19 | 9    | 28   |
| SEPT.| 10   | 29   | 17   | 7    | 26   |
| OCT. | 9    | 28   | 17   | 6    | 26   |
| NOV. | 8    | 27   | 15   | 5    | 24   |
| DEC. | 7    | 26   | 15   | 4    | 23   |

**Make your home more comfortable than ever**

# "To you, it's the **perfect lift chair.** To me, it's the **best sleep chair** I've ever had."

— J. Fitzgerald, VA

**NOW** also available in **Genuine Italian Leather** *(and new Chestnut color)*

**Three Chairs in One** Sleep/Recline/Lift

ACCREDITED BUSINESS **A+**

Pictured: Genuine Italian Leather chair chestnut color.

**You can't always lie down in bed and sleep. Heartburn, cardiac problems, hip or back aches – and dozens of other ailments and worries.** Those are the nights you'd give anything for a comfortable chair to sleep in: one that reclines to exactly the right degree, raises your feet and legs just where you want them, supports your head and shoulders properly, and <u>operates at the touch of a button</u>.

Our **Perfect Sleep Chair®** does all that and more. More than a chair or recliner, it's designed to provide total comfort. **Choose your preferred heat and massage settings, for hours of soothing relaxation.** Reading or watching TV? Our chair's recline technology allows you to pause the chair in an infinite number of settings. You'll love the other benefits, too. It helps with correct spinal alignment and promotes back pressure relief, to prevent back and muscle pain. The overstuffed,

oversized biscuit style back and unique seat design will cradle you in comfort. Generously filled, wide armrests provide enhanced arm support when sitting or reclining. **It even has a battery backup in case of a power outage.**

**White glove delivery** included in shipping charge. Professionals will deliver the chair to the exact spot in your home where you want it, unpack it, inspect it, test it, position it, and even carry the packaging away! You get your choice of Genuine Italian leather, stain and water repellent custom-manufactured DuraLux™ with the classic leather look or plush MicroLux™ microfiber in a variety of colors to fit any decor. **New Chestnut color only available in Genuine Italian Leather. Call now!**

## The Perfect Sleep Chair®
# 1-888-849-1623

Mention code 115047 when ordering.

Because each Perfect Sleep Chair is a made-to-order bedding product it cannot be returned, but if it arrives damaged or defective, at our option we will repair it or replace it. © 2021 *first*STREET for Boomers and Beyond, Inc.

46562

# BRIGHT STARS

## TRANSIT TIMES

This table shows the time (ET) and altitude of a star as it transits the meridian (i.e., reaches its highest elevation while passing over the horizon's south point) at Boston on the dates shown. The transit time on any other date differs from that of the nearest date listed by approximately 4 minutes per day. To find the time of a star's transit for your location, convert its time at Boston using Key Letter C (see Time Corrections, page 238).

| STAR | CONSTELLATION | MAGNITUDE | TIME OF TRANSIT (ET) BOLD = P.M. LIGHT = A.M. | | | | | | ALTITUDE (DEGREES) |
|------|---------------|-----------|--------|--------|-------|--------|---------|--------|----------|
| | | | JAN. 1 | MAR. 1 | MAY 1 | JULY 1 | SEPT. 1 | NOV. 1 | |
| Altair | Aquila | 0.8 | 12:51 | 8:59 | 5:59 | 1:59 | 9:51 | 5:51 | 56.3 |
| Deneb | Cygnus | 1.3 | 1:41 | 9:49 | 6:49 | 2:49 | 10:41 | 6:42 | 92.8 |
| Fomalhaut | Psc. Aus. | 1.2 | 3:57 | 12:05 | 9:05 | 5:05 | 1:02 | 8:58 | 17.8 |
| Algol | Perseus | 2.2 | 8:07 | 4:15 | 1:15 | 9:16 | 5:12 | 1:12 | 88.5 |
| Aldebaran | Taurus | 0.9 | 9:35 | 5:43 | 2:43 | 10:43 | 6:39 | 2:39 | 64.1 |
| Rigel | Orion | 0.1 | 10:13 | 6:21 | 3:21 | 11:21 | 7:17 | 3:18 | 39.4 |
| Capella | Auriga | 0.1 | 10:16 | 6:24 | 3:24 | 11:24 | 7:20 | 3:20 | 93.6 |
| Bellatrix | Orion | 1.6 | 10:24 | 6:32 | 3:32 | 11:32 | 7:28 | 3:28 | 54.0 |
| Betelgeuse | Orion | var. 0.4 | 10:53 | 7:02 | 4:02 | 12:02 | 7:58 | 3:58 | 55.0 |
| Sirius | Can. Maj. | −1.4 | 11:43 | 7:51 | 4:51 | 12:51 | 8:48 | 4:48 | 31.0 |
| Procyon | Can. Min. | 0.4 | 12:41 | 8:45 | 5:45 | 1:46 | 9:42 | 5:42 | 52.9 |
| Pollux | Gemini | 1.2 | 12:47 | 8:52 | 5:52 | 1:52 | 9:48 | 5:48 | 75.7 |
| Regulus | Leo | 1.4 | 3:10 | 11:14 | 8:14 | 4:14 | 12:11 | 8:11 | 59.7 |
| Spica | Virgo | var. 1.0 | 6:26 | 2:34 | 11:30 | 7:31 | 3:27 | 11:27 | 36.6 |
| Arcturus | Boötes | −0.1 | 7:16 | 3:24 | 12:25 | 8:21 | 4:17 | 12:17 | 66.9 |
| Antares | Scorpius | var. 0.9 | 9:30 | 5:38 | 2:38 | 10:35 | 6:31 | 2:31 | 21.3 |
| Vega | Lyra | 0 | 11:37 | 7:45 | 4:45 | 12:45 | 8:37 | 4:37 | 86.4 |

## RISE AND SET TIMES

To find the time of a star's rising at Boston on any date, subtract the interval shown at right from the star's transit time on that date; add the interval to find the star's setting time. To find the rising and setting times for your city, convert the Boston transit times above using the Key Letter shown at right before applying the interval (see Time Corrections, page 238). Deneb, Algol, Capella, and Vega are circumpolar stars—they never set but appear to circle the celestial north pole.

| STAR | INTERVAL (H.M.) | RISING KEY | DIR.* | SETTING KEY | DIR.* |
|------|-----------------|------------|-------|-------------|-------|
| Altair | 6 36 | B | EbN | E | WbN |
| Fomalhaut | 3 59 | E | SE | D | SW |
| Aldebaran | 7 06 | B | ENE | D | WNW |
| Rigel | 5 33 | D | EbS | B | WbS |
| Bellatrix | 6 27 | B | EbN | D | WbN |
| Betelgeuse | 6 31 | B | EbN | D | WbN |
| Sirius | 5 00 | D | ESE | B | WSW |
| Procyon | 6 23 | B | EbN | D | WbN |
| Pollux | 8 01 | A | NE | E | NW |
| Regulus | 6 49 | B | EbN | D | WbN |
| Spica | 5 23 | D | EbS | B | WbS |
| Arcturus | 7 19 | A | ENE | E | WNW |
| Antares | 4 17 | E | SEbE | A | SWbW |

*b = "by"

# SCIATICA BACK PAIN?

Are radiating pains down the back of your leg, or pain in your lower back or buttocks making it uncomfortable to sit, walk or sleep? Millions of people are suffering unnecessarily because they are not aware of this effective, topical treatment.

MagniLife® Leg & Back Pain Relief Cream combines seven active ingredients including Colocynthis to relieve burning pains and tingling sensations. This product is not intended to *treat or cure* sciatica, but can relieve painful symptoms. *"It provided me with the only relief for my sciatica."* - Mary.

MagniLife® Leg & Back Pain Relief Cream is **sold at Walgreens, CVS, Rite Aid and Amazon**. Order risk free for $19.99 +$5.95 S&H for a 4 oz jar. Get a **FREE** jar when you order two for $39.98 +$5.95 S&H. Send payment to: MagniLife SC-FA2, PO Box 6789, McKinney, TX 75071 or call **1-800-993-7691**. Money back guarantee. Order now at **www.LegBackCream.com**

# BURNING FOOT PAIN?

Do you suffer from burning, tingling or stabbing pain in your feet? You should know help is available. Many are suffering from these symptoms and live in pain because they are not aware of this proven treatment.

MagniLife® Pain Relieving Foot Cream contains eucalyptus oil and yellow jasmine, known to relieve tingling, burning, and stabbing pain while also restoring cracked, damaged, and itchy skin. *"It's the ONLY product that helps relieve the burning, and tingling feeling in my feet!"* - Mabel, NY

MagniLife® Pain Relieving Foot Cream is **sold at Walgreens, CVS, Rite Aid and Walmart** in footcare and diabetes care. Order risk free for $19.99 +$5.95 S&H for a 4 oz jar. **Get a FREE jar** when you order two for $39.98 +$5.95 S&H. Send payment to: MagniLife NC-FA2, PO Box 6789, McKinney, TX 75071, or call **1-800-993-7691**. Satisfaction guaranteed. Order at **www.MDFootCream.com**

# PSORIASIS ITCH OR PAIN?

Is itchy, painful, red or scaly skin causing you discomfort or embarrassment? Millions of Americans now suffer from psoriasis, which is becoming more prevalent among older adults. New treatments are now available without steroids or prescriptions.

MagniLife® Psoriasis Care+ can be used on the scalp, knees, elbows and body and contains Oat-derived Beta Glucan to relieve itching, pain and redness. Moisturizing gel deeply hydrates for visibly healthier skin. *"...for me this will take away the pain and burning overnight."* - Jessica.

MagniLife® Psoriasis Care+ is sold at **Walgreens** stores and **Amazon**. Order risk free for $17.99 +$5.95 S&H for a 2 oz jar. Get a FREE jar when you order two for $35.98 +$5.95 S&H. Send payment to: MagniLife OC-FA2, PO Box 6789, McKinney, TX 75071 or call **1-800-993-7691**. Satisfaction guaranteed. Order now at **www.PsoriasisCareGel.com**

# THE TWILIGHT ZONE/METEOR SHOWERS

Twilight is the time when the sky is partially illuminated preceding sunrise and again following sunset. The ranges of twilight are defined according to the Sun's position below the horizon. **Civil twilight** occurs when the Sun's center is between the horizon and 6 degrees below the horizon (visually, the horizon is clearly defined). **Nautical twilight** occurs when the center is between 6 and 12 degrees below the horizon (the horizon is distinct). **Astronomical twilight** occurs when the center is between 12 and 18 degrees below the horizon (sky illumination is imperceptible). When the center is at 18 degrees (**dawn** or **dark**) or below, there is no illumination.

## LENGTH OF ASTRONOMICAL TWILIGHT (HOURS AND MINUTES)

| LATITUDE | JAN. 1–APR. 10 | APR. 11–MAY 2 | MAY 3–MAY 14 | MAY 15–MAY 25 | MAY 26–JULY 22 | JULY 23–AUG. 3 | AUG. 4–AUG. 14 | AUG. 15–SEPT. 5 | SEPT. 6–DEC. 31 |
|---|---|---|---|---|---|---|---|---|---|
| 25°N to 30°N | 1 20 | 1 23 | 1 26 | 1 29 | 1 32 | 1 29 | 1 26 | 1 23 | 1 20 |
| 31°N to 36°N | 1 26 | 1 28 | 1 34 | 1 38 | 1 43 | 1 38 | 1 34 | 1 28 | 1 26 |
| 37°N to 42°N | 1 33 | 1 39 | 1 47 | 1 52 | 1 59 | 1 52 | 1 47 | 1 39 | 1 33 |
| 43°N to 47°N | 1 42 | 1 51 | 2 02 | 2 13 | 2 27 | 2 13 | 2 02 | 1 51 | 1 42 |
| 48°N to 49°N | 1 50 | 2 04 | 2 22 | 2 42 | – | 2 42 | 2 22 | 2 04 | 1 50 |

**TO DETERMINE THE LENGTH OF TWILIGHT:** The length of twilight changes with latitude and the time of year. See the **Time Corrections, page 238,** to find the latitude of your city or the city nearest you. Use that figure in the chart above with the appropriate date to calculate the length of twilight in your area.

**TO DETERMINE ARRIVAL OF DAWN OR DARK:** Calculate the sunrise/sunset times for your locality using the instructions in **How to Use This Almanac, page 116.**

Subtract the length of twilight from the time of sunrise to determine when dawn breaks. Add the length of twilight to the time of sunset to determine when dark descends.

### EXAMPLE:
**BOSTON, MASS. (LATITUDE 42°22')**

| | |
|---|---|
| Sunrise, August 1 | 5:37 A.M. ET |
| Length of twilight | – 1 52 |
| Dawn breaks | 3:45 A.M. |
| Sunset, August 1 | 8:04 P.M. ET |
| Length of twilight | +1 52 |
| Dark descends | 9:56 P.M. |

## PRINCIPAL METEOR SHOWERS

| SHOWER | BEST VIEWING | POINT OF ORIGIN | DATE OF MAXIMUM* | NO. PER HOUR** | ASSOCIATED COMET |
|---|---|---|---|---|---|
| Quadrantid | Predawn | N | Jan. 4 | 25 | – |
| Lyrid | Predawn | S | Apr. 22 | 10 | Thatcher |
| Eta Aquarid | Predawn | SE | May 4 | 10 | Halley |
| Delta Aquarid | Predawn | S | July 30 | 10 | – |
| **Perseid** | **Predawn** | **NE** | **Aug. 11–13** | **50** | **Swift-Tuttle** |
| Draconid | Late evening | NW | Oct. 9 | 6 | Giacobini-Zinner |
| Orionid | Predawn | S | Oct. 21–22 | 15 | Halley |
| Northern Taurid | Late evening | S | Nov. 9 | 3 | Encke |
| Leonid | Predawn | S | Nov. 17–18 | 10 | Tempel-Tuttle |
| Andromedid | Late evening | S | Nov. 25–27 | 5 | Biela |
| **Geminid** | **All night** | **NE** | **Dec. 13–14** | **75** | – |
| Ursid | Predawn | N | Dec. 22 | 5 | Tuttle |

*May vary by 1 or 2 days    **In a moonless, rural sky    **Bold** = most prominent

# NEW PROSTATE PILL HELPS RELIEVE SYMPTOMS WITHOUT DRUGS OR SURGERY

## Combats all-night bathroom urges and embarrassment... *Yet most doctors don't even know about it!*

By Health Writer, Peter Metler

Thanks to a brand new discovery made from a rare prostate relief plant; thousands of men across America are taking their lives back from "prostate hell". This remarkable new natural supplement helps you:

- **MINIMIZE** constant urges to urinate
- **END** embarrassing sexual "let-downs"
- **SUPPORT** a strong, healthy urine flow
- **GET** a restful night of uninterrupted sleep
- **STOP** false alarms, dribbles
- **ENJOY** a truly empty bladder

More men than ever before are dealing with prostate problems that range from annoying to downright EMBARRASSING! But now, research has discovered a new solution so remarkable that helps alleviate symptoms associated with an enlarged prostate (sexual failure, lost sleep, bladder discomfort and urgent runs to the bathroom). Like nothing before!

Yet 9 out of 10 doctors don't know about it! Here's why: Due to strict managed health care constrictions, many MD's are struggling to keep their practices afloat. "Unfortunately, there's no money in prescribing natural products. They aren't nearly as profitable," says a confidential source. Instead, doctors rely on toxic drugs that help, but could leave you sexually "powerless" (or a lot worse)!

On a CNN Special, Medical Correspondent Dr. Steve Salvatore shocked America by quoting a statistic from the prestigious Journal of American Medical Association that stated, "... about 60% of men who go under the knife for a prostatectomy are left UNABLE to perform sexually!"

### PROSTATE PROBLEM SOLVED!

But now you can now beat the odds. And enjoy better sleep, a powerful urine stream and a long and healthy love life. The secret? You need to load your diet with essential Phyto-Nutrients, (traditionally found in certain fruits, vegetables and grains).

The problem is, most Phyto-Nutrients never get into your bloodstream. They're destroyed

### HERE ARE 6 WARNING SIGNS YOU BETTER NOT IGNORE

- ✓ Waking up 2 to 6 times a night to urinate
- ✓ A constant feeling that you have to "go"... but can't
- ✓ A burning sensation when you do go
- ✓ A weak urine stream
- ✓ A feeling that your bladder is never completely empty
- ✓ Embarrassing sputtering, dripping & staining

by today's food preparation methods (cooking, long storage times and food additives).

### YEARS OF RESEARCH

Thankfully, a small company (Wellness Logix™) out of Maine, is on a mission to change that. They've created a product that arms men who suffer with prostate inflammation with new hope. And it's fast becoming the #1 Prostate formula in America.

*Prostate IQ*™ gives men the super-concentrated dose of Phyto-Nutrients they need to beat prostate symptoms. "You just can't get them from your regular diet" say Daniel. It's taken a long time to understand how to capture the prostate relieving power of this amazing botanical. But their hard work paid off. *Prostate IQ*™ is different than any other prostate supplement on the market...

### DON'T BE FOOLED BY CHEAP FORMULATIONS!

Many hope you won't notice, but a lot of prostate supplements fall embarrassingly short with their dosages. The formulas may be okay, but they won't do a darn thing for you unless you take 10 or more tablets a day. *Prostate IQ*™ contains a whopping 300mg of this special "Smart Prostate Plant". So it's loaded with Phyto-Nutrients. Plus, it gets inside your bloodstream faster and stays inside for maximum results!

### TRY IT RISK-FREE

#### SPECIAL OPPORTUNITY

Get a risk-free trial supply of *Prostate IQ*™ today - just for asking. But you must act now, supplies are limited!

**Call Now, Toll-Free at:**

# 1-800-380-0925

# THE VISIBLE PLANETS

Listed here for Boston are viewing suggestions for and the rise and set times (ET) of Venus, Mars, Jupiter, and Saturn on specific days each month, as well as when it is best to view Mercury. Approximate rise and set times for other days can be found by interpolation. Use the Key Letters at the right of each listing to convert the times for other localities **(see pages 116 and 238).**

**FOR ALL PLANET RISE AND SET TIMES BY ZIP CODE, VISIT ALMANAC.COM/2022.**

## VENUS

Venus will appear as a dazzling morning star, especially in February and March. The year opens with Venus low in the west in evening twilight, only to sink and vanish a few days later. Venus then emerges as a morning star in mid-January and remains striking through the summer, while gradually fading from its mid-February brilliance at magnitude –4.9. It plummets even lower until it sinks too low in September and finally vanishes behind the Sun in its superior conjunction on October 22. It slowly emerges again as an evening star to be glimpsed low in the western twilight in December. After forming a triangle with Jupiter and the Moon on April 27, it has a predawn conjunction with Jupiter on the 30th.

| | | | | | | | | | | | | | | | |
|---|---|---|---|---|---|---|---|---|---|---|---|---|---|---|---|
| Jan. 1 | set | **5:27** | B | Apr. 1 | rise | 4:38 | D | July 1 | rise | 3:17 | A | Oct. 1 | rise | 6:12 | C |
| Jan. 11 | rise | 6:34 | D | Apr. 11 | rise | 4:29 | D | July 11 | rise | 3:21 | A | Oct. 11 | rise | 6:36 | D |
| Jan. 21 | rise | 5:31 | D | Apr. 21 | rise | 4:19 | D | July 21 | rise | 3:31 | A | Oct. 21 | set | **5:56** | B |
| Feb. 1 | rise | 4:43 | D | May 1 | rise | 4:07 | C | Aug. 1 | rise | 3:48 | A | Nov. 1 | set | **5:47** | B |
| Feb. 11 | rise | 4:17 | E | May 11 | rise | 3:55 | C | Aug. 11 | rise | 4:08 | A | Nov. 11 | set | **4:41** | B |
| Feb. 21 | rise | 4:03 | E | May 21 | rise | 3:44 | B | Aug. 21 | rise | 4:31 | B | Nov. 21 | set | **4:41** | A |
| Mar. 1 | rise | 3:57 | E | June 1 | rise | 3:32 | B | Sept. 1 | rise | 4:58 | B | Dec. 1 | set | **4:47** | A |
| Mar. 11 | rise | 3:51 | E | June 11 | rise | 3:23 | B | Sept. 11 | rise | 5:22 | B | Dec. 11 | set | **4:58** | A |
| Mar. 21 | rise | 4:45 | D | June 21 | rise | 3:18 | B | Sept. 21 | rise | 5:47 | C | Dec. 21 | set | **5:16** | A |
| | | | | | | | | | | | | Dec. 31 | set | **5:38** | A |

## MARS

Mars achieves its brightest appearance on December 8, when it is higher in the sky for Northern Hemisphere observers than anytime in the past 15 years. The Red Planet starts the year as a predawn object subdued by dawn's twilight glare, shining at nearly its dimmest at magnitude 1.6. It slowly inches farther from the Sun and by April reaches the first magnitude. Steadily brightening as it glides eastward, it breaks the zero-magnitude threshold in August in Aries. Brightening through the summer as it crosses into Taurus, it starts rising before midnight and comes up soon after nightfall in November. Mars is closest on November 30 and reaches opposition on December 8 at a magnitude of –1.9, when it rises at sunset, is out all night long, and displays a disk 17 arc seconds in width.

| | | | | | | | | | | | | | | | |
|---|---|---|---|---|---|---|---|---|---|---|---|---|---|---|---|
| Jan. 1 | rise | 5:13 | E | Apr. 1 | rise | 4:33 | D | July 1 | rise | 1:15 | B | Oct. 1 | **rise** | **9:47** | A |
| Jan. 11 | rise | 5:08 | E | Apr. 11 | rise | 4:14 | D | July 11 | rise | 12:53 | B | Oct. 11 | **rise** | **9:18** | A |
| Jan. 21 | rise | 5:02 | E | Apr. 21 | rise | 3:53 | D | July 21 | rise | 12:31 | B | Oct. 21 | **rise** | **8:44** | A |
| Feb. 1 | rise | 4:54 | E | May 1 | rise | 3:32 | D | Aug. 1 | rise | 12:08 | B | Nov. 1 | **rise** | **8:01** | A |
| Feb. 11 | rise | 4:45 | E | May 11 | rise | 3:10 | D | Aug. 11 | **rise** | **11:44** | B | Nov. 11 | **rise** | **6:14** | A |
| Feb. 21 | rise | 4:34 | E | May 21 | rise | 2:48 | C | Aug. 21 | **rise** | **11:23** | B | Nov. 21 | **rise** | **5:22** | A |
| Mar. 1 | rise | 4:23 | E | June 1 | rise | 2:23 | C | Sept. 1 | **rise** | **10:59** | A | Dec. 1 | **rise** | **4:26** | A |
| Mar. 11 | rise | 4:09 | E | June 11 | rise | 2:00 | C | Sept. 11 | **rise** | **10:37** | A | Dec. 11 | set | 7:01 | E |
| Mar. 21 | rise | 4:53 | E | June 21 | rise | 1:38 | B | Sept. 21 | **rise** | **10:13** | A | Dec. 21 | set | 6:06 | E |
| | | | | | | | | | | | | Dec. 31 | set | 5:15 | E |

**BOLD** = P.M.   LIGHT = A.M.

## JUPITER

Jupiter opens the year as an evening star in Aquarius, low in the southwest evening. By month's end, it has sunk too low to be easily seen, but it reappears as a morning star in mid-April. Jupiter has a conjunction with Venus on April 30 in the predawn east and rises 2 hours earlier each month thereafter, until rising before midnight in August. Jupiter's opposition occurs on September 26, when it has a magnitude of –2.9. In autumn, it is increasingly an evening sky object. Jupiter remains visible in the west after sunset through the end of the year.

| | | | | | | | | | | | | | | | |
|---|---|---|---|---|---|---|---|---|---|---|---|---|---|---|---|
| Jan. 1 | set | 8:28 | B | Apr. 1 | rise | 5:48 | C | July 1 | rise | 12:27 | C | Oct. 1 | set | 6:20 | C |
| Jan. 11 | set | 7:59 | B | Apr. 11 | rise | 5:14 | C | July 11 | rise | 11:46 | C | Oct. 11 | set | 5:34 | C |
| Jan. 21 | set | 7:31 | B | Apr. 21 | rise | 4:40 | C | July 21 | rise | 11:08 | C | Oct. 21 | set | 4:49 | C |
| Feb. 1 | set | 7:01 | B | May 1 | rise | 4:05 | C | Aug. 1 | rise | 10:25 | C | Nov. 1 | set | 4:01 | C |
| Feb. 11 | set | 6:34 | B | May 11 | rise | 3:30 | C | Aug. 11 | rise | 9:45 | C | Nov. 11 | set | 2:18 | C |
| Feb. 21 | set | 6:07 | B | May 21 | rise | 2:55 | C | Aug. 21 | rise | 9:05 | C | Nov. 21 | set | 1:38 | C |
| Mar. 1 | set | 5:45 | C | June 1 | rise | 2:16 | C | Sept. 1 | rise | 8:19 | C | Dec. 1 | set | 12:59 | C |
| Mar. 11 | rise | 5:59 | D | June 11 | rise | 1:41 | C | Sept. 11 | rise | 7:38 | C | Dec. 11 | set | 12:22 | C |
| Mar. 21 | rise | 6:25 | D | June 21 | rise | 1:04 | C | Sept. 21 | rise | 6:56 | C | Dec. 21 | set | 11:43 | C |
| | | | | | | | | | | | | Dec. 31 | set | 11:09 | C |

## SATURN

Saturn starts the year low in the west at dusk, in Capricornus. Its rings are angled in open configuration easily observable through any telescope using more than 30× magnification. Saturn vanishes into solar glare by late January, reappears in the predawn east in March, and then rises 2 hours earlier each month. The Ringed Planet comes up before midnight in late June and slightly brightens until it reaches its opposition on August 14, when it is out all night. The Moon is near Saturn on May 22, June 18, and July 15 and closely meets Mars in the predawn hours of April 4 and 5 while standing 15 degrees high.

| | | | | | | | | | | | | | | | |
|---|---|---|---|---|---|---|---|---|---|---|---|---|---|---|---|
| Jan. 1 | set | 6:51 | B | Apr. 1 | rise | 4:38 | D | July 1 | rise | 10:44 | D | Oct. 1 | set | 2:33 | B |
| Jan. 11 | set | 6:18 | B | Apr. 11 | rise | 4:01 | D | July 11 | rise | 10:04 | D | Oct. 11 | set | 1:52 | B |
| Jan. 21 | set | 5:44 | B | Apr. 21 | rise | 3:24 | D | July 21 | rise | 9:23 | D | Oct. 21 | set | 1:12 | B |
| Feb. 1 | set | 5:08 | B | May 1 | rise | 2:46 | D | Aug. 1 | rise | 8:38 | D | Nov. 1 | set | 12:29 | B |
| Feb. 11 | rise | 6:36 | E | May 11 | rise | 2:08 | D | Aug. 11 | rise | 7:57 | D | Nov. 11 | set | 10:47 | B |
| Feb. 21 | rise | 6:00 | D | May 21 | rise | 1:30 | D | Aug. 21 | set | 5:27 | B | Nov. 21 | set | 10:10 | B |
| Mar. 1 | rise | 5:31 | D | June 1 | rise | 12:47 | D | Sept. 1 | set | 4:39 | B | Dec. 1 | set | 9:34 | B |
| Mar. 11 | rise | 4:55 | D | June 11 | rise | 12:08 | D | Sept. 11 | set | 3:56 | B | Dec. 11 | set | 8:58 | B |
| Mar. 21 | rise | 5:18 | D | June 21 | rise | 11:24 | D | Sept. 21 | set | 3:14 | B | Dec. 21 | set | 8:24 | B |
| | | | | | | | | | | | | Dec. 31 | set | 7:49 | B |

## MERCURY

Mercury dashes from the morning to the evening sky every few months. To observe Mercury, it must be at least 5 degrees above the horizon 40 minutes after sunset or before sunrise, at a time when its brightness exceeds magnitude 0.5. This year, its most favorable evening star conditions occur in twilight during the last half of April. It may be glimpsed less favorably as an evening star in the first half of January and from July 25 to September 1. In the eastern sky, Mercury is best seen as a morning star during the first 3 weeks of October, in the first 3 weeks of March, the last half of June, and from October 10 to 25.

**DO NOT CONFUSE:** *Mars with Saturn during their conjunction on April 4 and 5. Mars is orange, Saturn is brighter. • Jupiter with Venus on April 30 and during February through May, when both are visible before dawn. Venus is brighter. • Saturn with Mercury on February 2, low in the east before dawn. Mercury is slightly orange. • Venus, Mars, and Saturn when they form a triangle before dawn from March 24 to 26. Venus is brighter than the others, while Saturn is brighter than Mars.*

# ASTRONOMICAL GLOSSARY

**APHELION (APH.):** The point in a planet's orbit that is farthest from the Sun.

**APOGEE (APO.):** The point in the Moon's orbit that is farthest from Earth.

**CELESTIAL EQUATOR (EQ.):** The imaginary circle around the celestial sphere that can be thought of as the plane of Earth's equator projected out onto the sphere.

**CELESTIAL SPHERE:** An imaginary sphere projected into space that represents the entire sky, with an observer on Earth at its center. All celestial bodies other than Earth are imagined as being on its inside surface.

**CIRCUMPOLAR:** Always visible above the horizon, such as a circumpolar star.

**CONJUNCTION:** The time at which two or more celestial bodies appear closest in the sky. **Inferior (Inf.):** Mercury or Venus is between the Sun and Earth. **Superior (Sup.):** The Sun is between a planet and Earth. Actual dates for conjunctions are given on the **Right-Hand Calendar Pages, 121–147;** the best times for viewing the closely aligned bodies are given in **Sky Watch** on the **Left-Hand Calendar Pages, 120–146.**

**DECLINATION:** The celestial latitude of an object in the sky, measured in degrees north or south of the celestial equator; comparable to latitude on Earth. This Almanac gives the Sun's declination at noon.

**ECLIPSE, LUNAR:** The full Moon enters the shadow of Earth, which cuts off all or part of the sunlight reflected off the Moon. **Total:** The Moon passes completely through the umbra (central dark part) of Earth's shadow. **Partial:** Only part of the Moon passes through the umbra. **Penumbral:** The Moon passes through only the penumbra (area of partial darkness surrounding the umbra). See **page 102** for more information about eclipses.

**ECLIPSE, SOLAR:** Earth enters the shadow of the new Moon, which cuts off all or part of the Sun's light. **Total:** Earth passes through the umbra (central dark part) of the Moon's shadow, resulting in totality for observers within a narrow band on Earth. **Annular:** The Moon appears silhouetted against the Sun, with a ring of sunlight showing around it. **Partial:** The Moon blocks only part of the Sun.

**ECLIPTIC:** The apparent annual path of the Sun around the celestial sphere. The plane of the ecliptic is tipped 23½° from the celestial equator.

**ELONGATION:** The difference in degrees between the celestial longitudes of a planet and the Sun. **Greatest Elongation (Gr. Elong.):** The greatest apparent distance of a planet from the Sun, as seen from Earth.

**EPACT:** A number from 1 to 30 that indicates the Moon's age on January 1 at Greenwich, England; used in determining the date of Easter.

**EQUINOX:** When the Sun crosses the celestial equator. This event occurs two times each year: **Vernal** is around March 20 and **Autumnal** is around September 22.

**EVENING STAR:** A planet that is above the western horizon at sunset and less than 180° east of the Sun in right ascension.

**GOLDEN NUMBER:** A number in the 19-year Metonic cycle of the Moon, used in determining the date of Easter. See **page 149** for this year's Golden Number.

**MAGNITUDE:** A measure of a celestial object's brightness. **Apparent magnitude** measures the brightness of an object as seen from Earth. Objects with an apparent magnitude of 6 or less are observable to the naked eye. The lower the magnitude, the greater the brightness; an object with a magnitude of –1, e.g., is brighter than one with a magnitude of +1.

*(continued)*

# New Bladder Control Pill Sales May Surpass Adult Diapers By 2023

**Drug-free discovery works, say doctors. Many adults ditching diapers and pads for clinical strength pill that triggers day and night bladder support.**

By J.K. Roberts
*Interactive News Media*

INM — Over 150,000 doses have shipped to bladder sufferers so far, and sales continue to climb every day for the 'diaper replacing' new pill called BladderMax.

"We knew we had a great product, but it's even exceeded our expectations," said Keith Graham, Manager of Call Center Operations for BladderMax.

"People just keep placing orders, it's pretty amazing," he said.

But a closer look at this new bladder control sensation suggests that maybe the company shouldn't have been caught off guard by its success.

There are very good reasons for BladderMax's surging popularity.

To begin with, clinical studies show BladderMax not only reduces embarrassing bladder leakages quickly, but also works to strengthen and calm the bladder for lasting relief.

Plus, at just $2 per daily dose, it's very affordable.

This may be another reason why American diaper companies are starting to panic over its release.

## WHAT SCIENTISTS DISCOVERED

BladderMax contains a proprietary compound with a known ability to reduce stress, urgency, and overflow leakages in seniors suffering from overactive bladder.

This compound is not a drug. It is the active ingredient in BladderMax.

Studies show it naturally strengthens the bladder's muscle tone while relaxing the urination muscles resulting in a decrease in sudden urgency.

Many sufferers enjoy a reduction in bathroom trips both day and night. Others are able to get back to doing the things they love without worrying about embarrassing leakages.

"I couldn't sit through a movie without having to go to the bathroom 3-4

times," says Theresa Johnson of Duluth, GA, "but since using BladderMax I can not only sit through a movie, but I can drive on the freeway to another city without having to immediately go to the bathroom."

With so much positive feedback, it's easy to see why sales for this newly approved bladder pill continue to climb every day.

## SLASHES EMBARRASSING LEAKAGES BY 79%

The 6 week clinical study was carried out by scientists in Japan. The results were published in the Journal of Medicine and Pharmaceutical Science in 2001.

The study involved seniors who suffered from frequent and embarrassing bladder leakages. They were not instructed to change their daily routines. They were only told to take BladderMax's active ingredient every day.

The results were incredible.

Taking BladderMax's active ingredient significantly reduced both sudden urges to go and embarrassing urine leakages compared to the placebo.

In fact, many experienced a 79% reduction in embarrassing accidents when coughing, sneezing, laughing or physical activity at 6 weeks.

## HOW IT WORKS IS INCREDIBLE

Studies show that as many as one in six adults over age 40 suffers from an overactive bladder and embarrassing leakages.

"Losing control of when and how we go to the bathroom is just an indication of a weakening of the pelvic muscles caused by age-related hormonal changes," says Lewis.

"It happens in both men and women, and it is actually quite common."

The natural compound found in BladderMax contains the necessary

As new pill gains popularity, products like these will become unnecessary.

ingredients needed to help strengthen bladder muscles to relieve urgency, while reducing frequency.

Plus, it helps relax bladder muscles allowing for complete emptying of the bladder.

This proprietary compound is known as 'EFLA940'®.

And with over 17 years of medical use there have been no adverse side effects reported.

## RECOMMENDED BY U.S. MEDICAL DOCTORS

"Many of my patients used to complain that coughing, sneezing or even getting up quickly from a chair results in wetting themselves and they fear becoming a social outcast," reports Dr. Clifford James, M.D. "But BladderMax changes all that."

"BladderMax effectively treats urinary disorders, specifically overactive bladder," said Dr. Christie Wilkins, board certified doctor of natural medicine.

## OLD FARMER'S ALMANAC READERS GET SPECIAL DISCOUNT SUPPLY

This is the official release of BladderMax and so for a limited time, the company is offering a special discount supply to our readers. An Order Hotline has been set up for our readers to call, but don't wait. The special offer will not last forever. All you have to do is call TOLL FREE **1-800-615-9302**. The company will do the rest.

*These Statements Have Not Been Evaluated By The Food And Drug Administration. This Product Is Not Intended To Diagnose, Treat, Cure Or Prevent Any Disease. All Clinical Studies On BladderMax's Active Ingredient Were Independently Conducted And Were Not Sponsored By The Makers Of BladderMax. Offer Not Available To Iowa Residents.*

# ASTRONOMICAL GLOSSARY

**MIDNIGHT:** Astronomically, the time when the Sun is opposite its highest point in the sky. Both 12 hours before and after noon (so, technically, both A.M. and P.M.), midnight in civil time is usually treated as the beginning of the day. It is displayed as 12:00 A.M. on 12-hour digital clocks. On a 24-hour cycle, 00:00, not 24:00, usually indicates midnight.

**MOON ON EQUATOR:** The Moon is on the celestial equator.

**MOON RIDES HIGH/RUNS LOW:** The Moon is highest above or farthest below the celestial equator.

**MOONRISE/MOONSET:** When the Moon rises above or sets below the horizon.

**MOON'S PHASES:** The changing appearance of the Moon, caused by the different angles at which it is illuminated by the Sun. **First Quarter:** Right half of the Moon is illuminated. **Full:** The Sun and the Moon are in opposition; the entire disk of the Moon is illuminated. **Last Quarter:** Left half of the Moon is illuminated. **New:** The Sun and the Moon are in conjunction; the Moon is darkened because it lines up between Earth and the Sun.

**MOON'S PLACE, Astronomical:** The position of the Moon within the constellations on the celestial sphere at midnight. **Astrological:** The position of the Moon within the tropical zodiac, whose twelve 30° segments (signs) along the ecliptic were named more than 2,000 years ago after constellations within each area. Because of precession and other factors, the zodiac signs no longer match actual constellation positions.

**MORNING STAR:** A planet that is above the eastern horizon at sunrise and less than 180° west of the Sun in right ascension.

**NODE:** Either of the two points where a celestial body's orbit intersects the ecliptic. **Ascending:** When the body is moving from south to north of the ecliptic. **Descending:** When the body is moving from north to south of the ecliptic.

**OCCULTATION (OCCN.):** When the Moon or a planet eclipses a star or planet.

**OPPOSITION:** The Moon or a planet appears on the opposite side of the sky from the Sun (elongation 180°).

**PERIGEE (PERIG.):** The point in the Moon's orbit that is closest to Earth.

**PERIHELION (PERIH.):** The point in a planet's orbit that is closest to the Sun.

**PRECESSION:** The slowly changing position of the stars and equinoxes in the sky caused by a slight wobble as Earth rotates around its axis.

**RIGHT ASCENSION (R.A.):** The celestial longitude of an object in the sky, measured eastward along the celestial equator in hours of time from the vernal equinox; comparable to longitude on Earth.

**SOLSTICE, Summer:** When the Sun reaches its greatest declination (23½°) north of the celestial equator, around June 21. **Winter:** When the Sun reaches its greatest declination (23½°) south of the celestial equator, around December 21.

**STATIONARY (STAT.):** The brief period of apparent halted movement of a planet against the background of the stars shortly before it appears to move backward/westward (retrograde motion) or forward/eastward (direct motion).

**SUN FAST/SLOW:** When a sundial is ahead of (fast) or behind (slow) clock time.

**SUNRISE/SUNSET:** The visible rising/setting of the upper edge of the Sun's disk across the unobstructed horizon of an observer whose eyes are 15 feet above ground level.

**TWILIGHT:** See **page 106.** ∎

*Note: These definitions apply to the Northern Hemisphere; some do not hold true for locations in the Southern Hemisphere.*

## 2021

### JANUARY
| S | M | T | W | T | F | S |
|---|---|---|---|---|---|---|
|  |  |  |  |  | 1 | 2 |
| 3 | 4 | 5 | 6 | 7 | 8 | 9 |
| 10 | 11 | 12 | 13 | 14 | 15 | 16 |
| 17 | 18 | 19 | 20 | 21 | 22 | 23 |
| 24 | 25 | 26 | 27 | 28 | 29 | 30 |
| 31 |  |  |  |  |  |  |

### FEBRUARY
| S | M | T | W | T | F | S |
|---|---|---|---|---|---|---|
|  | 1 | 2 | 3 | 4 | 5 | 6 |
| 7 | 8 | 9 | 10 | 11 | 12 | 13 |
| 14 | 15 | 16 | 17 | 18 | 19 | 20 |
| 21 | 22 | 23 | 24 | 25 | 26 | 27 |
| 28 |  |  |  |  |  |  |

### MARCH
| S | M | T | W | T | F | S |
|---|---|---|---|---|---|---|
|  | 1 | 2 | 3 | 4 | 5 | 6 |
| 7 | 8 | 9 | 10 | 11 | 12 | 13 |
| 14 | 15 | 16 | 17 | 18 | 19 | 20 |
| 21 | 22 | 23 | 24 | 25 | 26 | 27 |
| 28 | 29 | 30 | 31 |  |  |  |

### APRIL
| S | M | T | W | T | F | S |
|---|---|---|---|---|---|---|
|  |  |  |  | 1 | 2 | 3 |
| 4 | 5 | 6 | 7 | 8 | 9 | 10 |
| 11 | 12 | 13 | 14 | 15 | 16 | 17 |
| 18 | 19 | 20 | 21 | 22 | 23 | 24 |
| 25 | 26 | 27 | 28 | 29 | 30 |  |

### MAY
| S | M | T | W | T | F | S |
|---|---|---|---|---|---|---|
|  |  |  |  |  |  | 1 |
| 2 | 3 | 4 | 5 | 6 | 7 | 8 |
| 9 | 10 | 11 | 12 | 13 | 14 | 15 |
| 16 | 17 | 18 | 19 | 20 | 21 | 22 |
| 23 | 24 | 25 | 26 | 27 | 28 | 29 |
| 30 | 31 |  |  |  |  |  |

### JUNE
| S | M | T | W | T | F | S |
|---|---|---|---|---|---|---|
|  |  | 1 | 2 | 3 | 4 | 5 |
| 6 | 7 | 8 | 9 | 10 | 11 | 12 |
| 13 | 14 | 15 | 16 | 17 | 18 | 19 |
| 20 | 21 | 22 | 23 | 24 | 25 | 26 |
| 27 | 28 | 29 | 30 |  |  |  |

### JULY
| S | M | T | W | T | F | S |
|---|---|---|---|---|---|---|
|  |  |  |  | 1 | 2 | 3 |
| 4 | 5 | 6 | 7 | 8 | 9 | 10 |
| 11 | 12 | 13 | 14 | 15 | 16 | 17 |
| 18 | 19 | 20 | 21 | 22 | 23 | 24 |
| 25 | 26 | 27 | 28 | 29 | 30 | 31 |

### AUGUST
| S | M | T | W | T | F | S |
|---|---|---|---|---|---|---|
| 1 | 2 | 3 | 4 | 5 | 6 | 7 |
| 8 | 9 | 10 | 11 | 12 | 13 | 14 |
| 15 | 16 | 17 | 18 | 19 | 20 | 21 |
| 22 | 23 | 24 | 25 | 26 | 27 | 28 |
| 29 | 30 | 31 |  |  |  |  |

### SEPTEMBER
| S | M | T | W | T | F | S |
|---|---|---|---|---|---|---|
|  |  |  | 1 | 2 | 3 | 4 |
| 5 | 6 | 7 | 8 | 9 | 10 | 11 |
| 12 | 13 | 14 | 15 | 16 | 17 | 18 |
| 19 | 20 | 21 | 22 | 23 | 24 | 25 |
| 26 | 27 | 28 | 29 | 30 |  |  |

### OCTOBER
| S | M | T | W | T | F | S |
|---|---|---|---|---|---|---|
|  |  |  |  |  | 1 | 2 |
| 3 | 4 | 5 | 6 | 7 | 8 | 9 |
| 10 | 11 | 12 | 13 | 14 | 15 | 16 |
| 17 | 18 | 19 | 20 | 21 | 22 | 23 |
| 24 | 25 | 26 | 27 | 28 | 29 | 30 |
| 31 |  |  |  |  |  |  |

### NOVEMBER
| S | M | T | W | T | F | S |
|---|---|---|---|---|---|---|
|  | 1 | 2 | 3 | 4 | 5 | 6 |
| 7 | 8 | 9 | 10 | 11 | 12 | 13 |
| 14 | 15 | 16 | 17 | 18 | 19 | 20 |
| 21 | 22 | 23 | 24 | 25 | 26 | 27 |
| 28 | 29 | 30 |  |  |  |  |

### DECEMBER
| S | M | T | W | T | F | S |
|---|---|---|---|---|---|---|
|  |  |  | 1 | 2 | 3 | 4 |
| 5 | 6 | 7 | 8 | 9 | 10 | 11 |
| 12 | 13 | 14 | 15 | 16 | 17 | 18 |
| 19 | 20 | 21 | 22 | 23 | 24 | 25 |
| 26 | 27 | 28 | 29 | 30 | 31 |  |

## 2022

### JANUARY
| S | M | T | W | T | F | S |
|---|---|---|---|---|---|---|
|  |  |  |  |  |  | 1 |
| 2 | 3 | 4 | 5 | 6 | 7 | 8 |
| 9 | 10 | 11 | 12 | 13 | 14 | 15 |
| 16 | 17 | 18 | 19 | 20 | 21 | 22 |
| 23 | 24 | 25 | 26 | 27 | 28 | 29 |
| 30 | 31 |  |  |  |  |  |

### FEBRUARY
| S | M | T | W | T | F | S |
|---|---|---|---|---|---|---|
|  |  | 1 | 2 | 3 | 4 | 5 |
| 6 | 7 | 8 | 9 | 10 | 11 | 12 |
| 13 | 14 | 15 | 16 | 17 | 18 | 19 |
| 20 | 21 | 22 | 23 | 24 | 25 | 26 |
| 27 | 28 |  |  |  |  |  |

### MARCH
| S | M | T | W | T | F | S |
|---|---|---|---|---|---|---|
|  |  | 1 | 2 | 3 | 4 | 5 |
| 6 | 7 | 8 | 9 | 10 | 11 | 12 |
| 13 | 14 | 15 | 16 | 17 | 18 | 19 |
| 20 | 21 | 22 | 23 | 24 | 25 | 26 |
| 27 | 28 | 29 | 30 | 31 |  |  |

### APRIL
| S | M | T | W | T | F | S |
|---|---|---|---|---|---|---|
|  |  |  |  |  | 1 | 2 |
| 3 | 4 | 5 | 6 | 7 | 8 | 9 |
| 10 | 11 | 12 | 13 | 14 | 15 | 16 |
| 17 | 18 | 19 | 20 | 21 | 22 | 23 |
| 24 | 25 | 26 | 27 | 28 | 29 | 30 |

### MAY
| S | M | T | W | T | F | S |
|---|---|---|---|---|---|---|
| 1 | 2 | 3 | 4 | 5 | 6 | 7 |
| 8 | 9 | 10 | 11 | 12 | 13 | 14 |
| 15 | 16 | 17 | 18 | 19 | 20 | 21 |
| 22 | 23 | 24 | 25 | 26 | 27 | 28 |
| 29 | 30 | 31 |  |  |  |  |

### JUNE
| S | M | T | W | T | F | S |
|---|---|---|---|---|---|---|
|  |  |  | 1 | 2 | 3 | 4 |
| 5 | 6 | 7 | 8 | 9 | 10 | 11 |
| 12 | 13 | 14 | 15 | 16 | 17 | 18 |
| 19 | 20 | 21 | 22 | 23 | 24 | 25 |
| 26 | 27 | 28 | 29 | 30 |  |  |

### JULY
| S | M | T | W | T | F | S |
|---|---|---|---|---|---|---|
|  |  |  |  |  | 1 | 2 |
| 3 | 4 | 5 | 6 | 7 | 8 | 9 |
| 10 | 11 | 12 | 13 | 14 | 15 | 16 |
| 17 | 18 | 19 | 20 | 21 | 22 | 23 |
| 24 | 25 | 26 | 27 | 28 | 29 | 30 |
| 31 |  |  |  |  |  |  |

### AUGUST
| S | M | T | W | T | F | S |
|---|---|---|---|---|---|---|
|  | 1 | 2 | 3 | 4 | 5 | 6 |
| 7 | 8 | 9 | 10 | 11 | 12 | 13 |
| 14 | 15 | 16 | 17 | 18 | 19 | 20 |
| 21 | 22 | 23 | 24 | 25 | 26 | 27 |
| 28 | 29 | 30 | 31 |  |  |  |

### SEPTEMBER
| S | M | T | W | T | F | S |
|---|---|---|---|---|---|---|
|  |  |  |  | 1 | 2 | 3 |
| 4 | 5 | 6 | 7 | 8 | 9 | 10 |
| 11 | 12 | 13 | 14 | 15 | 16 | 17 |
| 18 | 19 | 20 | 21 | 22 | 23 | 24 |
| 25 | 26 | 27 | 28 | 29 | 30 |  |

### OCTOBER
| S | M | T | W | T | F | S |
|---|---|---|---|---|---|---|
|  |  |  |  |  |  | 1 |
| 2 | 3 | 4 | 5 | 6 | 7 | 8 |
| 9 | 10 | 11 | 12 | 13 | 14 | 15 |
| 16 | 17 | 18 | 19 | 20 | 21 | 22 |
| 23 | 24 | 25 | 26 | 27 | 28 | 29 |
| 30 | 31 |  |  |  |  |  |

### NOVEMBER
| S | M | T | W | T | F | S |
|---|---|---|---|---|---|---|
|  |  | 1 | 2 | 3 | 4 | 5 |
| 6 | 7 | 8 | 9 | 10 | 11 | 12 |
| 13 | 14 | 15 | 16 | 17 | 18 | 19 |
| 20 | 21 | 22 | 23 | 24 | 25 | 26 |
| 27 | 28 | 29 | 30 |  |  |  |

### DECEMBER
| S | M | T | W | T | F | S |
|---|---|---|---|---|---|---|
|  |  |  |  | 1 | 2 | 3 |
| 4 | 5 | 6 | 7 | 8 | 9 | 10 |
| 11 | 12 | 13 | 14 | 15 | 16 | 17 |
| 18 | 19 | 20 | 21 | 22 | 23 | 24 |
| 25 | 26 | 27 | 28 | 29 | 30 | 31 |

## 2023

### JANUARY
| S | M | T | W | T | F | S |
|---|---|---|---|---|---|---|
| 1 | 2 | 3 | 4 | 5 | 6 | 7 |
| 8 | 9 | 10 | 11 | 12 | 13 | 14 |
| 15 | 16 | 17 | 18 | 19 | 20 | 21 |
| 22 | 23 | 24 | 25 | 26 | 27 | 28 |
| 29 | 30 | 31 |  |  |  |  |

### FEBRUARY
| S | M | T | W | T | F | S |
|---|---|---|---|---|---|---|
|  |  |  | 1 | 2 | 3 | 4 |
| 5 | 6 | 7 | 8 | 9 | 10 | 11 |
| 12 | 13 | 14 | 15 | 16 | 17 | 18 |
| 19 | 20 | 21 | 22 | 23 | 24 | 25 |
| 26 | 27 | 28 |  |  |  |  |

### MARCH
| S | M | T | W | T | F | S |
|---|---|---|---|---|---|---|
|  |  |  | 1 | 2 | 3 | 4 |
| 5 | 6 | 7 | 8 | 9 | 10 | 11 |
| 12 | 13 | 14 | 15 | 16 | 17 | 18 |
| 19 | 20 | 21 | 22 | 23 | 24 | 25 |
| 26 | 27 | 28 | 29 | 30 | 31 |  |

### APRIL
| S | M | T | W | T | F | S |
|---|---|---|---|---|---|---|
|  |  |  |  |  |  | 1 |
| 2 | 3 | 4 | 5 | 6 | 7 | 8 |
| 9 | 10 | 11 | 12 | 13 | 14 | 15 |
| 16 | 17 | 18 | 19 | 20 | 21 | 22 |
| 23 | 24 | 25 | 26 | 27 | 28 | 29 |
| 30 |  |  |  |  |  |  |

### MAY
| S | M | T | W | T | F | S |
|---|---|---|---|---|---|---|
|  | 1 | 2 | 3 | 4 | 5 | 6 |
| 7 | 8 | 9 | 10 | 11 | 12 | 13 |
| 14 | 15 | 16 | 17 | 18 | 19 | 20 |
| 21 | 22 | 23 | 24 | 25 | 26 | 27 |
| 28 | 29 | 30 | 31 |  |  |  |

### JUNE
| S | M | T | W | T | F | S |
|---|---|---|---|---|---|---|
|  |  |  |  | 1 | 2 | 3 |
| 4 | 5 | 6 | 7 | 8 | 9 | 10 |
| 11 | 12 | 13 | 14 | 15 | 16 | 17 |
| 18 | 19 | 20 | 21 | 22 | 23 | 24 |
| 25 | 26 | 27 | 28 | 29 | 30 |  |

### JULY
| S | M | T | W | T | F | S |
|---|---|---|---|---|---|---|
|  |  |  |  |  |  | 1 |
| 2 | 3 | 4 | 5 | 6 | 7 | 8 |
| 9 | 10 | 11 | 12 | 13 | 14 | 15 |
| 16 | 17 | 18 | 19 | 20 | 21 | 22 |
| 23 | 24 | 25 | 26 | 27 | 28 | 29 |
| 30 | 31 |  |  |  |  |  |

### AUGUST
| S | M | T | W | T | F | S |
|---|---|---|---|---|---|---|
|  |  | 1 | 2 | 3 | 4 | 5 |
| 6 | 7 | 8 | 9 | 10 | 11 | 12 |
| 13 | 14 | 15 | 16 | 17 | 18 | 19 |
| 20 | 21 | 22 | 23 | 24 | 25 | 26 |
| 27 | 28 | 29 | 30 | 31 |  |  |

### SEPTEMBER
| S | M | T | W | T | F | S |
|---|---|---|---|---|---|---|
|  |  |  |  |  | 1 | 2 |
| 3 | 4 | 5 | 6 | 7 | 8 | 9 |
| 10 | 11 | 12 | 13 | 14 | 15 | 16 |
| 17 | 18 | 19 | 20 | 21 | 22 | 23 |
| 24 | 25 | 26 | 27 | 28 | 29 | 30 |

### OCTOBER
| S | M | T | W | T | F | S |
|---|---|---|---|---|---|---|
| 1 | 2 | 3 | 4 | 5 | 6 | 7 |
| 8 | 9 | 10 | 11 | 12 | 13 | 14 |
| 15 | 16 | 17 | 18 | 19 | 20 | 21 |
| 22 | 23 | 24 | 25 | 26 | 27 | 28 |
| 29 | 30 | 31 |  |  |  |  |

### NOVEMBER
| S | M | T | W | T | F | S |
|---|---|---|---|---|---|---|
|  |  |  | 1 | 2 | 3 | 4 |
| 5 | 6 | 7 | 8 | 9 | 10 | 11 |
| 12 | 13 | 14 | 15 | 16 | 17 | 18 |
| 19 | 20 | 21 | 22 | 23 | 24 | 25 |
| 26 | 27 | 28 | 29 | 30 |  |  |

### DECEMBER
| S | M | T | W | T | F | S |
|---|---|---|---|---|---|---|
|  |  |  |  |  | 1 | 2 |
| 3 | 4 | 5 | 6 | 7 | 8 | 9 |
| 10 | 11 | 12 | 13 | 14 | 15 | 16 |
| 17 | 18 | 19 | 20 | 21 | 22 | 23 |
| 24 | 25 | 26 | 27 | 28 | 29 | 30 |
| 31 |  |  |  |  |  |  |

# A CALENDAR OF THE HEAVENS FOR 2022

**The Calendar Pages (120–147)** are the heart of *The Old Farmer's Almanac.* They present sky sightings and astronomical data for the entire year and are what make this book a true almanac, a "calendar of the heavens." In essence, these pages are unchanged since 1792, when Robert B. Thomas published his first edition. The long columns of numbers and symbols reveal all of nature's precision, rhythm, and glory, providing an astronomical look at the year 2022.

## HOW TO USE THE CALENDAR PAGES

The astronomical data on the **Calendar Pages (120–147)** are calculated for Boston (where Robert B. Thomas learned to calculate the data for his first Almanac). Guidance for calculating the times of these events for your locale appears on **pages 116–117.** Note that the results will be *approximate.* For the *exact* time of any astronomical event at your locale, go to **Almanac.com/ 2022** and enter your zip code. While you're there, print the month's "Sky Map," useful for viewing with "Sky Watch" in the Calendar Pages.

For a list of 2022 holidays and observances, see **pages 148–149.** Also check out the **Glossary of Almanac Oddities** on **pages 150–151,** which describes some of the more obscure entries traditionally found on the **Right-Hand Calendar Pages (121–147).**

**ABOUT THE TIMES:** All times are given in ET (Eastern Time), except where otherwise noted as AT (Atlantic Time, +1 hour), CT (Central Time, –1), MT (Mountain Time, –2), PT (Pacific Time, –3), AKT (Alaska Time, –4), or HAT (Hawaii-Aleutian Time, –5). Between 2:00 A.M., March 13, and 2:00 A.M., November 6, Daylight Saving Time is assumed in those locales where it is observed.

**ABOUT THE TIDES:** Tide times for Boston appear on **pages 120–146;** for Boston tide heights, see **pages 121–147.** Tide Corrections for East Coast locations appear on **pages 236–237.** Tide heights and times for locations across the United States and Canada are available via **Almanac.com/2022.**

CALENDAR

# The Left-Hand Calendar Pages, 120 to 146

On these pages are the year's astronomical predictions for Boston (42°22' N, 71°3' W). Learn how to calculate the times of these events for your locale here or go to **Almanac.com/2022** and enter your zip code.

## A SAMPLE MONTH

**SKY WATCH:** The paragraph at the top of each Left-Hand Calendar Page describes the best times to view conjunctions, meteor showers, planets, and more. (Also see **How to Use the Right-Hand Calendar Pages, page 118.**)

| | | | ☀ RISES H. M. | RISE KEY | ☀ SETS H. M. | SET KEY | LENGTH OF DAY H. M. | SUN FAST M. | SUN DECLINATION ° ' | HIGH TIDE TIMES BOSTON | ☾ RISES H. M. | RISE KEY | ☾ SETS H. M. | SET KEY | ☾ ASTRON. PLACE | ☾ AGE |
|---|---|---|---|---|---|---|---|---|---|---|---|---|---|---|---|---|
| DAY OF YEAR | DAY OF MONTH | DAY OF WEEK | | | | | | | | | | | | | | |
| 60 | 1 | Fr. | 6:20 | D | 5:34 | C | 11 14 | 4 | 7 s. 30 | 7¼  8 | 3:30 | E | 12:58 | B | SAG | 25 |
| 61 | 2 | Sa. | 6:18 | D | 5:35 | C | 11 17 | 4 | 7 s. 07 | 8¼  9 | 4:16 | E | 1:51 | B | SAG | 26 |
| 62 | 3 | **F** | 6:17 | D | 5:36 | C | 11 19 | 4 | 6 s. 44 | 9¼  9¾ | 4:56 | E | 2:47 | B | CAP | 27 |
| 63 | 4 | M. | 6:15 | D | 5:37 | C | 11 22 | 4 | 6 s. 21 | 10  10½ | 5:31 | E | 3:45 | C | CAP | 28 |

Column guide numbers: 1 (Rises/Rise Key and Sets/Set Key), 2 (Sets/Set Key), 3 (Length of Day), 4 (Sun Fast), 5 (Sun Declination / High Tide Times Boston), 6 (Moon Rises/Sets and keys), 7 (Astron. Place), 8 (Age)

**1.** To calculate the sunrise time in your locale: Choose a day. Note its Sun Rise Key Letter. Find your (nearest) city on **page 238**. Add or subtract the minutes that correspond to the Sun Rise Key Letter to/from the sunrise time for Boston.[†]

### EXAMPLE:

To calculate the sunrise time in Denver, Colorado, on day 1:

| Sunrise, Boston, with Key Letter D (above) | 6:20 A.M. ET |
|---|---|
| Value of Key Letter D for Denver (p. 238) | + 11 minutes |
| Sunrise, Denver | 6:31 A.M. MT |

To calculate your sunset time, repeat, using Boston's sunset time and its Sun Set Key Letter value.

**2.** To calculate the length of day: Choose a day. Note the Sun Rise and Sun Set Key Letters. Find your (nearest) city on **page 238**. Add or subtract the minutes that correspond to the Sun Set Key Letter to/from Boston's length of day. *Reverse* the sign (e.g., minus to plus) of the Sun Rise Key Letter minutes. Add or subtract it to/from the first result.

### EXAMPLE:

To calculate the length of day in Richmond, Virginia, on day 1:

| Length of day, Boston (above) | 11h.14m. |
|---|---|
| Sunset Key Letter C for Richmond (p. 242) | + 25m. |
| | 11h.39m. |
| Reverse sunrise Key Letter D for Richmond (p. 242, +17 to −17) | − 17m. |
| Length of day, Richmond | 11h.22m. |

**3.** Use Sun Fast to change sundial time to clock time. A sundial reads natural (Sun) time, which is neither Standard nor Daylight time. To calculate clock time on a sundial in Boston, subtract the minutes given in this column; add the minutes when preceded by an asterisk [*].

[†]For locations where Daylight Saving Time is never observed, subtract 1 hour from results between the second Sunday of March and first Sunday of November.

To convert the time to your (nearest) city, use Key Letter C on **page 238.**

**EXAMPLE:**

To change sundial to clock time in Boston or Salem, Oregon, on day 1:

| | |
|---|---|
| Sundial reading (Boston or Salem) | 12:00 noon |
| Subtract Sun Fast (p. 116) | - 4 minutes |
| Clock time, Boston | 11:56 A.M. ET** |
| Use Key Letter C for Salem (p. 241) | + 27 minutes |
| Clock time, Salem | 12:23 P.M. PT** |

**Note: Add 1 hour to the results in locations where Daylight Saving Time is currently observed.

**4.** This column gives the degrees and minutes of the Sun from the celestial equator at noon ET.

**5.** This column gives the approximate times of high tide in Boston. For example, the first high tide occurs at 7:15 A.M. and the second occurs at 8:00 P.M. the same day. (A dash indicates that high tide occurs on or after midnight and is recorded on the next day.) Figures for calculating approximate high tide times for localities other than Boston are given in the **Tide Corrections** table on page **236.**

**6.** To calculate the moonrise time in your locale: Choose a day. Note the Moon Rise Key Letter. Find your (nearest) city on **page 238.** Add or subtract the minutes that correspond to the Moon Rise Key Letter to/from the moonrise time given for Boston.

| LONGITUDE OF CITY | CORRECTION MINUTES | LONGITUDE OF CITY | CORRECTION MINUTES |
|---|---|---|---|
| 58°–76° | 0 | 116°–127° | +4 |
| 77°–89° | +1 | 128°–141° | +5 |
| 90°–102° | +2 | 142°–155° | +6 |
| 103°–115° | +3 | | |

(A dash indicates that the moonrise occurs on/after midnight and is recorded on the next day.) Find the longitude of your (nearest) city on **page 238.** Add a correction in minutes for your city's longitude (see table, bottom left). Use the same procedure with Boston's moonset time and the Moon Set Key Letter value to calculate the time of moonset in your locale.[†]

**EXAMPLE:**

To calculate the time of moonset in Lansing, Michigan, on day 1:

| | |
|---|---|
| Moonset, Boston, with Key Letter B (p. 116) | 12:58 P.M. ET |
| Value of Key Letter B for Lansing (p. 240) | + 53 minutes |
| Correction for Lansing longitude, 84°33' | + 1 minute |
| Moonset, Lansing | 1:52 P.M. ET |

**7.** This column gives the Moon's *astronomical* position among the constellations (not zodiac) at midnight. For *astrological* data, see **pages 224–227.**

Constellations have irregular borders; on successive nights, the midnight Moon may enter one, cross into another, and then move to a new area of the previous. It visits the 12 zodiacal constellations, as well as Auriga **(AUR),** a northern constellation between Perseus and Gemini; Cetus **(CET),** which lies south of the zodiac, just south of Pisces and Aries; Ophiuchus **(OPH),** primarily north of the zodiac but with a small corner between Scorpius and Sagittarius; Orion **(ORI),** whose northern limit first reaches the zodiac between Taurus and Gemini; and Sextans **(SEX),** which lies south of the zodiac except for a corner that just touches it near Leo.

**8.** This column gives the Moon's age: the number of days since the previous new Moon. (The average length of the lunar month is 29.53 days.) *(continued)*

# The Right-Hand Calendar Pages, 121 to 147

The Right-Hand Calendar Pages contain celestial events; religious obser-vances; proverbs and poems; civil holidays; historical events; folklore; tide heights; weather prediction rhymes; Farmer's Calendar essays; and more.

## A SAMPLE MONTH

**1 2 3 4 5 6 7 8 9 10**

| 1 | Fr. | ALL FOOLS' • | *If you want to make a fool of yourself, you'll find a lot of people ready to help you.* | *Flakes* | an inch long, who v |
| 2 | Sa. | Tap dancer Charles "Honi" Coles born, 1911 • Tides { 9.5 / 9.0 | | *alive!* | in fresh water, pro pond across the r |
| 3 | **B** | 2nd ♒. of Easter • | Writer F. Scott Fitzgerald married Zelda Sayre, 1920 | *Spring's* | emerged a month c |
| 4 | M. | Annunciation[T] • ♂♆☽ • | *Ben Hur* won 11 Academy Awards, 1960 | *arrived!* | to spend the next 3 on land before ret |
| 5 | Tu. | ☽AT ☊ • | Blizzard left 27.2" snow, St. John's, Nfld., 1999 • Tides { 10.8 / 10.8 | *Or is this* | their wet world. |
| 6 | W. | ☽ON EQ. • ♂♀☽ • | Twin mongoose lemurs born, Busch Gardens, Tampa, Fla., 2012 | *warmth* | You can't mis |

**1.** The bold letter is the Dominical Let-ter (from A to G), a traditional eccle-siastical designation for Sunday de-termined by the date on which the year's first Sunday falls. For 2022, the Dominical Letter is **B**.

**2.** Civil holidays and astronomical events.

**3.** Religious feasts: A [T] indicates a ma-jor feast that the church has this year temporarily transferred to a date other than its usual one.

**4.** Sundays and special holy days.

**5.** Symbols for notable celestial events. For example, ♂♆☽ on the 4th day means that a conjunction (♂) of Neptune (♆) and the Moon (☽) occurs.

**6.** Proverbs, poems, and adages.

**7.** Noteworthy historical events, folklore, and legends.

**8.** High tide heights, in feet, at Boston, Massachusetts.

**9.** Weather prediction rhyme.

**10.** Farmer's Calendar essay.

## Celestial Symbols

| | | | | |
|---|---|---|---|---|
| ☉ Sun | ⊕ Earth | ♅ Uranus | ♂ Conjunction (on the same celestial longitude) | ☋ Descending node |
| ○●☽ Moon | ♂ Mars | ♆ Neptune | | ☍ Opposition (180 degrees from Sun) |
| ☿ Mercury | ♃ Jupiter | ♇ Pluto | ☊ Ascending node | |
| ♀ Venus | ♄ Saturn | | | |

## PREDICTING EARTHQUAKES

Note the dates in the Right-Hand Calendar Pages when the Moon rides high or runs low. The date of the high begins the most likely 5-day period of earthquakes in the Northern Hemisphere; the date of the low indi-cates a similar 5-day period in the Southern Hemi-sphere. Also noted are the 2 days each month when the Moon is on the celestial equator, indicating the most likely time for earthquakes in either hemisphere.

### EARTH AT PERIHELION AND APHELION

**Perihelion:** January 4, 2022 (EST). Earth will be 91,406,842 miles from the Sun. **Aphelion:** July 4, 2022 (EDT). Earth will be 94,509,598 miles from the Sun.

CALENDAR

# Why We Have Seasons

The seasons occur because as Earth revolves around the Sun, its axis remains tilted at 23.5 degrees from the perpendicular. This tilt causes different latitudes on Earth to receive varying amounts of sunlight throughout the year.

In the Northern Hemisphere, the summer solstice marks the beginning of summer and occurs when the North Pole is tilted toward the Sun. The winter solstice marks the beginning of winter and occurs when the North Pole is tilted away from the Sun.

The equinoxes occur when the hemispheres equally face the Sun. At this time, the Sun rises due east and sets due west. The vernal equinox marks the beginning of spring; the autumnal equinox marks the beginning of autumn.

In the Southern Hemisphere, the seasons are the reverse of those in the Northern Hemisphere.

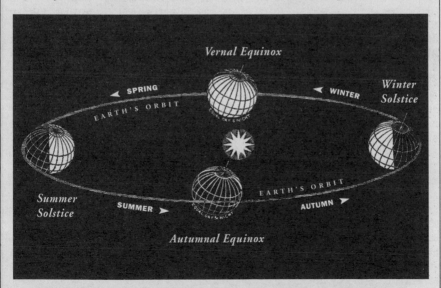

## THE FIRST DAYS OF THE 2022 SEASONS

**VERNAL (SPRING) EQUINOX:** March 20, 11:33 A.M. EDT

**SUMMER SOLSTICE:** June 21, 5:14 A.M. EDT

**AUTUMNAL (FALL) EQUINOX:** Sept. 22, 9:04 P.M. EDT

**WINTER SOLSTICE:** Dec. 21, 4:48 P.M. EST

# NOVEMBER

**SKY WATCH:** Venus, at a dazzling magnitude –4.33, crosses into Sagittarius and floats directly in front of our galaxy's center, which is off in the far distance. On the 7th, the crescent Moon joins Venus there. The Moon forms a triangle with Jupiter and Saturn on the 10th and then dangles beneath Jupiter on the 11th. Venus reaches its most southerly zodiac position at midmonth. Its declination of –27 degrees makes it set as far left as possible, in the southwest instead of the west. The night of the 18th–19th brings another nearly total lunar eclipse in the hours before dawn. This 98 percent–eclipsed Moon will be a strange, coppery sight—well worth a look by early risers and insomniacs who have unobstructed views of the low western sky.

● **NEW MOON** 4th day 5:15 P.M.  ○ **FULL MOON** 19th day 3:57 A.M.

◐ **FIRST QUARTER** 11th day 7:46 A.M.  ◑ **LAST QUARTER** 27th day 7:28 A.M.

*After 2:00 A.M. on November 7, Eastern Standard Time is given.*

**GET THESE PAGES WITH TIMES SET TO YOUR ZIP CODE VIA ALMANAC.COM/2022.**

| DAY OF YEAR | DAY OF MONTH | DAY OF WEEK | ☼ RISES H. M. | RISE KEY | ☼ SETS H. M. | SET KEY | LENGTH OF DAY H. M. | SUN FAST M. | SUN DECLINATION ° ′ | HIGH TIDE TIMES BOSTON | | ☾ RISES H. M. | RISE KEY | ☾ SETS H. M. | SET KEY | ☾ ASTRON. PLACE | ☾ AGE |
|---|---|---|---|---|---|---|---|---|---|---|---|---|---|---|---|---|---|
| 305 | 1 | M. | 7:18 | D | 5:37 | B | 10 19 | 32 | 14 s. 39 | 8¾ | 9¼ | 3:05 | D | 4:18 | D | LEO | 26 |
| 306 | 2 | Tu. | 7:19 | D | 5:36 | B | 10 17 | 32 | 14 s. 58 | 9½ | 10 | 4:17 | D | 4:42 | C | VIR | 27 |
| 307 | 3 | W. | 7:20 | D | 5:35 | B | 10 15 | 32 | 15 s. 16 | 10½ | 10¾ | 5:32 | E | 5:08 | C | VIR | 28 |
| 308 | 4 | Th. | 7:22 | D | 5:33 | B | 10 11 | 32 | 15 s. 35 | 11¼ | 11¾ | 6:51 | E | 5:37 | B | VIR | 0 |
| 309 | 5 | Fr. | 7:23 | D | 5:32 | B | 10 09 | 32 | 15 s. 53 | 12 | — | 8:11 | E | 6:11 | B | LIB | 1 |
| 310 | 6 | Sa. | 7:24 | E | 5:31 | B | 10 07 | 32 | 16 s. 11 | 12½ | 12¾ | 9:33 | E | 6:53 | B | SCO | 2 |
| 311 | 7 | C | 6:25 | E | 4:30 | B | 10 05 | 32 | 16 s. 28 | 1¼ | 12½ | 9:51 | E | 6:45 | A | OPH | 3 |
| 312 | 8 | M. | 6:27 | E | 4:29 | B | 10 02 | 32 | 16 s. 46 | 1¼ | 1½ | 11:01 | E | 7:47 | B | SAG | 4 |
| 313 | 9 | Tu. | 6:28 | E | 4:28 | B | 10 00 | 32 | 17 s. 03 | 2¼ | 2½ | 11:59 | E | 8:57 | B | SAG | 5 |
| 314 | 10 | W. | 6:29 | E | 4:27 | B | 9 58 | 32 | 17 s. 20 | 3¼ | 3½ | 12:44 | E | 10:09 | B | CAP | 6 |
| 315 | 11 | Th. | 6:30 | E | 4:26 | B | 9 56 | 32 | 17 s. 36 | 4¼ | 4½ | 1:20 | E | 11:21 | C | CAP | 7 |
| 316 | 12 | Fr. | 6:32 | E | 4:25 | B | 9 53 | 32 | 17 s. 52 | 5¼ | 5½ | 1:49 | E | — | - | AQU | 8 |
| 317 | 13 | Sa. | 6:33 | E | 4:24 | B | 9 51 | 32 | 18 s. 08 | 6½ | 6¾ | 2:13 | D | 12:30 | C | AQU | 9 |
| 318 | 14 | C | 6:34 | E | 4:23 | B | 9 49 | 31 | 18 s. 24 | 7½ | 7¾ | 2:35 | D | 1:36 | D | AQU | 10 |
| 319 | 15 | M. | 6:35 | E | 4:22 | B | 9 47 | 31 | 18 s. 39 | 8¼ | 8¾ | 2:56 | C | 2:40 | D | CET | 11 |
| 320 | 16 | Tu. | 6:37 | E | 4:21 | B | 9 44 | 31 | 18 s. 54 | 9 | 9½ | 3:17 | C | 3:43 | E | PSC | 12 |
| 321 | 17 | W. | 6:38 | E | 4:20 | B | 9 42 | 31 | 19 s. 09 | 9¾ | 10¼ | 3:39 | B | 4:45 | E | PSC | 13 |
| 322 | 18 | Th. | 6:39 | E | 4:19 | B | 9 40 | 31 | 19 s. 23 | 10¼ | 10¾ | 4:03 | B | 5:48 | E | ARI | 14 |
| 323 | 19 | Fr. | 6:40 | E | 4:19 | B | 9 39 | 30 | 19 s. 37 | 11 | 11½ | 4:32 | B | 6:51 | E | TAU | 15 |
| 324 | 20 | Sa. | 6:41 | E | 4:18 | B | 9 37 | 30 | 19 s. 50 | 11½ | — | 5:05 | B | 7:53 | E | TAU | 16 |
| 325 | 21 | C | 6:43 | E | 4:17 | B | 9 34 | 30 | 20 s. 03 | 12¼ | 12¼ | 5:45 | A | 8:53 | E | TAU | 17 |
| 326 | 22 | M. | 6:44 | E | 4:17 | A | 9 33 | 30 | 20 s. 16 | 12¾ | 12¾ | 6:33 | A | 9:48 | E | GEM | 18 |
| 327 | 23 | Tu. | 6:45 | E | 4:16 | A | 9 31 | 29 | 20 s. 29 | 1½ | 1½ | 7:27 | B | 10:38 | E | GEM | 19 |
| 328 | 24 | W. | 6:46 | E | 4:15 | A | 9 29 | 29 | 20 s. 41 | 2¼ | 2¼ | 8:27 | B | 11:20 | E | GEM | 20 |
| 329 | 25 | Th. | 6:47 | E | 4:15 | A | 9 28 | 29 | 20 s. 52 | 3 | 3 | 9:31 | B | 11:56 | E | CAN | 21 |
| 330 | 26 | Fr. | 6:48 | E | 4:14 | A | 9 26 | 28 | 21 s. 03 | 3¾ | 3¾ | 10:37 | C | 12:27 | E | LEO | 22 |
| 331 | 27 | Sa. | 6:50 | E | 4:14 | A | 9 24 | 28 | 21 s. 14 | 4½ | 4¾ | 11:45 | C | 12:54 | E | LEO | 23 |
| 332 | 28 | C | 6:51 | E | 4:14 | A | 9 23 | 28 | 21 s. 25 | 5½ | 5¾ | — | - | 1:19 | D | LEO | 24 |
| 333 | 29 | M. | 6:52 | E | 4:13 | A | 9 21 | 27 | 21 s. 35 | 6¼ | 6¾ | 12:54 | D | 1:42 | D | VIR | 25 |
| 334 | 30 | Tu. | 6:53 | E | 4:13 | A | 9 20 | 27 | 21 s. 45 | 7¼ | 7½ | 2:06 | D | 2:06 | C | VIR | 26 |

**To use this page, see p. 116; for Key Letters, see p. 238.** LIGHT = A.M. BOLD = P.M. **2022**

CALENDAR

THE ELEVENTH MONTH · 2021 **NOVEMBER** NOVEMBER HATH 30 DAYS

*The farmer sat there milking Bess, / A-whistling all the while;*
*He was a sunburnt, stalwart man, / And had a kindly smile.*
–**Mary E. Wilkins**

| DAY OF MONTH | DAY OF WEEK | DATES, FEASTS, FASTS, ASPECTS, TIDE HEIGHTS, AND WEATHER | |
|---|---|---|---|
| 1 | M. | All Saints' • Writer Stephen Crane born, 1871 • {9.5 9.9 | *Bundle* |
| 2 | Tu. | All Souls' • ELECTION DAY • ☾ ON EQ. • Tides {10.2 10.4 | *up* |
| 3 | W. | ☌☿☾ • John Adams elected 2nd U.S. president, 1796 • Tides {10.9 10.7 | *to* |
| 4 | Th. | NEW ● • ☌♂☾ • ⛢ AT ☍ • Tides {11.5 10.9 | *your* |
| 5 | Fr. | ☾ AT PERIG. • ☾ AT ☋ • *Better untaught than ill taught.* • Tides {12.0 — | *necks* |
| 6 | Sa. | Sadie Hawkins Day • Basketball-game inventor James Naismith born, 1861 • {10.9 12.2 | *for* |
| 7 | C | 24th S. af. P. • DAYLIGHT SAVING TIME ENDS, 2:00 A.M. • {10.7 12.1 | *the* |
| 8 | M. | ☾ RUNS LOW • ☌♀☾ • Astronomer Edmond Halley born, 1656 | *polar* |
| 9 | Tu. | ☌☿♂ • ☌♇☾ • Maj. Robert White flew X-15 rocket plane at Mach 6.04, 1961 | *vortex!* |
| 10 | W. | ☌♄☾ • 70+ tornadoes developed, eastern half of U.S., 2002 • Tides {9.6 10.7 | *Cold's* |
| 11 | Th. | St. Martin of Tours • VETERANS DAY • ☌♃☾ • Tides {9.3 10.2 | *injurious,* |
| 12 | Fr. | Indian Summer • *The wind in the west suits everyone best.* • Tides {9.2 9.8 | *flurries* |
| 13 | Sa. | ☌♆☾ • *Mariner 9* became 1st spacecraft to orbit another planet (Mars), 1971 • {9.3 9.6 | *furious.* |
| 14 | C | 25th S. af. P. • U.S. first lady Mamie Eisenhower born, 1896 • {9.5 9.5 | *Hunters* |
| 15 | M. | ☾ ON EQ. • America Recycles Day • Tides {9.7 9.5 | *find* |
| 16 | Tu. | 45°F plus 8.4" snow, Anchorage, Alaska, 2019 • Tides {9.9 9.4 | *plenty* |
| 17 | W. | St. Hugh of Lincoln • ☌⛢☾ • Social worker Grace Abbott born, 1878 • {10.1 9.4 | *of* |
| 18 | Th. | St. Hilda of Whitby • Standard Railway Time went into effect for most N.Am. railroads, 1883 | *snow* |
| 19 | Fr. | FULL BEAVER ○ • ECLIPSE ☾ • ☾ AT ☊ • Tides {10.2 9.2 | *for* |
| 20 | Sa. | ☾ AT APO. • Ballerina Maya Plisetskaya born, 1925 • {10.2 — | *tracking;* |
| 21 | C | 26th S. af. P. • H. Truman became 2nd U.S. pres. to dive in sub (T. Roosevelt 1st), 1946 | *turkey* |
| 22 | M. | ☾ RIDES HIGH • Agronomist William Evans born, 1786 • Comedian Rodney Dangerfield born, 1921 | *roasters,* |
| 23 | Tu. | St. Clement • Horseshoe manufacturing machine patented, 1835 • Tides {8.6 9.7 | *let's* |
| 24 | W. | Baseball player Warren Spahn died, 2003 • Tides {8.5 9.5 | *get* |
| 25 | Th. | THANKSGIVING DAY • *A good tale is none the worse for being twice told.* • {8.3 9.3 | *cracking!* |
| 26 | Fr. | Buoy recorded 75-foot wave off Cape Mendocino, Calif., 2019 • Tides {8.3 9.2 | *Woodstove* |
| 27 | Sa. | Microsoft's *Internet Explorer 2.0* released, starting 1st "browser war" (with Netscape's *Navigator*), 1995 | *owners* |
| 28 | C | 1st S. of Advent • Chanukah begins at sundown • ☿ IN SUP. ☌ | *better* |
| 29 | M. | ☾ ON EQ. • Ensemble of 1,013 cellists played in Kobe, Japan, setting world record, 1998 | *start* |
| 30 | Tu. | St. Andrew • Deadly tornado, Simsboro, La., 1996 • Tides {9.9 9.7 | *stacking!* |

## Farmer's Calendar

"Every man looks at his woodpile with a kind of affection," wrote American essayist Henry David Thoreau (1817–62). He's right, too, isn't he? An ample woodpile has a familiar, reassuring presence. It's a satisfactory object in a way that's a little hard to account for. We respond to the sight of a good woodpile with a level of contentment.

What is it that contents us? Not use, or not use alone.

It's not as fuel that a woodpile makes its particular appeal. It's as a symbol. We are cheered and comforted by our woodpile today because a woodpile is one of the stations of the year and expresses the essential ambiguity of all seasonal work. It represents a job that we know we can do well enough but that we also know will never finally be done: Woodpiles are built up that they may be torn down. Massive as they are, they're ephemeral. You'll have to build another next year, which you will then once more throw down. The woodpile reminds us of the fix we're in just by being alive on Earth. It connects us with the years, and so it connects us with one another. We may as well look at our woodpile with affection, then, for it makes us be philosophers.

**SKY WATCH:** On the 1st, Venus, now at its most brilliant, stands a comfortable 16 degrees high as the constellations emerge in the late evening twilight. On the 6th, it hovers just above the crescent Moon—a lovely sight. Also on the 6th, look for a planet bunch-up in the west after sunset: From lower right to upper left stand Venus, the Moon, Saturn, and Jupiter. The grouping remains on the 8th, with the crescent Moon now second from the top, below Jupiter, which moves back into Aquarius at midmonth. By the holidays, Mercury, at a bright magnitude –0.5, will be visible, too, dangling below Venus from the 24th to the 31st. It will stand left of Venus from the 29th to the 31st. The solstice brings winter to the Northern Hemisphere on the 21st at 10:59 A.M. EST.

● **NEW MOON** 4th day 2:43 A.M.   ○ **FULL MOON** 18th day 11:35 P.M.
◐ **FIRST QUARTER** 10th day 8:36 P.M.   ◑ **LAST QUARTER** 26th day 9:24 P.M.

*All times are given in Eastern Standard Time.*

GET THESE PAGES WITH TIMES SET TO YOUR ZIP CODE VIA ALMANAC.COM/2022.

| DAY OF YEAR | DAY OF MONTH | DAY OF WEEK | ☼ RISES H.M. | RISE KEY | ☼ SETS H.M. | SET KEY | LENGTH OF DAY H.M. | SUN FAST M. | SUN DECLINATION ° ' | HIGH TIDE TIMES BOSTON | ☽ RISES H.M. | RISE KEY | ☽ SETS H.M. | SET KEY | ☽ ASTRON. PLACE | ☽ AGE |
|---|---|---|---|---|---|---|---|---|---|---|---|---|---|---|---|---|
| 335 | 1 | W. | 6:54 | E | 4:12 | A | 9 18 | 27 | 21 s. 54 | 8     8½ | 3:20 | E | 2:33 | B | VIR | 27 |
| 336 | 2 | Th. | 6:55 | E | 4:12 | A | 9 17 | 26 | 22 s. 03 | 8¾    9½ | 4:38 | E | 3:03 | B | LIB | 28 |
| 337 | 3 | Fr. | 6:56 | E | 4:12 | A | 9 16 | 26 | 22 s. 11 | 9¾   10¼ | 6:00 | E | 3:41 | B | LIB | 29 |
| 338 | 4 | Sa. | 6:57 | E | 4:12 | A | 9 15 | 25 | 22 s. 19 | 10½  11¼ | 7:22 | E | 4:28 | B | OPH | 0 |
| 339 | 5 | C | 6:58 | E | 4:12 | A | 9 14 | 25 | 22 s. 27 | 11½       | 8:39 | E | 5:27 | A | SAG | 1 |
| 340 | 6 | M. | 6:59 | E | 4:12 | A | 9 13 | 25 | 22 s. 34 | 12    12¼ | 9:45 | E | 6:36 | B | SAG | 2 |
| 341 | 7 | Tu. | 7:00 | E | 4:11 | A | 9 11 | 24 | 22 s. 40 | 1     1¼ | 10:38 | E | 7:51 | B | SAG | 3 |
| 342 | 8 | W. | 7:01 | E | 4:11 | A | 9 10 | 24 | 22 s. 47 | 2     2 | 11:19 | E | 9:06 | B | CAP | 4 |
| 343 | 9 | Th. | 7:02 | E | 4:11 | A | 9 09 | 23 | 22 s. 52 | 3     3 | 11:51 | E | 10:18 | C | CAP | 5 |
| 344 | 10 | Fr. | 7:03 | E | 4:12 | A | 9 09 | 23 | 22 s. 58 | 4     4 | 12:18 | D | 11:27 | C | AQU | 6 |
| 345 | 11 | Sa. | 7:03 | E | 4:12 | A | 9 09 | 22 | 23 s. 03 | 5     5¼ | 12:41 | D | — | - | AQU | 7 |
| 346 | 12 | C | 7:04 | E | 4:12 | A | 9 08 | 22 | 23 s. 07 | 6     6¼ | 1:02 | C | 12:32 | D | PSC | 8 |
| 347 | 13 | M. | 7:05 | E | 4:12 | A | 9 07 | 21 | 23 s. 11 | 6¾    7¼ | 1:23 | C | 1:35 | E | PSC | 9 |
| 348 | 14 | Tu. | 7:06 | E | 4:12 | A | 9 06 | 21 | 23 s. 14 | 7¾    8¼ | 1:44 | C | 2:38 | E | PSC | 10 |
| 349 | 15 | W. | 7:06 | E | 4:12 | A | 9 06 | 20 | 23 s. 17 | 8½    9 | 2:08 | B | 3:40 | E | ARI | 11 |
| 350 | 16 | Th. | 7:07 | E | 4:13 | A | 9 06 | 20 | 23 s. 20 | 9¼    9¾ | 2:34 | B | 4:42 | E | ARI | 12 |
| 351 | 17 | Fr. | 7:08 | E | 4:13 | A | 9 05 | 19 | 23 s. 22 | 9¾   10½ | 3:06 | B | 5:45 | E | TAU | 13 |
| 352 | 18 | Sa. | 7:08 | E | 4:13 | A | 9 05 | 19 | 23 s. 24 | 10½  11¼ | 3:44 | A | 6:45 | E | TAU | 14 |
| 353 | 19 | C | 7:09 | E | 4:14 | A | 9 05 | 18 | 23 s. 25 | 11¼  11¾ | 4:29 | A | 7:43 | E | TAU | 15 |
| 354 | 20 | M. | 7:10 | E | 4:14 | A | 9 04 | 18 | 23 s. 26 | 11¾      | 5:21 | A | 8:35 | E | GEM | 16 |
| 355 | 21 | Tu. | 7:10 | E | 4:14 | A | 9 04 | 18 | 23 s. 26 | 12½  12½ | 6:20 | B | 9:20 | E | GEM | 17 |
| 356 | 22 | W. | 7:11 | E | 4:15 | A | 9 04 | 17 | 23 s. 25 | 1     1 | 7:23 | B | 9:58 | E | CAN | 18 |
| 357 | 23 | Th. | 7:11 | E | 4:16 | A | 9 05 | 17 | 23 s. 25 | 1¾    1¾ | 8:28 | C | 10:30 | E | CAN | 19 |
| 358 | 24 | Fr. | 7:11 | E | 4:16 | A | 9 05 | 16 | 23 s. 24 | 2½    2½ | 9:34 | C | 10:57 | E | LEO | 20 |
| 359 | 25 | Sa. | 7:12 | E | 4:17 | A | 9 05 | 16 | 23 s. 22 | 3¼    3¼ | 10:41 | D | 11:22 | D | LEO | 21 |
| 360 | 26 | C | 7:12 | E | 4:18 | A | 9 06 | 15 | 23 s. 20 | 4     4¼ | 11:49 | D | 11:45 | D | VIR | 22 |
| 361 | 27 | M. | 7:12 | E | 4:18 | A | 9 06 | 15 | 23 s. 17 | 4¾    5¼ | — | - | 12:08 | C | VIR | 23 |
| 362 | 28 | Tu. | 7:13 | E | 4:19 | A | 9 06 | 14 | 23 s. 14 | 5¾    6 | 12:59 | E | 12:32 | C | VIR | 24 |
| 363 | 29 | W. | 7:13 | E | 4:20 | A | 9 07 | 14 | 23 s. 11 | 6½    7 | 2:13 | E | 12:59 | B | VIR | 25 |
| 364 | 30 | Th. | 7:13 | E | 4:21 | A | 9 08 | 13 | 23 s. 07 | 7½    8 | 3:30 | E | 1:32 | B | LIB | 26 |
| 365 | 31 | Fr. | 7:13 | E | 4:22 | A | 9 09 | 13 | 23 s. 02 | 8½    9 | 4:50 | E | 2:12 | B | SCO | 27 |

# DECEMBER

*Let Joy light up in every breast, / And brighten every eye,*
*Distressing Care be lull'd to rest, / And hush'd be every sigh.*
–Peter Sherston

| DAY OF MONTH | DAY OF WEEK | DATES, FEASTS, FASTS, ASPECTS, TIDE HEIGHTS, AND WEATHER | |
|---|---|---|---|
| 1 | W. | ♆ STAT. • Holography pioneer Stephen Benton born, 1941 • {10.6 10.0 | *More* |
| 2 | Th. | St. Viviana • ☌♂☾ • 1st unmanned landing on Mars, by USSR *Mars 3*, 1971 • {11.3 10.3 | *snow* |
| 3 | Fr. | ☾ AT ☋ • 68°F, Portland, Maine, 2009 • Tides {11.8 10.5 | *than* |
| 4 | Sa. | NEW ● • ECLIPSE ⊙ • ☾ AT PERIG. • ☌☿☾ • ♀ GR. ILLUM. EXT. | *we* |
| 5 | C | **2nd S. of Advent** • ☾ RUNS LOW • Entrepreneur Walt Disney born, 1901 | *reckoned* |
| 6 | M. | St. Nicholas • ☌♀☾ • ☌♇☾ • Tides {10.5 12.2 | *for* |
| 7 | Tu. | St. Ambrose • NATIONAL PEARL HARBOR REMEMBRANCE DAY • ☌♄☾ | *piles* |
| 8 | W. | John McCrae's *In Flanders Fields* poem published, 1915 • Tides {10.0 11.3 | *up* |
| 9 | Th. | ☌♃☾ • Robert Cushman preached 1st known Christian sermon in America, Plymouth (Mass.), 1621 | *to* |
| 10 | Fr. | St. Eulalia • ☌♆☾ • Chemist Alfred Nobel died, 1896 • {9.5 10.0 | *the* |
| 11 | Sa. | ☌♀♇ • Statute of Westminster passed, 1931 • Tides {9.4 9.5 | *second* |
| 12 | C | **3rd S. of Advent** • ☾ ON EQ. • Astronomer Henrietta Swan Leavitt died, 1921 | *floor!* |
| 13 | M. | St. Lucia • Artist Grandma Moses died, 1961 • {9.4 8.9 | *Brief* |
| 14 | Tu. | Halcyon Days begin. • 5.6-lb. avocado set world record for heaviest, Kahului, Hawaii, 2018 | *relief,* |
| 15 | W. | Ember Day • ☌♅☾ • U.S. Bill of Rights ratified, 1791 • Tides {9.6 8.7 | *then* |
| 16 | Th. | ☾ AT ☊ • *In courtesy, rather pay a penny too much than too little.* • {9.8 8.8 | *good* |
| 17 | Fr. | Ember Day • ☾ AT APO. • 1st heart, lung, and liver transplant, 1986 • Tides {9.9 8.8 | *grief!* |
| 18 | Sa. | Ember Day • FULL COLD ○ • ♀ STAT. • Film director Steven Spielberg born, 1946 | *It's* |
| 19 | C | **4th S. of Advent** • ☾ RIDES HIGH • Mark Twain rec'd patent for suspenders, 1871 | *true:* |
| 20 | M. | Beware the Pogonip. • Astrophysicist Carl Sagan died, 1996 • Tides {10.0 — | *Even* |
| 21 | Tu. | St. Thomas • WINTER SOLSTICE • *After a rainy winter follows a fruitful spring.* • {8.7 10.0 | *Santa's* |
| 22 | W. | Grote Reber, builder of 1st radio telescope, born, 1911 • Tides {8.7 9.9 | *checking* |
| 23 | Th. | ☌♀♇ • *Voyager* aircraft completed 1st nonstop flight around world w/o refueling (9 days 4 min.), 1986 | *real* |
| 24 | Fr. | Eggnog Riot began, U.S. Military Academy at West Point, N.Y., 1826 • {8.7 9.6 | *estate* |
| 25 | Sa. | **Christmas** • Poet William Collins born, 1721 • Am. Red Cross founder Clara Barton born, 1821 | *in* |
| 26 | C | **1st S. af. Ch.** • BOXING DAY (CANADA) • FIRST DAY OF KWANZAA | *Malibu!* |
| 27 | M. | St. Stephen[T] • ☾ ON EQ. • Astronomer Johannes Kepler born, 1571 • {9.3 9.2 | *Lips* |
| 28 | Tu. | St. John[T] • ☌☿♀ • Iowa became 29th U.S. state, 1846 • 31.5" snow in 24 hrs., Victoria, B.C., 1996 | *will* |
| 29 | W. | Holy Innocents[T] • William Lyon Mackenzie King became 10th prime minister of Canada, 1921 | *be* |
| 30 | Th. | ☾ AT ☋ • ☌☿♇ • *A new broom sweeps clean.* • {10.7 9.5 | *blue* |
| 31 | Fr. | St. Sylvester • ☌♂☾ • Baltimore, Md., incorporated, 1796 • {11.2 9.6 | *in '22!* |

## Farmer's Calendar

Now, as the season of storms approaches, a bewildering multiplicity of snow shovels has been on display in practically every store in town. And what snow shovels they are! There are snow shovels with straight handles, snow shovels with bent handles, with fat blades, with thin blades, with D grips, with T grips. Some snow shovels are plastic and cost a couple of bucks; others are so expensive that it seems wrong to expose them to a substance, like snow, that comes for free.

What to do?

It took me a number of winters to discover that very often the best snow shovel is a simple broom, one with long, stiff straw. A broom will take care of better than half the snow you'll get in a winter, and it won't break your back, burst your heart, or dig up your grass by mistake. For cleaning snow off the car, the broom is far superior to the shovel because it can't scratch your paint job. And if you are equipped with a broom and you should, at last, get a fall of snow too deep to overcome, you can fly south until you get to a latitude where snow is unknown and the home centers sell only those shovels that come with pails for use at the beach.

# JANUARY

**SKY WATCH:** A fine, eclipse-filled year begins with the planets in the evening sky only at the very beginning and then in the final part of 2022. During the rest of the year, the action occurs in the predawn heavens. On the year's first evening, look low in the west 40 minutes after sunset to see Venus, Mercury, Saturn, and Jupiter, with the crescent Moon joining them on the 4th and 5th. Venus becomes too low after that, and the other planets sink lower, too, with only Mercury getting higher and hovering to Saturn's upper left from the 10th to the 14th. In the eastern sky, look for the crescent Moon to the right of Mars during the year's first dawn. By midmonth, Venus is a low morning star, but it rapidly gets higher each morning until easily seen to the left of the Moon and Mars 40 minutes before sunrise on the 29th.

● **NEW MOON** 2nd day 1:33 P.M.   ○ **FULL MOON** 17th day 6:48 P.M.
◐ **FIRST QUARTER** 9th day 1:11 P.M.   ◑ **LAST QUARTER** 25th day 8:41 A.M.

*All times are given in Eastern Standard Time.*

GET THESE PAGES WITH TIMES SET TO YOUR ZIP CODE VIA ALMANAC.COM/2022.

| DAY OF YEAR | DAY OF MONTH | DAY OF WEEK | RISES H. M. | RISE KEY | SETS H. M. | SET KEY | LENGTH OF DAY H. M. | SUN FAST M. | SUN DECLINATION ° ' | HIGH TIDE TIMES BOSTON | | RISES H. M. | RISE KEY | SETS H. M. | SET KEY | ASTRON. PLACE | AGE |
|---|---|---|---|---|---|---|---|---|---|---|---|---|---|---|---|---|---|
| 1 | 1 | Sa. | 7:13 | E | 4:22 | A | 9 09 | 12 | 22 s. 57 | 9¼ | 10 | 6:09 | E | 3:04 | B | OPH | 28 |
| 2 | 2 | **B** | 7:13 | E | 4:23 | A | 9 10 | 12 | 22 s. 52 | 10¼ | 11 | 7:22 | E | 4:09 | B | SAG | 0 |
| 3 | 3 | M. | 7:13 | E | 4:24 | A | 9 11 | 11 | 22 s. 46 | 11¼ | 11¾ | 8:22 | E | 5:23 | B | SAG | 1 |
| 4 | 4 | Tu. | 7:13 | E | 4:25 | A | 9 12 | 11 | 22 s. 40 | 12 | — | 9:11 | E | 6:41 | B | CAP | 2 |
| 5 | 5 | W. | 7:13 | E | 4:26 | A | 9 13 | 10 | 22 s. 33 | 12¾ | 1 | 9:48 | E | 7:57 | C | CAP | 3 |
| 6 | 6 | Th. | 7:13 | E | 4:27 | A | 9 14 | 10 | 22 s. 26 | 1¾ | 1¾ | 10:18 | E | 9:10 | C | AQU | 4 |
| 7 | 7 | Fr. | 7:13 | E | 4:28 | A | 9 15 | 10 | 22 s. 18 | 2½ | 2¾ | 10:43 | D | 10:19 | D | AQU | 5 |
| 8 | 8 | Sa. | 7:13 | E | 4:29 | A | 9 16 | 9 | 22 s. 10 | 3½ | 3¾ | 11:06 | D | 11:25 | D | PSC | 6 |
| 9 | 9 | **B** | 7:13 | E | 4:30 | A | 9 17 | 9 | 22 s. 02 | 4¼ | 4¾ | 11:27 | C | — | - | CET | 7 |
| 10 | 10 | M. | 7:13 | E | 4:31 | A | 9 18 | 8 | 21 s. 53 | 5¼ | 5½ | 11:48 | C | 12:29 | E | PSC | 8 |
| 11 | 11 | Tu. | 7:12 | E | 4:32 | A | 9 20 | 8 | 21 s. 43 | 6 | 6½ | 12:11 | B | 1:31 | E | ARI | 9 |
| 12 | 12 | W. | 7:12 | E | 4:33 | A | 9 21 | 7 | 21 s. 33 | 7 | 7½ | 12:37 | B | 2:34 | E | ARI | 10 |
| 13 | 13 | Th. | 7:12 | E | 4:35 | A | 9 23 | 7 | 21 s. 23 | 7¾ | 8½ | 1:07 | B | 3:36 | E | TAU | 11 |
| 14 | 14 | Fr. | 7:11 | E | 4:36 | A | 9 25 | 7 | 21 s. 13 | 8¾ | 9¼ | 1:42 | A | 4:38 | E | TAU | 12 |
| 15 | 15 | Sa. | 7:11 | E | 4:37 | A | 9 26 | 6 | 21 s. 02 | 9½ | 10 | 2:25 | A | 5:36 | E | TAU | 13 |
| 16 | 16 | **B** | 7:10 | E | 4:38 | A | 9 28 | 6 | 20 s. 50 | 10 | 10¾ | 3:15 | B | 6:30 | E | GEM | 14 |
| 17 | 17 | M. | 7:10 | E | 4:39 | A | 9 29 | 6 | 20 s. 38 | 10¾ | 11½ | 4:13 | B | 7:18 | E | GEM | 15 |
| 18 | 18 | Tu. | 7:09 | E | 4:41 | A | 9 32 | 5 | 20 s. 26 | 11½ | — | 5:15 | B | 7:58 | E | CAN | 16 |
| 19 | 19 | W. | 7:09 | E | 4:42 | A | 9 33 | 5 | 20 s. 14 | 12 | 12 | 6:21 | B | 8:32 | E | CAN | 17 |
| 20 | 20 | Th. | 7:08 | E | 4:43 | B | 9 35 | 5 | 20 s. 01 | 12¾ | 12¾ | 7:27 | C | 9:01 | E | LEO | 18 |
| 21 | 21 | Fr. | 7:07 | E | 4:44 | B | 9 37 | 5 | 19 s. 47 | 1¼ | 1¼ | 8:34 | C | 9:26 | E | LEO | 19 |
| 22 | 22 | Sa. | 7:06 | E | 4:45 | B | 9 39 | 4 | 19 s. 34 | 2 | 2 | 9:41 | D | 9:50 | D | LEO | 20 |
| 23 | 23 | **B** | 7:06 | E | 4:47 | B | 9 41 | 4 | 19 s. 20 | 2½ | 2¾ | 10:49 | E | 10:12 | C | VIR | 21 |
| 24 | 24 | M. | 7:05 | E | 4:48 | B | 9 43 | 4 | 19 s. 05 | 3¼ | 3¾ | 11:59 | E | 10:35 | C | VIR | 22 |
| 25 | 25 | Tu. | 7:04 | E | 4:49 | B | 9 45 | 4 | 18 s. 50 | 4¼ | 4½ | — | - | 11:00 | B | VIR | 23 |
| 26 | 26 | W. | 7:03 | E | 4:51 | B | 9 48 | 3 | 18 s. 35 | 5 | 5¾ | 1:12 | E | 11:29 | B | LIB | 24 |
| 27 | 27 | Th. | 7:02 | E | 4:52 | B | 9 50 | 3 | 18 s. 20 | 6 | 6¾ | 2:28 | E | 12:04 | B | LIB | 25 |
| 28 | 28 | F. | 7:02 | E | 4:53 | B | 9 51 | 3 | 18 s. 04 | 7 | 7¾ | 3:45 | E | 12:49 | B | OPH | 26 |
| 29 | 29 | Sa. | 7:01 | E | 4:54 | B | 9 53 | 3 | 17 s. 48 | 8 | 8¾ | 4:59 | E | 1:46 | B | SAG | 27 |
| 30 | 30 | **B** | 7:00 | E | 4:56 | B | 9 56 | 3 | 17 s. 31 | 9 | 9¾ | 6:04 | E | 2:55 | B | SAG | 28 |
| 31 | 31 | M. | 6:59 | E | 4:57 | B | 9 58 | 2 | 17 s. 15 | 10 | 10¾ | 6:58 | E | 4:11 | B | SAG | 29 |

To use this page, see p. 116; for Key Letters, see p. 238. LIGHT = A.M. **BOLD = P.M.**   2022

# JANUARY

*So the bells ring forth with might,*
*Heralding a future bright.*
–G. Weatherly

| DAY OF MONTH | DAY OF WEEK | DATES, FEASTS, FASTS, ASPECTS, TIDE HEIGHTS, AND WEATHER | |
|---|---|---|---|
| 1 | Sa. | Holy Name • **NEW YEAR'S DAY** • ☾ AT PERIG. • Tides {11.6 9.8 | *Solar* |
| 2 | **B** | **2nd S. af. Ch.** • NEW ● • ☾ RUNS LOW • {11.9 10.0 | *power!* |
| 3 | M. | ☌☿☾ • ☌♀☾ • ☌♇☾ • Aretha Franklin 1st woman inducted into Rock & Roll Hall of Fame, 1987 | |
| 4 | Tu. | St. Elizabeth Ann Seton • ☌♄☾ • ⊕ AT PERIHELION • {11.9 — | *An* |
| 5 | W. | Twelfth Night • ☌♃☾ • Antarctic explorer Sir Ernest Henry Shackleton died, 1922 | *inch* |
| 6 | Th. | **Epiphany** • New Mexico became 47th U.S. state, 1912 • Tides {10.0 11.1 | *an* |
| 7 | Fr. | Distaff Day • ☌♆☾ • ☿ GR. ELONG. (19° EAST) • Tides {9.9 10.5 | *hour!* |
| 8 | Sa. | ☾ ON EQ. • ♀ IN INF. ☌ • Entertainer Elvis Presley born, 1935 • {9.7 9.8 | *Flurries—* |
| 9 | **B** | **1st S. af. Ep.** • Apple introduced the iPhone, 2007 • Tides {9.5 9.1 | *you'll* |
| 10 | M. | Plough Monday • *If January calends be summerly gay, It will be winterly weather till the calends of May.* | *need* |
| 11 | Tu. | ☌♅☾ • 17 lb. 1 oz. ocean whitefish caught, Hurricane Bank, Calif., 2011 • {9.2 8.3 | *your* |
| 12 | W. | ☾ AT ☊ • Fictional Hal 9000 computer in film *2001: A Space Odyssey* became operational, 1992 | *furries!* |
| 13 | Th. | St. Hilary • ☿ STAT. • Naturalist/artist Maria Sibylla Merian died, 1717 • {9.3 8.1 | *Flakes* |
| 14 | Fr. | ☾ AT APO. • *Jan. 14–15:* –54°F to 49°F in a 24-hour period, setting record, Loma, Mont., 1972 | *spittin'—* |
| 15 | Sa. | Playwright Molière baptized, 1622 • 1st transpacific hot air balloon flight began, Japan to Canada, 1991 | *where* |
| 16 | **B** | **2nd S. af. Ep.** • ☾ RIDES HIGH • ☌♇☉ • Tides {9.8 8.5 | *are* |
| 17 | M. | **MARTIN LUTHER KING JR.'S BIRTHDAY, OBSERVED** • FULL WOLF ○ • Ben Franklin born, 1706 | *my* |
| 18 | Tu. | ♅ STAT. • *By going gains the mill, And not by standing still.* • Tides {10.1 — | *mittens?* |
| 19 | W. | Rare snowfall, Miami, Fla., 1977 • Poet James Dickey died, 1997 • {8.8 10.2 | *Mild:* |
| 20 | Th. | *Born Free* author Joy Adamson born, 1910 • {8.9 10.2 | *Rain and* |
| 21 | Fr. | 3-day, 81-tornado outbreak in Southeast U.S. began, 2017 • Raccoons mate now. • {9.1 10.1 | *snow* |
| 22 | Sa. | St. Vincent • Roberta Bondar became 1st Canadian woman in space, 1992 • {9.2 9.9 | *blend,* |
| 23 | **B** | **3rd S. af. Ep.** • ☾ ON EQ. • ☿ IN INF. ☌ • {9.4 9.7 | *then* |
| 24 | M. | Rover *Opportunity* landed on Mars, 2004 • Tides {9.6 9.4 | *it's* |
| 25 | Tu. | Conversion of Paul • January thaw traditionally begins about now. • {9.8 9.1 | *colder* |
| 26 | W. | Sts. Timothy & Titus • Canadian Coast Guard officially established, 1962 • {9.9 8.8 | *and* |
| 27 | Th. | ☾ AT ☋ • ☌☿♇ • *A little stone may upset a large cart.* • Tides {10.2 8.8 | *snowy,* |
| 28 | Fr. | St. Thomas Aquinas • Scottish-born Canadian statesman Alexander Mackenzie born, 1822 | *right* |
| 29 | Sa. | ☾ RUNS LOW • ☌♂☾ • ☌♀☾ • ♀ STAT. • {10.8 9.2 | *to* |
| 30 | **B** | ☾ AT PERIG. • ☌☿☾ • ☌♇☾ • Yerba Buena renamed San Francisco, 1847 | *the* |
| 31 | M. | Composer Franz Schubert born, 1797 • Baseball player Nolan Ryan born, 1947 • {11.5 9.9 | *end.* |

## Farmer's Calendar

Dashing through the snow? Check. In a one-horse open sleigh? You betcha—as o'er the fields we rode. Laughing all the way? Well, it was more like speechless awe. Crisp air stung our faces as we hurtled through the winter world in a vehicle without a windshield. Driver Linda Ward held the reins as she guided her Belgian draft horse, Ivy, along a snowy lane while her party of two snuggled under 100-year-old sleigh robes in the seat behind her. For an hour we lived the lyrics of "Jingle Bells" and "Over the River and Through the Woods"—our quiet ride accompanied only by the wooden sleigh's creak as it glided, its runners hissing against the snow and occasionally scrunching on ice—all powered by our equine engine. We watched Ivy's strong haunches as she conveyed as up hills and down them. Perhaps our great-great-grandparents would find our thrill at being pulled by a horse amusing. Our joy ride was their school bus and grocery getter. Yet for the duration of our jaunt, their scenery, what they knew—these arched-over birches, the burly mountain backdrop, the sugar woods, and the snow-smothered field—was our scenery, too. Oh, what fun? Heck, yeah!

# FEBRUARY

**SKY WATCH:** Only Jupiter remains in the evening sky, floating in the southwest to the upper right of the Moon on the 2nd. Besides this, February's action is focused in the predawn east, where Mercury brightens to magnitude zero and ascends a bit higher each morning, hovering to the left of Venus and Mars on the 13th. Look for dazzling Venus just above dim orange Mars and the slender waning crescent Moon on the 27th, followed on the next morning by an even thinner Moon floating just beneath Mercury, with Saturn to its left and the Venus–Mars duo to its right. This planet bunching is very low and challenging but will soon get much easier to see. Venus's supernal brilliance—at its brightest of the year during midmonth, a shadow-casting magnitude –4.9—grabs the attention of anyone gazing east before dawn.

| | | | |
|---|---|---|---|
| ● NEW MOON | 1st day 12:46 A.M. | ○ FULL MOON | 16th day 11:56 A.M. |
| ◐ FIRST QUARTER | 8th day 8:50 A.M. | ◑ LAST QUARTER | 23rd day 5:32 P.M. |

*All times are given in Eastern Standard Time.*

**GET THESE PAGES WITH TIMES SET TO YOUR ZIP CODE VIA ALMANAC.COM/2022.**

| DAY OF YEAR | DAY OF MONTH | DAY OF WEEK | ☼ RISES H. M. | RISE KEY | ☼ SETS H. M. | SET KEY | LENGTH OF DAY H. M. | SUN FAST M. | SUN DECLINATION ° | SUN DECLINATION ' | HIGH TIDE TIMES BOSTON | | ☾ RISES H. M. | RISE KEY | ☾ SETS H. M. | SET KEY | ☾ ASTRON. PLACE | ☾ AGE |
|---|---|---|---|---|---|---|---|---|---|---|---|---|---|---|---|---|---|---|
| 32 | 1 | Tu. | 6:58 | E | **4:58** | B | 10 00 | 2 | 16 | s. 57 | 11 | **11½** | 7:41 | E | **5:29** | C | CAP | 0 |
| 33 | 2 | W. | 6:57 | E | **5:00** | B | 10 03 | 2 | 16 | s. 40 | 11¾ | — | 8:14 | E | **6:45** | C | AQU | 1 |
| 34 | 3 | Th. | 6:56 | E | **5:01** | B | 10 05 | 2 | 16 | s. 22 | 12½ | **12¾** | 8:42 | D | **7:58** | D | AQU | 2 |
| 35 | 4 | Fr. | 6:54 | E | **5:02** | B | 10 08 | 2 | 16 | s. 05 | 1¼ | **1½** | 9:06 | D | **9:07** | D | AQU | 3 |
| 36 | 5 | Sa. | 6:53 | E | **5:04** | B | 10 11 | 2 | 15 | s. 46 | 2 | **2¼** | 9:28 | C | **10:14** | E | CET | 4 |
| 37 | 6 | **B** | 6:52 | D | **5:05** | B | 10 13 | 2 | 15 | s. 28 | 2¾ | **3¼** | 9:50 | C | **11:19** | E | PSC | 5 |
| 38 | 7 | M. | 6:51 | D | **5:06** | B | 10 15 | 2 | 15 | s. 09 | 3½ | **4** | 10:13 | B | — | - | CET | 6 |
| 39 | 8 | Tu. | 6:50 | D | **5:08** | B | 10 18 | 2 | 14 | s. 50 | 4½ | **5** | 10:37 | B | 12:22 | E | ARI | 7 |
| 40 | 9 | W. | 6:48 | D | **5:09** | B | 10 21 | 2 | 14 | s. 31 | 5¼ | **6** | 11:06 | B | 1:26 | E | TAU | 8 |
| 41 | 10 | Th. | 6:47 | D | **5:10** | B | 10 23 | 2 | 14 | s. 11 | 6¼ | **7** | 11:39 | B | 2:28 | E | TAU | 9 |
| 42 | 11 | Fr. | 6:46 | D | **5:11** | B | 10 25 | 2 | 13 | s. 52 | 7¼ | **8** | **12:19** | A | 3:28 | E | TAU | 10 |
| 43 | 12 | Sa. | 6:45 | D | **5:13** | B | 10 28 | 2 | 13 | s. 32 | 8 | **8¾** | **1:07** | A | 4:24 | E | GEM | 11 |
| 44 | 13 | **B** | 6:43 | D | **5:14** | B | 10 31 | 2 | 13 | s. 11 | 9 | **9½** | **2:02** | B | 5:13 | E | GEM | 12 |
| 45 | 14 | M. | 6:42 | D | **5:15** | B | 10 33 | 2 | 12 | s. 51 | 9¾ | **10¼** | **3:04** | B | 5:56 | E | CAN | 13 |
| 46 | 15 | Tu. | 6:41 | D | **5:17** | B | 10 36 | 2 | 12 | s. 30 | 10¼ | **11** | **4:09** | B | 6:33 | E | CAN | 14 |
| 47 | 16 | W. | 6:39 | D | **5:18** | B | 10 39 | 2 | 12 | s. 10 | 11 | **11½** | **5:16** | C | 7:03 | E | LEO | 15 |
| 48 | 17 | Th. | 6:38 | D | **5:19** | B | 10 41 | 2 | 11 | s. 49 | 11¾ | — | **6:24** | C | 7:30 | E | LEO | 16 |
| 49 | 18 | Fr. | 6:36 | D | **5:20** | B | 10 44 | 2 | 11 | s. 28 | 12¼ | **12¼** | **7:32** | D | 7:54 | D | LEO | 17 |
| 50 | 19 | Sa. | 6:35 | D | **5:22** | B | 10 47 | 2 | 11 | s. 06 | 12¾ | **1** | **8:41** | D | 8:17 | C | VIR | 18 |
| 51 | 20 | **B** | 6:33 | D | **5:23** | B | 10 50 | 2 | 10 | s. 45 | 1½ | **1¾** | **9:51** | E | 8:39 | C | VIR | 19 |
| 52 | 21 | M. | 6:32 | D | **5:24** | B | 10 52 | 2 | 10 | s. 23 | 2 | **2½** | **11:03** | E | 9:03 | C | VIR | 20 |
| 53 | 22 | Tu. | 6:30 | D | **5:25** | B | 10 55 | 2 | 10 | s. 01 | 2¾ | **3¼** | — | - | 9:31 | B | LIB | 21 |
| 54 | 23 | W. | 6:29 | D | **5:27** | B | 10 58 | 3 | 9 | s. 39 | 3¾ | **4¼** | 12:18 | E | 10:03 | B | LIB | 22 |
| 55 | 24 | Th. | 6:27 | D | **5:28** | B | 11 01 | 3 | 9 | s. 17 | 4½ | **5¼** | 1:33 | E | 10:44 | A | OPH | 23 |
| 56 | 25 | Fr. | 6:26 | D | **5:29** | B | 11 03 | 3 | 8 | s. 55 | 5¾ | **6½** | 2:46 | E | 11:35 | A | OPH | 24 |
| 57 | 26 | Sa. | 6:24 | D | **5:30** | C | 11 06 | 3 | 8 | s. 32 | 6¾ | **7½** | 3:53 | E | **12:37** | A | SAG | 25 |
| 58 | 27 | **B** | 6:23 | D | **5:32** | C | 11 09 | 3 | 8 | s. 10 | 7¾ | **8¾** | 4:49 | E | **1:48** | B | SAG | 26 |
| 59 | 28 | M. | 6:21 | D | **5:33** | C | 11 12 | 3 | 7 | s. 47 | 9 | **9¾** | 5:35 | E | **3:04** | B | CAP | 27 |

 To use this page, see p. 116; for Key Letters, see p. 238. LIGHT = A.M. **BOLD** = P.M. 

# FEBRUARY

FEBRUARY HATH 28 DAYS

*The hoar-frost crackles on the trees,*
*The rattling brook begins to freeze.*
–James Berry Bensel

| DAY OF MONTH | DAY OF WEEK | DATES, FEASTS, FASTS, ASPECTS, TIDE HEIGHTS, AND WEATHER | |
|---|---|---|---|
| 1 | Tu. | St. Brigid • LUNAR NEW YEAR (CHINA) • NEW ● • ☌♄☾ | *Groundhogs,* |
| 2 | W. | Candlemas • Groundhog Day • ☌♃☾ • {11.6 / — | *mixed up;* |
| 3 | Th. | ☌♆☾ • ☿ STAT. • Rare Feb. EF1 tornado, Gray/Roberts/Hemphill Cos., Tex., 2012 | *get* |
| 4 | Fr. | ☌♄☉ • *The Muses love the morning.* • {10.3 / 10.9 | *snowblowers* |
| 5 | Sa. | St. Agatha • ☾ ON EQ. • 3.7" snow, San Francisco, Calif., 1887 • {10.1 / 10.2 | *fixed* |
| 6 | **B** | Singer Natalie Cole born, 1950 • Tides {9.9 / 9.6 | *up!* |
| 7 | M. | ☌⛢☾ • Writer Charles Dickens born, 1812 • Tides {9.6 / 8.9 | *Keep* |
| 8 | Tu. | 1st radio installed in White House, D.C., 1922 • {9.2 / 8.3 | *them* |
| 9 | W. | ☾ AT ☊ • "War Time" (yr.-round daylight saving time) began in U.S., 1942 • {9.0 / 7.9 | *humming;* |
| 10 | Th. | ☾ AT APO. • *When the wind's in the north, You mustn't go forth.* • Tides {8.8 / 7.7 | *another* |
| 11 | Fr. | Inventor Thomas Edison born, 1847 • Track and field athlete Abby Hoffman born, 1947 | *big* |
| 12 | Sa. | ☾ RIDES HIGH • ☌☿♇ • ☌♀♂ • ♀ GR. ILLUM. EXT. • Abe Lincoln born, 1809 | *one's* |
| 13 | **B** | **Septuagesima** • 2nd Hubble Space Telescope tune-up began, 1997 | *coming!* |
| 14 | M. | Sts. Cyril & Methodius • VALENTINE'S DAY • {9.6 / 8.5 | *Valentine* |
| 15 | Tu. | NATIONAL FLAG OF CANADA DAY • Social reformer Susan B. Anthony born, 1820 • {9.9 / 8.9 | *gifts* |
| 16 | W. | FULL SNOW ○ • ☿ GR. ELONG. (26° WEST) • Winter's back breaks. • {10.2 / 9.2 | *obscured* |
| 17 | Th. | National Congress of Mothers, later known as PTA, founded, 1897 • Tides {10.4 / — | *by* |
| 18 | Fr. | Geochemist Wallace Broecker, who popularized term "global warming," died, 2019 • {9.5 / 10.4 | *drifts.* |
| 19 | Sa. | ☾ ON EQ. • 1st rescuers reached Donner Party in Sierra Nevada mtns., Calif., 1847 • {9.8 / 10.4 | *Rain and* |
| 20 | **B** | **Sexagesima** • Metropolitan Museum of Art opened, N.Y.C., 1872 • {10.0 / 10.2 | *snow* |
| 21 | M. | PRESIDENTS' DAY • Polaroid instant camera first demonstrated, 1947 • {10.2 / 9.8 | *alternating,* |
| 22 | Tu. | U.S. president George Washington born, 1732 • Tides {10.2 / 9.4 | *temperature* |
| 23 | W. | ☾ AT ☋ • 1st powered flight in Canada (by McCurdy in *Silver Dart*), Baddeck, N.S., 1909 | *elevating,* |
| 24 | Th. | St. Matthias • *Think today and speak tomorrow.* • {10.2 / 8.7 | *which* |
| 25 | Fr. | Actor Sean Astin born, 1971 • Tides {10.1 / 8.6 | *is* |
| 26 | Sa. | ☾ RUNS LOW • ☾ AT PERIG. • Buffalo Creek flood disaster, Logan Co., W.Va, 1972 | *well* |
| 27 | **B** | **Quinquagesima** • ☌♀☾ • ☌♂☾ • ☌♇☾ | *worth* |
| 28 | M. | St. Romanus • ☌☿☾ • ☌♄☾ • Skunks mate now. • {10.8 / 9.5 | *celebrating!* |

*Q: What is smarter than a hummingbird?*
*A: A spelling bee*

## Farmer's Calendar

A homegrown parsnip may take up to 400 days to raise, if you consider that the process begins the moment you place your seed order even as wind scatters more snow. Your single packet, when it arrives, contains plenty. I share my surplus seed with a neighbor because they lose viability if I try to hoard them for another season. Although the packet duly warns that these seeds germinate slowly, you may still lose faith. However, the moment your exasperation wins and you lug a flat of tomatoes over to transplant into the root bed instead, only then will you notice something so faint and delicate, you could mistake it for grass. Your parsnips have emerged; harvest is now merely nine months away. A full winter later, as the last snowbank thaws, and with only sprouting onions and tentacled potatoes remaining from last summer's harvest, you fetch the digging fork and revisit the roots that spent those bitter months buried in your forgotten garden, maturing. When forked loose and yanked free in late April, early May, the pale ivory roots resemble dirty icicles, albino carrots. But their flavor, thanks to the frost, is appreciably sweet—your edible prize for patience.

# MARCH

**SKY WATCH:** With the evening sky empty of planets, all the action happens in the east just before dawn. An oceanlike flat horizon may reveal a close meeting of Mercury and Saturn 40 minutes before sunrise on the 2nd, but they are only 3 degrees high. Far easier to view is dazzling Venus hovering above dimmer orange Mars. By midmonth, Mars and Saturn are higher up, Mercury is lower, and Venus is steady, if slightly less brilliant than before. Look for a triangle from the 24th to the 26th, with Mars on the right, Saturn to the left, and Venus at the top. On the 28th, the waning crescent Moon dangles below the triangle's remnant, a nice four-way conjunction. Jupiter is absent from all of these planet displays because it is in conjunction with the Sun on the 5th. Spring begins with the vernal equinox on the 20th at 11:33 A.M. EDT.

● **NEW MOON** 2nd day 12:35 P.M.   ○ **FULL MOON** 18th day 3:18 A.M.
◐ **FIRST QUARTER** 10th day 5:45 A.M.   ◑ **LAST QUARTER** 25th day 1:37 A.M.

*After 2:00 A.M. on March 13, Eastern Daylight Time is given.*

**GET THESE PAGES WITH TIMES SET TO YOUR ZIP CODE VIA ALMANAC.COM/2022.**

| DAY OF YEAR | DAY OF MONTH | DAY OF WEEK | ☼ RISES H. M. | RISE KEY | ☼ SETS H. M. | SET KEY | LENGTH OF DAY H. M. | SUN FAST M. | SUN DECLINATION ° ' | HIGH TIDE TIMES BOSTON | ☾ RISES H. M. | RISE KEY | ☾ SETS H. M. | SET KEY | ☾ ASTRON. PLACE | ☾ AGE |
|---|---|---|---|---|---|---|---|---|---|---|---|---|---|---|---|---|
| 60 | 1 | Tu. | 6:19 | D | **5:34** | C | 11 15 | 4 | 7 s. 24 | 10 — 10½ | 6:11 | E | **4:21** | C | CAP | 28 |
| 61 | 2 | W. | 6:18 | D | **5:35** | C | 11 17 | 4 | 7 s. 01 | 10¾ — 11¼ | 6:41 | E | **5:35** | C | AQU | 0 |
| 62 | 3 | Th. | 6:16 | D | **5:37** | C | 11 21 | 4 | 6 s. 38 | 11½ — — | 7:06 | D | **6:46** | D | AQU | 1 |
| 63 | 4 | Fr. | 6:15 | D | **5:38** | C | 11 23 | 4 | 6 s. 15 | 12 — 12¼ | 7:29 | D | **7:55** | D | PSC | 2 |
| 64 | 5 | Sa. | 6:13 | D | **5:39** | C | 11 26 | 4 | 5 s. 52 | 12¾ — 1 | 7:51 | C | **9:01** | E | PSC | 3 |
| 65 | 6 | **B** | 6:11 | D | **5:40** | C | 11 29 | 5 | 5 s. 29 | 1½ — 1¾ | 8:13 | B | **10:07** | E | PSC | 4 |
| 66 | 7 | M. | 6:10 | C | **5:41** | C | 11 31 | 5 | 5 s. 05 | 2¼ — 2½ | 8:37 | B | **11:12** | E | ARI | 5 |
| 67 | 8 | Tu. | 6:08 | C | **5:43** | C | 11 35 | 5 | 4 s. 42 | 2¾ — 3½ | 9:04 | B | — | - | TAU | 6 |
| 68 | 9 | W. | 6:06 | C | **5:44** | C | 11 38 | 5 | 4 s. 18 | 3¾ — 4¼ | 9:36 | A | 12:16 | E | TAU | 7 |
| 69 | 10 | Th. | 6:05 | C | **5:45** | C | 11 40 | 6 | 3 s. 55 | 4½ — 5¼ | 10:13 | A | 1:17 | E | TAU | 8 |
| 70 | 11 | Fr. | 6:03 | C | **5:46** | C | 11 43 | 6 | 3 s. 31 | 5½ — 6¼ | 10:58 | A | 2:15 | E | TAU | 9 |
| 71 | 12 | Sa. | 6:01 | C | **5:47** | C | 11 46 | 6 | 3 s. 08 | 6½ — 7¼ | 11:50 | A | 3:07 | E | GEM | 10 |
| 72 | 13 | **B** | 6:59 | C | **6:48** | C | 11 49 | 6 | 2 s. 44 | 8½ — 9¼ | **1:49** | B | 4:53 | E | GEM | 11 |
| 73 | 14 | M. | 6:58 | C | **6:50** | C | 11 52 | 7 | 2 s. 20 | 9¼ — 10 | **2:53** | B | 5:31 | E | CAN | 12 |
| 74 | 15 | Tu. | 6:56 | C | **6:51** | C | 11 55 | 7 | 1 s. 57 | 10 — 10¾ | **4:00** | B | 6:04 | E | LEO | 13 |
| 75 | 16 | W. | 6:54 | C | **6:52** | C | 11 58 | 7 | 1 s. 33 | 10¾ — 11¼ | **5:08** | C | 6:32 | E | LEO | 14 |
| 76 | 17 | Th. | 6:53 | C | **6:53** | C | 12 00 | 7 | 1 s. 09 | 11½ — — | **6:17** | D | 6:57 | D | LEO | 15 |
| 77 | 18 | Fr. | 6:51 | C | **6:54** | C | 12 03 | 8 | 0 s. 45 | 12 — 12¼ | **7:27** | D | 7:20 | D | VIR | 16 |
| 78 | 19 | Sa. | 6:49 | C | **6:55** | C | 12 06 | 8 | 0 s. 22 | 12½ — 1 | **8:39** | E | 7:43 | C | VIR | 17 |
| 79 | 20 | **B** | 6:47 | C | **6:57** | C | 12 10 | 8 | 0 N. 01 | 1¼ — 1¾ | **9:52** | E | 8:06 | C | VIR | 18 |
| 80 | 21 | M. | 6:46 | C | **6:58** | C | 12 12 | 9 | 0 N. 25 | 2 — 2½ | **11:07** | E | 8:33 | B | LIB | 19 |
| 81 | 22 | Tu. | 6:44 | C | **6:59** | C | 12 15 | 9 | 0 N. 48 | 2¾ — 3¼ | — | - | 9:04 | B | LIB | 20 |
| 82 | 23 | W. | 6:42 | C | **7:00** | C | 12 18 | 9 | 1 N. 12 | 3½ — 4 | 12:24 | E | 9:42 | B | SCO | 21 |
| 83 | 24 | Th. | 6:40 | C | **7:01** | C | 12 21 | 10 | 1 N. 36 | 4¼ — 5 | 1:39 | E | 10:30 | A | OPH | 22 |
| 84 | 25 | Fr. | 6:39 | C | **7:02** | C | 12 23 | 10 | 1 N. 59 | 5¼ — 6¼ | 2:47 | E | 11:28 | A | SAG | 23 |
| 85 | 26 | Sa. | 6:37 | C | **7:03** | C | 12 26 | 10 | 2 N. 23 | 6½ — 7¼ | 3:46 | E | **12:35** | B | SAG | 24 |
| 86 | 27 | **B** | 6:35 | C | **7:04** | C | 12 29 | 11 | 2 N. 46 | 7½ — 8½ | 4:33 | E | **1:49** | B | CAP | 25 |
| 87 | 28 | M. | 6:33 | C | **7:06** | C | 12 33 | 11 | 3 N. 10 | 8¾ — 9½ | 5:11 | E | **3:04** | B | CAP | 26 |
| 88 | 29 | Tu. | 6:32 | C | **7:07** | C | 12 35 | 11 | 3 N. 33 | 9¾ — 10½ | 5:42 | E | **4:17** | C | AQU | 27 |
| 89 | 30 | W. | 6:30 | C | **7:08** | D | 12 38 | 11 | 3 N. 56 | 10¾ — 11¼ | 6:08 | D | **5:28** | D | AQU | 28 |
| 90 | 31 | Th. | 6:28 | C | **7:09** | D | 12 41 | 12 | 4 N. 20 | 11½ — — | 6:31 | D | **6:37** | D | PSC | 29 |

To use this page, see p. 116; for Key Letters, see p. 238. LIGHT = A.M. BOLD = P.M.   2022

# MARCH

MARCH HATH 31 DAYS

*Fled now the sullen murmurs of the North,*
*The splendid raiment of the Spring peeps forth.*
–**Robert Bloomfield**

| DAY OF MONTH | DAY OF WEEK | DATES, FEASTS, FASTS, ASPECTS, TIDE HEIGHTS, AND WEATHER | |
|---|---|---|---|
| 1 | Tu. | Shrove Tuesday • St. David • 1st U.S. national park (Yellowstone) established, 1872 | *Sun-splashed* |
| 2 | W. | **Ash Wednesday** • NEW ● • ☌☿♄ • ☌♃☾ • {11.2 / 10.3 | *and* |
| 3 | Th. | ☌♂♇ • ☌♆☾ • Athlete Jackie Joyner-Kersee born, 1962 • {11.2 / — | *strangely* |
| 4 | Fr. | ☾ ON EQ. • ☌♀♇ • Bertha Wilson 1st woman appointed to Supreme Court of Canada, 1982 | *vernal;* |
| 5 | Sa. | St. Piran • ☌♃⊙ • *Many littles make a mickle* [large amount]. • {10.5 / 10.5 | *hopes* |
| 6 | **B** | **1st S. in Lent** • Bandmaster John Philip Sousa died, 1932 • Tides {10.3 / 10.0 | *dashed* |
| 7 | M. | Orthodox Lent begins • St. Perpetua • ☌⛢☾ • {10.0 / 9.4 | *by* |
| 8 | Tu. | ☾ AT ☊ • Joseph Lee, father of playground movement, born, 1862 • {9.7 / 8.8 | *rain* |
| 9 | W. | Ember Day • Hummingbirds migrate north now. • Tides {9.3 / 8.2 | *that* |
| 10 | Th. | ☾ AT APO. • Uranus rings discovered, 1977 • *Pay as you go, And what you have you know.* | *seems* |
| 11 | Fr. | Ember Day • ☾ RIDES HIGH • "Faster than it looks" cow wanted by police, Pembroke Pines, Fla., 2020 | *eternal.* |
| 12 | Sa. | Ember Day • ☌♀♂ • Singer Liza Minnelli born, 1946 • Tides {8.7 / 7.7 | *Saint* |
| 13 | **B** | **2nd S. in Lent** • **Daylight Saving Time begins, 2:00 a.m.** • ☌♆⊙ | *Patrick's* |
| 14 | M. | Gordie Howe 2nd player in NHL history to score 500 career goals, 1962 • Tides {9.2 / 8.4 | *Day* |
| 15 | Tu. | Beware the ides of March. • Mi'kmaq poet Rita Joe born, 1932 • Tides {9.6 / 8.8 | *is* |
| 16 | W. | United States Military Academy established, West Point, N.Y., 1802 • Tides {9.9 / 9.3 | *damp* |
| 17 | Th. | **St. Patrick's Day** • 1,263 people dressed as leprechauns (Bandon, Ireland) set world record, 2012 | *and* |
| 18 | Fr. | **FULL WORM** ○ • ☾ ON EQ. • Feb. 2019 world's 5th warmest Feb. since 1880, NOAA announced, 2019 | *gray.* |
| 19 | Sa. | St. Joseph • Elvis Presley paid $1,000 deposit to buy Graceland, Memphis, Tenn., 1957 • {10.3 / 10.6 | *No* |
| 20 | **B** | **3rd S. in Lent** • **VERNAL EQUINOX** • ☌☿♃ • ♀ GR. ELONG. (47° WEST) | *relief;* |
| 21 | M. | Twitter founded, 2006 • Astronomer Halton Christian Arp born, 1927 • {10.8 / 10.3 | *the* |
| 22 | Tu. | ☾ AT ☋ • Animatronic T-rex caught fire, Canon City, Colo., 2018 • Tides {10.9 / 9.9 | *warmth* |
| 23 | W. | ☾ AT PERIG. • ☌☿♆ • *Halifax Gazette* became Canada's 1st newspaper, 1752 | *is* |
| 24 | Th. | Explorer John W. Powell born, 1834 • Tides {10.6 / 9.1 | *brief—* |
| 25 | Fr. | **Annunciation** • ☾ RUNS LOW • Musician Elton John born, 1947 • {10.3 / 8.7 | *we* |
| 26 | Sa. | ☌♇☾ • 12-pound walleye caught with fly tackle, Manistee River, Mich., 1999 • {10.1 / 8.7 | *sing* |
| 27 | **B** | **4th S. in Lent** • ☌♂☾ • *March many weathers.* • Tides {10.1 / 8.9 | *of* |
| 28 | M. | ☌♀☾ • ☌♄☾ • Fireball seen around 6:15 a.m. EDT, northeastern U.S., 2019 • {10.2 / 9.3 | *spring* |
| 29 | Tu. | ☌♀♄ • Vesta, brightest asteroid known, discovered, 1807 • Tides {10.4 / 9.8 | *through* |
| 30 | W. | ☌♃☾ • ☌♆☾ • Last rum ration issued in Royal Canadian Navy, 1972 | *chattering* |
| 31 | Th. | ☾ ON EQ. • ☌☿☾ • Chipmunks emerge from hibernation now. • {10.7 / 10.5 | *teeth!* |

## Farmer's Calendar

Soil is a celebrity at the Main Street Museum in White River Junction, Vermont. The brown powders displayed in clear jars are reminiscent of samples farmers trowel out of their fields and send off to the Extension Service to determine nitrogen and phosphorous levels. This exhibited dirt, however, bears labels that announce: "Silt from the 1927 Flood" and "Sandy Thin Sample from the birthplace of Henry Leland [designer of the Cadillac] near Barton, Vermont." It forces one to consider: What *isn't* sacred, or at least special, ground? A museum in Sidney, Iowa, also possesses an earthly collection, featuring labeled jars filled with two spoonfuls, resembling spices in a pantry. Begun as a farmwife's hobby—gathered in Missouri and Texas, and brought to her from France and the North Pole—they became her legacy. When a museum trustee first unpacked the donation—157 samples—she thought, "Why would we want a bunch of dirt?" Seen as separate from the field, one could forget this humble medium furnishes our food and wood. Or, as the trustee realized, it reminds us the world is bound to the soil. Now, as snow recedes and reveals the long-hidden mud, we might celebrate by the acre and spoonful.

CALENDAR

# APRIL

**SKY WATCH:** The month's first sunrise is heralded by a crooked line of planets in the predawn southeast, with Mars on the right, Saturn in the middle, and dazzling Venus on the left. On the 4th and 5th, Mars and Saturn come extremely close together. With Venus to their left, they float a comfortable 15 degrees high; Saturn is slightly brighter than orange Mars. On the 27th, the night's three brightest objects—the Moon, Venus, and Jupiter—form a lovely triangle 15 degrees high in the morning twilight. The latter two planets come extremely close together on the 30th in a don't-miss conjunction. Unfortunately, the partial solar eclipse created by the new Moon on the 30th is visible only from southern South America and Antarctica.

● NEW MOON    1st day  2:24 A.M.    ◐ LAST QUARTER  23rd day  7:56 A.M.
◐ FIRST QUARTER  9th day  2:48 A.M.    ● NEW MOON    30th day  4:28 P.M.
○ FULL MOON  16th day  2:55 P.M.

*All times are given in Eastern Daylight Time.*

**GET THESE PAGES WITH TIMES SET TO YOUR ZIP CODE VIA ALMANAC.COM/2022.**

| DAY OF YEAR | DAY OF MONTH | DAY OF WEEK | ☀ RISES H.M. | RISE KEY | ☀ SETS H.M. | SET KEY | LENGTH OF DAY H.M. | SUN FAST M. | SUN DECLINATION ° ' | HIGH TIDE TIMES BOSTON | | ☽ RISES H.M. | RISE KEY | ☽ SETS H.M. | SET KEY | ☽ ASTRON. PLACE | ☽ AGE |
|---|---|---|---|---|---|---|---|---|---|---|---|---|---|---|---|---|---|
| 91 | 1 | Fr. | 6:27 | C | **7:10** | D | 12 43 | 12 | 4 N. 43 | 12 | 12¼ | 6:53 | C | **7:44** | E | CET | 0 |
| 92 | 2 | Sa. | 6:25 | C | **7:11** | D | 12 46 | 12 | 5 N. 06 | 12½ | 1 | 7:15 | C | **8:51** | E | PSC | 1 |
| 93 | 3 | **B** | 6:23 | C | **7:12** | D | 12 49 | 13 | 5 N. 29 | 1¼ | 1¾ | 7:38 | B | **9:56** | E | ARI | 2 |
| 94 | 4 | M. | 6:21 | C | **7:14** | D | 12 53 | 13 | 5 N. 52 | 2 | 2½ | 8:03 | B | **11:02** | E | ARI | 3 |
| 95 | 5 | Tu. | 6:20 | C | **7:15** | D | 12 55 | 13 | 6 N. 15 | 2½ | 3 | 8:33 | B | — | - | TAU | 4 |
| 96 | 6 | W. | 6:18 | C | **7:16** | D | 12 58 | 13 | 6 N. 37 | 3¼ | 3¾ | 9:08 | A | 12:05 | E | TAU | 5 |
| 97 | 7 | Th. | 6:16 | C | **7:17** | D | 13 01 | 14 | 7 N. 00 | 4 | 4¾ | 9:49 | A | 1:05 | E | TAU | 6 |
| 98 | 8 | Fr. | 6:15 | B | **7:18** | D | 13 03 | 14 | 7 N. 22 | 4¾ | 5½ | 10:39 | A | 2:00 | E | GEM | 7 |
| 99 | 9 | Sa. | 6:13 | B | **7:19** | D | 13 06 | 14 | 7 N. 45 | 5¾ | 6½ | 11:35 | A | 2:48 | E | GEM | 8 |
| 100 | 10 | **B** | 6:11 | B | **7:20** | D | 13 09 | 15 | 8 N. 07 | 6¾ | 7½ | **12:36** | E | 3:29 | E | CAN | 9 |
| 101 | 11 | M. | 6:10 | B | **7:21** | D | 13 11 | 15 | 8 N. 29 | 7¾ | 8½ | **1:41** | B | 4:03 | E | CAN | 10 |
| 102 | 12 | Tu. | 6:08 | B | **7:23** | D | 13 15 | 15 | 8 N. 51 | 8½ | 9¼ | **2:48** | C | 4:32 | E | LEO | 11 |
| 103 | 13 | W. | 6:06 | B | **7:24** | D | 13 18 | 15 | 9 N. 13 | 9½ | 10 | **3:57** | C | 4:58 | E | LEO | 12 |
| 104 | 14 | Th. | 6:05 | B | **7:25** | D | 13 20 | 16 | 9 N. 34 | 10¼ | 10¾ | **5:07** | D | 5:21 | D | LEO | 13 |
| 105 | 15 | Fr. | 6:03 | B | **7:26** | D | 13 23 | 16 | 9 N. 56 | 11 | 11¼ | **6:18** | E | 5:44 | D | VIR | 14 |
| 106 | 16 | Sa. | 6:02 | B | **7:27** | D | 13 25 | 16 | 10 N. 17 | 11¾ | — | **7:32** | E | 6:07 | C | VIR | 15 |
| 107 | 17 | **B** | 6:00 | B | **7:28** | D | 13 28 | 16 | 10 N. 38 | 12 | 12½ | **8:49** | E | 6:33 | B | VIR | 16 |
| 108 | 18 | M. | 5:58 | B | **7:29** | D | 13 31 | 16 | 10 N. 59 | 12¾ | 1¼ | **10:08** | E | 7:03 | B | LIB | 17 |
| 109 | 19 | Tu. | 5:57 | B | **7:30** | D | 13 33 | 17 | 11 N. 20 | 1½ | 2 | **11:26** | E | 7:39 | B | SCO | 18 |
| 110 | 20 | W. | 5:55 | B | **7:32** | D | 13 37 | 17 | 11 N. 40 | 2¼ | 3 | — | - | 8:24 | A | OPH | 19 |
| 111 | 21 | Th. | 5:54 | B | **7:33** | D | 13 39 | 17 | 12 N. 01 | 3¼ | 4 | 12:39 | E | 9:20 | A | SAG | 20 |
| 112 | 22 | Fr. | 5:52 | B | **7:34** | D | 13 42 | 17 | 12 N. 21 | 4 | 5 | 1:43 | E | 10:26 | B | SAG | 21 |
| 113 | 23 | Sa. | 5:51 | B | **7:35** | D | 13 44 | 17 | 12 N. 41 | 5 | 6 | 2:34 | E | 11:39 | B | CAP | 22 |
| 114 | 24 | **B** | 5:49 | B | **7:36** | D | 13 47 | 18 | 13 N. 01 | 6¼ | 7 | 3:14 | E | **12:53** | B | CAP | 23 |
| 115 | 25 | M. | 5:48 | B | **7:37** | D | 13 49 | 18 | 13 N. 20 | 7½ | 8¼ | 3:46 | E | **2:06** | C | AQU | 24 |
| 116 | 26 | Tu. | 5:46 | B | **7:38** | D | 13 52 | 18 | 13 N. 39 | 8½ | 9¼ | 4:13 | E | **3:17** | C | AQU | 25 |
| 117 | 27 | W. | 5:45 | B | **7:39** | D | 13 54 | 18 | 13 N. 59 | 9½ | 10 | 4:36 | D | **4:25** | D | AQU | 26 |
| 118 | 28 | Th. | 5:43 | B | **7:41** | D | 13 58 | 18 | 14 N. 18 | 10½ | 10¾ | 4:58 | C | **5:32** | D | CET | 27 |
| 119 | 29 | Fr. | 5:42 | B | **7:42** | D | 14 00 | 18 | 14 N. 36 | 11¼ | 11½ | 5:19 | C | **6:37** | E | PSC | 28 |
| 120 | 30 | Sa. | 5:41 | B | **7:43** | E | 14 02 | 19 | 14 N. 55 | 12 | — | 5:41 | B | **7:43** | E | PSC | 0 |

CALENDAR

THE FOURTH MONTH · 2022 **APRIL** APRIL HATH 30 DAYS

*Did you dip your wings in azure dye,*
*When April began to paint the sky?*
–**Susan Hartley Swett, of a blue jay**

| DAY OF MONTH | DAY OF WEEK | DATES, FEASTS, FASTS, ASPECTS, TIDE HEIGHTS, AND WEATHER | |
|---|---|---|---|
| 1 | Fr. | ALL FOOLS' • NEW ● • *One fool makes a hundred.* • {10.6 / — | *Cold* |
| 2 | Sa. | Ramadan begins at sundown • ☿ IN SUP. ☌ • Inventor Samuel Morse died, 1872 | *and* |
| 3 | **B** | 5th S. in Lent • St. Richard of Chichester • ☌♅☾ • Actress Doris Day born, 1922 | *mucky:* |
| 4 | M. | ☾ AT ☊ • ☌♂♄ • Astronomer Jérôme Lalande died, 1807 • {10.4 / 9.6 | *yucky!* |
| 5 | Tu. | Anne Sullivan conveyed meaning of word "water" to blind/deaf student Helen Keller, 1887 | *Thunder's* |
| 6 | W. | Vancouver, B.C., incorporated, 1886 • Microsoft released Windows 3.1, 1992 • {9.8 / 8.7 | *tympani* |
| 7 | Th. | ☾ AT APO. • NASA's *Mars Odyssey* spacecraft launched, 2001 • Tides {9.4 / 8.3 | *rumbles* |
| 8 | Fr. | ☾ RIDES HIGH • Honolulu Academy of Arts opened, Hawaii, 1927 • Tides {9.0 / 8.0 | *in* |
| 9 | Sa. | Battle of Vimy Ridge (WWI) began, France, 1917 • Tides {8.8 / 7.8 | *a* |
| 10 | **B** | **Palm Sunday** • 1st Arbor Day, Nebr., 1872 • Tides {8.7 / 7.9 | *spring* |
| 11 | M. | Jackie Robinson became 1st African-American MLB player, 1947 • Tides {8.9 / 8.2 | *symphony,* |
| 12 | Tu. | ☌♃♆ • Stubbs the Cat, honorary mayor of Talkeetna, Alaska, born, 1997 • {9.1 / 8.7 | *but* |
| 13 | W. | U.S. president Thomas Jefferson born, 1743 • Tides {9.5 / 9.3 | *don't* |
| 14 | Th. | Maundy Thursday • *April weather, rain and sunshine, both together.* • {9.9 / 9.9 | *put* |
| 15 | Fr. | **Good Friday** • Passover begins at sundown • ☾ ON EQ. • {10.2 / 10.5 | *away* |
| 16 | Sa. | FULL PINK ○ • Aviator Wilbur Wright born, 1867 • {10.5 / — | *your* |
| 17 | **B** | **Easter** • Writer Thornton Wilder born, 1897 • Tides {11.0 / 10.6 | *galoshes:* |
| 18 | M. | Easter Monday • ☾ AT ☋ • ☌☿♅ • {11.4 / 10.6 | *Everything* |
| 19 | Tu. | ☾ AT PERIG. • 1st Boston Marathon, 1897 • Tides {11.5 / 10.3 | *sloshes!* |
| 20 | W. | 54 lb. 8 oz. freshwater drum caught, Nickajack Lake, Tenn., 1972 • Tides {11.5 / 10.0 | *We grope* |
| 21 | Th. | ☾ RUNS LOW • Environmentalist Aldo Leopold died, 1948 • Tides {11.2 / 9.6 | *for* |
| 22 | Fr. | EARTH DAY • ☌♇☾ • Red River crested at 54.35 ft., Grand Forks, N.Dak., 1997 • {10.9 / 9.3 | *hope:* |
| 23 | Sa. | St. George • Canadian prime minister Lester Pearson born, 1897 • Tides {10.4 / 9.1 | *nope.* |
| 24 | **B** | 2nd S. of Easter • **Orthodox Easter** • ☌♄☾ • *Almanac* founder Robert B. Thomas born, 1766 | |
| 25 | M. | St. Mark • ☌♂☾ • *Patience wears out stones.* • {10.0 / 9.3 | *Blessed* |
| 26 | Tu. | ☌♀☾ • ☌♆☾ • Landscape architect Frederick Law Olmsted born, 1822 | *sight!* |
| 27 | W. | ☌♀♆ • ☌♃☾ • U.S. president Ulysses S. Grant born, 1822 | *It's* |
| 28 | Th. | ☾ ON EQ. • Poplars leaf out about now. • Tides {10.0 / 10.3 | *warm* |
| 29 | Fr. | ☿ GR. ELONG. (21° EAST) • Proposed Nfld. flag design revealed, 1980 • {10.0 / 10.5 | *and* |
| 30 | Sa. | NEW ● • ECLIPSE ⊙ • ☌♀♃ • ♇ STAT. • {9.9 / — | *bright!* |

## Farmer's Calendar

Where the earth produced enough corn to feed a farmer's herd through the winter, a man now wanders, searching for yet another harvest. His boots crunch on thawing stubble and he's wearing headphones as he swings a metal detector, listening for the song of lost things, pieces of the past: treasures. Throughout winter he studies old atlases, town records, and topographical maps to determine the best hunting grounds. Then, in the interval following snowmelt, before the growing season begins, he meanders the grounds of yesteryear's stagecoach stops, boardinghouses, farm dumps, churchyards—places where tools, coins, jewelry, and buttons might still reside. In the decade he's spent hunting Vermont's dirt, he's racked up scores of intriguing finds: a galaxy of buttons, a commissary of soldiers' things, and an exchequer's purse of ancient coins. Now, as he homes in on a signal, he hunches close to the bare soil and remnant stalks. Detaching his microphone-like probe from his detector, he plunges it into the ground. As the beeping grows ever stronger and more constant, he clears away the dirt, searching for the source with tempered optimism, knowing "a diamond ring makes the same sound as a pop-top."

# MAY

**SKY WATCH:** Before dawn in the east on the 1st, Venus and Jupiter are still wonderfully close together. From the 3rd to the 20th, look for an easy planet lineup featuring, from left to right, Venus, Jupiter, Mars, and Saturn. The crescent Moon serves as an easy guide to all of the planets beginning on the 22nd, when it's just below Saturn. The Moon will dangle below Jupiter and Mars on the 25th and below Venus on the 27th. From the 27th to the 30th, Jupiter will be very close to Mars. A total lunar eclipse appears on the night of the 15th–16th, with the entire eclipse visible from the eastern half of the U.S. and Canada and all of South America. West of the Mississippi, the Moon will rise already eclipsed, offering intriguing photography opportunities.

| | | | | | |
|---|---|---|---|---|---|
| ◐ FIRST QUARTER | 8th day | 8:21 P.M. | ◑ LAST QUARTER | 22nd day | 2:43 P.M. |
| ○ FULL MOON | 16th day | 12:14 A.M. | ● NEW MOON | 30th day | 7:30 A.M. |

*All times are given in Eastern Daylight Time.*

**GET THESE PAGES WITH TIMES SET TO YOUR ZIP CODE VIA ALMANAC.COM/2022.**

| DAY OF YEAR | DAY OF MONTH | DAY OF WEEK | ☼ RISES | RISE KEY | ☼ SETS | SET KEY | LENGTH OF DAY | SUN FAST | SUN DECLINATION | | HIGH TIDE TIMES BOSTON | | ☾ RISES | RISE KEY | ☾ SETS | SET KEY | ☾ ASTRON. PLACE | ☾ AGE |
|---|---|---|---|---|---|---|---|---|---|---|---|---|---|---|---|---|---|---|
| | | | H. M. | | H. M. | | H. M. | M. | ° | ' | | | H. M. | | H. M. | | | |
| 121 | 1 | **B** | 5:39 | B | **7:44** | E | 14 05 | 19 | 15 N. | 13 | 12¼ | **12¾** | 6:05 | B | **8:48** | E | ARI | 1 |
| 122 | 2 | M. | 5:38 | B | **7:45** | E | 14 07 | 19 | 15 N. | 31 | 12¾ | **1¼** | 6:33 | B | **9:53** | E | TAU | 2 |
| 123 | 3 | Tu. | 5:37 | B | **7:46** | E | 14 09 | 19 | 15 N. | 48 | 1½ | **2** | 7:05 | B | **10:55** | E | TAU | 3 |
| 124 | 4 | W. | 5:35 | B | **7:47** | E | 14 12 | 19 | 16 N. | 06 | 2 | **2¾** | 7:44 | A | **11:52** | E | TAU | 4 |
| 125 | 5 | Th. | 5:34 | B | **7:48** | E | 14 14 | 19 | 16 N. | 23 | 2¾ | **3½** | 8:30 | A | — | - | GEM | 5 |
| 126 | 6 | Fr. | 5:33 | B | **7:49** | E | 14 16 | 19 | 16 N. | 40 | 3½ | **4¼** | 9:24 | A | 12:43 | E | GEM | 6 |
| 127 | 7 | Sa. | 5:32 | B | **7:51** | E | 14 19 | 19 | 16 N. | 56 | 4¼ | **5** | 10:23 | B | 1:26 | E | CAN | 7 |
| 128 | 8 | **B** | 5:30 | B | **7:52** | E | 14 22 | 19 | 17 N. | 13 | 5 | **5¾** | 11:26 | B | 2:02 | E | CAN | 8 |
| 129 | 9 | M. | 5:29 | B | **7:53** | E | 14 24 | 19 | 17 N. | 29 | 6 | **6¾** | **12:31** | C | 2:33 | E | LEO | 9 |
| 130 | 10 | Tu. | 5:28 | B | **7:54** | E | 14 26 | 19 | 17 N. | 44 | 7 | **7½** | **1:37** | C | 2:59 | E | LEO | 10 |
| 131 | 11 | W. | 5:27 | B | **7:55** | E | 14 28 | 19 | 18 N. | 00 | 7¾ | **8½** | **2:45** | D | 3:23 | D | LEO | 11 |
| 132 | 12 | Th. | 5:26 | B | **7:56** | E | 14 30 | 19 | 18 N. | 15 | 8¾ | **9¼** | **3:54** | D | 3:45 | D | VIR | 12 |
| 133 | 13 | Fr. | 5:25 | B | **7:57** | E | 14 32 | 19 | 18 N. | 30 | 9½ | **10** | **5:06** | E | 4:08 | C | VIR | 13 |
| 134 | 14 | Sa. | 5:24 | B | **7:58** | E | 14 34 | 19 | 18 N. | 44 | 10½ | **10¾** | **6:22** | E | 4:32 | C | VIR | 14 |
| 135 | 15 | **B** | 5:23 | A | **7:59** | E | 14 36 | 19 | 18 N. | 58 | 11¼ | **11½** | **7:41** | E | 4:59 | B | LIB | 15 |
| 136 | 16 | M. | 5:22 | A | **8:00** | E | 14 38 | 19 | 19 N. | 12 | **12** | — | **9:03** | E | 5:32 | B | LIB | 16 |
| 137 | 17 | Tu. | 5:21 | A | **8:01** | E | 14 40 | 19 | 19 N. | 26 | 12¼ | **1** | **10:21** | E | 6:14 | B | OPH | 17 |
| 138 | 18 | W. | 5:20 | A | **8:02** | E | 14 42 | 19 | 19 N. | 39 | 1 | **1¾** | **11:32** | E | 7:07 | A | OPH | 18 |
| 139 | 19 | Th. | 5:19 | A | **8:03** | E | 14 44 | 19 | 19 N. | 52 | 2 | **2¾** | — | - | 8:12 | B | SAG | 19 |
| 140 | 20 | Fr. | 5:18 | A | **8:04** | E | 14 46 | 19 | 20 N. | 04 | 3 | **3¾** | 12:30 | E | 9:25 | B | SAG | 20 |
| 141 | 21 | Sa. | 5:17 | A | **8:05** | E | 14 48 | 19 | 20 N. | 16 | 4 | **4¾** | 1:15 | E | 10:42 | B | CAP | 21 |
| 142 | 22 | **B** | 5:16 | A | **8:06** | E | 14 50 | 19 | 20 N. | 28 | 5 | **5¾** | 1:50 | E | 11:57 | C | CAP | 22 |
| 143 | 23 | M. | 5:16 | A | **8:07** | E | 14 51 | 19 | 20 N. | 40 | 6 | **6¾** | 2:18 | E | **1:09** | C | AQU | 23 |
| 144 | 24 | Tu. | 5:15 | A | **8:08** | E | 14 53 | 19 | 20 N. | 51 | 7 | **7¾** | 2:42 | D | **2:17** | D | AQU | 24 |
| 145 | 25 | W. | 5:14 | A | **8:09** | E | 14 55 | 19 | 21 N. | 02 | 8¼ | **8¾** | 3:04 | D | **3:24** | D | PSC | 25 |
| 146 | 26 | Th. | 5:13 | A | **8:10** | E | 14 57 | 19 | 21 N. | 12 | 9¼ | **9½** | 3:25 | C | **4:29** | E | PSC | 26 |
| 147 | 27 | Fr. | 5:13 | A | **8:11** | E | 14 58 | 18 | 21 N. | 22 | 10 | **10¼** | 3:46 | C | **5:34** | E | PSC | 27 |
| 148 | 28 | Sa. | 5:12 | A | **8:11** | E | 14 59 | 18 | 21 N. | 32 | 10¾ | **11** | 4:09 | B | **6:38** | E | ARI | 28 |
| 149 | 29 | **B** | 5:11 | A | **8:12** | E | 15 01 | 18 | 21 N. | 41 | 11½ | **11¾** | 4:35 | B | **7:43** | E | TAU | 29 |
| 150 | 30 | M. | 5:11 | A | **8:13** | E | 15 02 | 18 | 21 N. | 50 | **12¼** | — | 5:06 | A | **8:46** | E | TAU | 0 |
| 151 | 31 | Tu. | 5:10 | A | **8:14** | E | 15 04 | 18 | 21 N. | 58 | 12¼ | **1** | 5:42 | A | **9:45** | E | TAU | 1 |

 To use this page, see p. 116; for Key Letters, see p. 238. LIGHT = A.M. **BOLD** = P.M. 

# THE FIFTH MONTH • 2022 MAY MAY HATH 31 DAYS

*Now the bright morning star, day's harbinger, / Comes dancing from the East, and leads with her / The flowery May.*
–John Milton

| DAY OF MONTH | DAY OF WEEK | DATES, FEASTS, FASTS, ASPECTS, TIDE HEIGHTS, AND WEATHER | |
|---|---|---|---|
| 1 | B | 3rd S. of Easter • MAY DAY • ☾ AT ☊ • ☌♅☾ • {10.6 / 9.7 | *Dank,* |
| 2 | M. | Sts. Philip & James[T] • ☌☿☾ • 1st FBI director J. Edgar Hoover died, 1972 • {10.5 / 9.5 | *dismal—* |
| 3 | Tu. | Magician Doug Henning born, 1947 • Tides {10.3 / 9.2 | *abysmal!* |
| 4 | W. | Educator Horace Mann born, 1796 • Damaging windstorm in southern Ont. produced 78-mph gusts in Hamilton, 2018 | *But* |
| 5 | Th. | ☾ RIDES HIGH • ☾ AT APO. • ☌♅☉ • *It rains by planets.* • {9.8 / 8.6 | *never* |
| 6 | Fr. | Writer Henry David Thoreau died, 1862 • *Hindenburg* disaster, 1937 • {9.5 / 8.4 | *pine—* |
| 7 | Sa. | Bigfoot reported seen in Hollis, N.H., 1977 • Tides {9.3 / 8.2 | *now* |
| 8 | B | 4th S. of Easter • MOTHER'S DAY • *A mother's love changes never.* • {9.0 / 8.2 | *it's* |
| 9 | M. | St. Gregory of Nazianzus • 1st May snow in Boston in 107 years, Mass., 1977 • Tides {8.9 / 8.4 | *fine!* |
| 10 | Tu. | ☿ STAT. • Victoria Woodhull 1st woman nominated for U.S. president, 1872 • {9.0 / 8.7 | *Summer* |
| 11 | W. | 20-ton meteor fell to ground near Blackstone, Va., 1922 • Three • Tides {9.2 / 9.2 | *to the* |
| 12 | Th. | ☾ ON EQ. • Susie Maroney swam from Cuba to Fla. in 24.5 hours, 1997 • Chilly • {9.4 / 9.8 | *rescue,* |
| 13 | Fr. | Cranberries in bud now. • Saints • Tides {9.8 / 10.5 | *with* |
| 14 | Sa. | Botanist Mikhail Semyonovich Tsvet, inventor of chromatography, born, 1872 • Tides {10.1 / 11.1 | *clover* |
| 15 | B | 5th S. of Easter • ☾ AT ☋ • Writer Emily Dickinson died, 1886 | *and* |
| 16 | M. | Vesak • FULL FLOWER ○ • ECLIPSE ☾ • Tides {10.4 / — | *fescue!* |
| 17 | Tu. | ☾ AT PERIG. • ☌♂♆ • Singer Donna Summer died, 2012 • {11.9 / 10.4 | *Everything's* |
| 18 | W. | ☾ RUNS LOW • Film director Frank Capra born, 1897 • Tides {12.0 / 10.3 | *growing;* |
| 19 | Th. | St. Dunstan • Paraplegic Anna Sarol took steps across grad stage to receive H.S. diploma, Kans., 2019 | *soon* |
| 20 | Fr. | ☌♇☾ • 3.5-week study of dust devils began, Eloy, Ariz., 2002 • Tides {11.5 / 9.8 | *you'll* |
| 21 | Sa. | ☿ IN INF. ☌ • Aviator Charles Lindbergh completed 1st nonstop solo flight across Atlantic, N.Y. to Paris, 1927 | *be* |
| 22 | B | Rogation Sunday • ☌♄☾ • Hubble 'scope detected at least two more Saturn moons, 1995 | *mowing!* |
| 23 | M. | VICTORIA DAY (CANADA) • Historian David Ludlum died, 1997 • {10.1 / 9.6 | *Spring* |
| 24 | Tu. | ☌♂☾ • ☌♃☾ • ☌♆☾ • *Aurora 7* spacecraft launched, 1962 • {9.8 / 9.7 | *has* |
| 25 | W. | St. Bede • ☾ ON EQ. • Original *Star Wars* released in theaters, 1977 | *sprung,* |
| 26 | Th. | Ascension • ☌♀☾ • Announced: Dumbo octopus sighted 22,825 ft. down, setting record, 2020 | |
| 27 | Fr. | German ship *Bismarck* sunk, WWII, 1941 • Tides {9.4 / 10.3 | *winter is* |
| 28 | Sa. | ☾ AT ☊ • ☌♂♃ • ☌♅☾ • Jell-O gelatin introduced, 1897 • {9.4 / 10.3 | *going!* |
| 29 | B | 1st S. af. Asc. • ☌☿☾ • Historian Marcel Trudel born, 1917 • {9.3 / 10.3 | *No* |
| 30 | M. | MEMORIAL DAY • NEW ● • Lincoln Memorial dedicated, D.C., 1922 | *more* |
| 31 | Tu. | Visit. of Mary • *A good word extinguishes more than a pail full of water.* • {10.3 / 9.1 | *snowing!* |

## Farmer's Calendar

One spring, a local museum assembled oxen to move its 1823 schoolhouse a third of a mile up the road. The crowd gawked as 22 teams lined up before their 105-ton load. The oxen ranged in size from Jim and John, a diminutive pair of 1-year-olds no bigger than Saint Bernards, to Pick and Axe, 8-year-olds standing as high as the cab on a dump truck, and each weighing more than a ton. At the coordinator's signal, whips swung and oxen pulled; the school inched forward. "A lot of these oxen have never pulled on pavement before," a farmer commented as he hovered by his sons and their straining team. "Oxen need to dig into the ground to really pull a load; they can't do that here." Then he exposed the truth, that theoretically, each ox can pull half its weight. If this building were to be entirely moved by animal power, the farmer calculated, "we'd need about 100 teams." Fortunately, the schoolhouse was on a carriage with hydrostatic drive, so the oxen's success of progressively tugging the building uphill was a mirage. And yet what a sight—the animals' patient, unwavering dedication, I thought, accelerating my car wistfully into this century.

# JUNE

**SKY WATCH:** The predawn action continues, with Venus now getting low in the east, bright Jupiter above dimmer orange Mars, and Saturn highest up and to the right of the others. From the 16th until month's end, all of the planets form a line like a string of pearls. Moreover, they appear in their true order from the Sun. From lower left to upper right, some 45 minutes before sunrise, look for Mercury, Venus, Mars, Jupiter, and Saturn! The crescent Moon visits each; look for the Moon below Saturn on the 18th, below Jupiter on the 21st, to the right of Mars on the 22nd, above Venus on the 26th, and above Mercury on the 27th. Summer in the Northern Hemisphere begins with the solstice on the 21st at 5:14 A.M. EDT.

◐ **FIRST QUARTER** 7th day 10:48 A.M.    ◑ **LAST QUARTER** 20th day 11:11 P.M.
○ **FULL MOON** 14th day 7:52 A.M.    ● **NEW MOON** 28th day 10:52 P.M.

*All times are given in Eastern Daylight Time.*

GET THESE PAGES WITH TIMES SET TO YOUR ZIP CODE VIA ALMANAC.COM/2022.

| DAY OF YEAR | DAY OF MONTH | DAY OF WEEK | ☼ RISES H. M. | RISE KEY | ☼ SETS H. M. | SET KEY | LENGTH OF DAY H. M. | SUN FAST M. | SUN DECLINATION ° ' | HIGH TIDE TIMES BOSTON | | ☾ RISES H. M. | RISE KEY | ☾ SETS H. M. | SET KEY | ☾ ASTRON. PLACE | ☾ AGE |
|---|---|---|---|---|---|---|---|---|---|---|---|---|---|---|---|---|---|
| 152 | 1 | W. | 5:10 | A | 8:15 | E | 15 05 | 18 | 22 N. 07 | 1 | 1½ | 6:26 | A | 10:38 | E | TAU | 2 |
| 153 | 2 | Th. | 5:09 | A | 8:15 | E | 15 06 | 18 | 22 N. 14 | 1½ | 2¼ | 7:17 | A | 11:24 | E | GEM | 3 |
| 154 | 3 | Fr. | 5:09 | A | 8:16 | E | 15 07 | 17 | 22 N. 22 | 2¼ | 3 | 8:14 | B | — | – | GEM | 4 |
| 155 | 4 | Sa. | 5:09 | A | 8:17 | E | 15 08 | 17 | 22 N. 29 | 3 | 3¾ | 9:15 | B | 12:02 | E | CAN | 5 |
| 156 | 5 | **B** | 5:08 | A | 8:18 | E | 15 10 | 17 | 22 N. 35 | 3¾ | 4½ | 10:19 | B | 12:34 | E | LEO | 6 |
| 157 | 6 | M. | 5:08 | A | 8:18 | E | 15 10 | 17 | 22 N. 42 | 4½ | 5¼ | 11:23 | C | 1:02 | E | LEO | 7 |
| 158 | 7 | Tu. | 5:08 | A | 8:19 | E | 15 11 | 17 | 22 N. 47 | 5½ | 6 | 12:29 | C | 1:26 | D | LEO | 8 |
| 159 | 8 | W. | 5:07 | A | 8:19 | E | 15 12 | 17 | 22 N. 53 | 6¼ | 6¾ | 1:35 | D | 1:48 | D | VIR | 9 |
| 160 | 9 | Th. | 5:07 | A | 8:20 | E | 15 13 | 16 | 22 N. 58 | 7¼ | 7¾ | 2:44 | E | 2:09 | C | VIR | 10 |
| 161 | 10 | Fr. | 5:07 | A | 8:21 | E | 15 14 | 16 | 23 N. 02 | 8 | 8½ | 3:56 | E | 2:32 | C | VIR | 11 |
| 162 | 11 | Sa. | 5:07 | A | 8:21 | E | 15 14 | 16 | 23 N. 06 | 9 | 9¼ | 5:12 | E | 2:57 | B | VIR | 12 |
| 163 | 12 | **B** | 5:07 | A | 8:22 | E | 15 15 | 16 | 23 N. 10 | 10 | 10¼ | 6:32 | E | 3:26 | B | LIB | 13 |
| 164 | 13 | M. | 5:07 | A | 8:22 | E | 15 15 | 16 | 23 N. 14 | 10¾ | 11 | 7:53 | E | 4:03 | B | SCO | 14 |
| 165 | 14 | Tu. | 5:07 | A | 8:23 | E | 15 16 | 15 | 23 N. 17 | 11¾ | — | 9:10 | E | 4:51 | A | OPH | 15 |
| 166 | 15 | W. | 5:07 | A | 8:23 | E | 15 16 | 15 | 23 N. 19 | 12 | 12¾ | 10:16 | E | 5:51 | A | SAG | 16 |
| 167 | 16 | Th. | 5:07 | A | 8:23 | E | 15 16 | 15 | 23 N. 21 | 12¾ | 1½ | 11:08 | E | 7:03 | B | SAG | 17 |
| 168 | 17 | Fr. | 5:07 | A | 8:24 | E | 15 17 | 15 | 23 N. 23 | 1¾ | 2½ | 11:49 | E | 8:22 | B | CAP | 18 |
| 169 | 18 | Sa. | 5:07 | A | 8:24 | E | 15 17 | 14 | 23 N. 24 | 2¾ | 3½ | — | – | 9:40 | C | CAP | 19 |
| 170 | 19 | **B** | 5:07 | A | 8:24 | E | 15 17 | 14 | 23 N. 25 | 3¾ | 4½ | 12:20 | E | 10:56 | C | AQU | 20 |
| 171 | 20 | M. | 5:07 | A | 8:24 | E | 15 17 | 14 | 23 N. 26 | 4¾ | 5½ | 12:46 | D | 12:08 | D | AQU | 21 |
| 172 | 21 | Tu. | 5:07 | A | 8:25 | E | 15 18 | 14 | 23 N. 26 | 5¾ | 6¼ | 1:09 | D | 1:16 | D | PSC | 22 |
| 173 | 22 | W. | 5:08 | A | 8:25 | E | 15 17 | 14 | 23 N. 25 | 6¾ | 7¼ | 1:30 | C | 2:22 | E | CET | 23 |
| 174 | 23 | Th. | 5:08 | A | 8:25 | E | 15 17 | 13 | 23 N. 24 | 7¾ | 8¼ | 1:51 | C | 3:27 | E | PSC | 24 |
| 175 | 24 | Fr. | 5:08 | A | 8:25 | E | 15 17 | 13 | 23 N. 23 | 8¾ | 9 | 2:14 | B | 4:31 | E | ARI | 25 |
| 176 | 25 | Sa. | 5:09 | A | 8:25 | E | 15 16 | 13 | 23 N. 22 | 9¾ | 9¾ | 2:39 | B | 5:35 | E | ARI | 26 |
| 177 | 26 | **B** | 5:09 | A | 8:25 | E | 15 16 | 13 | 23 N. 20 | 10½ | 10½ | 3:08 | B | 6:38 | E | TAU | 27 |
| 178 | 27 | M. | 5:09 | A | 8:25 | E | 15 16 | 13 | 23 N. 18 | 11¼ | 11¼ | 3:42 | A | 7:38 | E | TAU | 28 |
| 179 | 28 | Tu. | 5:10 | A | 8:25 | E | 15 15 | 12 | 23 N. 15 | 12 | — | 4:23 | A | 8:33 | E | TAU | 0 |
| 180 | 29 | W. | 5:10 | A | 8:25 | E | 15 15 | 12 | 23 N. 11 | 12 | 12½ | 5:12 | A | 9:22 | E | GEM | 1 |
| 181 | 30 | Th. | 5:11 | A | 8:25 | E | 15 14 | 12 | 23 N. 08 | 12½ | 1¼ | 6:07 | B | 10:02 | E | GEM | 2 |

# THE SIXTH MONTH · 2022 JUNE JUNE HATH 30 DAYS

*O summer is here with its breezy train*
*I know by the robin's roundelay.*
**–Richard Kendall Munkittrick**

| DAY OF MONTH | DAY OF WEEK | DATES, FEASTS, FASTS, ASPECTS, TIDE HEIGHTS, AND WEATHER | |
|---|---|---|---|
| 1 | W. | ☾ RIDES HIGH • ☾ AT APO. • Ky. became 15th U.S. state, 1792 • {10.2 / 8.9} | *Showers* |
| 2 | Th. | **Orthodox Ascension** • ☿ STAT. • *Surveyor 1* landed on Moon, 1966 • {10.1 / 8.8} | *are* |
| 3 | Fr. | Tenor Roland Hayes born, 1887 • Tides {9.9 / 8.7} | *pattering,* |
| 4 | Sa. | Shavuot begins at sundown • Sierra Club incorporated, 1892 • {9.7 / 8.6} | *not* |
| 5 | **B** | **Whit S.** • **Pentecost** • ♄ STAT. • Tides {9.5 / 8.6} | *so* |
| 6 | M. | D-Day, 1944 • Barbara Washburn 1st woman to summit Denali (Mount McKinley), Alaska, 1947 | *chilly.* |
| 7 | Tu. | Comedian Bill Hader born, 1978 • Extreme Ultraviolet Explorer (EUVE) satellite launched, 1992 | *More* |
| 8 | W. | Ember Day • Posted: Restaurant rec'd rare blue lobster in seafood shipment, Eastham, Mass., 2019 | *showers,* |
| 9 | Th. | ☾ ON EQ. • *When need is greatest, help is nearest.* • Tides {9.2 / 9.7} | *but* |
| 10 | Fr. | Ember Day • Singer Judy Garland born, 1922 • Tides {9.3 / 10.3} | *just* |
| 11 | Sa. | St. Barnabas • Ember Day • ☌♀♅ • Tides {9.5 / 10.9} | *a* |
| 12 | **B** | **Trinity** • Orthodox Pentecost • ☾ AT ☋ • {9.8 / 11.4} | *smattering,* |
| 13 | M. | Queen Victoria took her 1st train ride, 1842 • {10.0 / 11.8} | *silly.* |
| 14 | Tu. | St. Basil • FLAG DAY • FULL STRAWBERRY ○ • ☾ AT PERIG. | *Still* |
| 15 | W. | ☾ RUNS LOW • *June damp and warm / Does the farmer no harm.* • {10.2 / —} | *more showers,* |
| 16 | Th. | ☌♇☾ • ☿ GR. ELONG. (23° WEST) • Henry Berliner made 1st controlled horizontal helicopter flight in U.S., 1922 | |
| 17 | Fr. | Double-hulled, 62-ft. Polynesian voyaging canoe *Hōkūle'a* returned to Hawaii after world trip, 2017 | *but* |
| 18 | Sa. | ☌♄☾ • 143-lb. blue catfish caught, Kerr Lake, Buggs Island, Va., 2011 • {11.6 / 10.1} | *not* |
| 19 | **B** | **Corpus Christi** • Orthodox All Saints' • FATHER'S DAY • JUNETEENTH • {11.1 / 10.0} | *a* |
| 20 | M. | ☌♆☾ • New National Library and Archives building opened, Ottawa, 1967 • {10.6 / 9.9} | *battering.* |
| 21 | Tu. | SUMMER SOLSTICE • ☾ ON EQ. • ☌♃☾ • Tides {10.0 / 9.9} | *Glory* |
| 22 | W. | St. Alban • ☌♂☾ • 12" rain in 42 mins., Holt, Mo., 1947 • Tides {9.5 / 9.9} | *be!* |
| 23 | Th. | From opposite ends, Nik and Lijana Wallenda crossed high wire 25 stories high, N.Y.C., 2019 • {9.2 / 9.9} | *We're* |
| 24 | Fr. | Nativ. John the Baptist • MIDSUMMER DAY • ☌♅☾ • {8.9 / 10.0} | *shower-* |
| 25 | Sa. | ☾ AT ☊ • Oceanographer Jacques-Yves Cousteau died, 1997 • Tides {8.8 / 10.0} | *free!* |
| 26 | **B** | **3rd S. af. P.** • ☌♀☾ • 1st Harry Potter book debuted in UK, 1997 | *Sunny,* |
| 27 | M. | ☌☿☾ • Poet Paul Laurence Dunbar born, 1872 • Tides {8.7 / 10.1} | *cool—* |
| 28 | Tu. | St. Irenaeus • NEW ● • ♆ STAT. • *Love makes labor light.* • {8.7 / 10.1} | *no* |
| 29 | W. | Sts. Peter & Paul • ☾ RIDES HIGH • ☾ AT APO. • Tides {8.8 / —} | *more* |
| 30 | Th. | 1st leap second introduced to Coordinated Universal Time (UTC), 1972 • Tides {10.1 / 8.8} | *school!* |

## Farmer's Calendar

There are many ways to arrive at the magisterial white barn at the University of Vermont's Morgan Horse Farm in Weybridge. If you're a horse, however, you were probably born here, as part of the longest continuous breeding program of Morgans in the nation, one devoted to perpetuating the traits of an extraordinary horse. The breed originated when a Vermont teacher named Justin Morgan accepted a debt repayment in the form of a colt that proved legendary. He grew to clear timber and haul stones; later he raced two horses—one after the other—and won both times. As well, he won a pulling contest. Then, in July 1817, he bore President Monroe through the streets of Montpelier. No wonder the breed became the state's animal, as "it could outdraw, outrun, and out trot any other horse." Mares often deliver their foals in the chilly days of spring. If you find your way to the farm in June, you'll discover those month-old colts in a corral, bumping and nuzzling their mothers, like mischievous shadows. Then, one of the newest progeny, oblivious to both the nearby statue of its famous ancestor and its own storied pedigree, may nibble your bare elbow, sniff opportunistically at your wrist.

# JULY

**SKY WATCH:** Earth reaches its annual solar far point, or aphelion, on the 4th. In the predawn eastern sky, the lineup is still happening, but Mercury is now lower and harder to see and the other planets are now farther apart and less eye-catching. After the 4th, Mercury is too low to see, but Saturn, rising a half hour earlier each week, now comes up by 11 P.M., with Jupiter, in Pisces, following the Ringed Planet to appear low in the east after midnight. Both giant planets are now at their highest at dawn. Mars, too, is gaining in visibility at a very bright magnitude 0.3, as it rises at 2 A.M. in Aries. Planet viewing has now shifted from the exclusively predawn stage of winter and spring to summer's middle-of-the-night venue.

◑ **FIRST QUARTER** 6th day 10:14 P.M.　◐ **LAST QUARTER** 20th day 10:19 A.M.
○ **FULL MOON** 13th day 2:38 P.M.　● **NEW MOON** 28th day 1:55 P.M.

*All times are given in Eastern Daylight Time.*

**GET THESE PAGES WITH TIMES SET TO YOUR ZIP CODE VIA ALMANAC.COM/2022.**

| DAY OF YEAR | DAY OF MONTH | DAY OF WEEK | ☼ RISES H. M. | RISE KEY | ☼ SETS H. M. | SET KEY | LENGTH OF DAY H. M. | SUN FAST M. | SUN DECLINATION ° ' | HIGH TIDE TIMES BOSTON | | ☽ RISES H. M. | RISE KEY | ☽ SETS H. M. | SET KEY | ☽ ASTRON. PLACE | ☽ AGE |
|---|---|---|---|---|---|---|---|---|---|---|---|---|---|---|---|---|---|
| 182 | 1 | Fr. | 5:11 | A | 8:25 | E | 15 14 | 12 | 23 N. 04 | 1¼ | 2 | 7:08 | B | 10:36 | E | CAN | 3 |
| 183 | 2 | Sa. | 5:12 | A | 8:25 | E | 15 13 | 12 | 22 N. 59 | 2 | 2½ | 8:11 | B | 11:05 | E | CAN | 4 |
| 184 | 3 | **B** | 5:12 | A | 8:25 | E | 15 13 | 11 | 22 N. 55 | 2½ | 3¼ | 9:15 | C | 11:30 | E | LEO | 5 |
| 185 | 4 | M. | 5:13 | A | 8:24 | E | 15 11 | 11 | 22 N. 49 | 3¼ | 4 | 10:19 | C | 11:52 | D | LEO | 6 |
| 186 | 5 | Tu. | 5:13 | A | 8:24 | E | 15 11 | 11 | 22 N. 44 | 4 | 4¾ | 11:24 | D | — | - | LEO | 7 |
| 187 | 6 | W. | 5:14 | A | 8:24 | E | 15 10 | 11 | 22 N. 38 | 4¾ | 5½ | 12:30 | D | 12:13 | D | VIR | 8 |
| 188 | 7 | Th. | 5:15 | A | 8:23 | E | 15 08 | 11 | 22 N. 31 | 5¾ | 6¼ | 1:38 | E | 12:34 | C | VIR | 9 |
| 189 | 8 | Fr. | 5:15 | A | 8:23 | E | 15 08 | 11 | 22 N. 24 | 6½ | 7 | 2:50 | E | 12:57 | C | VIR | 10 |
| 190 | 9 | Sa. | 5:16 | A | 8:23 | E | 15 07 | 10 | 22 N. 17 | 7½ | 8 | 4:06 | E | 1:23 | B | LIB | 11 |
| 191 | 10 | **B** | 5:17 | A | 8:22 | E | 15 05 | 10 | 22 N. 10 | 8½ | 8¾ | 5:25 | E | 1:55 | B | LIB | 12 |
| 192 | 11 | M. | 5:18 | A | 8:22 | E | 15 04 | 10 | 22 N. 02 | 9½ | 9¾ | 6:43 | E | 2:36 | B | OPH | 13 |
| 193 | 12 | Tu. | 5:18 | A | 8:21 | E | 15 03 | 10 | 21 N. 53 | 10½ | 10¾ | 7:55 | E | 3:29 | A | SAG | 14 |
| 194 | 13 | W. | 5:19 | A | 8:20 | E | 15 01 | 10 | 21 N. 45 | 11½ | 11¾ | 8:54 | E | 4:36 | B | SAG | 15 |
| 195 | 14 | Th. | 5:20 | A | 8:20 | E | 15 00 | 10 | 21 N. 36 | 12½ | — | 9:41 | E | 5:53 | B | SAG | 16 |
| 196 | 15 | Fr. | 5:21 | A | 8:19 | E | 14 58 | 10 | 21 N. 26 | 12½ | 1¼ | 10:18 | E | 7:14 | B | CAP | 17 |
| 197 | 16 | Sa. | 5:22 | A | 8:19 | E | 14 57 | 10 | 21 N. 16 | 1½ | 2¼ | 10:47 | E | 8:34 | C | AQU | 18 |
| 198 | 17 | **B** | 5:22 | A | 8:18 | E | 14 56 | 10 | 21 N. 06 | 2½ | 3 | 11:12 | D | 9:50 | D | AQU | 19 |
| 199 | 18 | M. | 5:23 | A | 8:17 | E | 14 54 | 9 | 20 N. 56 | 3¼ | 4 | 11:34 | C | 11:02 | D | AQU | 20 |
| 200 | 19 | Tu. | 5:24 | A | 8:16 | E | 14 52 | 9 | 20 N. 45 | 4¼ | 4¾ | 11:55 | C | 12:11 | D | CET | 21 |
| 201 | 20 | W. | 5:25 | A | 8:16 | E | 14 51 | 9 | 20 N. 34 | 5¼ | 5¾ | — | - | 1:17 | E | PSC | 22 |
| 202 | 21 | Th. | 5:26 | A | 8:15 | E | 14 49 | 9 | 20 N. 22 | 6¼ | 6¾ | 12:18 | B | 2:23 | E | ARI | 23 |
| 203 | 22 | Fr. | 5:27 | A | 8:14 | E | 14 47 | 9 | 20 N. 10 | 7¼ | 7½ | 12:42 | B | 3:28 | E | ARI | 24 |
| 204 | 23 | Sa. | 5:28 | A | 8:13 | E | 14 45 | 9 | 19 N. 58 | 8¼ | 8½ | 1:09 | B | 4:31 | E | TAU | 25 |
| 205 | 24 | **B** | 5:29 | A | 8:12 | E | 14 43 | 9 | 19 N. 45 | 9¼ | 9¼ | 1:42 | A | 5:32 | E | TAU | 26 |
| 206 | 25 | M. | 5:30 | A | 8:11 | E | 14 41 | 9 | 19 N. 32 | 10 | 10 | 2:21 | A | 6:29 | E | TAU | 27 |
| 207 | 26 | Tu. | 5:31 | A | 8:10 | E | 14 39 | 9 | 19 N. 19 | 10¾ | 10¾ | 3:08 | A | 7:19 | E | GEM | 28 |
| 208 | 27 | W. | 5:32 | A | 8:09 | E | 14 37 | 9 | 19 N. 05 | 11½ | 11½ | 4:01 | A | 8:02 | E | GEM | 29 |
| 209 | 28 | Th. | 5:33 | B | 8:08 | E | 14 35 | 9 | 18 N. 52 | 12¼ | — | 5:01 | B | 8:38 | E | CAN | 0 |
| 210 | 29 | Fr. | 5:34 | B | 8:07 | E | 14 33 | 9 | 18 N. 37 | 12¼ | 12¾ | 6:03 | B | 9:08 | E | CAN | 1 |
| 211 | 30 | Sa. | 5:35 | B | 8:06 | E | 14 31 | 9 | 18 N. 23 | 12¾ | 1½ | 7:08 | B | 9:34 | E | LEO | 2 |
| 212 | 31 | **B** | 5:36 | B | 8:05 | E | 14 29 | 9 | 18 N. 08 | 1½ | 2 | 8:12 | C | 9:57 | D | LEO | 3 |

To use this page, see p. 116; for Key Letters, see p. 238. LIGHT = A.M. **BOLD** = P.M.

*'Tis Summer's noon: High rides the fervid Sun*
*O'er fresh-mown meads and fields of waving corn.*
–**John Askham**

| DAY OF MONTH | DAY OF WEEK | DATES, FEASTS, FASTS, ASPECTS, TIDE HEIGHTS, AND WEATHER | |
|---|---|---|---|
| 1 | Fr. | CANADA DAY • Dominion of Canada created, 1867 • Tides {10.1 8.8 | *Fireworks* |
| 2 | Sa. | Aviatrix Amelia Earhart and navigator Fred Noonan disappeared during flight, Pacific Ocean, 1937 | *(both* |
| 3 | **B** | 4th S. af. P. • Dog Days begin. • *Fruit, Garden and Home* magazine debuted, 1922 | *natural* |
| 4 | M. | INDEPENDENCE DAY • ⊕ AT APHELION • U.S. president Calvin Coolidge born, 1872 | *and* |
| 5 | Tu. | 110°F, Regina, Sask., 1937 • Burt's Bees cofounder Burt Shavitz died, 2015 • Tides {9.5 9.2 | *patriotic)* |
| 6 | W. | ☾ ON EQ. • Althea Gibson won women's singles title at Wimbledon, 1957 • {9.4 9.4 | *amaze* |
| 7 | Th. | Sci-fi writer Robert Heinlein born, 1907 • Armadillos mate now. • {9.2 9.8 | *our* |
| 8 | Fr. | Military press release stated "flying disc" recovered near Roswell, N.Mex., 1947 • Tides {9.2 10.1 | *gazes;* |
| 9 | Sa. | ☾ AT ☋ • 98°F, Buffalo, N.Y., 2020 • Tides {9.2 10.6 | *it's* |
| 10 | **B** | 5th S. af. P. • Folksinger Arlo Guthrie born, 1947 • Tides {9.3 11.0 | *hot* |
| 11 | M. | *A heart free from care is better than a full purse.* • {9.4 11.4 | *as* |
| 12 | Tu. | ☾ RUNS LOW • Cornscateous air is everywhere. • {9.7 11.8 | *blazes!* |
| 13 | W. | FULL BUCK ○ • ☾ AT PERIG. • ☌♇☾ • Tides {10.0 12.0 | *Here's* |
| 14 | Th. | Bastille Day • Manufacturer Frederick Louis Maytag born, 1857 • Tides {10.2 — | *a* |
| 15 | Fr. | St. Swithin • ☌♄☾ • Official production of 1958 Edsel began, 1957 • {12.1 10.3 | *friendly* |
| 16 | Sa. | ☿ IN SUP. ☌ • Washington, D.C., became capital of U.S., 1790 • {11.9 10.4 | *warning:* |
| 17 | **B** | 6th S. af. P. • ☌♆☾ • Mathematician Jules Henri Poincaré died, 1912 | *No* |
| 18 | M. | ☾ ON EQ. • ☌♃☾ • Astrogeologist Eugene Shoemaker died, 1997 • Tides {11.0 10.3 | *key,* |
| 19 | Tu. | ♇ AT ☍ • Horace Tuttle (after Lewis Swift 3 days earlier) discovered what is now Comet 109P/Swift-Tuttle, 1862 | |
| 20 | W. | 78-lb. 14-oz. flathead catfish caught, Neuse River, N.C., 2020 • Tides {9.8 10.0 | *no kite,* |
| 21 | Th. | ☌♂☾ • *If corn is hard to husk, expect a hard winter.* • Tides {9.2 9.8 | *stay* |
| 22 | Fr. | St. Mary Magdalene • ☾ AT ☊ • ☌♅☾ • Geneticist Gregor Mendel born, 1822 • {8.7 9.6 | *in* |
| 23 | Sa. | Black-eyed Susans in bloom now. • Tides {8.5 9.6 | *at* |
| 24 | **B** | 7th S. af. P. • Lightning stroke measured at 345,000 amperes, Pittsburgh, Pa., 1947 | *night!* |
| 25 | M. | St. James • Moon crater named after scientist Michael Wargo, 2017 • {8.4 9.7 | *(Ben* |
| 26 | Tu. | St. Anne • ☾ RIDES HIGH • ☾ AT APO. • ☌♀☾ • Tides {8.4 9.8 | *Franklin,* |
| 27 | W. | Naturalist Thomas Say born, 1787 • Adult gypsy moths emerge. • {8.6 10.0 | *though* |
| 28 | Th. | NEW ● • 1st U.S. railway post office, Hannibal and St. Joseph Railroad, 1862 • {8.7 — | *plucky,* |
| 29 | Fr. | St. Martha • First of Muharram begins at sundown • ☌☿☾ • ♃ STAT. • {10.1 8.9 | *was* |
| 30 | Sa. | Politician/actor Arnold Schwarzenegger born, 1947 • Tides {10.1 9.0 | *mighty* |
| 31 | **B** | 8th S. af. P. • *Life is half spent before we know what it is.* • Tides {10.1 9.2 | *lucky!)* |

## Farmer's Calendar

You expect tractor pulls, tilt-a-whirls, and prizewinning sows at a county fair. But the "Field Days" in Johnson, Vermont, also host the "Ladies' Underhanded Skillet Toss," wherein females ages 3 to 83 competed in flinging a cast-iron frying pan. This reinforced skillet was manufactured at a local foundry specifically for this opportunity. One year, when the staff couldn't find the special skillet, they destroyed nine regular ones, Jessica, a Field Days board member, informs the crowd, seated safely away from the pitching lane: "Yep, ladies, it's heavier than it looks." As toddlers, then grade schoolers, then preteens, then women all the way up through their golden years each take their turn wielding the skillet and throwing it away, it flies farther and farther across the field, a distance duly noted by Jessica's boyfriend, who uses a measuring wheel. In the last division, "Young at Heart," a first-timer named Vicki steps up. She needs to surpass the current record of 47 feet 9 inches to win. Getting ready, she draws her right hand back like a tennis player readying her serve. Then she sends it hurtling with all her might, tossing that bacon-cooking, egg-scrambling, pancake-flipping pan into the sizzling sky.

CALENDAR

# AUGUST

**SKY WATCH:** With the famous Perseid meteor shower ruined by a full Moon, this month's spotlight remains on the planets, with Saturn's earlier 10 P.M. rising offering viewing opportunities to night owls. The Ringed Planet reaches opposition, its closest and brightest of 2022, on the 14th. Still, as morning twilight begins from the 1st to the 3rd, look for bright Mars, now at magnitude 0, halfway between far-apart Venus, low in the east, and Jupiter, nicely up in the south. On these mornings, binocular users can easily see green Uranus next to orange Mars. On the 14th, the Moon is near Jupiter. On the 19th, look for the Moon closely above Mars, a gorgeous conjunction that is at its highest at dawn. On the 25th, the crescent Moon hovers above Venus, with the Moon to the planet's lower left on the next morning.

◑ **FIRST QUARTER** 5th day 7:07 A.M.   ◐ **LAST QUARTER** 19th day 12:36 A.M.
○ **FULL MOON** 11th day 9:36 P.M.   ● **NEW MOON** 27th day 4:17 A.M.

*All times are given in Eastern Daylight Time.*

GET THESE PAGES WITH TIMES SET TO YOUR ZIP CODE VIA ALMANAC.COM/2022.

| DAY OF YEAR | DAY OF MONTH | DAY OF WEEK | ☀ RISES H. M. | RISE KEY | ☀ SETS H. M. | SET KEY | LENGTH OF DAY H. M. | SUN FAST M. | SUN DECLINATION ° ' | HIGH TIDE TIMES BOSTON | | ☾ RISES H. M. | RISE KEY | ☾ SETS H. M. | SET KEY | ASTRON. PLACE | ☾ AGE |
|---|---|---|---|---|---|---|---|---|---|---|---|---|---|---|---|---|---|
| 213 | 1 | M. | 5:37 | B | 8:04 | E | 14 27 | 9 | 17 N. 53 | 2¼ | 2¾ | 9:17 | D | 10:18 | D | LEO | 4 |
| 214 | 2 | Tu. | 5:38 | B | 8:03 | E | 14 25 | 10 | 17 N. 38 | 2¾ | 3¼ | 10:22 | D | 10:38 | C | VIR | 5 |
| 215 | 3 | W. | 5:39 | B | 8:01 | E | 14 22 | 10 | 17 N. 22 | 3½ | 4 | 11:28 | E | 11:00 | C | VIR | 6 |
| 216 | 4 | Th. | 5:40 | B | 8:00 | E | 14 20 | 10 | 17 N. 06 | 4¼ | 4¾ | 12:37 | E | 11:24 | B | VIR | 7 |
| 217 | 5 | Fr. | 5:41 | B | 7:59 | E | 14 18 | 10 | 16 N. 50 | 5¼ | 5½ | 1:49 | E | 11:53 | B | LIB | 8 |
| 218 | 6 | Sa. | 5:42 | B | 7:58 | E | 14 16 | 10 | 16 N. 33 | 6¼ | 6½ | 3:05 | E | — | - | LIB | 9 |
| 219 | 7 | **B** | 5:43 | B | 7:56 | E | 14 13 | 10 | 16 N. 16 | 7¼ | 7½ | 4:21 | E | 12:29 | B | SCO | 10 |
| 220 | 8 | M. | 5:44 | B | 7:55 | E | 14 11 | 10 | 15 N. 59 | 8¼ | 8½ | 5:34 | E | 1:14 | A | OPH | 11 |
| 221 | 9 | Tu. | 5:45 | B | 7:54 | E | 14 09 | 10 | 15 N. 42 | 9¼ | 9½ | 6:38 | E | 2:13 | A | SAG | 12 |
| 222 | 10 | W. | 5:46 | B | 7:52 | E | 14 06 | 10 | 15 N. 25 | 10¼ | 10½ | 7:30 | E | 3:25 | B | SAG | 13 |
| 223 | 11 | Th. | 5:47 | B | 7:51 | D | 14 04 | 11 | 15 N. 07 | 11¼ | 11½ | 8:11 | E | 4:44 | B | CAP | 14 |
| 224 | 12 | Fr. | 5:48 | B | 7:50 | D | 14 02 | 11 | 14 N. 49 | 12 | — | 8:44 | E | 6:06 | C | CAP | 15 |
| 225 | 13 | Sa. | 5:49 | B | 7:48 | D | 13 59 | 11 | 14 N. 31 | 12¼ | 1 | 9:11 | D | 7:25 | C | AQU | 16 |
| 226 | 14 | **B** | 5:50 | B | 7:47 | D | 13 57 | 11 | 14 N. 12 | 1¼ | 1¾ | 9:35 | D | 8:41 | D | AQU | 17 |
| 227 | 15 | M. | 5:51 | B | 7:45 | D | 13 54 | 11 | 13 N. 53 | 2 | 2½ | 9:57 | C | 9:53 | D | PSC | 18 |
| 228 | 16 | Tu. | 5:52 | B | 7:44 | D | 13 52 | 12 | 13 N. 34 | 3 | 3½ | 10:19 | C | 11:02 | E | PSC | 19 |
| 229 | 17 | W. | 5:53 | B | 7:42 | D | 13 49 | 12 | 13 N. 15 | 3¾ | 4¼ | 10:43 | B | 12:10 | E | ARI | 20 |
| 230 | 18 | Th. | 5:55 | B | 7:41 | D | 13 46 | 12 | 12 N. 56 | 4¾ | 5 | 11:10 | B | 1:17 | E | ARI | 21 |
| 231 | 19 | Fr. | 5:56 | B | 7:39 | D | 13 43 | 12 | 12 N. 36 | 5¾ | 6 | 11:41 | B | 2:22 | E | TAU | 22 |
| 232 | 20 | Sa. | 5:57 | B | 7:38 | D | 13 41 | 12 | 12 N. 17 | 6½ | 7 | — | | 3:25 | E | TAU | 23 |
| 233 | 21 | **B** | 5:58 | B | 7:36 | D | 13 38 | 13 | 11 N. 57 | 7½ | 7¾ | 12:18 | A | 4:23 | E | TAU | 24 |
| 234 | 22 | M. | 5:59 | B | 7:35 | D | 13 36 | 13 | 11 N. 36 | 8½ | 8¾ | 1:02 | A | 5:16 | E | GEM | 25 |
| 235 | 23 | Tu. | 6:00 | B | 7:33 | D | 13 33 | 13 | 11 N. 16 | 9½ | 9½ | 1:54 | A | 6:01 | E | GEM | 26 |
| 236 | 24 | W. | 6:01 | B | 7:31 | D | 13 30 | 14 | 10 N. 56 | 10¼ | 10½ | 2:51 | B | 6:40 | E | GEM | 27 |
| 237 | 25 | Th. | 6:02 | B | 7:30 | D | 13 28 | 14 | 10 N. 35 | 11 | 11 | 3:54 | B | 7:11 | E | CAN | 28 |
| 238 | 26 | Fr. | 6:03 | B | 7:28 | D | 13 25 | 14 | 10 N. 14 | 11¾ | 11¾ | 4:58 | B | 7:38 | E | LEO | 29 |
| 239 | 27 | Sa. | 6:04 | B | 7:27 | D | 13 23 | 14 | 9 N. 53 | 12¼ | — | 6:04 | C | 8:02 | D | LEO | 0 |
| 240 | 28 | **B** | 6:05 | B | 7:25 | D | 13 20 | 15 | 9 N. 32 | 12½ | 1 | 7:09 | C | 8:23 | D | LEO | 1 |
| 241 | 29 | M. | 6:06 | B | 7:23 | D | 13 17 | 15 | 9 N. 11 | 1 | 1½ | 8:15 | D | 8:44 | C | VIR | 2 |
| 242 | 30 | Tu. | 6:07 | B | 7:22 | D | 13 15 | 15 | 8 N. 49 | 1¾ | 2 | 9:21 | E | 9:05 | C | VIR | 3 |
| 243 | 31 | W. | 6:08 | B | 7:20 | D | 13 12 | 16 | 8 N. 27 | 2½ | 2¾ | 10:29 | E | 9:28 | B | VIR | 4 |

**To use this page, see p. 116; for Key Letters, see p. 238.** LIGHT = A.M. **BOLD = P.M.**   **2022**

# AUGUST

*How stealthily the twilight steals around,*
*Infolding all in the sweet zone of peace!*
–J. Dawson

| DAY OF MONTH | DAY OF WEEK | DATES, FEASTS, FASTS, ASPECTS, TIDE HEIGHTS, AND WEATHER | |
|---|---|---|---|
| 1 | M. | Lammas Day • CIVIC HOLIDAY (CANADA) • ☌♂♅ • Tides {10.0 9.4 | *Keep* |
| 2 | Tu. | ☾ ON EQ. • Inventor Alexander Graham Bell died, 1922 • {9.9 9.5 | *an* |
| 3 | W. | Canadian governor-general John Campbell Hamilton-Gordon born, 1847 • {9.7 9.7 | *eye* |
| 4 | Th. | Major geomagnetic storm, 1972 • *Keep some till furthermore come.* • Tides {9.5 9.9 | *on* |
| 5 | Fr. | ☾ AT ☋ • NASA's *Juno* spacecraft, to study Jupiter, launched, 2011 • Tides {9.2 10.1 | *the* |
| 6 | Sa. | Transfiguration • Radio astronomer Sir Bernard Lovell died, 2012 • Tides {9.0 10.3 | *sky* |
| 7 | **B** | 9th S. af. P. • Badge of Military Merit (succeeded by Purple Heart) established, 1782 | *if* |
| 8 | M. | St. Dominic • International Cat Day • Paleontologist Henry Fairfield Osborn born, 1857 | *you're* |
| 9 | Tu. | ☾ RUNS LOW • For charity, "East Coasters for Kids" group rode 74 roller coasters in 24 hours, setting world record, 2001 | |
| 10 | W. | St. Lawrence • ☾ AT PERIG. • ☌♇☾ • Tides {9.6 11.6 | *swimming* |
| 11 | Th. | St. Clare • Dog Days end. • FULL STURGEON ○ • ☌♄☾ | *or golfing.* |
| 12 | Fr. | Botanist Thomas Andrew Knight born, 1759 • Gray squirrels have second litters now. | *Wetter—* |
| 13 | Sa. | *If larks fly high and sing long, expect fine weather.* • {11.8 10.6 | *you* |
| 14 | **B** | 10th S. af. P. • ☌♆☾ • ♄ AT ☍ • Tides {11.7 10.7 | *might* |
| 15 | M. | Assumption • ☾ ON EQ. • ☌♃☾ • Tides {11.3 10.7 | *need a* |
| 16 | Tu. | Battle of Bennington, Vt., 1777 • U.S./Canadian Migratory Bird Treaty signed, 1916 | *sweater.* |
| 17 | W. | Cat Nights commence. • Asaph Hall discovered Mars's moon Phobos, 1877 • Tides {10.1 10.2 | *Dark* |
| 18 | Th. | ☾ AT ☊ • ☌♅☾ • Ragweed in bloom. • Tides {9.4 9.8 | *glasses* |
| 19 | Fr. | ☌♂☾ • Poet Ogden Nash born, 1902 • Tides {8.8 9.5 | *are* |
| 20 | Sa. | Damaging widespread early frost, Man. and Sask., 2004 • Tides {8.4 9.3 | *wise to* |
| 21 | **B** | 11th S. af. P. • Total solar eclipse across N.Am. biggest online event yet measured by NASA, 2017 | |
| 22 | M. | ☾ RIDES HIGH • ☾ AT APO. • Composer Claude Debussy born, 1862 • {8.1 9.3 | *protect* |
| 23 | Tu. | Fannie Farmer opened cooking school, Boston, Mass., 1902 • Tides {8.2 9.5 | *the* |
| 24 | W. | St. Bartholomew • ♅ STAT. • Quebec premier René Lévesque born, 1922 • {8.4 9.7 | *eyes;* |
| 25 | Th. | ☌♀☾ • Astronaut Neil Armstrong died, 2012 • {8.7 9.9 | *you'll* |
| 26 | Fr. | National Dog Day • Hummingbirds migrate south. • {9.0 10.1 | *feel* |
| 27 | Sa. | NEW ● • ☿ GR. ELONG. (27° EAST) • Railroad crossing gate patented, 1867 • {9.3 — | *bereft* |
| 28 | **B** | 12th S. af. P. • *Take heed will surely speed.* • Tides {10.2 9.5 | *if* |
| 29 | M. | St. John the Baptist • ☾ ON EQ. • ☌☿☾ • Tides {10.3 9.8 | *not* |
| 30 | Tu. | Rosemary Brown 1st black woman elected to Canadian provincial legislature, B.C., 1972 • {10.2 10.0 | *properly* |
| 31 | W. | Congress authorized what became U.S. Naval Observatory, 1842 • Princess Diana died, 1997 | *SPF'd.* |

## Farmer's Calendar

As Vermont's loon population rebounds from 29 birds in 1983 to an estimated 365 in 2020, Eric Hanson's waking hours, especially between April to November, are preoccupied with the birds' yodeling, mating, nesting, chick-rearing, and migrating. As the state's Loon Biologist, Eric also serves as a public relations director for them, joking that more of his time is spent on people than on the speckled birds with a spooky song. He fields questions, concerns, and sometimes their unfortunate discoveries, such as when a farmer delivers a dead loon he scooped off his manure pit. Nevertheless, sometimes the two species in Eric's work converge beautifully. Twinges of sadness for this recent casualty are replaced with hope when, through Eric's binoculars, he spots the unmistakable profile of a nesting loon jutting from the lake island's edge. Although one has been lost, perhaps one, possibly two, will hatch—that's encouraging math. We paddle his canoe on another lake where Eric spots three mature birds. Two dive below while one remains floating, in a sort of, *"Hey? Guys?"*—then it too dips under. We wait, silent, our paddles hanging, dripping above the water, scanning to discover where they'll bob up next.

**SKY WATCH:** The planets' long, predawn repertory performance is coming to a close, with Venus getting very low and finishing its run as a morning star. The scene shifts to the evening sky, with Jupiter and Saturn both up in the east after 9 P.M. Saturn hovers to the left of the Moon on the 7th and to its right on the 8th. Jupiter stands to the left of the Moon on the 10th and just above it on the 11th. On the 16th, Mars, now rising at 11:30 P.M., floats to the left of the Moon. Jupiter reaches its opposition on the 26th, when it makes its closest, biggest, and brightest appearance of the year. Autumn begins with the autumnal equinox at 9:04 P.M. EDT on the night of the 22nd.

◗ **FIRST QUARTER** 3rd day 2:08 P.M.   ◑ **LAST QUARTER** 17th day 5:52 P.M.
○ **FULL MOON** 10th day 5:59 A.M.   ● **NEW MOON** 25th day 5:55 P.M.

*All times are given in Eastern Daylight Time.*

GET THESE PAGES WITH TIMES SET TO YOUR ZIP CODE VIA ALMANAC.COM/2022.

| DAY OF YEAR | DAY OF MONTH | DAY OF WEEK | ☀ RISES H.M. | RISE KEY | ☀ SETS H.M. | SET KEY | LENGTH OF DAY H.M. | SUN FAST M. | SUN DECLINATION ° ' | HIGH TIDE TIMES BOSTON | | ☾ RISES H.M. | RISE KEY | ☾ SETS H.M. | SET KEY | ☾ ASTRON. PLACE | ☾ AGE |
|---|---|---|---|---|---|---|---|---|---|---|---|---|---|---|---|---|---|
| 244 | 1 | Th. | 6:09 | B | 7:18 | D | 13 09 | 16 | 8 N. 06 | 3¼ | 3½ | 11:40 | E | 9:55 | B | VIR | 5 |
| 245 | 2 | Fr. | 6:10 | B | 7:16 | D | 13 06 | 16 | 7 N. 44 | 4 | 4¼ | 12:54 | E | 10:27 | B | LIB | 6 |
| 246 | 3 | Sa. | 6:11 | B | 7:15 | D | 13 04 | 17 | 7 N. 22 | 4¾ | 5¼ | 2:08 | E | 11:08 | A | SCO | 7 |
| 247 | 4 | **B** | 6:13 | B | 7:13 | D | 13 00 | 17 | 7 N. 00 | 5¾ | 6 | 3:21 | E | — | A | OPH | 8 |
| 248 | 5 | M. | 6:14 | B | 7:11 | D | 12 57 | 17 | 6 N. 37 | 6¾ | 7¼ | 4:27 | E | 12:00 | – | SAG | 9 |
| 249 | 6 | Tu. | 6:15 | C | 7:10 | D | 12 55 | 18 | 6 N. 15 | 8 | 8¼ | 5:22 | E | 1:05 | A | SAG | 10 |
| 250 | 7 | W. | 6:16 | C | 7:08 | D | 12 52 | 18 | 5 N. 53 | 9 | 9¼ | 6:06 | E | 2:19 | B | CAP | 11 |
| 251 | 8 | Th. | 6:17 | C | 7:06 | D | 12 49 | 18 | 5 N. 30 | 10 | 10¼ | 6:41 | E | 3:39 | B | CAP | 12 |
| 252 | 9 | Fr. | 6:18 | C | 7:04 | D | 12 46 | 19 | 5 N. 07 | 11 | 11¼ | 7:10 | E | 4:58 | C | AQU | 13 |
| 253 | 10 | Sa. | 6:19 | C | 7:03 | C | 12 44 | 19 | 4 N. 45 | 11¾ | — | 7:35 | D | 6:16 | D | AQU | 14 |
| 254 | 11 | **B** | 6:20 | C | 7:01 | C | 12 41 | 19 | 4 N. 22 | 12 | 12½ | 7:58 | C | 7:30 | D | PSC | 15 |
| 255 | 12 | M. | 6:21 | C | 6:59 | C | 12 38 | 20 | 3 N. 59 | 1 | 1¼ | 8:20 | C | 8:41 | E | CET | 16 |
| 256 | 13 | Tu. | 6:22 | C | 6:57 | C | 12 35 | 20 | 3 N. 36 | 1¾ | 2 | 8:43 | B | 9:51 | E | PSC | 17 |
| 257 | 14 | W. | 6:23 | C | 6:56 | C | 12 33 | 20 | 3 N. 13 | 2½ | 2¾ | 9:09 | B | 11:00 | E | ARI | 18 |
| 258 | 15 | Th. | 6:24 | C | 6:54 | C | 12 30 | 21 | 2 N. 50 | 3¼ | 3½ | 9:38 | B | 12:08 | E | ARI | 19 |
| 259 | 16 | Fr. | 6:25 | C | 6:52 | C | 12 27 | 21 | 2 N. 27 | 4¼ | 4½ | 10:13 | A | 1:13 | E | TAU | 20 |
| 260 | 17 | Sa. | 6:26 | C | 6:50 | C | 12 24 | 21 | 2 N. 04 | 5 | 5¼ | 10:55 | A | 2:15 | E | TAU | 21 |
| 261 | 18 | **B** | 6:27 | C | 6:49 | C | 12 22 | 22 | 1 N. 41 | 6 | 6¼ | 11:44 | A | 3:10 | E | TAU | 22 |
| 262 | 19 | M. | 6:28 | C | 6:47 | C | 12 19 | 22 | 1 N. 17 | 7 | 7¼ | — | – | 3:58 | E | GEM | 23 |
| 263 | 20 | Tu. | 6:29 | C | 6:45 | C | 12 16 | 22 | 0 N. 54 | 8 | 8¼ | 12:40 | B | 4:39 | E | GEM | 24 |
| 264 | 21 | W. | 6:30 | C | 6:43 | C | 12 13 | 23 | 0 N. 31 | 9 | 9 | 1:41 | B | 5:13 | E | CAN | 25 |
| 265 | 22 | Th. | 6:32 | C | 6:41 | C | 12 09 | 23 | 0 N. 07 | 9¾ | 9¾ | 2:45 | B | 5:41 | E | LEO | 26 |
| 266 | 23 | Fr. | 6:33 | C | 6:40 | C | 12 07 | 24 | 0 S. 15 | 10½ | 10½ | 3:51 | C | 6:06 | E | LEO | 27 |
| 267 | 24 | Sa. | 6:34 | C | 6:38 | C | 12 04 | 24 | 0 S. 38 | 11 | 11¼ | 4:56 | C | 6:28 | D | LEO | 28 |
| 268 | 25 | **B** | 6:35 | C | 6:36 | C | 12 01 | 24 | 1 S. 02 | 11¾ | — | 6:03 | D | 6:49 | C | VIR | 0 |
| 269 | 26 | M. | 6:36 | C | 6:34 | C | 11 58 | 25 | 1 S. 25 | 12 | 12¼ | 7:10 | D | 7:10 | C | VIR | 1 |
| 270 | 27 | Tu. | 6:37 | C | 6:33 | C | 11 56 | 25 | 1 S. 48 | 12½ | 1 | 8:19 | E | 7:32 | C | VIR | 2 |
| 271 | 28 | W. | 6:38 | C | 6:31 | C | 11 53 | 25 | 2 S. 12 | 1¼ | 1½ | 9:30 | E | 7:58 | B | VIR | 3 |
| 272 | 29 | Th. | 6:39 | C | 6:29 | C | 11 50 | 26 | 2 S. 35 | 2 | 2¼ | 10:44 | E | 8:28 | B | LIB | 4 |
| 273 | 30 | Fr. | 6:40 | C | 6:27 | C | 11 47 | 26 | 2 S. 58 | 2¾ | 3 | 12:00 | E | 9:06 | A | SCO | 5 |

**CALENDAR**

# SEPTEMBER

*My teacher says, little by little / To the mountaintops we climb,*
*It isn't all done in a minute, / But only a step at a time.*
–Carlotta Perry

| DAY OF MONTH | DAY OF WEEK | DATES, FEASTS, FASTS, ASPECTS, TIDE HEIGHTS, AND WEATHER | |
|---|---|---|---|
| 1 | Th. | ☾ AT ☋ • *September rain is much liked by the farmer.* • Tides {9.8 / 10.3 | *Sunny,* |
| 2 | Fr. | Chess rematch between Bobby Fischer and Boris Spassky began, 1992 • Tides {9.5 / 10.3 | *cool, for* |
| 3 | Sa. | Poet e. e. cummings died, 1962 • Tides {9.2 / 10.3 | *back to school.* |
| 4 | **B** | **13th S. af. P.** • U.S. swimmer Mark Spitz 1st person to win 7 gold medals in single Olympics, 1972 | |
| 5 | M. | **LABOR DAY** • ☾ RUNS LOW • Saint Teresa of Calcutta died, 1997 • Tides {8.8 / 10.4 | *Apple* |
| 6 | Tu. | ☌♇☾ • Canadian highway signs converted to metric in many areas, 1977 • {8.9 / 10.7 | *pickers* |
| 7 | W. | ☾ AT PERIG. • 109°F, Weldon, N.C., 1954 • Tides {9.2 / 10.9 | *gather* |
| 8 | Th. | ☌♄☾ • Cranberry bog harvest begins, Cape Cod, Mass. • Tides {9.7 / 11.2 | *red* |
| 9 | Fr. | ☿ STAT. • Montreal founder Paul de Chomedey de Maisonneuve died, 1676 • {10.2 / 11.4 | *fruit* |
| 10 | Sa. | **FULL HARVEST** ○ • ☌♆☾ • New pterosaur species *Cryodrakon boreas,* from Alta., announced, 2019 | *in* |
| 11 | **B** | **14th S. af. P.** • **PATRIOT DAY** • ☾ ON EQ. • ☌♃☾ | *yellow* |
| 12 | M. | JFK: "*We choose to go to the Moon . . . not because* [it is] *easy, but because* [it is] *hard,*" 1962 • {11.2 / 10.9 | *slickers,* |
| 13 | Tu. | Astrophysicist Dilhan Eryurt died, 2012 • Tides {10.8 / 10.8 | *pausing* |
| 14 | W. | Holy Cross • ☾ AT ☊ • ☌⛢☾ • First date of Gregorian calendar used by British Empire, 1752 | *to* |
| 15 | Th. | *Nothing is easy to the unwilling.* • Tides {9.7 / 10.1 | *admire* |
| 16 | Fr. | ☌♂☾ • ♆ AT ☍ • Botanist Robert Fortune born, 1813 • Tides {9.1 / 9.7 | *the* |
| 17 | Sa. | Battle of Antietam, U.S. Civil War, near Sharpsburg, Md., 1862 • Tides {8.5 / 9.3 | *foliage* |
| 18 | **B** | **15th S. af. P.** • ☾ RIDES HIGH • Central Intelligence Agency (CIA) founded, 1947 | *fire.* |
| 19 | M. | ☾ AT APO. • Deadly hurricane made landfall near Chandeleur Islands, La., 1947 • Tides {8.0 / 8.9 | *Only* |
| 20 | Tu. | Expectant dog stranded on bridge ledge rescued (and later adopted), Natchez, Miss., 2020 • {8.0 / 9.0 | *thunder* |
| 21 | W. | St. Matthew • Ember Day • N.Y. *Sun*'s Frank Church replied, "Yes, Virginia, there is a Santa Claus," 1897 | |
| 22 | Th. | Harvest Home • **AUTUMNAL EQUINOX** • Zoologist Victor Ernest Shelford born, 1877 | *stops them* |
| 23 | Fr. | Ember Day • ☿ IN INF. ☌ • Judy Reed rec'd patent for dough kneader and roller, 1884 | *reaping* |
| 24 | Sa. | Ember Day • *Least said is soonest mended.* • Tides {9.4 / 10.1 | *crops,* |
| 25 | **B** | Rosh Hashanah begins at sundown • **NEW** ● • ☌☿☾ • ☌♀☾ • ☌☿♀ | *while* |
| 26 | M. | ☾ ON EQ. • ♃ AT ☍ • 1st Shrine Temple organized, N.Y.C., 1872 • Tides {10.2 / — | *random* |
| 27 | Tu. | St. Vincent de Paul • U.S. statesman Samuel Adams born, 1722 • {10.3 / 10.5 | *raindrops* |
| 28 | W. | ☾ AT ☋ • Woodchucks hibernate now. • Tides {10.3 / 10.7 | *speckle* |
| 29 | Th. | St. Michael • Writer Miguel de Cervantes likely born, 1547 • Tides {10.1 / 10.8 | *the* |
| 30 | Fr. | St. Gregory the Illuminator • Meteor fireball seen in morning sky, eastern half of U.S., 2020 | *treetops.* |

## Farmer's Calendar

"Excuse me, do you have a white horse?" the man at my door asked one foggy morning. I followed him out, and there, standing in the mists, was a phantom stallion with lustrous eyes and alert ears. Oh, that's Petey, I explained. He belonged to my way-down-the-road neighbor. I'd never seen him roam beyond his ample pasture girded by electrified tape. Yet here he was, looming in a lane trafficked mostly by pickup trucks and tractors, and spooking this driver. Those who tend livestock know: Creatures sometimes go where you least want them. A fencing expert once taught me: An electrical fence is just a psychological boundary. "You've got a 500-pound animal, obeying a 1/16-inch strand of aluminum wire that carries a volt every other second—it's only a discouragement." But, he assured, if the shock carried a strong charge, the fence would be effective. Until it wasn't. Many animal husbands know the phone call, sometimes shrill or gruff, but always urgent: *"Hey! Your animal is out!"* One evening I arrived late for chores at another farm because I'd been rounding up my wayward sheep. I apologized to my boss, but he grinned sympathetically and told me, *"You're farming now."*

# OCTOBER

**SKY WATCH:** The action now mostly remains in the evening sky at nightfall, where the Moon is below Saturn on the 5th, closely below Jupiter on the 8th, and close to Mars on the 14th. All three planets are now worthy targets for backyard telescopes. The Red Planet (Mars), which actually appears orange, reaches a brilliant magnitude –0.86 and rises at 10 P.M. in Taurus. Venus has its superior conjunction on the 22nd. Mercury, which reaches a very bright magnitude –1.0, rises for its best 2022 appearance as a morning star, especially after the 12th. A partial solar eclipse, not visible from the U.S. or Canada, appears over parts of Greenland, Iceland, Europe, northeastern Africa, the Middle East, western Asia, India, and western China on the 25th.

◖ **FIRST QUARTER** 2nd day 8:14 P.M.　◗ **LAST QUARTER** 17th day 1:15 P.M.
○ **FULL MOON** 9th day 4:55 P.M.　● **NEW MOON** 25th day 6:49 A.M.

*All times are given in Eastern Daylight Time.*

GET THESE PAGES WITH TIMES SET TO YOUR ZIP CODE VIA ALMANAC.COM/2022.

| DAY OF YEAR | DAY OF MONTH | DAY OF WEEK | ☼ RISES H. M. | RISE KEY | ☼ SETS H. M. | SET KEY | LENGTH OF DAY H. M. | SUN FAST M. | SUN DECLINATION ° ' | HIGH TIDE TIMES BOSTON | | ☾ RISES H. M. | RISE KEY | ☾ SETS H. M. | SET KEY | ☾ ASTRON. PLACE | ☾ AGE |
|---|---|---|---|---|---|---|---|---|---|---|---|---|---|---|---|---|---|
| 274 | 1 | Sa. | 6:41 | C | 6:26 | C | 11 45 | 26 | 3 s. 22 | 3¾ | 3¾ | 1:13 | E | 9:55 | A | OPH | 6 |
| 275 | 2 | **B** | 6:42 | C | 6:24 | C | 11 42 | 27 | 3 s. 45 | 4½ | 4¾ | 2:21 | E | 10:55 | A | SAG | 7 |
| 276 | 3 | M. | 6:43 | C | 6:22 | C | 11 39 | 27 | 4 s. 08 | 5½ | 5¾ | 3:18 | E | — | - | SAG | 8 |
| 277 | 4 | Tu. | 6:45 | C | 6:20 | C | 11 35 | 27 | 4 s. 31 | 6¾ | 7 | 4:04 | E | 12:05 | B | SAG | 9 |
| 278 | 5 | W. | 6:46 | C | 6:19 | C | 11 33 | 27 | 4 s. 54 | 7¾ | 8 | 4:41 | E | 1:21 | B | CAP | 10 |
| 279 | 6 | Th. | 6:47 | D | 6:17 | C | 11 30 | 28 | 5 s. 17 | 8¾ | 9¼ | 5:11 | E | 2:38 | C | AQU | 11 |
| 280 | 7 | Fr. | 6:48 | D | 6:15 | C | 11 27 | 28 | 5 s. 40 | 9¾ | 10 | 5:36 | D | 3:55 | D | AQU | 12 |
| 281 | 8 | Sa. | 6:49 | D | 6:14 | C | 11 25 | 28 | 6 s. 03 | 10¾ | 11 | 5:59 | D | 5:09 | D | AQU | 13 |
| 282 | 9 | **B** | 6:50 | D | 6:12 | C | 11 22 | 29 | 6 s. 26 | 11½ | 11¾ | 6:21 | C | 6:20 | D | CET | 14 |
| 283 | 10 | M. | 6:51 | D | 6:10 | C | 11 19 | 29 | 6 s. 49 | 12¼ | — | 6:44 | C | 7:31 | E | PSC | 15 |
| 284 | 11 | Tu. | 6:52 | D | 6:09 | C | 11 17 | 29 | 7 s. 11 | 12½ | 12¾ | 7:08 | B | 8:41 | E | ARI | 16 |
| 285 | 12 | W. | 6:54 | D | 6:07 | C | 11 13 | 29 | 7 s. 34 | 1¼ | 1½ | 7:36 | B | 9:50 | E | ARI | 17 |
| 286 | 13 | Th. | 6:55 | D | 6:05 | C | 11 10 | 30 | 7 s. 56 | 2 | 2¼ | 8:09 | A | 10:57 | E | TAU | 18 |
| 287 | 14 | Fr. | 6:56 | D | 6:04 | B | 11 08 | 30 | 8 s. 19 | 2¾ | 3 | 8:48 | A | 12:02 | E | TAU | 19 |
| 288 | 15 | Sa. | 6:57 | D | 6:02 | B | 11 05 | 30 | 8 s. 41 | 3¾ | 3¾ | 9:34 | A | 1:01 | E | TAU | 20 |
| 289 | 16 | **B** | 6:58 | D | 6:01 | B | 11 03 | 30 | 9 s. 03 | 4½ | 4½ | 10:28 | A | 1:53 | E | GEM | 21 |
| 290 | 17 | M. | 6:59 | D | 5:59 | B | 11 00 | 30 | 9 s. 25 | 5½ | 5½ | 11:27 | B | 2:36 | E | GEM | 22 |
| 291 | 18 | Tu. | 7:01 | D | 5:57 | B | 10 56 | 31 | 9 s. 47 | 6¼ | 6½ | — | - | 3:12 | E | CAN | 23 |
| 292 | 19 | W. | 7:02 | D | 5:56 | B | 10 54 | 31 | 10 s. 08 | 7¼ | 7½ | 12:30 | B | 3:42 | E | CAN | 24 |
| 293 | 20 | Th. | 7:03 | D | 5:54 | B | 10 51 | 31 | 10 s. 30 | 8¼ | 8¼ | 1:34 | C | 4:08 | E | LEO | 25 |
| 294 | 21 | Fr. | 7:04 | D | 5:53 | B | 10 49 | 31 | 10 s. 51 | 9 | 9¼ | 2:40 | C | 4:31 | D | LEO | 26 |
| 295 | 22 | Sa. | 7:05 | D | 5:51 | B | 10 46 | 31 | 11 s. 12 | 9¾ | 10 | 3:46 | C | 4:52 | D | LEO | 27 |
| 296 | 23 | **B** | 7:06 | D | 5:50 | B | 10 44 | 32 | 11 s. 33 | 10¼ | 10¾ | 4:53 | D | 5:13 | C | VIR | 28 |
| 297 | 24 | M. | 7:08 | D | 5:48 | B | 10 40 | 32 | 11 s. 54 | 11 | 11½ | 6:02 | E | 5:35 | C | VIR | 29 |
| 298 | 25 | Tu. | 7:09 | D | 5:47 | B | 10 38 | 32 | 12 s. 15 | 11¾ | — | 7:13 | E | 5:59 | B | VIR | 0 |
| 299 | 26 | W. | 7:10 | D | 5:46 | B | 10 36 | 32 | 12 s. 35 | 12¼ | 12¼ | 8:28 | E | 6:28 | B | LIB | 1 |
| 300 | 27 | Th. | 7:11 | D | 5:44 | B | 10 33 | 32 | 12 s. 56 | 1 | 1 | 9:45 | E | 7:04 | B | LIB | 2 |
| 301 | 28 | Fr. | 7:13 | D | 5:43 | B | 10 30 | 32 | 13 s. 16 | 1¾ | 1¾ | 11:02 | E | 7:50 | A | OPH | 3 |
| 302 | 29 | Sa. | 7:14 | D | 5:41 | B | 10 27 | 32 | 13 s. 36 | 2½ | 2¾ | 12:14 | E | 8:47 | A | OPH | 4 |
| 303 | 30 | **B** | 7:15 | D | 5:40 | B | 10 25 | 32 | 13 s. 55 | 3½ | 3½ | 1:15 | E | 9:55 | B | SAG | 5 |
| 304 | 31 | M. | 7:16 | D | 5:39 | B | 10 23 | 32 | 14 s. 15 | 4¼ | 4½ | 2:05 | E | 11:10 | B | SAG | 6 |

# OCTOBER

*See how the great old forest vies*
*With all the glory of the skies.*
–Alexander M'Lachlan

| DAY OF MONTH | DAY OF WEEK | DATES, FEASTS, FASTS, ASPECTS, TIDE HEIGHTS, AND WEATHER | |
|---|---|---|---|
| 1 | Sa. | ☿ STAT. • 1st agricultural fair in U.S. held, Pittsfield, Mass., 1810 • Tides {9.5 / 10.6} | *Light* |
| 2 | **B** | **17th S. af. P.** • ☾ RUNS LOW • Tides {9.1 / 10.4} | *rain* |
| 3 | M. | ☌♇☾ • Watch for banded woolly bear caterpillars now. • Tides {8.9 / 10.3} | *(or* |
| 4 | Tu. | St. Francis of Assisi • Yom Kippur begins at sundown • ☾ AT PERIG. • {8.9 / 10.3} | *harder)* |
| 5 | W. | ☌♄☾ • Businessman Ray Kroc born, 1902 • Professor Robert Goddard born, 1882 | *never* |
| 6 | Th. | *Respect out of fear is never genuine; reverence out of respect is never false.* • Tides {9.5 / 10.6} | *dampens* |
| 7 | Fr. | ☌♆☾ • Tornado struck Jenner, Alta., 2017 • {10.0 / 10.8} | *the* |
| 8 | Sa. | ☌♃☾ • ♇ STAT. • ☿ GR. ELONG. (18° WEST) • Tides {10.5 / 10.8} | *ardor* |
| 9 | **B** | **18th S. af. P.** • Sukkoth begins at sundown • FULL HUNTER'S ○ • ☾ ON EQ. | *of* |
| 10 | M. | COLUMBUS DAY, OBSERVED • INDIGENOUS PEOPLES' DAY • THANKSGIVING DAY (CANADA) | *the* |
| 11 | Tu. | ☾ AT ☊ • Little brown bats hibernate now. • Wildlife artist John Ruthven died, 2020 | *foliage* |
| 12 | W. | NATIONAL FARMER'S DAY • OCCN. ♅☾ • Musician John Denver died, 1997 | *pilgrims;* |
| 13 | Th. | 58-lb. muskie caught, Lake Bellaire, Mich., 2012 • Tides {9.8 / 10.4} | *sunny* |
| 14 | Fr. | Charles Yeager 1st to break sound barrier, reaching Mach 1.06 in Bell X-1 jet, 1947 • Tides {9.3 / 10.0} | *skies* |
| 15 | Sa. | ☌♂☾ • Andy Green 1st to break sound barrier in land-based vehicle, at 763.035 mph, 1997 | *couldn't* |
| 16 | **B** | **19th S. af. P.** • ☾ RIDES HIGH • 4.0 earthquake occurred near Hollis Center, Maine, 2012 | *be* |
| 17 | M. | St. Ignatius of Antioch • ☾ AT APO. • Tides {8.1 / 8.9} | *better for* |
| 18 | Tu. | St. Luke • St. Luke's little summer. • British Broadcasting Co. (BBC) formed, 1922 | *maple-red,* |
| 19 | W. | *Blow the wind never so fast, It will lower at last.* • Tides {8.1 / 8.9} | *ash-gold,* |
| 20 | Th. | Physicist John Bardeen 1st to win 2nd Nobel Prize in same field (1st, 1956), 1972 • {8.4 / 9.1} | *and* |
| 21 | Fr. | Poet Samuel Taylor Coleridge born, 1772 • USS *Constitution* launched, 1797 • {8.8 / 9.4} | *beech-butter;* |
| 22 | Sa. | ♀ IN SUP. ☌ • At 0.575 $mm^2$, OmniVision OV6948 set world record as tiniest commercial image sensor, 2019 | |
| 23 | **B** | **20th S. af. P.** • ☾ ON EQ. • ♄ STAT. • Tides {9.8 / 9.9} | *dazzled* |
| 24 | M. | St. James of Jerusalem[T] • ☌☿☾ • "Father of Microbiology" Antonie van Leeuwenhoek born, 1632 | *and* |
| 25 | Tu. | NEW ● • ECLIPSE ☉ • ☌♀☾ • Tides {10.8 / —} | *awed,* |
| 26 | W. | ☾ AT ☋ • *Pac-Man* arcade game released in U.S., 1980 • Timber rattlesnakes move to winter dens. | *they* |
| 27 | Th. | At 16, violinist Jascha Heifetz made his American debut at Carnegie Hall, N.Y., 1917 • {10.2 / 11.3} | *surrender* |
| 28 | Fr. | Sts. Simon & Jude • *All is not butter that comes from the cow.* • Tides {10.1 / 11.3} | *to* |
| 29 | Sa. | ☾ RUNS LOW • ☾ AT PERIG. • Artist Bob Ross born, 1942 • Tides {9.8 / 11.2} | *the* |
| 30 | **B** | **21st S. af. P.** • ♂ STAT. • Bodybuilder Charles Atlas born, 1892 | *autumn* |
| 31 | M. | All Hallows' Eve • Reformation Day • ☌♇☾ • {9.2 / 10.6} | *splendor.* |

## Farmer's Calendar

Plenty of people commute *to work,* but our mail lady drives 88 miles a day, over mostly dirt roads, *for work,* delivering letters, catalogs, and rototiller parts on her starfish-shaped circuit around town. As she feeds each of the 350-plus mailboxes on her rural route, she knows the truth: She knows where she'll have to yield for crossing cows, for fawns and does, and for "big old, roly-poly black bears" in the middle of the road. Her Jeep rattles as she zips beneath the canopies of goldening maples. Our town exists thanks to a trail hacked out of wilderness with an ax in 1779—the Bayley-Hazen Military Road—a route that later delivered settlers, including one so determined to get here in 1789 that he took over the yoke when one of his oxen sickened and dragged his sled the last hundred miles. Some 230 years on, this ancient thoroughfare constitutes just one leg of the mail lady's daylong journey to bring us our bills. Her grumbly vehicle pauses at box after box, the way a bee visits each blossom. Here she comes. There she goes—Godspeeding to all the other unpaved places, roads aptly named King Farm, Black River, Auld Lang Syne, and Mud Island.

# NOVEMBER

**SKY WATCH:** Now and for the remainder of the year, the action happens solely in the evening sky, except for on the night of the 7th–8th, when a very nice total eclipse of the Moon is at least partially visible from the entire U.S. and Canada during the second half of the night. West of the Mississippi, the eclipse may be seen in its entirety. The Moon features prominently throughout this month, as it dangles below Saturn on the 1st, closely below Jupiter on the 4th, above Mars on the 10th, below Mars on the 11th, to the left of Virgo's blue star Spica on the 21st, below Saturn again on the 28th, and halfway between Jupiter and Saturn on the 30th.

◖ **FIRST QUARTER**   1st day   2:37 A.M.      ● **NEW MOON**        23rd day   5:57 P.M.
○ **FULL MOON**          8th day   6:02 A.M.      ◗ **FIRST QUARTER** 30th day   9:37 A.M.
◑ **LAST QUARTER**   16th day   8:27 A.M.

*After 2:00 A.M. on November 6, Eastern Standard Time is given.*

GET THESE PAGES WITH TIMES SET TO YOUR ZIP CODE VIA ALMANAC.COM/2022.

| DAY OF YEAR | DAY OF MONTH | DAY OF WEEK | ☀ RISES H. M. | RISE KEY | ☀ SETS H. M. | SET KEY | LENGTH OF DAY H. M. | SUN FAST M. | SUN DECLINATION ° ' | HIGH TIDE TIMES BOSTON | | ☾ RISES H. M. | RISE KEY | ☾ SETS H. M. | SET KEY | ☾ ASTRON. PLACE | ☾ AGE |
|---|---|---|---|---|---|---|---|---|---|---|---|---|---|---|---|---|---|
| 305 | 1 | Tu. | 7:18 | D | 5:37 | B | 10 19 | 32 | 14 s. 34 | 5½ | 5¾ | 2:44 | E | — | - | CAP | 7 |
| 306 | 2 | W. | 7:19 | D | 5:36 | B | 10 17 | 32 | 14 s. 53 | 6½ | 6¾ | 3:15 | E | 12:27 | B | CAP | 8 |
| 307 | 3 | Th. | 7:20 | D | 5:35 | B | 10 15 | 32 | 15 s. 12 | 7½ | 8 | 3:41 | D | 1:42 | C | AQU | 9 |
| 308 | 4 | Fr. | 7:21 | E | 5:34 | B | 10 13 | 32 | 15 s. 30 | 8½ | 9 | 4:03 | D | 2:55 | D | AQU | 10 |
| 309 | 5 | Sa. | 7:22 | E | 5:33 | B | 10 11 | 32 | 15 s. 49 | 9½ | 10 | 4:25 | C | 4:05 | D | PSC | 11 |
| 310 | 6 | **B** | 6:24 | E | 4:31 | B | 10 07 | 32 | 16 s. 07 | 9¼ | 9¾ | 3:47 | C | 4:15 | E | PSC | 12 |
| 311 | 7 | M. | 6:25 | E | 4:30 | B | 10 05 | 32 | 16 s. 24 | 10 | 10½ | 4:10 | B | 5:24 | E | PSC | 13 |
| 312 | 8 | Tu. | 6:26 | E | 4:29 | B | 10 03 | 32 | 16 s. 42 | 10¾ | 11¼ | 4:36 | B | 6:33 | E | ARI | 14 |
| 313 | 9 | W. | 6:27 | E | 4:28 | B | 10 01 | 32 | 16 s. 59 | 11½ | — | 5:06 | B | 7:41 | E | TAU | 15 |
| 314 | 10 | Th. | 6:29 | E | 4:27 | B | 9 58 | 32 | 17 s. 16 | 12 | 12 | 5:43 | A | 8:47 | E | TAU | 16 |
| 315 | 11 | Fr. | 6:30 | E | 4:26 | B | 9 56 | 32 | 17 s. 32 | 12¾ | 12¾ | 6:26 | A | 9:49 | E | TAU | 17 |
| 316 | 12 | Sa. | 6:31 | E | 4:25 | B | 9 54 | 32 | 17 s. 48 | 1½ | 1½ | 7:17 | A | 10:45 | E | GEM | 18 |
| 317 | 13 | **B** | 6:32 | E | 4:24 | B | 9 52 | 31 | 18 s. 04 | 2¼ | 2¼ | 8:14 | B | 11:32 | E | GEM | 19 |
| 318 | 14 | M. | 6:34 | E | 4:23 | B | 9 49 | 31 | 18 s. 20 | 3 | 3 | 9:16 | B | 12:11 | E | GEM | 20 |
| 319 | 15 | Tu. | 6:35 | E | 4:22 | B | 9 47 | 31 | 18 s. 35 | 3¾ | 3¾ | 10:19 | B | 12:43 | E | CAN | 21 |
| 320 | 16 | W. | 6:36 | E | 4:21 | B | 9 45 | 31 | 18 s. 50 | 4¾ | 4¾ | 11:23 | C | 1:10 | E | LEO | 22 |
| 321 | 17 | Th. | 6:37 | E | 4:20 | B | 9 43 | 31 | 19 s. 05 | 5½ | 5¾ | — | - | 1:33 | E | LEO | 23 |
| 322 | 18 | Fr. | 6:39 | E | 4:20 | B | 9 41 | 31 | 19 s. 19 | 6½ | 6½ | 12:28 | C | 1:54 | D | LEO | 24 |
| 323 | 19 | Sa. | 6:40 | E | 4:19 | B | 9 39 | 30 | 19 s. 33 | 7¼ | 7½ | 1:33 | D | 2:15 | C | VIR | 25 |
| 324 | 20 | **B** | 6:41 | E | 4:18 | B | 9 37 | 30 | 19 s. 47 | 8 | 8¼ | 2:40 | D | 2:36 | C | VIR | 26 |
| 325 | 21 | M. | 6:42 | E | 4:17 | B | 9 35 | 30 | 20 s. 00 | 8¾ | 9¼ | 3:50 | E | 2:59 | B | VIR | 27 |
| 326 | 22 | Tu. | 6:43 | E | 4:17 | A | 9 34 | 30 | 20 s. 13 | 9½ | 10 | 5:03 | E | 3:25 | B | VIR | 28 |
| 327 | 23 | W. | 6:45 | E | 4:16 | A | 9 31 | 29 | 20 s. 26 | 10¼ | 10¾ | 6:21 | E | 3:58 | B | LIB | 0 |
| 328 | 24 | Th. | 6:46 | E | 4:16 | A | 9 30 | 29 | 20 s. 38 | 11 | 11½ | 7:40 | E | 4:41 | A | SCO | 1 |
| 329 | 25 | Fr. | 6:47 | E | 4:15 | A | 9 28 | 29 | 20 s. 50 | 11¾ | — | 8:57 | E | 5:35 | A | OPH | 2 |
| 330 | 26 | Sa. | 6:48 | E | 4:15 | A | 9 27 | 28 | 21 s. 01 | 12¼ | 12½ | 10:05 | E | 6:42 | B | SAG | 3 |
| 331 | 27 | **B** | 6:49 | E | 4:14 | A | 9 25 | 28 | 21 s. 12 | 1¼ | 1½ | 11:01 | E | 7:57 | B | SAG | 4 |
| 332 | 28 | M. | 6:50 | E | 4:14 | A | 9 24 | 27 | 21 s. 22 | 2¼ | 2¼ | 11:44 | E | 9:15 | B | CAP | 5 |
| 333 | 29 | Tu. | 6:52 | E | 4:13 | A | 9 21 | 27 | 21 s. 33 | 3¼ | 3¼ | 12:18 | D | 10:32 | C | CAP | 6 |
| 334 | 30 | W. | 6:53 | E | 4:13 | A | 9 20 | 27 | 21 s. 42 | 4¼ | 4½ | 12:46 | D | 11:46 | C | AQU | 7 |

# NOVEMBER

*Fill your hearts with old-time cheer:*
*Heaven be thanked for one more year.*
–G. P. Lathrop

| DAY OF MONTH | DAY OF WEEK | DATES, FEASTS, FASTS, ASPECTS, TIDE HEIGHTS, AND WEATHER | |
|---|---|---|---|
| 1 | Tu. | All Saints' • ☌♄☾ • Space Coast's 321 area code went into effect, Brevard Co., Fla., 1999 • {9.1 10.2 | *Mild* |
| 2 | W. | All Souls' • Howard Hughes's *Hercules* (aka *Spruce Goose*) wooden aircraft flew 1 mile, 1947 • {9.1 10.1 | *and* |
| 3 | Th. | *Common sense is not always true.* • Tides {9.4 10.0 | *drizzly.* |
| 4 | Fr. | ☌♃☾ • ☌♆☾ • Composer Felix Mendelssohn died, 1847 • {9.8 10.1 | *Suddenly* |
| 5 | Sa. | Sadie Hawkins Day • ☾ ON EQ. • Susan B. Anthony cast ballot, earning $100 fine, 1872 | *grisly:* |
| 6 | **B** | **22nd S. af. P.** • **Daylight Saving Time ends, 2:00 A.M.** • {10.6 10.1 | *raining* |
| 7 | M. | Magnitude 6.3 earthquake struck off coast of Vancouver Island, B.C., 2012 • {10.8 10.0 | *and sleeting* |
| 8 | Tu. | **Election Day** • **Full Beaver** ○ • **Eclipse** ☾ • ☾ AT ☊ • ☌♅☾ • ☿ IN SUP. ☌ | |
| 9 | W. | ♅ AT ☍ • Great Boston fire began, 1872 • 1st launch of NASA's *Saturn V* rocket, 1967 • {10.7 — | *and* |
| 10 | Th. | Montreal Canadiens' Armand Mondou awarded 1st penalty shot in NHL, 1934 • Tides {9.6 10.5 | *freezing,* |
| 11 | Fr. | St. Martin of Tours • **Veterans Day** • ☌♂☾ • Tides {9.3 10.3 | *before* |
| 12 | Sa. | Indian Summer • ☾ RIDES HIGH • *Rain at seven, fine at eleven.* • {8.9 9.9 | *easing.* |
| 13 | **B** | **23rd S. af. P.** • Wall of Vietnam Veterans Memorial dedicated, D.C., 1982 • {8.6 9.6 | *Don't* |
| 14 | M. | ☾ AT APO. • Insulin co-discoverer Sir Frederick Banting born, 1891 • Tides {8.3 9.2 | *drop* |
| 15 | Tu. | Artist Georgia O'Keeffe born, 1887 • 49 tornadoes tore through Midwest, 2005 • {8.2 9.0 | *your* |
| 16 | W. | Last Hawaiian king, Kalakaua, born, 1836 • Tides {8.1 8.8 | *guard—* |
| 17 | Th. | St. Hugh of Lincoln • 1st U.S. patent for clock granted to Eli Terry, 1797 • Tides {8.3 8.8 | *snowing* |
| 18 | Fr. | St. Hilda of Whitby • 1st dated book printed in England, *Dictes or Sayengis of the Philosophres,* 1477 | *hard!* |
| 19 | Sa. | ☾ ON EQ. • Cat, missing for 3 yrs., reunited w/ owner after walking into hospital, Berlin, N.H., 2020 | *You'll* |
| 20 | **B** | **24th. S. af. P.** • Princess Elizabeth (later, Queen Elizabeth II) wed Lt. Philip Mountbatten, 1947 | *suffer* |
| 21 | M. | "Tweety Bird" cartoon character debuted, 1942 • {10.2 9.6 | *without* |
| 22 | Tu. | ☾ AT ☋ • ☌☿♀ • Filmmaker Gil Cardinal died, 2015 • {10.7 9.9 | *a* |
| 23 | W. | St. Clement • **New** ● • *Pleasant hours fly fast.* • Tides {11.2 10.0 | *muffler!* |
| 24 | Th. | **Thanksgiving Day** • ☌☿☾ • ☌♀☾ • ♃ STAT. • {11.6 10.1 | *May* |
| 25 | Fr. | ☾ AT PERIG. • Record 4-min., 17.9-sec. mile run by P. Robinson in Antarctica (–13°F windchill), 2017 | *your* |
| 26 | Sa. | ☾ RUNS LOW • *Peanuts* cartoonist Charles Schulz born, 1922 • Tides {10.0 11.7 | *feast* |
| 27 | **B** | **1st S. of Advent** • ☌♇☾ • Announced: Britain's Prince Harry engaged to Meghan Markle, 2017 | |
| 28 | M. | ☌♄☾ • 1st ad via skywriting, N.Y.C., 1922 • {9.7 11.1 | *be feastly:* |
| 29 | Tu. | *Pong* coin-operated video game debuted, 1972 • Tides {9.5 10.7 | *Outside's* |
| 30 | W. | St. Andrew • ♂ AT CLOSEST APPROACH • 405-lb. yellowfin tuna caught, Magdalena Bay, Mexico, 2010 | *beastly!* |

## Farmer's Calendar

You can measure a kestrel's life span on one hand. But if you're handy, you can increase the chances that this smallest falcon may have a place to lay its eggs, as my neighbor did some 30 years ago.

In 1989, Dave nailed together boards from rough-cut pine, with a hole big enough for his fist to fit. He stationed the box 16 feet up his telephone pole. The first spring, the place stayed vacant. But the second year and ever since, kestrels have been in residence—arriving as early as March 25 or delayed until April 16—depending on the amount of bare ground nearby. Kestrels need snowless patches to hunt mice and other small rodents, and, as the season warms, insects. In late June, Dave spies the nestlings' faces squeezed into the opening; by mid-July, the box is again hollow. In autumn, Dave fetches a ladder to clean his chimney, then he leans it against the pole and climbs up to rake out old bedding. From his pocket he delivers a fistful of clean shavings. On this dim, chill afternoon, he's preparing for the next handful of kestrels that will perch at this opening, taking their first peek at the world.

CALENDAR

# DECEMBER

**SKY WATCH:** The Moon is again the star of the celestial show throughout this month, as it dangles below Jupiter on the 1st; floats closely and beautifully above Mars on the 7th, when it is full; dangles below Saturn on the 26th; hangs below Jupiter on the 28th; and stands to the left of Jupiter on the 29th. (It is again beautifully close to Mars on January 3, 2023.) Unfortunately, the Moon plays the role of villain for the Geminid meteors on December 13, when its fat gibbous phase casts unwelcome light. During the final week of the year, Venus may be glimpsed as it returns as an evening star, very low in the southwest. Winter in the Northern Hemisphere begins with the solstice on December 21 at 4:48 P.M. EST.

| | | | | |
|---|---|---|---|---|
| ○ **FULL MOON** | 7th day 11:08 P.M. | ● **NEW MOON** | 23rd day 5:17 A.M. |
| ◑ **LAST QUARTER** | 16th day 3:56 A.M. | ◐ **FIRST QUARTER** | 29th day 8:21 P.M. |

*All times are given in Eastern Standard Time.*

GET THESE PAGES WITH TIMES SET TO YOUR ZIP CODE VIA ALMANAC.COM/2022.

| DAY OF YEAR | DAY OF MONTH | DAY OF WEEK | ☼ RISES H.M. | RISE KEY | ☼ SETS H.M. | SET KEY | LENGTH OF DAY H. M. | SUN FAST M. | SUN DECLINATION ° ' | HIGH TIDE TIMES BOSTON | | ☽ RISES H.M. | RISE KEY | ☽ SETS H.M. | SET KEY | ☽ ASTRON. PLACE | ☽ AGE |
|---|---|---|---|---|---|---|---|---|---|---|---|---|---|---|---|---|---|
| 335 | 1 | Th. | 6:54 | E | 4:13 | A | 9 19 | 27 | 21 s. 52 | 5¼ | 5½ | 1:09 | D | — | - | AQU | 8 |
| 336 | 2 | Fr. | 6:55 | E | 4:12 | A | 9 17 | 26 | 22 s. 01 | 6¼ | 6¾ | 1:31 | C | 12:57 | D | PSC | 9 |
| 337 | 3 | Sa. | 6:56 | E | 4:12 | A | 9 16 | 26 | 22 s. 09 | 7¼ | 7¾ | 1:52 | C | 2:05 | E | PSC | 10 |
| 338 | 4 | **B** | 6:57 | E | 4:12 | A | 9 15 | 25 | 22 s. 17 | 8 | 8¾ | 2:14 | B | 3:13 | E | PSC | 11 |
| 339 | 5 | M. | 6:58 | E | 4:12 | A | 9 14 | 25 | 22 s. 25 | 9 | 9½ | 2:38 | B | 4:21 | E | ARI | 12 |
| 340 | 6 | Tu. | 6:59 | E | 4:12 | A | 9 13 | 25 | 22 s. 32 | 9¾ | 10¼ | 3:07 | B | 5:28 | E | ARI | 13 |
| 341 | 7 | W. | 7:00 | E | 4:11 | A | 9 11 | 24 | 22 s. 39 | 10¼ | 11 | 3:40 | A | 6:35 | E | TAU | 14 |
| 342 | 8 | Th. | 7:01 | E | 4:11 | A | 9 10 | 24 | 22 s. 45 | 11 | 11¾ | 4:21 | A | 7:38 | E | TAU | 15 |
| 343 | 9 | Fr. | 7:02 | E | 4:11 | A | 9 09 | 23 | 22 s. 51 | 11¾ | — | 5:09 | A | 8:36 | E | TAU | 16 |
| 344 | 10 | Sa. | 7:02 | E | 4:11 | A | 9 09 | 23 | 22 s. 56 | 12¼ | 12¼ | 6:05 | A | 9:27 | E | GEM | 17 |
| 345 | 11 | **B** | 7:03 | E | 4:12 | A | 9 09 | 22 | 23 s. 01 | 1 | 1 | 7:05 | B | 10:09 | E | GEM | 18 |
| 346 | 12 | M. | 7:04 | E | 4:12 | A | 9 08 | 22 | 23 s. 06 | 1¾ | 1¾ | 8:07 | B | 10:43 | E | CAN | 19 |
| 347 | 13 | Tu. | 7:05 | E | 4:12 | A | 9 07 | 22 | 23 s. 10 | 2½ | 2½ | 9:11 | B | 11:11 | E | LEO | 20 |
| 348 | 14 | W. | 7:06 | E | 4:12 | A | 9 06 | 21 | 23 s. 14 | 3¼ | 3¼ | 10:14 | C | 11:36 | E | LEO | 21 |
| 349 | 15 | Th. | 7:06 | E | 4:12 | A | 9 06 | 21 | 23 s. 17 | 4 | 4 | 11:17 | D | 11:57 | D | LEO | 22 |
| 350 | 16 | Fr. | 7:07 | E | 4:13 | A | 9 06 | 20 | 23 s. 19 | 4¾ | 5 | — | - | 12:17 | D | VIR | 23 |
| 351 | 17 | Sa. | 7:08 | E | 4:13 | A | 9 05 | 20 | 23 s. 22 | 5½ | 5¾ | 12:21 | D | 12:37 | C | VIR | 24 |
| 352 | 18 | **B** | 7:08 | E | 4:13 | A | 9 05 | 19 | 23 s. 23 | 6¼ | 6¾ | 1:28 | E | 12:58 | C | VIR | 25 |
| 353 | 19 | M. | 7:09 | E | 4:14 | A | 9 05 | 19 | 23 s. 25 | 7¼ | 7¾ | 2:38 | E | 1:22 | B | VIR | 26 |
| 354 | 20 | Tu. | 7:09 | E | 4:14 | A | 9 05 | 18 | 23 s. 25 | 8 | 8½ | 3:52 | E | 1:51 | B | LIB | 27 |
| 355 | 21 | W. | 7:10 | E | 4:15 | A | 9 05 | 18 | 23 s. 26 | 8¾ | 9½ | 5:10 | E | 2:28 | B | LIB | 28 |
| 356 | 22 | Th. | 7:10 | E | 4:15 | A | 9 05 | 17 | 23 s. 26 | 9¾ | 10¼ | 6:29 | E | 3:17 | A | SCO | 29 |
| 357 | 23 | Fr. | 7:11 | E | 4:16 | A | 9 05 | 17 | 23 s. 25 | 10½ | 11¼ | 7:44 | E | 4:19 | A | SAG | 0 |
| 358 | 24 | Sa. | 7:11 | E | 4:16 | A | 9 05 | 16 | 23 s. 24 | 11½ | — | 8:48 | E | 5:33 | B | SAG | 1 |
| 359 | 25 | **B** | 7:12 | E | 4:17 | A | 9 05 | 16 | 23 s. 22 | 12 | 12¼ | 9:38 | E | 6:54 | B | CAP | 2 |
| 360 | 26 | M. | 7:12 | E | 4:18 | A | 9 06 | 15 | 23 s. 20 | 1 | 1¼ | 10:17 | E | 8:15 | C | CAP | 3 |
| 361 | 27 | Tu. | 7:12 | E | 4:18 | A | 9 06 | 15 | 23 s. 18 | 2 | 2 | 10:48 | E | 9:33 | C | AQU | 4 |
| 362 | 28 | W. | 7:13 | E | 4:19 | A | 9 06 | 14 | 23 s. 15 | 2¾ | 3 | 11:13 | D | 10:47 | D | AQU | 5 |
| 363 | 29 | Th. | 7:13 | E | 4:20 | A | 9 07 | 14 | 23 s. 11 | 3¾ | 4 | 11:36 | D | 11:57 | D | PSC | 6 |
| 364 | 30 | Fr. | 7:13 | E | 4:21 | A | 9 08 | 13 | 23 s. 08 | 4¾ | 5¼ | 11:57 | C | — | - | CET | 7 |
| 365 | 31 | Sa. | 7:13 | E | 4:21 | A | 9 08 | 13 | 23 s. 03 | 5¾ | 6¼ | 12:19 | C | 1:05 | E | PSC | 8 |

**To use this page, see p. 116; for Key Letters, see p. 238.** LIGHT = A.M. BOLD = P.M. **2022**

# DECEMBER

*Holly, fir, and spruce boughs / Green upon the wall,*
*Spotless snow upon the road— / More going to fall.*
–Unknown

| DAY OF MONTH | DAY OF WEEK | DATES, FEASTS, FASTS, ASPECTS, TIDE HEIGHTS, AND WEATHER | |
|---|---|---|---|
| 1 | Th. | ☌♃☾ • ☌♆☾ • Writer/USN Capt. Edward L. Beach died, 2002 • {9.5 9.8 | *Numb* |
| 2 | Fr. | St. Viviana • ☾ ON EQ. • 1st pizza party in space, ISS, 2017 • Tides {9.7 9.6 | *and* |
| 3 | Sa. | *If things were to be done twice, all would be wise.* • {9.9 9.4 | *number,* |
| 4 | **B** | **2nd S. of Advent** • ♆ STAT. • Tides {10.2 9.4 | *with flakes* |
| 5 | M. | ☾ AT ☊ • ☌♅☾ • Ship *Mary Celeste* found abandoned, 1872 • {10.4 9.3 | *aswirl;* |
| 6 | Tu. | St. Nicholas • Everglades Nat'l Park dedicated, Fla., 1947 • Tides {10.4 9.2 | *bluster* |
| 7 | W. | St. Ambrose • **NATIONAL PEARL HARBOR REMEMBRANCE DAY** • **FULL COLD** ○ • OCCN. ♂☾ | |
| 8 | Th. | ♂ AT ☍ • 896 couples in N.H./Mo./Col. kissed under mistletoe, setting world record, 2019 | *ceases,* |
| 9 | Fr. | ☾ RIDES HIGH • Canada's 1st coin club, Numismatic Society of Montreal, formed, 1862 • {10.3 — | *sun* |
| 10 | Sa. | St. Eulalia • Poet Emily Dickinson born, 1830 • Tides {8.9 10.1 | *increases.* |
| 11 | **B** | **3rd S. of Advent** • ☾ AT APO. • *Good words cost naught.* • {8.7 9.9 | *Hang* |
| 12 | M. | **OUR LADY OF GUADALUPE** • *Apollo 17* astronauts discovered orange soil on Moon, 1972 • {8.6 9.7 | *your* |
| 13 | Tu. | St. Lucia • National Day of the Horse • Tides {8.5 9.4 | *holly:* |
| 14 | W. | Ember Day • Halcyon Days begin. • *Mariner 2* passed Venus (1st successful planetary flyby), 1962 | *Don't* |
| 15 | Th. | Baseball player Dick Stuart died, 2002 • Tides {8.4 8.9 | *go* |
| 16 | Fr. | Ember Day • Lillian Disney (wife of Walt Disney) died, 1997 • Tides {8.6 8.7 | *out* |
| 17 | Sa. | Ember Day • ☾ ON EQ. • France formally recognized American independence, 1777 | *without* |
| 18 | **B** | **4th S. of Advent** • Chanukah begins at sundown • Tides {9.3 8.8 | *your* |
| 19 | M. | ☾ AT ☋ • 1st season of National Hockey League (NHL), 1917 • Tides {9.7 9.0 | *brolly!* |
| 20 | Tu. | Beware the Pogonip. • J. Russell Coffey, oldest known U.S. WWI veteran at time, died at age 109, 2007 | *Leave* |
| 21 | W. | St. Thomas • **WINTER SOLSTICE** • ☿ GR. ELONG. (20° EAST) • Tides {10.9 9.5 | *Santa* |
| 22 | Th. | U.S. first lady Claudia "Lady Bird" Johnson born, 1912 • Tides {11.4 9.8 | *a* |
| 23 | Fr. | NEW ● • ☾ RUNS LOW • Saturn's moon Rhea discovered, 1672 • Tides {11.7 10.0 | *snack* |
| 24 | Sa. | ☾ AT PERIG. • ☌☿☾ • ☌♀☾ • ☌♇☾ • Tides {12.0 — | *to* |
| 25 | **B** | **Christmas** • *If windy on Christmas Day, trees will bring much fruit.* • Tides {10.1 11.9 | *be* |
| 26 | M. | St. Stephen • **BOXING DAY (CANADA)** • **FIRST DAY OF KWANZAA** • ☌♄☾ • {10.1 11.7 | *sure* |
| 27 | Tu. | St. John • Chemist Louis Pasteur born, 1822 • 141-lb. 8-oz. Pacific sailfish caught on 4# test line, Piñas Bay, Panama, 1992 | |
| 28 | W. | Holy Innocents • ☌♆☾ • ☿ STAT. • Comic book writer Stan Lee born, 1922 | *he comes* |
| 29 | Th. | ☾ ON EQ. • ☌☿♀ • ☌♃☾ • *Dec. 28–29:* 25.5" snow in 24 hrs., Victoria, B.C., 1996 | *back.* |
| 30 | Fr. | Samoa skipped this day to move from eastern to western side of International Date Line, 2011 • {9.8 9.5 | *Adieu,* |
| 31 | Sa. | St. Sylvester • Gymnast Gabby Douglas born, 1995 • Tides {9.8 9.0 | *'22!* |

## Farmer's Calendar

Plowing the roads of Cabot, Vermont, is the second-best job Walter "Rusty" Churchill's ever had. First best? Dairy farming, which he did for 30 years. He didn't know what he'd do after he sold his cows. He thought about taking a shift at the Cabot Creamery; then someone mentioned a job opening at the town garage and encouraged Rusty to throw his name in for it. They hired another guy, but he didn't last. So that's how, for over a decade now, Rusty's knack for spreading lime and manure and tilling soil makes him an ace at scattering salt and sand and plowing for his hometown. The hours are similar—Thanksgiving, Christmas, New Year's, Easter—he works them all. But, he admits, it's satisfying to clear a path after a huge storm: "Then it seems like you're doing something." Rusty's route includes some of the town's 65 miles of blacktop, hilltop, and back roads. "There aren't too many out this early," he says of clearing snow long before sunrise. "You've got Creamery help—they have a shift that starts at 4:00 A.M.—and milk trucks. Otherwise, it's just me. Kinda peaceful. As long as the radio works, I'm all set."

CALENDAR

# HOLIDAYS AND OBSERVANCES

## 2022 HOLIDAYS
### FEDERAL HOLIDAYS ARE LISTED IN BOLD.

**JAN. 1:** New Year's Day

**JAN. 17: Martin Luther King Jr.'s Birthday, observed**

**FEB. 2:** Groundhog Day

**FEB. 12:** Abraham Lincoln's Birthday

**FEB. 14:** Valentine's Day

**FEB. 15:** Susan B. Anthony's Birthday *(Fla.)*

**FEB. 21: Presidents' Day**

**FEB. 22:** George Washington's Birthday

**MAR. 1:** Mardi Gras *(Baldwin & Mobile counties, Ala.; La.)*
Town Meeting Day *(Vt.)*

**MAR. 2:** Texas Independence Day

**MAR. 8:** International Women's Day

**MAR. 13:** Daylight Saving Time begins at 2:00 A.M.

**MAR. 17:** St. Patrick's Day
Evacuation Day *(Suffolk Co., Mass.)*

**MAR. 28:** Seward's Day *(Alaska)*

**MAR. 31:** César Chávez Day

**APR. 2:** Pascua Florida Day

**APR. 18:** Patriots Day *(Maine, Mass.)*

**APR. 21:** San Jacinto Day *(Tex.)*

**APR. 22:** Earth Day

**APR. 29:** National Arbor Day

**MAY 5:** Cinco de Mayo

**MAY 8:** Mother's Day
Truman Day *(Mo.)*

**MAY 21:** Armed Forces Day

**MAY 22:** National Maritime Day

**MAY 23:** Victoria Day *(Canada)*

**MAY 30: Memorial Day**

**JUNE 5:** World Environment Day

**JUNE 11:** King Kamehameha I Day *(Hawaii)*

**JUNE 14:** Flag Day

**JUNE 17:** Bunker Hill Day *(Suffolk Co., Mass.)*

**JUNE 19:** Father's Day
Juneteenth

**JUNE 20:** West Virginia Day

**JULY 1:** Canada Day

**JULY 4: Independence Day**

**JULY 23:** National Day of the Cowboy

**JULY 24:** Pioneer Day *(Utah)*

**AUG. 1:** Colorado Day
Civic Holiday *(parts of Canada)*

**AUG. 16:** Bennington Battle Day *(Vt.)*

**AUG. 19:** National Aviation Day

**AUG. 26:** Women's Equality Day

**SEPT. 5: Labor Day**

**SEPT. 9:** Admission Day *(Calif.)*

**SEPT. 11:** Patriot Day
Grandparents Day

**SEPT. 17:** Constitution Day

**SEPT. 21:** International Day of Peace

**OCT. 3:** Child Health Day

**OCT. 9:** Leif Eriksson Day

**OCT. 10: Columbus Day, observed**
Indigenous Peoples' Day *(parts of U.S.)*
Thanksgiving Day *(Canada)*

**OCT. 12:** National Farmer's Day

**OCT. 18:** Alaska Day

**OCT. 24:** United Nations Day

**OCT. 28:** Nevada Day

**OCT. 31:** Halloween

**NOV. 4:** Will Rogers Day *(Okla.)*

**NOV. 6:** Daylight Saving Time ends at 2:00 A.M.

**NOV. 8:** Election Day

**NOV. 11: Veterans Day**
Remembrance Day *(Canada)*

| | |
|---|---|
| **NOV. 19:** Discovery of Puerto Rico Day | **DEC. 15:** Bill of Rights Day |
| **NOV. 24: Thanksgiving Day** | **DEC. 17:** Wright Brothers Day |
| **NOV. 25:** Acadian Day *(La.)* | **DEC. 25: Christmas Day** |
| **DEC. 7:** National Pearl Harbor Remembrance Day | **DEC. 26:** Boxing Day *(Canada)* First day of Kwanzaa |

## Movable Religious Observances

| | |
|---|---|
| **FEB. 13:** Septuagesima Sunday | **MAY 26:** Ascension Day |
| **MAR. 1:** Shrove Tuesday | **JUNE 5:** Whitsunday–Pentecost |
| **MAR. 2:** Ash Wednesday | **JUNE 12:** Trinity Sunday |
| **APR. 2:** Ramadan begins at sundown | **JUNE 19:** Corpus Christi |
| **APR. 10:** Palm Sunday | **SEPT. 25:** Rosh Hashanah begins at sundown |
| **APR. 15:** Good Friday Passover begins at sundown | **OCT. 4:** Yom Kippur begins at sundown |
| **APR. 17:** Easter | **NOV. 27:** First Sunday of Advent |
| **APR. 24:** Orthodox Easter | **DEC. 18:** Chanukah begins at sundown |
| **MAY 22:** Rogation Sunday | |

## CHRONOLOGICAL CYCLES

Dominical Letter **B**

Epact **27**

Golden Number (Lunar Cycle) **9**

Roman Indiction **15**

Solar Cycle **15**

Year of Julian Period **6735**

## ERAS

| ERA | YEAR | BEGINS |
|---|---|---|
| Byzantine | 7531 | September 14 |
| Jewish (A.M.)* | 5783 | September 25 |
| Chinese (Lunar) [Year of the Tiger] | 4720 | February 1 |
| Roman (A.U.C.) | 2775 | January 14 |
| Nabonassar | 2771 | April 18 |
| Japanese | 2682 | January 1 |
| Grecian (Seleucidae) | 2334 | September 14 (or October 14) |
| Indian (Saka) | 1944 | March 22 |
| Diocletian | 1739 | September 11 |
| Islamic (Hegira)* | 1444 | July 29 |
| Bahá'í* | 179 | March 20 |

*Year begins at sundown.

# GLOSSARY OF ALMANAC ODDITIES

Many readers have expressed puzzlement over the rather obscure entries that appear on our **Right-Hand Calendar Pages, 121–147.** These "oddities" have long been fixtures in the Almanac, and we are pleased to provide some definitions. Once explained, they may not seem so odd after all!

**EMBER DAYS:** These are the Wednesdays, Fridays, and Saturdays that occur in succession following (1) the First Sunday in Lent; (2) Whitsunday–Pentecost; (3) the Feast of the Holy Cross, September 14; and (4) the Feast of St. Lucia, December 13. The word *ember* is perhaps a corruption of the Latin *quatuor tempora,* "four times." The four periods are observed by some Christian denominations for prayer, fasting, and the ordination of clergy.

Folklore has it that the weather on each of the 3 days foretells the weather for the next 3 months; that is, in September, the first Ember Day, Wednesday, forecasts the weather for October; Friday predicts November; and Saturday foretells December.

**DISTAFF DAY (JANUARY 7):** This was the day after Epiphany, when women were expected to return to their spinning following the Christmas holiday. A distaff is the staff that women used for holding the flax or wool in spinning. (Hence the term "distaff" refers to women's work or the maternal side of the family.)

**PLOUGH MONDAY (JANUARY):** Traditionally, the first Monday after Epiphany was called Plough Monday because it was the day when men returned to their plough, or daily work, following the Christmas holiday. (Every few years, Plough Monday and Distaff Day fall on the same day.) It was customary at this time for farm laborers to draw a plough through the village, soliciting money for a "plough light,"

which was kept burning in the parish church all year. This traditional verse captures the spirit of it:

> *Yule is come and Yule is gone,*
> *and we have feasted well;*
> *so Jack must to his flail again*
> *and Jenny to her wheel.*

**THREE CHILLY SAINTS (MAY):** Mamertus, Pancras, and Gervais were three early Christian saints whose feast days, on May 11, 12, and 13, respectively, are traditionally cold; thus they have come to be known as the Three Chilly Saints. An old French saying translates to "St. Mamertus, St. Pancras, and St. Gervais do not pass without a frost."

**MIDSUMMER DAY (JUNE 24):** To the farmer, this day is the midpoint of the growing season, halfway between planting and harvest. The Anglican Church considered it a "Quarter Day," one of the four major divisions of the liturgical year. It also marks the feast day of St. John the Baptist. (Midsummer Eve is an occasion for festivity and celebrates fertility.)

**CORNSCATEOUS AIR (JULY):** First used by early almanac makers, this term signifies warm, damp air. Although it signals ideal climatic conditions for growing corn, warm, damp air poses a danger to those affected by asthma and other respiratory problems.

**DOG DAYS (JULY 3–AUGUST 11):** These 40 days are traditionally the year's hottest and unhealthiest. They once coincided with the year's heliacal (at sunrise) rising of the Dog Star, Sirius. Ancient folks thought that the "combined heat" of Sirius and the Sun caused summer's swelter.

**LAMMAS DAY (AUGUST 1):** Derived from the Old English *hlaf maesse,* meaning "loaf mass," Lammas Day marked the beginning of the harvest. Traditionally, loaves of bread were baked from the first-ripened grain and brought to the churches to be consecrated. In Scotland, Lammastide fairs became famous as the time when trial marriages could be made. These marriages could end after a year with no strings attached.

**CAT NIGHTS COMMENCE (AUGUST 17):** This term harks back to the days when people believed in witches. An Irish legend says that a witch could turn into a cat and regain herself eight times, but on the ninth time (August 17), she couldn't change back and thus began her final life permanently as a cat. Hence the saying "A cat has nine lives."

**HARVEST HOME (SEPTEMBER):** In Britain and other parts of Europe, this marked the conclusion of the harvest and a period of festivals for feasting and thanksgiving. It was also a time to hold elections, pay workers, and collect rents. These festivals usually took place around the autumnal equinox. Certain groups in the United States, e.g., the Pennsylvania Dutch, have kept the tradition alive.

**ST. LUKE'S LITTLE SUMMER (OCTOBER):** This is a period of warm weather that occurs on or near St. Luke's feast day (usually October 18) and is sometimes called Indian summer.

**INDIAN SUMMER (NOVEMBER):** A period of warm weather following a cold spell or a hard frost, Indian summer can occur between St. Martin's Day (November 11) and November 20. Although there are differing dates for its occurrence, for more than 225 years the Almanac has adhered to the saying "If All Saints' [November 1] brings out winter, St. Martin's brings out Indian summer." The term may have come from early Native Americans, some of whom believed that the condition was caused by a warm wind sent from the court of their southwestern god, Cautantowwit.

**HALCYON DAYS (DECEMBER):** This period of about 2 weeks of calm weather often follows the blustery winds at autumn's end. Ancient Greeks and Romans experienced this weather at around the time of the winter solstice, when the halcyon, or kingfisher, was thought to brood in a nest floating on the sea. The bird was said to have charmed the wind and waves so that waters were especially calm at this time.

**BEWARE THE POGONIP (DECEMBER):** The word *pogonip* refers to frozen fog and was coined by Native Americans to describe the frozen fogs of fine ice needles that occur in the mountain valleys of the western United States and Canada. According to tradition, breathing the fog is injurious to the lungs. ■

# OUR AMAZING
# NORTH STAR

The steady sentinel of our northern sky
is more than meets the eye.

BY BOB BERMAN

It's the most famous star. And the most useful. Yet nothing else in the heavens generates as much confusion as Polaris, the North Star.

Go ahead, ask your friends: "What makes the North Star special?" Most will say its brightness. Some will merely shrug. Odds are, none will give the right answer:

*It's the only object in the sky that doesn't appear to move—and this is absolutely astounding!*

Make no mistake; Polaris's brightness is notable. Of the 6,000 stars visible to the naked eye, it ranks a respectable 45th in brightness. It's bright enough to appear in polluted city skies (on every clear night, it's visible to 88 percent of Earth's humans), but it's not brilliant enough to catch your eye. It is 2nd-magnitude—a medium star, matching those of Orion's Belt and the ones forming the Big Dipper. It's no dim bulb but not a standout, either; its strength is its stability while all else is in perpetual motion.

Thanks to our planet's rotation, the Moon, Sun, and stars rise in the east, cross the sky, and then set in the west. Look up, then an hour later glance skyward again, and you'll notice that nearly everything's shifted rightward (or leftward, for those in the Southern Hemisphere)—except Polaris. It shares this stationary quality with nothing else in the universe. If it's halfway up the sky as you look out your north-facing window, it'll still be there next month, next year, and when your grandchildren are old.

Think of it this way: Imagine you painted hundreds of polka dots on your floor, walls, and ceiling and then performed ballet pirouettes in the middle of the room. As you spun, the dots would seem to whirl around you. Except for one. The polka dot on the ceiling right over your head wouldn't move because your axis of spin points straight up in its direction.

Earth's axis of spin has to point somewhere, too. By chance, it's angled

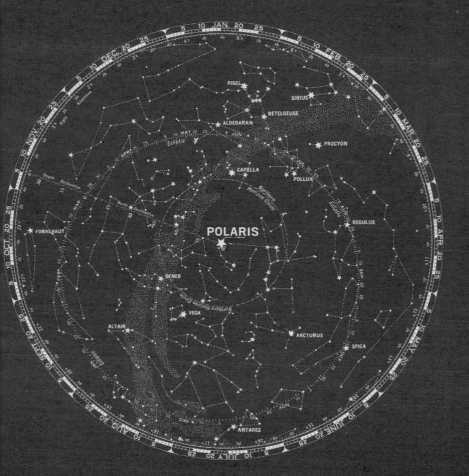

## DEGREES OF SEPARATION

As mariners have always known, if you measure the North Star's height in the sky, you'll ascertain your latitude. Latitude is expressed in degrees, with the North Pole at 90°, most U.S. cities at 30° to 40°, and the Equator at 0° latitude. From the North Pole, latitude 90°, Polaris stands almost exactly 90° high—straight up. At the Equator, latitude 0°, Polaris stands 0° high as it hovers atop the horizon. From Denver or New York City, both of which are at approximately latitude 40°, Polaris is 40° high, about halfway up the northern sky.

Measure Polaris's elevation above the horizon and you instantly know your latitude. Here's how to do it: A clenched adult fist held at arm's length blocks 10° of the sky, so, for example, Polaris appears to hover four stacked fists high—approximately 40° up— as seen from Denver. (Longitude is a different matter and requires an onboard clock.)

toward Polaris. So, like that one dot on the ceiling, Polaris doesn't seem to move. If you visited the North Pole, you'd see Polaris almost exactly straight overhead. When you moved away from the pole, Polaris would be high overhead but no longer straight up. The farther you traveled from the pole, the lower Polaris would appear, until you reached the Equator, when Polaris would sit on the northern horizon and it wouldn't budge as the hours wore on each night.

If you're south of the Equator, Polaris is below the horizon and invisible. You will find no comparable "South Star" at the south celestial pole—the sky-spot at which the other end of Earth's axis points as our world spins. Serious astronomers can identify 5th-magnitude Sigma Octantis, the very dim southern pole star that hovers over Aussie-land, but it's no standout.

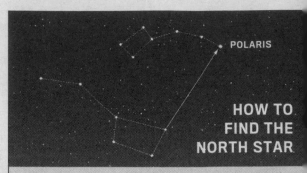

**POLARIS**

# HOW TO FIND THE NORTH STAR

The easiest way to find Polaris is to first locate the Big Dipper. It is visible throughout the year—highest up in spring and quite low in autumn, especially for those in the most southerly states. The Big Dipper has a curved handle and a bowl. Find the two stars at the edge of the bowl that's farthest from the handle. Follow a line from the star at the base of the bowl through the star at the top of that edge onward to a single star that's the same brightness as they are—that's Polaris!

P olaris is unique. The fact that it just happens to sit within a single degree of the celestial pole, the precise motionless spot

in the sky around which everything pivots, is an unlikely reality. The odds can be easily calculated. There are 41,253 square degrees of sky, and only some 45 stars are as bright or brighter than Polaris. The chance of such a noticeable star occupying the right spot is nearly a thousand to one against. The odds against both poles being occupied by medium-bright stars would be nearly a million to one.

What's more, Polaris is—for all practical purposes—precise. It shows us true north

with far greater accuracy than a compass, which merely follows the magnetic pole and is badly in error from most locations. From Boston, for instance, compasses point a whopping 16 degrees to the left of north, while instruments on the Pacific coast point nearly as erroneously in the other direction. In fact, if we drop an imaginary plumb bob straight down from Polaris, it touches the northern horizon to a precision of better than a degree.

Yet Polaris is not permanent. While our North

Image: ScienceSparks.co[m]

Star appears constant for centuries, it is not in its position for eternity. The wobbly motion of our planet's axis, called precession, gradually creates new stationary sky positions and new north stars over a cycle of 25,780 years. Like a spinning toy top tilting around in a slow drunken circle as its rotation speed decreases, Earth's leisurely wobble once caused our northern axis to point toward a relatively dim star in Draco named Thuban when the Pyramids were being built. And 12,000 years from now, brilliant Vega will be our north star, although it will never be as visually glued in place as our own Polaris.

The north celestial pole, the spot of sky that doesn't move each night, is moving incrementally slowly in Polaris's direction. At present, 2022, Polaris hovers within 1 degree of this pole, but it will stand at less than a half-degree at its closest, an event that is expected to occur within 3 years of 2109 (no one can be more precise on the timing). After that, the celestial pole will start to slowly pull away, and, within a few centuries, Polaris will trace out tiny but noticeable nightly circles. Now, Polaris sits so close to the celestial pole that the circle that it makes each night is too small to notice—but it does show up on long exposure photos. The diameter of Polaris's nocturnal arc will increase over time, and thus will the epoch of Polaris gradually conclude. We'll then have to wait another 260 centuries—a full precessional cycle—before it once again becomes our "North Star."

U sing recent astrophysical discoveries, we know that the distant star to which Earth's axis points is remarkable.
• First, it's no ordinary star; it's a giant. At about 440 light-years distant, it lies some four times farther away than the Big Dipper's two "pointer" stars that guide our eyes to it.
• Being at that distance yet so prominently visible means that it is exceptionally luminous. In fact, Polaris shines with extraordinary brilliance, emitting the light of thousands of Suns.
• Even more remarkable is that Polaris's north rotation pole is located dead center to our observations. This means that we are *its* "north star"!

Viewers using small telescopes with lenses or mirrors at least 3 inches in diameter are encouraged to observe the North Star and see its small companion star. Studies of Polaris's light indicate a second companion star as well.

Or try this more restful exercise: Point your instrument at Polaris and leave it there. Unplug the drive motor. Take a 20-, 30-, or even 40-year sabbatical. When you return, the constant star will still be in the same position, waiting for you. ∎

**Bob Berman,** our astronomy editor, ran the astronomy program at Yellowstone Park for 15 years and was an adjunct professor of astronomy and physics at Marymount College in New York's Westchester County. He writes and hosts the "Strange Universe" show heard weekly during NPR's *Weekend Edition* on Northeast Public Radio.

# WHAT, THE HAIL?

## TRACKING THE PLAGUE OF "WATERY METEORS"

BY CHRISTOPHER C. BURT

**HEAVY WEATHER**
Have you experienced a hailstorm?
Share your pics on f @theoldfarmersalmanac

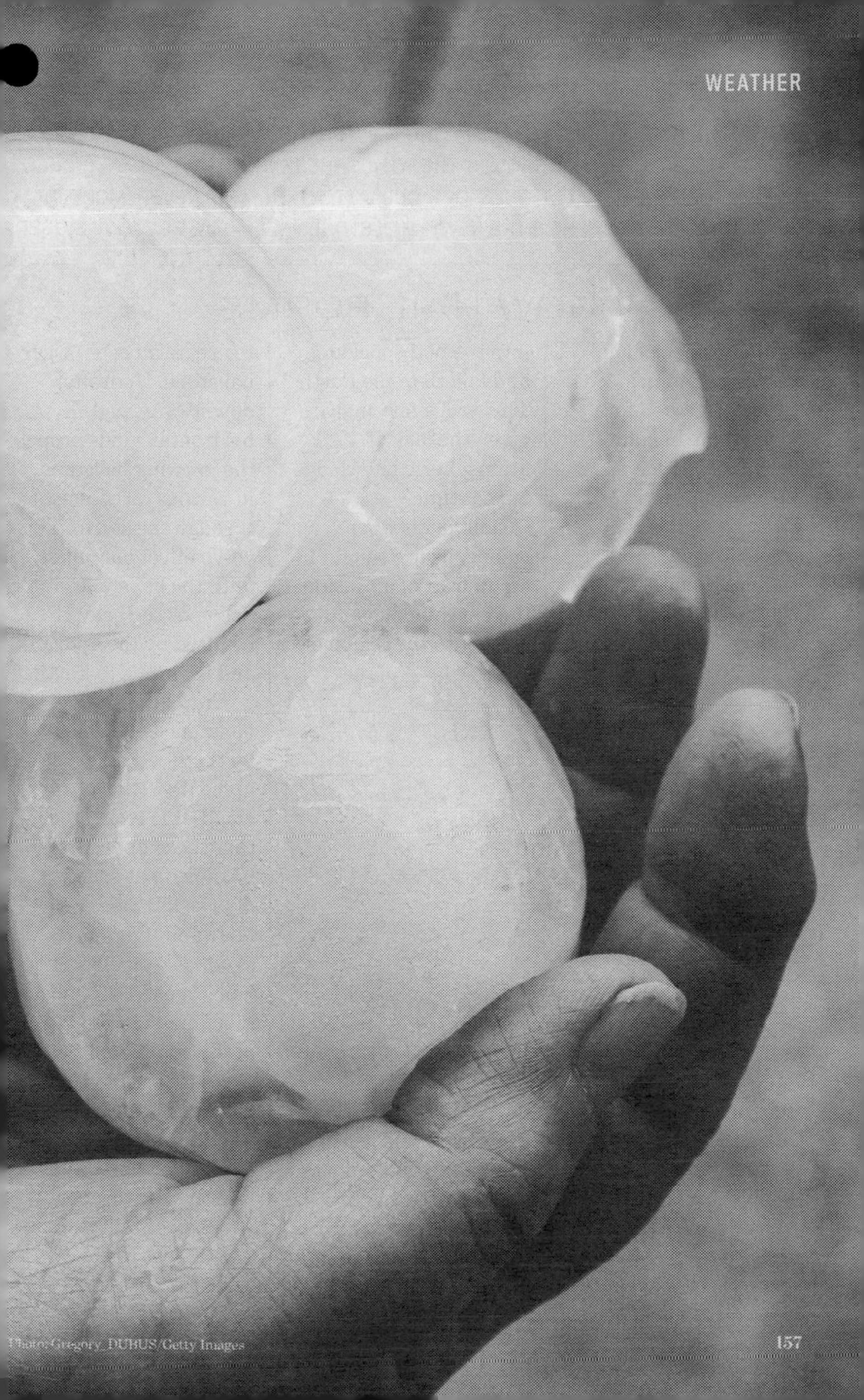

Photo: Gregory_DUBUS/Getty Images

ONE OF NATURE'S MOST FASCINATING AND FEARSOME WEATHER EVENTS IS A HAILSTORM. BORN OF CHAOS IN THE ATMOSPHERE AND THE CAUSE OF CHAOS WHERE THEY FALL, HAILSTONES GET OUR ATTENTION—AND NEVER MORE THAN WHEN THEY ARE BIG. HERE'S THE NEWS: HAILSTONES SEEM TO BE GETTING BIGGER.

# HOW HAIL FORMS

The science of hail formation has been understood for a long time. In John Tulley's *Almanac of 1693* (Cambridge, Massachusetts), while speculating on the "Natural Causes of Watery Meteors, such as snow, hail, rain, into the body of cloud, and falleth to the Earth." This was a fair analysis given the lack of atmospheric knowledge at that time.

Hail forms when raindrops are caught in an updraft of air inside the parent cloud and lifted into the region of to create an ever larger hailstone. Updrafts, downdrafts, and horizontal winds propel the growing hailstone in various directions through the storm. This yo-yo effect continues until the hailstone becomes too heavy to be lifted by the updrafts and thus falls to Earth.

The size of the hailstone is determined by the strength of the updrafts in the storm cloud. It is estimated that these updrafts can be moving at speeds of over 150 miles per hour and thus can produce grapefruit-size hailstones (5 to 6 inches in diameter). The tops of the cumulonimbus clouds that host large hail can soar as high as 70,000 feet into the atmosphere, well into the stratosphere, which begins at around 35,000 feet in the midlatitudes of the Northern Hemisphere.

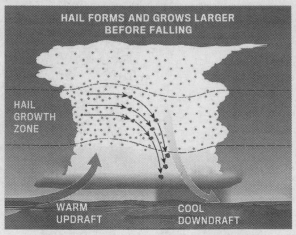

HAIL FORMS AND GROWS LARGER BEFORE FALLING

HAIL GROWTH ZONE

WARM UPDRAFT

COOL DOWNDRAFT

etc.," he wrote ". . . hail is engendered of rain, congealed into ice, freezing the drops perfectly . . . in the middle region of the air, whereby the extremity of cold, it is thickened the cloud that is below freezing (which varies depending on what the surface temperature might be). Once frozen, the raindrop can then grow by colliding with still-unfrozen droplets

Illustration: Australian Bureau of Meteorology

## GOING UP

Of course, not every hailstone is citrus-size (the U.S. National Weather Service actually did away with hail descriptions related to food products some time ago). They range from the size of bb's to as big as DVDs. Weak thunderstorms normally produce smaller hailstones and powerful ones larger ones, but in recent years there has been an apparent increase in the frequency of large-hail (2-inch or greater diameter) events, the kind that can put dents in a car's hood and roof—especially if you're foolish enough to drive through a storm producing hail that size, as I once did on I-80 over the Donner Summit in the Sierra Nevada.

Why this increase in hail size? The science is still unclear, but it appears that the most

| HAIL SIZE DESCRIPTION | | |
|---|---|---|
| Hailstone Size | Diameter in. | cm |
| BB | <$1/4$ | <0.64 |
| PEA | $1/4$ | 0.64 |
| DIME | $7/10$ | 1.8 |
| PENNY | $3/4$ | 1.9 |
| NICKEL | $7/8$ | 2.2 |
| QUARTER | 1 | 2.5 |
| HALF-DOLLAR | $1 1/4$ | 3.2 |
| GOLF BALL | $1 3/4$ | 4.4 |
| BILLIARD BALL | $2 1/8$ | 5.4 |
| TENNIS BALL | $2 1/2$ | 6.4 |
| BASEBALL | $2 3/4$ | 7.0 |
| SOFTBALL | 3.8 | 9.7 |
| CD/DVD | $4 3/4$ | 12.1 |

-Hendricks County (Ind.) Radio Amateur Civil Emergency Service

extreme hail days now tend to have greater instability (the contrast between warm, moist air near Earth's surface and cold air aloft), perhaps as a result of long-term warming. (This is happening in hail-prone areas around the world.)

Curiously, however, some studies suggest that the actual number of hail events (not just large-hail ones) is decreasing. We do not fully understand why, but comparisons of the number of hail days and average hailstone sizes reported from before and after the year 2000 have shown this to be true. *(continued)*

Photo: Henrik Norway/Getty Images

# MATTERS OF SIZE

Hail occurs at some time everywhere in the U.S. and Canada south of the Arctic Circle, but the majority of hail reports emanate from the Plains/Prairies regions because it is here where the most severe

across and 18.5 inches around, with a weight of almost 2 pounds—was collected by Lee Scott near Vivian, South Dakota, on July 23, 2010. Scott claims that it actually measured close to 11 inches across when he picked it up

largest hailstone on record was a 4.5-inch–diameter head-knocker that was measured in Cedoux, Saskatchewan, on August 27, 1973.

Very large hail (4-inch or greater diameter) is rare outside of the U.S. Midwest and Plains states, but it can occur—-even in Hawaii: At Kailua on Oahu Island, on March 9, 2012, hailstones measuring 4.25 inches in diameter pummeled the ground.

A SCIENTIST PREPARES TO MAKE A THREE-DIMENSIONAL MODEL OF THE VIVIAN HAILSTONE, THE LARGEST EVER RECORDED IN THE U.S.

thunderstorms and— not coincidentally—the most tornadoes occur.

Large hail and tornadoes go together. The months of May through August account for 85 percent of all annual hailstorm reports in the U.S. and Canada, with June being the peak month. It's perhaps no surprise, then, that the largest hailstone ever recorded in the U.S.—8 inches

and placed it in his freezer. This was before a power outage (a result of the storm), during which the stone melted to *only* 8 inches before it refroze when the power returned. Scott eventually turned the stone over to the NWS for preservation and analysis. Vermont's record hailstone measured 3.3 inches in diameter in Westford on July 16, 2009. Canada's

Even larger hailstones have been reported from other places. On February 8, 2018, a thunderstorm in Cordoba province, Argentina, produced a stone collected and measured at 7.1 inches in diameter. Video taken of the stones falling through the air has been analyzed by meteorologists who estimated that some of them were as large as 9.3 inches in diameter. The experts even proposed a new size category— "gargantuan"—for hailstones that are at least 6 inches in diameter.

Photo: University Corporation for Atmospheric Research

# HAILING A STORM TRAIN

That's big, but it pales when compared to the glacial effect: Training thunderstorms, a series of storms passing over the same location, can dump hail for hours and result in massive accumulations of it. Such an event took place in Selden, Kansas, on June 3, 1959, when, during an 85-minute storm, hailstones piled up to 18 inches deep. Often, rainfall accompanying such events will wash the

**HAIL CLIFFS IN CLAYTON, NEW MEXICO, 2004**

hail to a low point in the terrain and pile it up into fantastic heaps. This occurred near Clayton, New Mexico, on August 13, 2004, when an accumulation of hail washed into a creek bed and backed up behind a clogged culvert. Hail cliffs resembling the edge of a glacier rose some 15 feet high and took weeks to melt.

# UNDERRATED IMPACT

Although the vast majority of hailstorms cause no significant damage, hail is an underrated economic hazard in the U.S. In most years, it causes more damage than tornadoes—and its havoc can rival that of hurricanes. Canada is not immune to its impact, as evidenced in the Calgary, Alberta, area on June 13, 2020, when a massive hailstorm became the fourth costliest natural disaster in that country's history. Just as they were in 1693 and before, "watery meteors" are but one more awesome example of Mother Nature's powerful potential. *(continued)*

**HAIL DAMAGE IN CALGARY, ALBERTA, 2020**

Photos, from top: National Weather Service; NOAA

# THE COLD REALITY: HAILSTONE DAMAGE

**H**ailstones can hurt or even kill randomly. Only a few documented human fatalities as a result of being struck have been recorded in modern U.S. history; Canada has experienced none. Fatalities to animals are more numerous, and injuries to both people and animals caught in hailstorms are relatively common— and can be painful. Dollar costs based on structural damage are well documented and can run into the billions for a single event.

Take these precautions if you are caught in a "watery meteor" barrage:

• Indoors—Close curtains, blinds, and shades to prevent injury from glass broken by hailstones. Remain indoors until the storm passes and the hailstones melt; they can be slippery underfoot.

• Outdoors—Seek shelter, but not under trees; lightning, which often accompanies hailstorms, can strike a tree—and thus you. Tree limbs can break and also strike you. Protect your head while moving to safety.

• In a car or other vehicle—Pull off the road. Remain inside. Instruct passengers to turn away from the windows and cover their eyes and head (with a sweatshirt, jacket, etc.) to protect against any glass broken by hailstones. If possible before the storm, seek safety nearby—for example, under an overpass or service station awning or in a garage. ■

---

**Christopher C. Burt** is the weather historian for Weather Underground, an IBM Company, and author of *Extreme Weather: A Guide and Record Book* (W. W. Norton & Co., 2007).

# THE TOOTH,
## THE WHOLE TOOTH,
## AND NOTHING BUT THE TOOTH

### AN EXAMINATION OF TEETH, FROM CRADLE TO GRAVE

BY TIM CLARK

## NATAL TEETH

About 1 in 1,000 babies is born with teeth. Some cultures celebrate the "natal teeth," as they are called. Ancient Romans considered such babies lucky, and they were often named "Dentatus." However, other cultures considered natal teeth as a bad omen. The children were thought likely to become vampires. Some were killed.

## MILK TEETH

Most babies are born with 20 milk teeth, which usually erupt (appear in the mouth) within the first 3 years after birth. They start to get pushed out of the jaw at around age 5 by adult teeth growing in. The Vikings paid children for their milk teeth, which warriors wore around their necks in battle, believing that they would bring good luck.

Many cultures have strong beliefs about the disposal of these teeth. The most common practice involves offering the tooth to rodents like mice, rats, or even beavers. Known for their strong teeth, rodents were thought to give the child's succeeding teeth strength and beauty in return.

Rodents appeared in a book called *The Tooth Fairy,* written by Lee Rogow in 1949, which popularized the custom (already old by then) of putting a child's lost tooth under his or her pillow, to be miraculously replaced by money—perhaps a penny in colonial days but rising with inflation to an average of $3.19 these days, according to researchers at Visa.

## PROPHETIC TEETH

While the baby teeth are falling out, a child starts growing his or her 32 adult teeth. Once the complete set has formed, several long-held superstitions take over.

Teeth set close together mean that a girl will live near her parents, while a space between the two front upper incisors means that she will make her eventual home far away—and she'll live a long life, be lucky, make a lot of money and, oddly enough, marry twice.

If a young man loses his teeth before he is 21, he won't live long; if after 21, he will live to be 100.

## WISDOM TEETH

The last teeth to emerge, usually between the ages of 17 and 21, are called "wisdom teeth." This third pair of molars, at the back of the mouth, are surrounded by folklore, including the belief that a child will never gain any knowledge or be wise until his wisdom teeth appear—an observation upheld by science, which has found that the part of the brain responsible for decision-making and judgment is not completely developed until the early 20s.

The Romani people of central Europe deeply respect wisdom teeth and believe that those who have all four of them are spiritually strong. To keep wisdom teeth healthy, they may cast a spell on them by using water that reflects a full Moon as a mouthwash, while saying, "Wisdom is mine, protection is mine, but pain and diseases are not mine."

## TOOTHACHE CURES

Sumerians living 7,000 years ago frequently complained of "tooth worms" drilling into their teeth and causing toothaches. This was not such a crazy idea at the time. Cavities produced holes that looked like the ones tiny worms made when digging into the ground or fruit.

The belief in tooth worms persisted well into the 18th century. The English thought that the worms looked like eels, while Germans favored something more like maggots. People suffering from toothaches would inhale smoke or spread honey on their teeth to persuade the worms to come out.

Weird, you say? Here are five of the strangest toothache cures suggested by American folklore:
• Run three times around a church without thinking of a fox.
• Cook earthworms in oil, then place them in the ear opposite the toothache.
• Plug the cavity with your own earwax.
• Chase a cat across a plowed field (perpendicular to the furrows) until it sweats, then rub the sweat on the aching tooth.
• Eat the eyes of a vulture.

## MISSING TEETH

The most common cure for a toothache in years past was to pull the tooth. Then you had to dispose of the pulled tooth properly, and folk wisdom has plenty of suggestions on how to do it:
• Put the tooth in a glass of water, and in 24 hours, it will become money.
• Throw the tooth over your left shoulder, and you'll have good luck.
• Carry a wisdom tooth on your person for luck.
• After a tooth is pulled, if you swallow a bubble from milk, a gold tooth will come into your mouth to replace it.

• If you throw away your first tooth and a chicken picks it up, you will get chicken teeth.

### UNHELPFUL HYGIENE
If you've heard it, don't believe it:
• Chew tobacco to preserve your teeth.
• Clean your teeth with cigar ashes to preserve them and make them white.
• Eat bread crusts to make teeth white.

## WATERLOO TEETH

Long ago, the best source of replacement teeth was corpses. The demand was so great that dentists and doctors employed men called "resurrectionists" to dig up graves and remove teeth from dead bodies.

But this was slow and inefficient. The best source of vast numbers of teeth—and teeth from young, healthy men—was the battlefield. Such teeth came to be called "Waterloo teeth" after the 1815 showdown that ended Napoleon's reign. More than 50,000 men died there, and a British resurrectionist named Butler was ready. "There'll be no want of teeth," he boasted before the fight. "I'll draw them as fast as the men are knocked down."

Dentists cheerfully advertised their dentures as "Waterloo teeth" or "Waterloo ivory." Fifty years later, dental catalogs still advertised the teeth of freshly killed soldiers. But these came from the casualties of the American Civil War (1861–65) and were shipped across the Atlantic. ■

**Tim Clark** still has all four of his wisdom teeth.

# Top Digestive Aid Pill Quietly Slows Premature Aging, Users Report Big Health Boost

Clinical research shows how a gastrointestinal "tonic" can restore GI health and slow an accelerated aging process; studies find the pill helps protect users from metabolic decline, cardiovascular issues, and serious conditions that accompany premature aging

**Seattle, WA** – A published study on a leading acid buffer shows that its key ingredient improves digestive health while supporting healthy inflammation response that slows down signs of premature aging in men and women.

And, if consumer sales are any indication of a product's effectiveness, this 'GI-tonic turned anti-aging phenomenon' is nothing short of a miracle.

Sold under the brand name AloeCure®, its ingredient was already backed by research showing its ability to neutralize acid levels and improve gastric discomfort.

But soon doctors started reporting some incredible results...

"With AloeCure, my patients started reporting better sleep, more energy, stronger immune systems... even less stress and better skin, hair, and nails," explains Dr. Liza Leal, a leading integrative health specialist and company spokesperson.

AloeCure contains an active ingredient that helps optimize the pH balance of your stomach.

Scientists now believe that having optimal acid levels could be a major contributing factor to a healthy immune system.

The daily allowance of AloeCure has been shown to optimize the acid levels needed to manage healthy immune function which is why AloeCure is so effective.

It relieves other stressful issues related to GI health like discomfort, excess gas and bloating, and bathroom times.

Now, backed with new scientific studies, AloeCure is being doctor-recommended to help improve digestive function, help build better bones, support healthy joint function.

## FIX YOUR GUT & SUPPORT HEALTHY INFLAMMATION

Since hitting the market, sales for AloeCure have taken off and there are some very good reasons why. To start, the clinical studies have been impressive.

Virtually all participants reported stunning improvement in digestive symptoms including gastric discomfort.

Users can also experience higher energy levels and endurance, less discomfort and better sleep,.

An unhealthy gut can wreak havoc on the human body. Doctors say this is why AloeCure works on so many aspects of your health.

## EXCITING USER REPORTS

To date millions of bottles of AloeCure have been sold, and the community seeking non-pharma therapy for their GI health continues to grow.

According to Dr. Leal, her patients are absolutely thrilled with their results and are often shocked by how fast it works.

"I recommend it to everyone who wants to improve GI health."

"All the problems with my stomach are gone. Completely gone. I can say AloeCure is a miracle. It's a miracle." Another user turned spokesperson said, "I started to notice a difference because I was sleeping through the night and that was great. AloeCure does work for me. It's made a huge difference."

With so much positive feedback, it's easy to see why the community of believers is growing and sales for the new pill are soaring.

## THE SCIENCE BEHIND ALOECURE

AloeCure is a gastric and digestive tonic.

The active ingredient is a compound only found in Aloe Vera called Acemannan.

Millions spent in developing a proprietary process for extracting acemannan resulted in the highest quality, most bio-available levels of acemannan known to exist, and it's made from organic aloe.

According to Dr. Leal and leading experts, improving the pH balance of your stomach and restoring gut health is the key to revitalizing your entire body.

When your digestive system isn't healthy, it causes unwanted stress on your immune system and that might lead to unhealthy inflammation.

The recommended daily allowance of AloeCure has been proven to support digestive health, manage healthy immune function, and promote healthy inflammation response without side effects or drugs.

This would explain why so many users are experiencing impressive results so quickly.

---

**AloeCure Taken Daily**

- Helps End Digestion Nightmares
- Reduces appearance of Wrinkles & Increases Elasticity
- Supports Healthy Immune System
- Supports Joint Health
- Promotes Healthy Inflammation Response
- Supports Bowel Health & Regularity

---

## REVITALIZE YOUR ENTIRE BODY

With daily use, AloeCure helps users look and feel decades younger and defend against premature aging that can make life hard.

By helping acid levels stay optimal and promoting gut health, AloeCure's ingredient supports joint health…helps skin appear smooth…maintains healthy cholesterol and oxidative stress…improves sleep and associated weight loss….and supports brain function by way of gut biome…without side effects or expense.

Readers can now support their energy, vitality, and youth regardless of age.

## HOW TO CLAIM A FREE SUPPLY TODAY

This is an exclusive offer for our readers. And so, AloeCure is offering up to 3 FREE bottles and FREE S&H with their order. While supplies last you may also receive a FREE book on Aloe Vera health benefits.

A special hotline number has been created. All you have to do is call **TOLL-FREE 1-800-561-6637**, and the special promotion will be automatically applied. This is the best way to try AloeCure with their 100% satisfaction guarantee, and any free gifts are yours to keep no matter what.

Important: Due to a surge in sales supplies are not guaranteed. Call now to not lose out on this offer.

# THE ART AND SCIENCE OF ANIMAL TRACKING

**SHOW US YOUR ANIMAL TRACKS!**
Share pics on
@theoldfarmersalmanac

## BY R. SCOTT SEMMENS

Humans have been animal tracking since the dawn of our species. The ancient art and science of animal tracking has its practical uses even today. There are two aspects of animal tracking: (1) studying the tracks and signs that animals leave behind, which is like reading the headlines about an animal, and (2) trailing an animal with the hope of seeing it while you remain undetected. *(continued)*

Photo: habrda/Getty Images

## NATURE

"Track and sign" is a basic skill that helps you to recognize little scenes from the lives of animals. If there is snow on the ground, you can find tracks everywhere. Otherwise, they appear in sandy, dusty, or muddy areas.

"Trailing" builds on tracks and signs to reveal a more comprehensive story. It is more complex and requires more skills, such as knowledge of how to "age" a trail and of the animal's ecology and seasonal behavior, which helps to predict where an animal may go when you lose the trail. Familiarity with the topography and an ability to move stealthily through it also help.

Animals seldom leave perfect tracks. Those of some species overlap in size and shape, making them difficult to identify. Through practice, your observation skills will be sharpened. By identifying some key features, you will be able to place the tracks within a family or order and then narrow them down to species, usually with the aid of animal track guidebooks.

### THE FINE POINTS OF THE FOOT

Learning about foot morphology can help you to understand how the foot leaves the tracks behind.

---

### A TRACKER'S TECHNIQUE

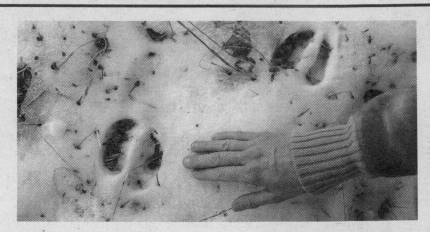

Before I identify a track, I look for similar tracks in the vicinity to ascertain the morphology, or form. I count the number of toes, examine their shapes and relationship to the pads, and determine whether they are front or hind feet. This can help to identify the family or order of the animal. I try to find associative signs (scats, scrapes, etc.) and evaluate the animal's gait, if possible, to understand its behavior. I note the context, such as habitat, ground, season, and specific location. Then I mentally match the evidence collected to a master list of possible animals that may reside in the area.

---

## TREAD MARKS
### (HIND FOOT AT LEFT, FRONT FOOT AT RIGHT)

RACCOON    STRIPED SKUNK    COYOTE    DOG    EASTERN COTTONTAIL

BLACK BEAR    MINK    BOBCAT    GRAY FOX    RED FOX

Mammals in the same order or family group often have similar foot morphology. Take the gray squirrel: Its front feet have four toes, plus one vestigial toe (toe #1, equivalent to our thumb). The hind feet have five toes. These toe patterns—especially the arrangement of toes #2, #3, and #4 in the hind feet—and the number of toes are characteristics of most members of the Sciuridae family. Similar patterns exist in the tracks of the squirrel's cousins, the chipmunk and the woodchuck.

The foot patterns of the canids (the dog family, which includes coyotes, foxes, wolves, and domestic dogs) are also similar to each other.

Measuring the size of the tracks can give some clue as to "owner"—but often not enough for identification. Consider that gray fox and red fox tracks can be similar in size; to know which is which, you have to examine the overall shapes of the tracks, the clarity of the toe pads, and the shapes of the metacarpal (front paw) pads. (Canids, unlike members of the squirrel family, have no heel pads.)

Here is how they differ:
• Overall, the gray fox print shape is round; that of the red fox is oval.
• The nails of the gray fox often do not show up on their tracks because their claws are semi-retractable; not so for the red fox, whose claws do appear.
• The toe pads in the gray fox show up clear and defined, while those of the red fox appear fuzzy—and that's a clue: The red fox's foot is furrier, thus blurring

GRAY FOX

RED FOX

the overall appearance. Plus, the red fox metacarpal pad is shaped like a chevron and can have a distinct "bar" running through it, caused by a raised ridge on the pad.

Sometimes a red fox track can be confused with a small coyote track because both are oval. But look again: The pads on coyote tracks are well defined, unlike those of the red fox, which are blurred because of the fur on the bottom of its feet.

Domestic dog tracks can also be confused with coyote tracks—even though dog tracks vary considerably in shape and size. However, there are some commonalities that distinguish domestic dog tracks from those of wild canids.

Domestic dog tracks usually have clear pads.

The metacarpal (front) and metatarsal (hind) pads are often nearly equal in size. The toe pads on domestic dog tracks are usually more splayed, while those of wild canids are tighter, as if more disciplined. Also, the nails of the domestic dog are blunt and large, whereas the nails of wild canids are sharp and fine.

Here are a few more commonly found animal families and the characteristics of their tracks:

## FELIDAE FAMILY
### E.G., BOBCAT

• Four toes front and hind. (A fifth toe is in the front but too high to register on the track.)
• Toes are asymmetrical. Note leading toe #3. (Only in the dog family are they symmetrical on both feet.)
• Large pads when

compared to toe size
• Three lobes (bumps) on the posterior edge of the pads
• The front and hind feet are round. The hind foot may be a little longer than it is wide.

## LAGOMORPH FAMILY
### E.G., EASTERN COTTONTAIL

• Five toes in the front foot and four toes in the hind foot
• Toe #1 is not always present. If present, it drops very low on the inside of the foot.
• Both feet are J-shape

---

### WHEN IN THE WILD . . .

When you first encounter a set of tracks, look at them as if it's your first time tracking. Notice the details without bias or expectations. Take measurements. Make notes on the texture, overall shape, color, and shading. Draw the tracks; this forces you to notice even more details. Any photos that you take should have some scale (e.g., a measuring tape) associated with them.

---

(especially the hind)
• Metacarpal and metatarsal pads rarely show up.

## MEPHITIDAE FAMILY
### E.G., STRIPED SKUNK

• Five toes front and hind
• Nails in the front foot are longer than those in the hind foot.
• Toes are partially fused in the front and hind feet.
• Toe #1 is the smallest and lowest on both feet.

## MUSTELIDAE FAMILY
### E.G., MINK

• Five toes front and hind
• Pads are arch-shape, with a relatively large

amount of space between pads and toes.
• Toe #1 is small on front and hind feet. All toes are distinct. In mink and otter, the hind foot toe #1 drops lower than toe #5.

## PROCYONIDAE FAMILY
### E.G., RACCOON

• Five toes front and hind
• Long, fingerlike toes, especially in the front feet
• Toe #1 is the lowest and smallest on front and hind.

• The front is distinguished by an abrupt anterior ridge of the metacarpal pad leading toward the toes in the front foot, as opposed to the more tapering anterior edge of the metatarsal pad transitioning to the toes in the hind foot.

## URSIDAE FAMILY
### E.G., BLACK BEAR

• Five toes front and hind
• Toe #1 is the smallest

and lowest on both feet.
• In the front foot, the inside lobe of the metacarpal pad is narrower and forms a distinct arch around toe #5.
• The hind foot has a continuous pad leading to the heel.

Animal tracking is a great way to enjoy the great outdoors. Now that you've learned the steps and acquired some skills in track identification, go outside and track! ■

**R. Scott Semmens** of Stoddard, New Hampshire, tracks animals around the world and teaches animal tracking to people of all ages—especially children—to get them excited about learning biology, ecology, and other sciences. He recommends that enthusiasts read Mark Elbroch's *Mammal Tracks & Sign: A Guide to North American Species,* 2nd ed. (Stackpole Books, 2019).

# NATURE'S SIGNS
# MEAN FISH
# ON LINES

## BY GLENN SAPIR • ILLUSTRATIONS BY TIM ROBINSON

**W**hen the telephone rang, the screen showed that it was my old fishing buddy, Ray Goodson, calling.

"The shadbushes are flowering," he said excitedly. "You know what *that* means!"

The Caller ID feature on my phone may have been newfangled when he made that call decades ago, but the message was one that has been repeated by shad fishermen all along the Delaware River year after year since people first figured out how to catch these anadromous fish on artificial lures. The American shad, prized for its fight in the water and its roe on the table, makes its annual spawning run every spring from the Atlantic Ocean through Delaware Bay and then along the Pennsylvania–New Jersey and then Pennsylvania–New York borders, which the river defines.

You could never be sure when the first shad might find their way into the commercial fishing nets, but you knew that when the shadbush was in bloom, it was time to go fishing.

Scientists call this

"phenology," the study of cyclic and seasonal natural phenomena. Anglers across the continent, in both the United States and Canada, however, simply call it Mother Nature. These fishermen believe that her plants and wildlife—even tiny insects—can tell them when to grab their rods and reels.

Fly-fishers seeking trout, especially in streams, base their strategy on the somewhat predictable timing of the emergence of aquatic insects that hatch in the water, sometimes fly into the air and then, often, lay their eggs before their brief life ends. During this time, these insects provide trout with a feast and fishermen

with obvious clues as to what to tie to their leaders. Simply put, it's called "matching the hatch," and those anglers who can tie on convincing imitations when they are in the right place at the right time—that is, when these insects are hatching, emerging, and falling back to the surface—might have fishing action that they will never forget.

What other natural indicators signal good fishing? One inquiry posted on Facebook and an email to several in-the-know anglers drew a variety of examples for both fresh and salt waters.

## SIGNS IN SPRING

Shad enthusiasts in Quebec know that when the yellow flowers of dandelions are replaced by wispy white tufts, typically in mid-May, it's time to head for the Rivière des Prairies, which flows into the St. Lawrence River, to cash in on the run.

The shadbush that flowers along the Delaware telling fishermen to get to the river sends a

different message when it blooms on Martha's Vineyard in Massachusetts. There, fishermen then know to head for the salt ponds and estuaries because the striped bass have arrived.

Lilacs are another of nature's indicators that deliver a message to fishermen on various parts of the continent. Their blooming on Long Island, New York, is a welcome sign, hinting at the arrival of weakfish. In Great Lakes country, fishermen know that when that bush produces its fragrant flowers, it's time to hit Lake Erie for walleyes, one of freshwater's tastiest catches. In Saskatchewan, too, when the lilacs bloom, anglers know that walleyes are ready to go on a post-spawn feeding frenzy.

Some fishermen attentively watch for dogwood blossoms. One angler swears that when dogwood blossoms are the size of a squirrel's ear, bass are ready for the taking.

This same fisher-man, who grew up in the Chicago area, notes another cyclical activity that suggests good bass fishing. "When you see people collecting young dandelion leaves from plants, the bass are on the beds."

Another flower sends the same signal on the West Coast.

"When the poppies start blooming, the bass are heading into the shallows for the spawn," says one Californian, a veteran fisherman.

He's observed an-other of nature's indica-tors in the Southwest: When the yuccas start blooming, the bluegills move into the shallows to spawn, he reports.

Why is such informa-tion important?

First, it's a clue that fish have moved from

the deep area of a body of water to its shallows. Second, when fish head for the spawning beds, the males—loaded with milt (semen)—and the females—laden with roe (eggs)—are at their heaviest weight. Third, the fish are in a protec-tive mode, guarding the area that they have

## SIGNS OF CHANGE

Climate change—specifically, water temperature—may threaten the dependability of some of these observations in coming years. For example, the Long Island Sound habitat along the New York and Connecticut coasts has warmed by 3 degrees in a 38-year period (1976-2014), changing the area from one characteristic of New England to one more like New Jersey, Delaware, and Maryland. This has triggered a northward migration of two-thirds of 82 northeastern marine species, according to the National Oceanic and Atmospheric Administration. At least two warm-water species, black sea bass and red hake, have moved about 200 miles north, according to the the Environmental Protection Agency.

Scientists can only watch and wonder how quickly fish will evolve or adapt, while fishermen keep an eye out for new signs. In parts of the U.S. Northeast, spring now arrives a full week earlier than it did a few decades ago.

staked out as a nursery and likely to attack anything, including your bait, that threatens their territory.

Bass and bluegill aren't the only species for which nature drops clues that fish are on their spawning beds.

In the Ozarks, it's said that there are often a few days when the redbud blooms start to fade and the dogwoods begin flowering simultaneously. When this happens, the crappie are shallow and spawning.

In central Missouri, when the black locusts are in bloom, the walleye spawning run is in full swing.

## AUTUMNAL INDICATORS

Not all of nature's indicators arrive in spring and summer.

In the Rocky Mountain states and provinces, when the aspens turn yellow in the fall, the lake brown trout are moving into stream mouths for their spawning run. This is when they are aggressive and vulnerable.

In coastal New England, anglers believe that when apples fall from the trees in October, the false albacore, a prized gamefish, migrate. This indicator has earned the species a nickname of "apple-knockers."

## FEATHERED FORECASTERS

Year after year, birds, too, serve as a seasonal signal corps for anglers.

In mid-Atlantic region coastal waters, laughing gulls arrive at

the same time that summer flounder, aka fluke, make their appearance.

When New Englanders see flocks of night herons standing watch on the shoreline of a river, they know that the alewife and herring spawning run is under way and large striped bass will be close to shore, eager to attack anything that disturbs the surface along the bank. This presents fishermen with a perfect opportunity for action on topwater plugs.

It is not serendipity that lends validity to all of these observations. The day length and angle of sunlight and the rising and lowering of water and air temperatures are key factors that trigger these coincidental occurrences in nature that repeat themselves year after year. Successful anglers have long known that following the weather and nature's signs are surefire keys to a great catch. ∎

**Glenn Sapir** of Putnam County, New York, is an award-winning writer and editor who has devoted his 50-plus-year career to communicating about the outdoors. He has served on the editorial staffs of major outdoors publications and is the author and/or editor of several books, including *A Sapir Sampler: Favorites by an Outdoor Writer* (Ashmark Communications, 2018).

Robert Heft holds his original 50-star flag.

**RAISE THE FLAG!**
Share pics of your national flag
on @ @theoldfarmersalmanac

# The **Star-Spangled** School Project

### BY JAY COPP

Who designed the American flag? Betsy Ross, of course, when the country consisted of 13 states. But who created the current version—the one with a star for each of the 50 states?

A high school student.

Born in 1941, 17-year-old Robert Heft of Lancaster, Ohio, learned from the news in 1958 that Alaska and Hawaii might be admitted to the Union as states. Later, when his history teacher, Stanley Pratt, required students to come up with a project, Heft had a bold idea.

He took the 48-star U.S. flag given to his parents as a wedding gift and considered how to artfully add two stars. Inspired, he pedaled his bike to a downtown department store and purchased $2.87 worth of blue cotton broadcloth. His breakthrough design idea was to insert the two stars by arranging all 50 stars in five rows of six alternating with four rows of five.

One problem: Heft was no seamstress. "I had never sewn in my life," he said.

He asked his grandmother to help, but she angrily rebuffed

Photo: Associated Press

him, saying that he was "desecrating" the flag. So he did it all on his own. Crouching down on the floor of the family living room, he traced the white stars on cardboard before cutting them out. He did the best he could with a foot-operated Singer sewing machine. It took him 12 hours over a weekend to arrange and sew the new pattern of stars.

However, Mr. Pratt was not impressed. He gave Heft a B-minus, and Heft was miffed. With a stern smile, Pratt told Heft that he would give him a better grade if the U.S. Congress ever accepted his design.

Undaunted, Heft pedaled to the nearby home of his congressman, Walter Moeller, explained what he had done, and left the flag with him. The following year, the congressman called Heft and told him some incredible news. More than 1,500 flag designs had been submitted to a special committee for a new flag. Many of them proposed alternating rows of five and six stars. Three designs were identical to Heft's—but the persistent, perfectionist teenager was the only one to stitch together a model flag. President Eisenhower had been given five finalists, and he had chosen Heft's design.

Eisenhower later called Heft at work to invite him to the official raising of the flag. The young man actually put the

president on hold to see if his boss would give him time off. "Yes, you can go," he was told.

On July 4, 1960, Heft was part of the festive ceremonies at Fort McHenry in Maryland, whose bombardment by the British had inspired the writing of "The Star-Spangled Banner."

This was gratifying for Heft, but not as satisfying as his return to his old high school, where his taskmaster, Pratt, gladly changed his grade to an A.

For years after, Heft traveled the world with his handmade flag, recounting his saga. "He was the greatest patriot I ever knew," said his friend Wil Hufton. Heft visited all of the states and nearly 60 nations. He traveled to the White House as an invited guest more than a dozen times, flew on *Air Force One*, toured with celebrities, and appeared on TV shows. His original flag flew over every state capitol and 88 U.S. embassies. He once declined an offer of $250,000 for it. (He had insured it for $1 million.)

Heft died in 2009 at the age of 67, allegedly in possession of the copyright for a design for a 51-star flag. His grandnephews and -nieces inherited the one that he had made in high school. ∎

**Jay Copp** is a former magazine editor and longtime freelance writer whose work has been published in dozens of magazines. He lives near Chicago with his wife and three sons.

# BEYOND THE

WHAT HAPPENED ON THE ICE WAS ONLY PART

PHIL ESPOSITO (7) OF TEAM CANADA
PLAYS AGAINST TEAM USSR
DURING THE 1972 SUMMIT SERIES

# BOARDS

## OF THE 1972 CANADA-SOVIET HOCKEY SUMMIT. BY PAT HICKEY

This year marks the 50th anniversary of the eight-game clash of hockey and political ideologies between Canada and the Soviet Union known as the Summit Series. Stats and stories of the games, the first ever between Canadian pros and the Soviet national team, are legendary; less well known are some of these off-ice incidents.

## THE GOLDEN JET IS GROUNDED

There was controversy over the roster before the series. High-scoring winger Bobby Hull, aka The Golden Jet, was named to the team but later dropped because the competition was limited to National Hockey League players and he had signed a contract with the Winnipeg Jets of the rival World Hockey Association. Prime Minister Pierre Trudeau joined fans and the media to protest Hull's exclusion, but their pleas fell on deaf ears. Derek Sanderson, Gerry Cheevers, and J. C. Tremblay were also excluded after signing with the WHA.

## ORR CASHES IN

Bobby Orr, who was the top defenseman in the NHL, was named to the team but unable to play because he was recovering from knee surgery. However, he was a big winner financially. With some help from agent Alan Eagleson, who also served as the main organizer of the series, Orr and Toronto Maple Leafs owner Harold Ballard secured the TV rights for the series for $750,000. They later walked away with a profit of $1.2 million.

## TROUBLE WITH SHOTS?

When Team Canada scouts Bob David-son and John McLellan saw Soviet goaltender Vladislav Tretiak give up eight goals in an intrasquad game, they weren't impressed. What they didn't know was that the 20-year-old was playing on the night before he got married and—perhaps more important—the night after his bachelor party.

## READY TO FIGHT

Soviet coach Vsevolod Bobrov recalled being roughed up by the Penticton Vees when he was playing in the 1955 world championships, so he added boxing lessons to his team's training program.

## COSTLY FENDER BENDER

When the Soviets arrived in Montreal for Game 1 of the series, their equipment was seized at the airport after a Montreal resident filed a suit claiming that his car had been damaged by Soviet tanks during the invasion of Prague in 1968. The equipment was released after Eagleson wrote a check to cover the damages.

## SHOCKER AT THE FORUM

When Phil Esposito scored 30 seconds into the opening game and then Paul Henderson scored to make it 2–0, fans were expecting a high-scoring romp

**BOXING LESSONS WERE ADDED TO TEAM USSR'S TRAINING PROGRAM.**

for Canada on the Montreal Forum ice. In the end, the Soviets proved to be a better-conditioned team that baffled the Canadians with their precision passing. The visitors led 3–2 after the first period and went on to win 7–3.

## TO BOO OR NOT TO BOO

Canada rebounded for a 4–1 win in Toronto and had to settle for a 4–4 tie in Game 3 in Winnipeg, but the final home contest in Vancouver was a disaster. The crowd at the PNE Coliseum booed the Canadian players as they stumbled to a 5–3 loss. The Soviets dominated the game, and only a late goal by Dennis Hull made the final score respectable. Phil Esposito, who was named the player of the game for Canada, was interviewed on television after the game and expressed the players' frustration

at being booed. He assured fans that the players were giving 150 percent against a very good team and ended with the promise: "We're gonna get better." The Canadian portion of the series ended with one win, two losses and a tie.

## THE BIG M'S PARANOIA

As the series shifted to the Soviet Union, Frank Mahovlich, whose parents had emigrated to Canada from Yugoslavia, was deeply suspicious of the Soviets, who were the de facto rulers of the Balkan country—and he may have been right to suspect that the Canadians' hotel rooms were bugged. Wayne Cashman believed that the Russians were using two-way mirrors to monitor the players, so he threw any reflective items in his room into the hallway. One story that was never verified concerned

## IT WAS US VERSUS THEM. AND KHARLAMOV WAS KILLING US.

players who discovered a suspicious metal plate under a carpet. When they unscrewed the plate, a lighting fixture in the room below crashed to the floor.

### THE CASE OF THE SHRINKING STEAKS

The Canadians brought their own food to Moscow, including a supply of inch-thick steaks. When the steaks were served, they were found to have been cut in half diagonally. After the players complained, at their next steak dinner they were properly served their full-size steaks—but the pieces had been cut down to ½ inch in thickness. Team Canada also brought its own beer, which disappeared on the tarmac at the Moscow airport.

### KEEPING THE WIVES HAPPY

While the Canadian players were experiencing frustration on and off the ice, the situation was no better for the wives who accompanied them to Moscow. They were originally booked into a second-class hotel, but Eagleson pulled strings to move them into the Intourist hotel, which housed the players. The wives also complained about the quality of the available food and received handouts from their husbands.

### THE FERGY FACTOR

Canada lost the first game in Moscow, 5–4, but there were no boos, as nearly 3,000 visiting Canadian fans showed their support. Canada was on the verge of defeat in the series, but the fans and a controversial incident in Game 6

changed the momentum. Bobby Clarke took a two-handed swipe at Soviet star Valeri Kharlamov's ankle. Assistant coach John Ferguson, who had been a hard-nosed enforcer in his playing days, later recalled: "I told Clarke, 'I think he needs a tap on the ankle.' I didn't think twice about it. It was Us versus Them. And Kharlamov was killing us. I mean, somebody had to do it." Kharlamov missed Game 7 and was not at his best in the final game.

### A HALL OF FAME PERFORMANCE?

Paul Henderson, who almost skipped the series because he and his wife had planned a European vacation, became a national hero when he scored the winning goal with 34 seconds remaining in Game 8, the final. Many fans believe that the goal, which was watched by an estimated 4.26 million television viewers, should have earned Henderson a place in the Hockey Hall of Fame. The selection committee hasn't shared that view, deciding that Henderson's career fell short of recognition. In a 2019 interview with CTV, Henderson said: "The worst thing they could do would be to put me in the Hall of Fame, because people get ticked off all the time, saying, 'You should be in the Hall of Fame!' and they talk about it. If I get put in, they'll forget all about me." ■

Pat Hickey has been writing about sports for 55 years. He covered the opening games of the 1972 Summit Series and is currently a hockey columnist and beat writer for the *Montreal Gazette*.

Photo: Frank Lennon/Toronto Star/Getty Image

YVAN COURNOYER (12) HUGS
PAUL HENDERSON AFTER
HENDERSON'S GOAL SEALED
CANADA'S WIN IN THE
FINAL SUMMIT SERIES GAME.

# REMAINS to BE SEEN

## BY TIM CLARK

From earliest human times, the bodies of deceased dictators, saints, philosophers, criminals, eccentrics, and beloved animals have been preserved often for the edification of future generations. Here are a few that are still on display.

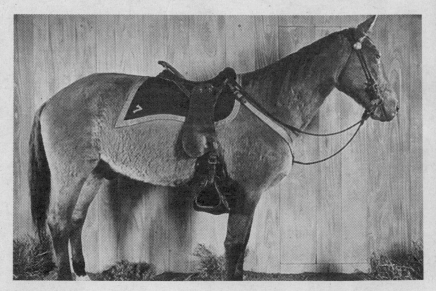

## Sole Survivor

Comanche, a horse belonging to an officer of the U.S. 7th Cavalry–the unit that was wiped out at the Little Bighorn in 1876–is often described as the sole survivor of Custer's Last Stand. It's now clear that other horses were captured or scattered by the victorious Lakota Sioux and Cheyenne warriors. But Comanche's story is the only one we know. Suffering from seven bullet wounds, he was found by U.S. troops who arrived too late to save Custer and his 210 soldiers. Nursed back to health at Ft. Abraham Lincoln in the Dakota Territory, Comanche was given the honorary title of "second-in-command" of the 7th Cavalry. Upon his death in 1890, he was given a funeral with full military honors, and his body was sent to the University of Kansas to be stuffed. It is currently on display there.

## POSTAL PUP

At the end of the 19th century, a terrier named Owney was informally adopted by the post office in Albany, New York. The employees declared him an official mail dog and let him ride the trains that delivered it across the nation. He is said to have visited all 48 contiguous states and made a 'round-the-world trip in 1895—to deliver the mail, of course. After his death in 1897, he was stuffed and displayed at the 1904 World's Fair as the mascot of the U.S. Post Office. He's still on display at the Smithsonian National Postal Museum in Washington, D.C.

# Trigger Happy

When the Roy Rogers and Dale Evans Museum closed in 2009, many of its fans wondered, "What will happen to Trigger?" Trigger, of course, was the name of several golden palomino horses that Roy Rogers (1911–98) rode in nearly 100 cowboy films and two TV series. When the original Trigger died in 1965, Rogers had him stuffed, and eventually he went on display in the museum, along with Buttermilk, the horse that his wife and co-star Dale rode, and Bullet, a German shepherd that also appeared in the films. The contents of the museum were auctioned off in 2010. The rural cable network WRFD-TV paid $266,500 for Trigger and $35,000 for Bullet. In 2019, Trigger and Bullet made their way to The Cowboy Channel TV and Live Recording Studio in the Fort Worth Stockyards, Texas.          *(continued)*

# Goofy Gophers

In the mid-1990s, folks in Torrington, Alberta (pop. approx. 200), sought to attract visitors. It was a challenge: Torrington is on the prairie, 90 minutes from Calgary. It has no hotels and only two restaurants, one a gas station that sells pizza. What Torrington had was gophers—Richardson's Ground Squirrels—that hibernate 7 months of the year and are only sporadically active when they're awake. Hearing opportunity knock, in 1996, folks opened the Gopher Hole Museum. It houses 47 dioramas of stuffed, costumed, posed gophers. Want to see gophers at the beauty parlor? This is the place.

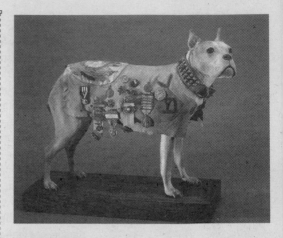

## WAR HERO

In 1917, Pvt. J. Robert Conroy found a brindle puppy on the playing fields at Yale University, where his unit, part of the 26th "Yankee" Division, was training to be deployed in World War I. Although animals were not allowed in camp, officers let "Stubby" stay and even taught him to salute. When the 26th shipped out, Stubby (named for his short tail) was smuggled on board and served as mascot for the 102nd Infantry Regiment. Stubby recognized the scent of poisonous gas and barked when he detected it. He found lost or wounded men between the lines and led them back or barked until medics arrived. After capturing a German infiltrator by biting his leg and holding on, Stubby was promoted to sergeant. Wounded by shrapnel, he visited other patients in the hospital while convalescing. He served in 17 battles, won medals for bravery, and met three presidents. When Conroy went to law school at Georgetown after the war, Stubby came along to become the university's mascot. He died in 1926, and his preserved body is in the National Museum of American History in Washington, D.C.

Photos, from left: Gopher Hole Museum; National Museum of American Histor

## Political Posers

Vladimir Ilich Lenin, father of the Soviet Revolution, died in 1924. His embalmed body rests under glass in a tomb in Moscow's Red Square, where scientists continue to work to halt its deterioration. According to Alexei Yurchak, a professor of social anthropology at the University of California-Berkeley, the Russians focus not on preserving the original body, but "substitute occasional parts of skin and flesh with plastics and other materials . . . so the body is less and less of what it used to be."

Soviet experts were also called in to preserve the bodies of Vietnam's Ho Chi Minh (d. 1969), who rests in a mausoleum in Hanoi, and father-and-son North Korean dictators Kim Il-Sung (d. 1994) and Kim Jong-Il (d. 2011) in Pyongyang.

VLADIMIR LENIN

HO CHI MINH

KIM IL-SUNG

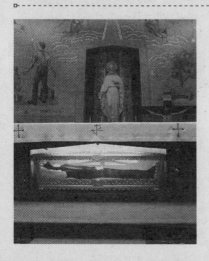

## WHOLLY DEVOTED

For centuries, devout Catholics have believed that God has preserved unchanged the bodies of saints. One "incorruptible saint" is Mother Cabrini, the first American saint. Born in Italy, Sister Frances Cabrini (1850–1917) emigrated to America and worked tirelessly in the United States on behalf of her countrymen and -women who were struggling to assimilate. Her mummified remains are visible at her chapel in Manhattan (N.Y.). *(continued)*

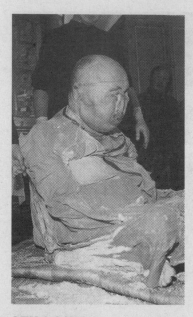

## STILL LIFE

Dashi-Dorzho Itigilov, a Russian Buddhist monk who died in 1927, had ordered his followers to bury him exactly as he was found. They followed his instructions and interred him sitting up in the lotus position of meditation. When he was exhumed 30 years later, his body was still soft and flexible. Reinterred, his body was re-exhumed in 1973, with no changes evident. After extensive study, in 2002 his body was declared a Buddhist relic and placed in Russia's Ivolginsky monastery, where it may be seen seven times a year on Buddhist holidays.

# Headmaster

Political philosopher and reformer Jeremy Bentham showed his commitment to Utilitarianism (a doctrine best summarized by his motto, "The greatest good for the greatest number") by leaving his body to the University of Edinburgh, where he taught. It can be seen today at University College London's student center, in a glass cabinet, stuffed with straw and clothed in 18th-century garments. The head on the body is not Bentham's; he had asked that it be removed from his body and mummified, but the result was so terrifying that it was replaced with a wax replica. The mummified head was placed in a box between his feet. Student pranksters once stole it and held it for ransom, which was duly paid and donated to charity, but the head was hidden away to prevent further outrages. It is now part of an exhibit called "What Does It Mean to Be Human? Curating Heads at UCL."

## HOME AT LAST

Samuel P. Dinsmoor started building his "cabin home" in Lucas, Kansas, in 1907. After construction was done, he began developing his yard into a "Garden of Eden" full of unique sculptures. The project's *pièce de résistance* was a Dinsmoor-designed concrete coffin with glass top to be placed inside the house as the permanent resting place for his remains after his demise—which occurred in 1932. After the death of his wife Emilie in 1967, the site was opened to the public as a tourist attraction. It's now on the National Register of Historic Places and receives some 10,000 visitors a year who can meet the architect of the "Garden of Eden" face to face. ∎

**Tim Clark** lives in Dublin, New Hampshire, with his wife and two dogs.

# FINE-TUNE
# YOUR FAMILY TREE

## 10 SIMPLE TIPS FOR DIGGING DOWN DEEP
## TO REACH ALL OF YOUR ROOTS

by the editors of *Family Tree* magazine

Whether you're an experienced genealogist or someone whose family tree still grows only in the imagination, these techniques for researching your past will ensure that your search is thorough and fun!

**1. GATHER WHAT YOU ALREADY KNOW ABOUT YOUR FAMILY.** Scour your basement, attic, and closets (and those of your family members!) and collect family records, old photos, letters, diaries, photocopies from family Bibles and religious books, even newspaper clippings.

**2. TALK TO YOUR RELATIVES.** Ask your parents, grandparents, aunts, and uncles about their memories. Don't ask just about facts and dates; get the stories of their growing up and of the ancestors whom they remember. Try to phrase questions with "why?," "how?," and "what?" Reach out to far-flung relatives to ask whether they have records that may be of help in your genealogy quest.

**BEST CONVERSATION STARTERS:**
Familytreemagazine.com/interviews

**3. PUT IT ON "PAPER."** Write down (physically or digitally) what you know so that you can decide what you don't yet know.

**BEST WORKSHEETS:**
Familytreemagazine.com/freeforms

**4. FOCUS YOUR SEARCH.** What are the blanks in your family tree? Don't try to fill them in all at once; focus on someone from the most recent generation where your chart is missing information. Try to answer that "mystery" first, then work backward in time.

**BEST SEARCH TIPS:**
Familytreemagazine.com/google

**5. SEARCH THE INTERNET.** The Internet is a terrific place to find leads and share information, but don't expect to "find your whole family tree" online. Check on whether your local library offers an Ancestry.com subscription free on its computers. You can also search many of the Web's biggest databases of names with one click by using "One-Step Webpages by Stephen Morse."

**BEST DATABASE FOR ANCESTRY.COM OR FAMILYSEARCH.ORG:**
stevemorse.org/      *(continued)*

**6. EXPLORE SPECIFIC WEB SITES.** Once you've searched for the surnames in your family, try Web sites specifically about your ethnic heritage or parts of the country where your relatives lived. You may even find Web sites about your family created by distant relatives researching the same family tree. A good place to start is with *Family Tree*'s international directory of more than 100 sources.

**BEST DIRECTORY:** Familytreemagazine.com/101websites

**7. DISCOVER YOUR LOCAL FAMILY HISTORY CENTER.** The Church of Jesus Christ of Latter-day Saints has more than 4,000 Family History Centers where anyone can tap the world's largest collection of genealogical information. Using your local center, you can view microfilm of records such as the birth, marriage, or death certificates of your ancestors. More than 2 million rolls of microfilmed records from all over the world are available. Compare the information in these sources with what you already know, fill in the blanks in your family tree, and look for clues to more answers to the puzzles of your past.

**BEST FAMILY HISTORY CENTER SOURCE:** Familysearch.org/locations/

**8. ORGANIZE YOUR NEW INFORMATION.** Enter your findings in family tree software programs or on paper charts. (Make sure that you note your sources!) File photocopies and notes by family, geography, or source so that you can refer to them easily. Decide what you want to focus on next.

**BEST WAYS TO CITE SOURCES:** Familytreemagazine.com/sources

**9. PLAN YOUR NEXT STEP.** Once you've exhausted your family sources, the Internet, and your Family History Center, you may want to travel to places where your ancestors lived to visit courthouses, churches, cemeteries, and other places where old records are kept. This is also a rewarding way to walk in the footsteps of your ancestors and bring your heritage to life. You'll find that the quest to discover where you came from is fun, as exciting as a detective story, and never-ending.

**BEST SOURCE FOR DIGGING DEEPER:** Pinterest.com/familytreemagazine/genealogy-for-beginners/

**10. SHARE YOUR RESEARCH.** Now that you've planted your family tree, show it off! Print family trees or start a family history Web site to share your research with loved ones. Looping others into your genealogy can help you to add more stories and family members to your research—not to mention that it's always exciting to learn more!

**BEST PLACE TO PRINT FAMILY TREES:** Familytreemagazine.com/print

Using the tips and links in this article should bring you not just a host of information, but also a great deal of satisfaction. Plus, your ancestors will be proud of you! ∎

For more information about *Family Tree* magazine and all things genealogical, go to Familytreemagazine.com.

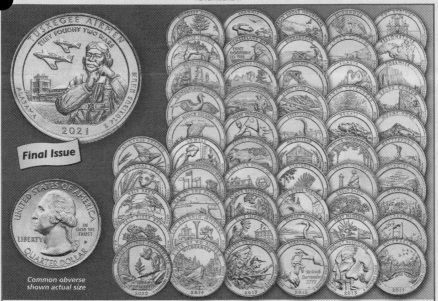
195

*(continued from page 56)*

## PUT UP YOUR POTPOURRI

Use the ingredients in one of the recipes here while following these basic directions: Measure and gently mix all of the dry ingredients in a fragrance throughout the mixture. Check the fragrance after several days and add more oil(s), if desired. Let your nose be your guide. Cure for 2 to 6 weeks, then place the mixture in glass bowls or candy dishes.

After about 3 months,

## Essential Advice

Avoid essential oils sold in clear glass or plastic bottles; buy only those in amber or other dark glass bottles. Store them in a cool, dark place, well out of the reach of children.

Before using oils from already open bottles, place a drop on a paper towel, wait a minute or two, and then sniff to evaluate. As oils age, they lose their fragrance, generally in 1 to 3 years.

Never use powdered spices in your potpourri mixtures. They quickly lose their scent and stick to glass containers.

large, nonmetallic bowl (or paper bag). Scatter drops of essential oil(s) over the mixture, stirring (or shaking) gently until thoroughly blended. Fill a widemouthed glass or ceramic jar ¾ full, cover tightly, and store in a cool, dark place. Gently shake the jar every day to distribute the the scent of the potpourri will start to diminish. Revive it by adding small amounts of essential oil, as needed. Dry potpourri seldom keeps its true scent for longer than 2 years.

## DRYING TIPS

All ingredients in a potpourri must be thoroughly dried. You don't need any fancy equipment—just air!

The secret to successfully air-drying *flowers and herbs* for maximum color retention is to dry them as quickly as possible. Gather bunches of flowers and herbs, tie them together with string in small bundles, and hang them upside down in a warm, dry, dark area—in an attic or empty closet or from the ceiling of an unused room. Air-drying times vary with the humidity, but most flowers and herbs will be dry enough to use within 7 to 15 days.

To prepare *citrus peels,* cut long, thin spirals of peel from whole fruit. Air-dry them on a baking sheet or inside a paper-towel–lined gift box for 10 to 15 days.

Using small *pinecones and evergreen sprigs?* Lay them flat on a baking sheet and dry them until the evergreen needles are brittle and the sap on the cones is dry to the touch—usually 2 to 3 weeks.

## ESSENCE-OF-ROSE POTPOURRI

3 cups mixed rose petals (pink, yellow, rose, lavender, red)
1 cup small rose blossoms
1 cup small rose leaves
½ cup statice blossoms (white)
½ cup globe amaranth blossoms (white or pale pink)
¼ cup cut orrisroot*
10 drops rose oil*

## MIXED FLOWER POTPOURRI

2 cups mixed rose petals
2 cups mixed herbs
1 cup lavender
2 cups mixed colorful blossoms
1 stick cinnamon, broken into small pieces
½ vanilla bean, chopped into small pieces
½ cup rosemary
½ cup cut orrisroot*
6 drops rose oil*
2 drops lavender oil*
2 drops carnation oil*
2 drops nutmeg oil*
1 drop lemon oil*
1 drop frankincense oil*

## SPICY BLEND POTPOURRI

½ cup orange peel
½ cup lemon peel
2 cups mixed marigold petals, chamomile flowers, scented geranium leaves (lemon and orange), globe amaranth blossoms
¼ cup broken cinnamon sticks
¼ cup whole cloves
¼ cup whole allspice
¼ cup cut orrisroot*
8 to 10 drops orange oil*

## WOODLAND POTPOURRI

½ cup bayberry leaves
½ cup globe amaranth blossoms
½ cup snipped balsam needles
½ cup miniature pinecones
½ cup rose hips
½ cup lemon verbena leaves
½ cup broken cinnamon sticks
¼ cup whole coriander
¼ cup juniper berries
¼ cup cut orrisroot*
8 to 10 drops evergreen oil*

## YOUR OWN BLEND POTPOURRI

Create your own bewitching blends using almost anything from your flower or herb garden. Use this formula as a starting point:

4 cups mixed flower petals
2 cups herbs
1 cup whole or broken spices or citrus peel
¼ cup cut orrisroot*
10 to 15 drops essential oil* ■

## Orris Origins

Orrisroot is the dried and ground rhizome of several iris species, including *Iris pallida*, an eastern Mediterranean native (also known as zebra, sweet, or Dalmatian iris) that bears an especially fragrant flower. Dried orrisroot has been used since medieval times as a fragrance fixative as well as a perceived magical medicinal. Its oil is used as a flavoring agent.

**Betty Earl** is an author, photographer, and speaker. Her books include *Fairy Gardens: A Guide to Growing an Enchanted Miniature World* (B. B. Mackey, 2012) and the forthcoming *Enchanting Miniature Gardens: Captivating Ideas for Special Occasions* (B. B. Mackey).

*(continued from page 72)*

## SPRING
# RHUBARB CHUTNEY

*Serve this tangy chutney alongside chicken or pork or as an appetizer with goat cheese and apples.*

2 cups diced rhubarb
1 tart apple, peeled and chopped
½ cup raisins
½ cup brown sugar
¼ cup apple cider vinegar
1 tablespoon lemon juice
1 teaspoon ground ginger
½ teaspoon ground cumin

Combine all of the ingredients in a heavy, nonaluminum saucepan. Bring slowly to a boil, then reduce heat and simmer for 10 minutes, or until the rhubarb and apple are very soft but still hold their shape. Do not allow them to turn into mush. Taste and adjust seasonings. Cool and chill before serving.

**Makes about 2½ cups.**

## SUMMER
# TOMATO AND STRAWBERRY SALSA

*Serve with tortilla chips or as an accompaniment to grilled fish, chicken, or pork.*

1 pint (about 12 ounces) fresh strawberries, diced
1 pint (about 10 ounces) ripe cherry or grape tomatoes, diced
1 small or medium-size jalapeño pepper, seeded and minced
1 clove garlic, minced
½ cup diced red onion
½ cup loosely packed cilantro leaves, roughly chopped
¼ cup freshly squeezed lime juice
2 tablespoons honey
½ teaspoon kosher salt

In a bowl, combine all of the ingredients. Chill in the refrigerator before serving.

**Makes about 3 cups.**

*(continued)*

Photos: Samantha Jones/Quinn Brein Communications

## SUMMER
# GARDEN PATCH POTATO SALAD

*Serve this salad at room temperature or after chilling in the refrigerator.*

1 cup fresh green
  beans, trimmed
5 small potatoes,
  peeled
1 cup fresh or frozen
  green peas
½ cup thinly sliced
  zucchini
½ cup thinly sliced
  carrot
¼ cup finely chopped
  onion
¾ cup mayonnaise
1½ teaspoons salt
⅛ teaspoon freshly
  ground black pepper
chives, for garnish

In a pot of salted water, simmer green beans until just tender and bright green, about 3 to 5 minutes. Reserving the cooking liquid, remove beans and transfer to a bowl of ice water to stop cooking, then drain.

Add potatoes to cooking water and simmer until tender, about 12 minutes. Remove potatoes with a slotted spoon, then slice them.

Add peas to cooking water and simmer until tender, about 2 to 3 minutes.

In a bowl, combine zucchini, carrots, and onions with beans, potatoes, and peas. Add mayonnaise, salt, and pepper and stir to coat vegetables. Garnish with chives.

**Makes 8 servings.** ■

---

*(continued from page 78)*

## HONORABLE MENTION
# CHICKPEA, ORZO, RAISIN, AND CARROT SALAD
# IN FIG BALSAMIC VINEGAR

1 can (15 ounces) chickpeas, drained and rinsed
1 cup cooked orzo
1 cup freshly grated carrots
⅓ cup fig balsamic vinegar
¼ cup raisins (softened in warm water if hard)
2 grinds fresh black pepper
¼ teaspoon salt

In a large bowl, combine all ingredients.

Place in the refrigerator and chill for at least 1 hour.

**Makes 4 to 6 servings.**

*–Susan Skrtich,*
*Hamilton, Ontario* ■

Photo: Samantha Jones/Quinn Brein Communications

# HOW WE PREDICT THE WEATHER

We derive our weather forecasts from a secret formula that was devised by the founder of this Almanac, Robert B. Thomas, in 1792. Thomas believed that weather on Earth was influenced by sunspots, which are magnetic storms on the surface of the Sun.

Over the years, we have refined and enhanced this formula with state-of-the-art technology and modern scientific calculations. We employ three scientific disciplines to make our long-range predictions: solar science, the study of sunspots and other solar activity; climatology, the study of prevailing weather patterns; and meteorology, the study of the atmosphere. We predict weather trends and events by comparing solar patterns and historical weather conditions with current solar activity.

Our forecasts emphasize temperature and precipitation deviations from averages, or normals. These are based on 30-year statistical averages prepared by government meteorological agencies and updated every 10 years. Our forecasts are based on the tabulations that span the period 1981 through 2010.

The borders of the 16 weather regions of the contiguous states (page 205) are based primarily on climatology and the movement of weather systems. For example, while the average weather in Richmond, Virginia, and Boston, Massachusetts, is very different (although both are in Region 2), both areas tend to be affected by the same storms and high-pressure centers and have weather deviations from normal that are similar.

We believe that nothing in the universe happens haphazardly, that there is a cause-and-effect pattern to all phenomena. However, although neither we nor any other forecasters have as yet gained sufficient insight into the mysteries of the universe to predict the weather with total accuracy, our results are almost always very close to our traditional claim of 80%.

# WEATHER PHOBIAS

| FEAR OF | PHOBIA |
| --- | --- |
| Clouds | Nephophobia |
| Cold | Cheimatophobia<br>Frigophobia<br>Psychrophobia |
| Dampness, moisture | Hygrophobia |
| Daylight, sunshine | Heliophobia<br>Phengophobia |
| Extreme cold, frost, ice | Cryophobia<br>Pagophobia |
| Floods | Antlophobia |
| Fog | Homichlophobia<br>Nebulaphobia |
| Heat | Thermophobia |
| Hurricanes, tornadoes | Lilapsophobia |
| Lightning, thunder | Astraphobia<br>Brontophobia<br>Keraunophobia |
| Northern lights, southern lights | Auroraphobia |
| Rain | Ombrophobia<br>Pluviophobia |
| Snow | Chionophobia |
| Thunder | Ceraunophobia<br>Tonitrophobia |
| Wind | Ancraophobia<br>Anemophobia |

# HOW ACCURATE WAS OUR FORECAST LAST WINTER?

Our overall accuracy rate in forecasting the direction of the change in temperature compared with the previous winter season across the 18 regions of the United States was 72.2%, while our accuracy rate in forecasting the change in precipitation was 77.8%. So, our overall accuracy rate was 75%, which is slightly below our traditional average rate of 80%. Our temperature forecasts were incorrect for the Intermountain, Desert Southwest, and Pacific Southwest regions. We also count the Northeast and Hawaii as "misses," even though in these regions we came infinitesimally close to predicting the proper temperature trends. In precipitation, we were correct in all regions except for the Southeast, Lower Lakes, Heartland, and Intermountain.

Our forecast that snowfall would be greater than normal in the Northeast was close, but the actual area was from Connecticut to Philadelphia. We were also close in forecasting above-normal snowfall in Wisconsin, with the actual area from southern Wisconsin to Chicago. Our forecasts of above-normal snowfall in the High Plains and northern Alaska were correct. Upper Michigan had mostly below-normal snowfall, despite our forecast for above, while the northern Ohio Valley, portions of the Deep South and Texas, from Omaha to Des Moines, and portions of Washington and Idaho had more snow than we forecast. In most other areas, our forecast of below-normal snowfall was correct.

The table below shows how the actual average temperature differed from our forecast for November through March for one city in each region. On average, these actual winter temperatures differed from our forecasts by 0.68 degree F.

| REGION/ CITY | Nov.-Mar. Temp Variations From Normal (degrees) PREDICTED | ACTUAL | REGION/ CITY | Nov.-Mar. Temp Variations From Normal (degrees) PREDICTED | ACTUAL |
|---|---|---|---|---|---|
| 1. Albany, NY | 0.0 | 0.5 | 10. St. Louis, MO | 3.9 | 2.4 |
| 2. Boston, MA | 1.6 | 1.9 | 11. San Antonio, TX | 2.2 | 0.9 |
| 3. Asheville, NC | 2.0 | 2.0 | 12. Rapid City, SD | 2.2 | 1.4 |
| 4. Raleigh, NC | 1.0 | 0.9 | 13. Reno, NV | –0.3 | 0.0 |
| 5. Orlando, FL | 0.4 | 1.5 | 14. Albuquerque, NM | –0.8 | 0.5 |
| 6. Detroit, MI | 2.3 | 2.3 | 15. Seattle, WA | 0.2 | 0.7 |
| 7. Cincinnati, OH | 2.1 | 1.7 | 16. Los Angeles, CA | –0.8 | 0.3 |
| 8. Jackson, MS | 1.5 | 1.5 | 17. Juneau, AK | 0.8 | 0.9 |
| 9. Minneapolis, MN | 2.1 | 3.1 | 18. Honolulu, HI | 0.0 | 1.9 |

# WEATHER REGIONS

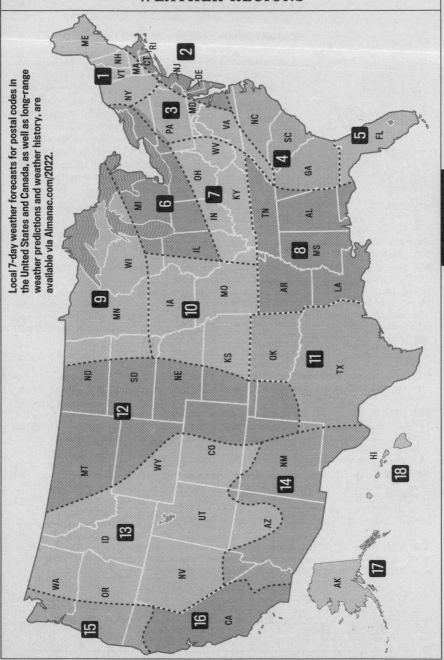

Local 7-day weather forecasts for postal codes in the United States and Canada, as well as long-range weather predictions and weather history, are available via Almanac.com/2022.

WEATHER

Illustrations of U.S. map and regional maps 1–16: Rob Schuster

**SUMMARY: Winter** will be colder than normal, on average, with near- to below-normal snowfall. Precipitation will be above normal in the north and below normal in the south. The coldest periods will be in early December, early to mid- and late January, and mid-February, with the snowiest periods in mid- to late December, early January, and early and mid-February. **April** and **May** will be warmer and drier than normal. **Summer** temperatures will be slightly cooler than normal, on average, with above-normal rainfall. The hottest periods will be in early to mid-July and mid- to late August. **September** and **October** will bring temperatures below normal in the north and above normal in the south and be rainier than normal.

**NOV. 2021:** Temp. 36° (4° below avg.); precip. 2.5" (1" below avg.). 1–7 Snow showers, cold. 8–11 Sunny, cold. 12–18 Flurries, cold. 19–21 Showers, mild. 22–29 Snow, then flurries, cold. 30 Rain to snow.

**DEC. 2021:** Temp. 25° (3° below avg.); precip. 3" (1" above avg. north, 1" below south). 1–7 Snow showers, very cold. 8–10 Sunny, mild. 11–18 Snow showers, cold. 19–25 Snowy periods, cold. 26–31 Snow showers; cold north, mild south.

**JAN. 2022:** Temp. 19° (4° below avg.); precip. 3" (1" above avg. north, 1" below south). 1–2 Sunny, cold. 3–12 Snowstorm, then flurries, frigid. 13–17 Snow showers, cold. 18–22 Periods of rain and snow, mild. 23–31 Snow showers, cold.

**FEB. 2022:** Temp. 26° (3° above avg.); precip. 3.5" (1" above avg.). 1–5 Snow showers, turning mild. 6–12 Snowstorm, then flurries, cold. 13–17 Snowstorm, then sunny, cold. 18–28 Periods of rain and snow, mild.

**MAR. 2022:** Temp. 40° (6° above avg.); precip. 4" (1" above avg.). 1–5 Sunny, quite warm. 6–11 Rainy periods, turning colder. 12–18 Periods of rain and snow, cold. 19–24 Rainy periods, warm. 25–31 Periods of rain and snow, chilly.

**APR. 2022:** Temp. 48° (2° above avg.); precip. 2" (1" below avg.). 1–4 Rain and snow showers, chilly. 5–12 T-storms, then sunny, mild.

13–17 Showers, warm. 18–26 A few showers, cool. 27–30 Sunny, warm.

**MAY 2022:** Temp. 57° (2° above avg.); precip. 2.5" (1" below avg.). 1–8 Showers, cool. 9–17 Sunny, turning hot. 18–22 A few showers, cool. 23–24 Sunny, warm. 25–31 Rainy periods, cool.

**JUNE 2022:** Temp. 64° (1° below avg.); precip. 3.5" (1" above avg. north, 1" below south). 1–8 Showers; cool, then warm. 9–15 Showers, cool. 16–23 Scattered showers, warm. 24–30 Sunny, cool.

**JULY 2022:** Temp. 71° (1° above avg.); precip. 5" (1" above avg.). 1–6 Scattered t-storms, cool. 7–12 Sunny, turning hot. 13–23 Scattered t-storms, cool. 24–31 T-storms, warm.

**AUG. 2022:** Temp. 65° (1° above avg.); precip. 5" (1" above avg.). 1–9 Scattered t-storms, cool. 10–19 A few showers, cool. 20–22 Sunny, hot. 23–27 A few t-storms, warm. 28–31 Showers, cool.

**SEPT. 2022:** Temp. 57.5° (3° below avg. north, avg. south); precip. 6" (2" above avg.). 1–4 Sunny, cool. 5–9 Showers, cool. 10–19 Rainy periods, cool. 20–22 T-storms, then sunny, cool. 23–30 Rainy periods, cool.

**OCT. 2022:** Temp. 50° (2° above avg.); precip. 4.5" (1" above avg.). 1–3 Rainy periods, warm. 4–10 Showers, cool. 11–15 A few showers, warm. 16–27 Sunny, warm. 28–31 Rainy periods, mild.

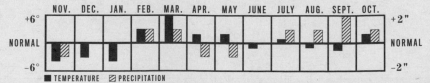

# ATLANTIC CORRIDOR

**SUMMARY: Winter** temperatures and precipitation will be below normal, on average, with above-normal snowfall in the north and below-normal in the south. The coldest periods will be in early, mid-, and late December; mid-January; and early to mid-February. The snowiest periods will occur in mid- and late December, from early to mid-January, and in mid-March. **April** and **May** will be warmer than normal, with rainfall near normal in the north and below normal in the south. **Summer** will be hotter and slightly drier than normal, with the hottest periods in mid-June and early to mid-July, from late July into early August, and in late August. **September** and **October** will bring temperatures near normal in the north and above normal in the south and be rainier than normal.

**WEATHER**

**NOV. 2021:** Temp. 42° (5° below avg.); precip. 2" (2" below avg. north, avg. south). 1–8 Rain and snow showers, cold. 9–18 Sunny, cool. 19–21 Rainy, mild. 22–28 Flurries north, sunny south; cold. 29–30 Rainy, mild.

**DEC. 2021:** Temp. 35° (4° below avg.); precip. 3.5" (1" below avg.). 1–3 Sunny, cold. 4–8 Rain to snow, then sunny, cold. 9–17 Rainy periods, cool. 18–28 Snowy periods, cold. 29–31 Snowstorm.

**JAN. 2022:** Temp. 29° (6° below avg.); precip. 2.5" (1" below avg.). 1–6 Rain to snow, then snow showers, cold. 7–15 Snowstorm, then sunny, very cold. 16–21 Snow showers north, sunny south; cold. 22–26 Sunny, cold. 27–31 Rain and snow showers.

**FEB. 2022:** Temp. 38° (4° above avg.); precip. 2" (1" below avg.). 1–7 Sunny, mild. 8–14 Snow showers, cold. 15–26 Rainy periods, mild. 27–28 Sunny, mild.

**MAR. 2022:** Temp. 49° (5° above avg.); precip. 5" (2" above avg. north, avg. south). 1–5 Sunny, warm. 6–9 Rainy periods, mild. 10–16 Heavy snow, then rain north; rain south. 17–19 Sunny, cold. 20–24 Showers, warm. 25–31 Rainy periods, turning cool.

**APR. 2022:** Temp. 57° (5° above avg.); precip. 2.5" (1" below avg.). 1–3 Showers, cool. 4–15 Sunny, warm. 16–21 Rainy, turning cooler. 22–30 A few t-storms, warm.

**MAY 2022:** Temp. 64° (2° above avg.); precip. 2.5" (1" above avg. north, 2" below south). 1–3 Heavy rain north, sunny south; cool. 4–10 Sunny, turning hot. 11–19 Showers, cool, then sunny, hot. 20–31 Scattered t-storms, cool.

**JUNE 2022:** Temp. 72° (1° above avg.); precip. 2.5" (1" below avg.). 1–4 Rainy periods, cool. 5–10 Showers, mild. 11–13 Sunny, hot. 14–26 Scattered t-storms, warm. 27–30 T-storms; hot, then cool.

**JULY 2022:** Temp. 78° (2° above avg.); precip. 4" (avg.). 1–5 A few t-storms; cool north, hot south. 6–14 Scattered t-storms, hot. 15–17 Sunny, warm. 18–22 T-storms, then sunny, cool. 23–31 A few t-storms, hot.

**AUG. 2022:** Temp. 76° (2° above avg.); precip. 4" (avg.). 1–10 A few t-storms, hot. 11–14 Sunny, cool. 15–19 Rain, then sunny, cool. 20–22 Sunny, hot. 23–31 Scattered t-storms, hot.

**SEPT. 2022:** Temp. 67.5° (1° below avg. north, 2° above south); precip. 3.5" (2" above avg. north, 2" below south). 1–9 Rainy periods, cool. 10–12 Scattered t-storms, warm. 13–18 Rainy, cool north; sunny, warm south. 19–25 A few t-storms, warm. 26–30 Sunny, cool.

**OCT. 2022:** Temp. 57° (1° above avg.); precip. 5" (avg. north, 3" above south). 1–2 Heavy rain, cool. 3–13 Rainy periods, cool. 14–18 Sunny, warm. 19–21 T-storms, warm. 22–26 Sunny, cool. 27–31 Rainy, warm.

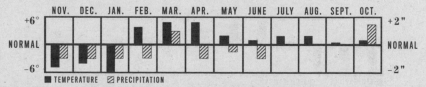

# APPALACHIANS

Elmira
Scranton
Harrisburg
Frederick
Roanoke
Asheville

**SUMMARY: Winter** will be colder and drier than normal, with near-normal snowfall. The coldest periods will be in early, mid-, and late December; through much of January; and in early and mid-February. The snowiest periods will be in early December, early January, and mid-February. **April** and **May** will be warmer and drier than normal, with an early hot spell in early to mid-May. **Summer** will be hotter and drier than normal, with the hottest periods in early and mid- to late August. **September** and **October** will bring near-normal temperatures and be rainier than normal.

**NOV. 2021:** Temp. 39° (5° below avg.); precip. 2.5" (1" below avg.). 1–6 Rain and snow showers, chilly. 7–12 Sunny, mild. 13–18 Flurries, cold. 19–21 Rainy periods, warm. 22–28 Flurries, cold. 29–30 Rainy, mild.

**DEC. 2021:** Temp. 32° (4° below avg.); precip. 2" (1" below avg.). 1–3 Snow, then flurries, cold. 4–7 Rain, then flurries, cold. 8–9 Showers, mild. 10–22 Snow showers, cold. 23–25 Flurries, frigid. 26–31 Snow showers, cold.

**JAN. 2022:** Temp. 25° (5° below avg.); precip. 1" (1.5" below avg.). 1–6 Snow, then flurries, cold. 7–12 Snow, then sunny, frigid. 13–20 Snow showers, cold. 21–25 Sunny, frigid. 26–31 Snow showers; mild, then cold.

**FEB. 2022:** Temp. 31° (1° above avg.); precip. 2" (0.5" below avg.). 1–2 Flurries, cold. 3–7 Rain and snow showers, mild. 8–11 Flurries, cold. 12–15 Snow, then sunny, cold. 16–20 Rainy periods, mild. 21–24 Sunny, cold. 25–28 Rainy, mild.

**MAR. 2022:** Temp. 45° (5° above avg.); precip. 5.5" (2.5" above avg.). 1–4 Sunny, warm. 5–9 Rainy, mild. 10–16 Snow, cold north; rain, mild south. 17–20 Sunny, cool. 21–24 Showers, warm. 25–31 Rainy periods, cool.

**APR. 2022:** Temp. 55° (5° above avg.); precip. 2" (0.5" below avg.). 1–7 Sunny; cool, then warm. 8–15 Sunny, turning very warm. 16–21 Rainy periods, cool. 22–24 Sunny, warm. 25–30 Showers, warm.

**MAY 2022:** Temp. 61° (1° above avg.); pre-cip. 3.5" (1" below avg.). 1–2 Rainy, cool. 3–10 Sunny, turning hot. 11–18 Scattered t-storms, warm. 19–21 Sunny, warm. 22–29 Scattered t-storms, cool. 30–31 Rainy, chilly.

**JUNE 2022:** Temp. 67° (avg.); precip. 3" (1" below avg.). 1–5 Rainy periods, cool. 6–13 A few t-storms, turning warm. 14–21 Rainy periods, cool. 22–25 Sunny, warm. 26–30 Rainy, cool north; sunny, hot south.

**JULY 2022:** Temp. 75° (2° above avg.); precip. 3.5" (avg.). 1–6 Scattered t-storms, warm. 7–9 Sunny, hot. 10–18 Scattered t-storms; hot, then cool. 19–23 Sunny, cool. 24–31 A few t-storms, warm north; sunny, hot south.

**AUG. 2022:** Temp. 75° (2° above avg.); precip. 3" (0.5" below avg.). 1–4 Scattered t-storms, hot. 5–10 A few t-storms; cool north, hot south. 11–19 Scattered showers, cool. 20–23 Sunny, hot. 24–31 Scattered t-storms; warm north, hot south.

**SEPT. 2022:** Temp. 63° (1° below avg.); pre-cip. 4" (2" above avg. north, 1" below south). 1–6 Showers, then sunny, cool. 7–12 T-storms, turning warm. 13–20 Rainy periods, cool north; sunny, warm south. 21–30 Showers, cool.

**OCT. 2022:** Temp. 54° (1° above avg.); pre-cip. 5" (1" above avg. north, 3" above south). 1–5 Rain, then sunny, cool. 6–10 Rainy, cool. 11–17 Showers, mild. 18–22 Sunny north, rain south; mild. 23–25 Sunny, cool. 26–31 Rainy periods, mild.

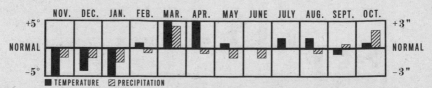

# SOUTHEAST

**SUMMARY:** Winter temperatures will be below normal, on average, with the coldest periods in mid- and late December, throughout much of January, and in early to mid-February. Precipitation will be below normal in the north and above normal in the south. Snowfall will be near normal, with the best chances for snow in mid- to late January and early to mid-February. **April** and **May** will be warmer than normal, with rainfall below normal in the north and above normal in the south. **Summer** will be hotter and drier than normal, with the hottest periods in mid- and late June and early and late July. Watch for a tropical storm in mid- to late August. **September** and **October** will be a bit cooler than normal, with rainfall above normal in the north and below normal in the south. Watch for a hurricane in mid-September.

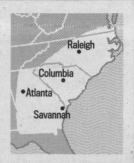

WEATHER

**NOV. 2021:** Temp. 51° (4° below avg.); precip. 4.5" (avg. north, 3" above south). 1–3 Sunny, cold. 4–9 Rainy, chilly. 10–18 Sunny, cold. 19–22 Rainy periods, mild. 23–28 Sunny, cold. 29–30 Heavy rain.

**DEC. 2021:** Temp. 44° (3° below avg.); precip. 4.5" (1" above avg.). 1–3 Rain, then sunny, cold. 4–9 Rainy periods. 10–12 Sunny, mild. 13–17 Rain, then sunny, cold. 18–24 Rainy periods, chilly. 25–27 Sunny, cold. 28–31 Rainy periods, cold.

**JAN. 2022:** Temp. 38° (6° below avg.); precip. 2.5" (2" below avg.). 1–7 Rainy periods, cold. 8–16 Sunny, cold. 17–24 Rain and snow showers, cold. 25–31 Sunny, cold.

**FEB. 2022:** Temp. 48° (2° above avg.); precip. 4.5" (0.5" above avg.). 1–4 Sunny, turning mild. 5–8 Rainy periods, mild. 9–11 Snow showers, cold. 12–15 Sunny, cold. 16–20 Rainy periods, warm. 21–24 Sunny, cold. 25–28 Rainy, cool.

**MAR. 2022:** Temp. 60° (5° above avg.); precip. 4.5" (avg.). 1–6 A few t-storms, turning warm. 7–12 Sunny, warm. 13–15 Rainy, cool. 16–20 Sunny, cool. 21–31 Rainy periods, warm.

**APR. 2022:** Temp. 68° (5° above avg.); precip. 1.5" (1.5" below avg.). 1–11 Sunny; cool, then warm. 12–20 Scattered showers, turning cool. 21–30 Scattered t-storms, turning warm.

**MAY 2022:** Temp. 71° (avg.); precip. 4" (1" below avg. north, 2" above south). 1–11 Sunny; cool, then hot. 12–19 A few t-storms, warm. 20–31 Isolated t-storms, warm.

**JUNE 2022:** Temp. 79° (1° above avg.); precip. 2.5" (2" below avg.). 1–13 Scattered t-storms; cool, then hot. 14–18 T-storms, then sunny, cool. 19–30 Scattered t-storms, hot.

**JULY 2022:** Temp. 83° (1° above avg.); precip. 3.5" (1" below avg.). 1–3 Scattered t-storms, hot. 4–10 Sunny, hot. 11–19 Isolated t-storms, turning cooler. 20–22 Heavy rain, cool. 23–31 A few t-storms, turning hot.

**AUG. 2022:** Temp. 81° (1° above avg.); precip. 4.5" (0.5" below avg.). 1–11 A few t-storms, warm. 12–22 Sunny north, t-storms south; warm. 23–25 Tropical storm threat. 26–31 A few t-storms, warm.

**SEPT. 2022:** Temp. 74.5° (0.5° above avg.); precip. 3.5" (avg. north, 2" below south). 1–6 Rain, then sunny, cool. 7–10 T-storms, warm. 11–15 Hurricane threat. 16–23 Sunny north, t-storms south; warm. 24–30 T-storms, then sunny, cool.

**OCT. 2022:** Temp. 63° (1° below avg.); precip. 5.5" (3" above avg. north, avg. south). 1–7 Rainy periods, chilly. 8–17 Sunny, cool. 18–22 Rainy periods, warm. 23–31 A few t-storms, warm.

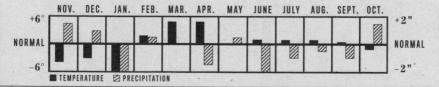

# FLORIDA

Jacksonville

Orlando

Tampa

Miami

**SUMMARY: Winter** will be cooler than normal, with the coldest temperatures in mid- and late December and mid-January and from late January into early February. Precipitation will be above normal in the north and below normal in the south. **April** and **May** will be slightly cooler than normal, on average, with near-normal rainfall in the north and well above-normal rainfall in the south. **Summer** will be hotter and slightly drier than normal, with the hottest periods in mid-June, early and late July, and early to mid-August. **September** and **October** will be slightly warmer and much drier than normal, with the hottest period in early September.

**NOV. 2021:** Temp. 66° (5° below avg. north, 1° below south); precip. 2.3" (1" above avg. north, 1.5" below south). 1–4 Sunny, cool. 5–10 Rainy periods; cool north, warm south. 11–14 Showers, warm. 15–18 Sunny, chilly. 19–27 A few showers; warm, then chilly. 28–30 Rainy, mild.

**DEC. 2021:** Temp. 62° (1° below avg.); precip. 4.5" (3" above avg. north, avg. south). 1–3 Showers, cool. 4–13 Showers, warm. 14–20 Rainy periods, cool. 21–31 Showers, cool.

**JAN. 2022:** Temp. 55° (5° below avg.); precip. 2.5" (avg.). 1–2 Sunny, cool. 3–9 Rainy periods, mild. 10–16 Sunny, cold. 17–25 Rainy periods, chilly. 26–31 T-storms, then sunny, cool.

**FEB. 2022:** Temp. 60° (1° below avg.); precip. 2" (0.5" below avg.). 1–9 Sunny north, showers south; cool. 10–16 Sunny, cool. 17–20 Showers, warm. 21–24 Sunny, cool. 25–28 Rainy, warm.

**MAR. 2022:** Temp. 71° (4° above avg.); precip. 1" (2" below avg.). 1–12 T-storms, then sunny, warm. 13–19 Showers, then sunny, cool. 20–28 Sunny, warm. 29–31 Showers.

**APR. 2022:** Temp. 71° (avg.); precip. 4" (1" below avg. north, 4" above south). 1–9 Sunny north, t-storms south; cool. 10–13 Sunny, warm. 14–17 T-storms, warm. 18–25 Sunny, mild. 26–30 T-storms, warm.

**MAY 2022:** Temp. 76° (1° below avg.); precip. 7" (1" above avg. north, 5" above south). 1–15 Rain, then sunny, warm. 16–22 Rainy periods, warm. 23–31 T-storms, warm.

**JUNE 2022:** Temp. 84° (2° above avg.); precip. 3.5" (3" below avg.). 1–3 Sunny, warm. 4–12 Scattered t-storms, hot. 13–23 Scattered t-storms, north, sunny south; hot. 24–30 A few t-storms, warm.

**JULY 2022:** Temp. 84° (1° above avg.); precip. 5.5" (1" below avg.). 1–6 Sunny, hot. 7–18 Scattered t-storms, warm. 19–22 Sunny, hot. 23–31 Daily t-storms, hot.

**AUG. 2022:** Temp. 82.5° (0.5° above avg.); precip. 10.5" (3" above avg.). 1–4 Sunny north, t-storms south; warm. 5–14 A few t-storms, hot. 15–21 Sunny north, t-storms south; warm. 22–31 A few t-storms, warm.

**SEPT. 2022:** Temp. 81.5° (1.5° above avg.); precip. 2.5" (3" below avg.). 1–7 Sunny, hot. 8–14 A few t-storms, warm. 15–21 Sunny, hot north; t-storms, warm south. 22–30 Sunny, turning cool.

**OCT. 2022:** Temp. 74° (1° below avg.); precip. 2" (2" below avg.). 1–5 Scattered showers, warm. 6–13 Sunny, chilly. 14–19 Rainy periods, mild. 20–27 A few showers north, sunny south; cool. 28–31 Showers, warm.

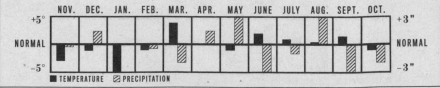

# LOWER LAKES

**SUMMARY: Winter** will be colder and drier than normal, with the coldest temperatures in mid- to late November, through most of December and January, and in early to mid-February. Snowfall will be near normal in most areas, although a few places south of the Lakes will have much-above-normal snowfall. The snowiest periods will be in late November, mid- and late December, early and mid- to late January, early to mid-February, and mid-March. **April** and **May** will be much warmer and slightly drier than normal. **Summer** will be warmer and slightly rainier than normal, with the hottest periods in mid- and late June, early to mid-July, and mid-August. **September** and **October** will be warmer and rainier than normal.

WEATHER

**NOV. 2021:** Temp. 36° (5° below avg.); precip. 1" (1.5" below avg.). 1–5 Snow showers, cold. 6–10 Sunny, cold. 11–17 Snow showers, cold. 18–20 Showers, mild. 21–28 Lake snows, very cold. 29–30 Rain and snow showers.

**DEC. 2021:** Temp. 28° (4° below avg.); precip. 1.5" (1.5" below avg.). 1–7 Snow showers, cold. 8–13 Rain and snow showers, mild. 14–20 Lake snows, cold. 21–24 Snow showers, very cold. 25–31 Snowy periods, cold.

**JAN. 2022:** Temp. 20° (7° below avg.); precip. 1.5" (1" below avg.). 1–6 Lake snows, very cold. 7–11 Snowy periods; mild, then very cold. 12–16 Snow showers, cold. 17–24 Snowy periods; mild, then very cold. 25–31 Snowy periods; mild, then cold.

**FEB. 2022:** Temp. 29° (2° above avg.); precip. 2.5" (1" below avg. east, 2" above west). 1–6 Rain and snow showers, mild. 7–14 Lake snows, cold. 15–19 Rainy periods, mild. 20–28 Flurries, cold, then showers, mild.

**MAR. 2022:** Temp. 45° (7° above avg.); precip. 3.5" (0.5" above avg.). 1–4 Sunny, warm. 5–9 Rainy periods, warm. 10–17 Snowy periods, cold. 18–23 Rainy periods, turning warm. 24–31 Snow showers, cold east; rainy, mild west.

**APR. 2022:** Temp. 55° (7° above avg.); precip. 3.5" (avg.). 1–6 Sunny, turning warm. 7–14 Showers, warm. 15–18 Rainy, cool. 19–24 Sunny; chilly, then warm. 25–30 Rainy periods, turning cool.

**MAY 2022:** Temp. 62° (2° above avg. east, 6° above west); precip. 2" (1.5" below avg.). 1–7 Sunny, cool. 8–17 Scattered showers, turning hot. 18–23 Sunny, cooler east; a few showers, warm west. 24–31 Scattered t-storms, turning cool.

**JUNE 2022:** Temp. 67° (1° above avg.); precip. 3.5" (avg.). 1–7 Sunny east, a few t-storms west; cool. 8–16 Scattered t-storms; warm, then cool. 17–21 A few t-storms, hot. 22–30 Scattered t-storms; cool, then hot.

**JULY 2022:** Temp. 72.5° (2° above avg.); precip. 3.5" (avg.). 1–14 A few t-storms, turning hot. 15–21 T-storms, then sunny. cool. 22–31 T-storms, warm.

**AUG. 2022:** Temp. 69° (avg.); precip. 5" (1" above avg.). 1–8 T-storms, cool. 9–13 Sunny, cool. 14–17 T-storms, cool. 18–21 Sunny, turning hot. 22–31 Scattered t-storms, warm.

**SEPT. 2022:** Temp. 62° (avg.); precip. 7" (2.5" above avg.). 1–5 Sunny, turning cool. 6–13 Rainy periods, turning warm. 14–20 A few t-storms; cool, then warm. 21–30 Showers, cool.

**OCT. 2022:** Temp. 55° (3° above avg.); precip. 2" (0.5" below avg.). 1–11 Showers, cool. 12–20 Sunny, turning warm. 21–24 Scattered showers, mild. 25–31 Rainy periods, warm.

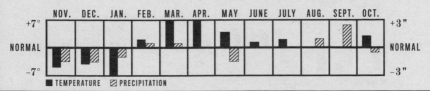

# OHIO VALLEY

**SUMMARY: Winter** will be colder than normal, with below-normal precipitation but above-normal snowfall, especially in the west. The coldest periods will occur in mid- to late November and through much of the period from mid-December through January. The snowiest periods will arrive in mid-December, early and mid-January, and mid- to late February. **April** and **May** will be much warmer than normal, with below-normal precipitation. **Summer** will be slightly cooler and drier than normal in the east, with above-normal temperatures and rainfall in the west. The hottest periods will be in late June, early to mid-July, and early August. **September** and **October** will be warmer than normal, with normal precipitation.

**NOV. 2021:** Temp. 39° (7° below avg.); precip. 2.5" (1" below avg.). 1–12 Rain and snow showers, then sunny, cold. 13–18 Snow showers, cold. 19–28 Rain to snow, then flurries, very cold. 29–30 Rainy, mild.

**DEC. 2021:** Temp. 32° (5° below avg.); precip. 1.5" (1.5" below avg.). 1–5 Rain and snow showers; cold, then mild. 6–11 Sunny, mild. 12–19 Rain to snow, then snow showers, cold. 20–31 Snowy periods, cold.

**JAN. 2022:** Temp. 24° (9° below avg.); precip. 2" (1" below avg.). 1–6 Snow, then flurries, bitter cold. 7–16 Snowy periods, cold. 17–24 Snowstorm, then flurries, frigid. 25–31 Snow showers, cold.

**FEB. 2022:** Temp. 35° (1° above avg.); precip. 2" (1" below avg.). 1–4 Sunny, turning mild. 5–14 Rain to snow, then flurries, cold. 15–20 Showers, warm. 21–28 Snow, then showers, turning mild.

**MAR. 2022:** Temp. 50° (5° above avg.); precip. 6" (2" above avg.). 1–4 Sunny, warm. 5–9 Showers, warm. 10–16 Rainy periods, cool. 17–19 Sunny, cool. 20–28 Rainy periods, mild. 29–31 Rain to snow.

**APR. 2022:** Temp. 62° (7° above avg.); precip. 1.5" (avg. east, 1" below west). 1–9 Sunny, turning warm. 10–16 T-storms, warm. 17–23 Showers, cool. 24–30 Rainy periods, warm.

**MAY 2022:** Temp. 66° (3° above avg.); precip. 1.5" (2" below avg.). 1–5 Sunny, cool. 6–17 Isolated t-storms, warm. 18–25 Sunny, warm. 26–31 Rainy periods, cool.

**JUNE 2022:** Temp. 71° (1° below avg.); precip. 5" (avg. east, 2" above west). 1–2 Rainy, cool. 3–13 A few t-storms, turning warm. 14–23 Scattered t-storms, cool. 24–31 A few t-storms, turning hot.

**JULY 2022:** Temp. 76° (1° below avg. east, 3° above west); precip. 4" (avg.). 1–5 A few t-storms, warm. 6–14 Sun, then scattered t-storms; hot. 15–24 Showers, cool. 25–31 Scattered t-storms, turning warm.

**AUG. 2022:** Temp. 74° (1° above avg.); precip. 4.5" (1" below avg. east, 2" above west). 1–9 A few t-storms, very warm. 10–13 Sunny, cool. 14–19 Showers, then sunny, cool. 20–31 Scattered t-storms, warm.

**SEPT. 2022:** Temp. 68° (1° above avg.); precip. 3" (avg.). 1–6 Showers, mild. 7–13 Rainy periods; cool, then warm. 14–16 Sunny. 17–24 Scattered t-storms, warm. 25–30 Showers, cool.

**OCT. 2022:** Temp. 59° (2° above avg.); precip. 2.5" (avg.). 1–12 Showers, cool. 13–17 Sunny, warm. 18–26 T-storms, then sunny, warm. 27–31 T-storms, warm.

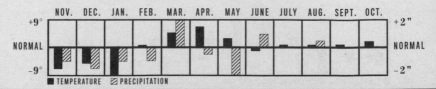

# DEEP SOUTH

**SUMMARY: Winter** will be colder than normal, on average, with the coldest periods in mid-December, early and mid- to late January, and early to mid-February. Rainfall will be near normal in the north and above normal in the south, with the best threats for snow in the north from late December into early January and in mid- to late January. **April** and **May** will be much warmer than normal, with below-normal rainfall. **Summer** will be hotter and rainier than normal, with the hottest periods in late June, early July, and mid-August. Watch for a tropical storm in mid- to late July. **September** and **October** will bring near-normal temperatures and be rainier than normal. Watch for a tropical storm in late October.

**WEATHER**

**NOV. 2021:** Temp. 49° (avg. north, 6° below south); precip. 5" (2" below avg. north, 2" above south). 1–3 Sunny, chilly. 4–13 Rainy periods, cool. 14–18 Sunny, cold. 19–26 Rain, then sunny, cold. 27–30 Rainy, cool.

**DEC. 2021:** Temp. 45° (3° below avg.); precip. 6.5" (2" below avg. north, 5" above south). 1–2 Sunny, cold. 3–5 Rainy, mild. 6–11 Sunny north, rainy periods south. 12–17 Rain, then sunny, cold. 18–21 Showers, mild. 22–26 Rain to snow. 27–31 Rain and snow north, rain south.

**JAN. 2022:** Temp. 37° (8° below avg.); precip. 5" (avg.). 1–5 Snow north, rain south, then sunny, cold. 6–9 Rainy periods, turning mild. 10–15 Snow showers north, sunny south; cold. 16–22 Snow north, rain south, then sunny, very cold. 23–26 Sunny north, rain and snow south. 27–31 Sunny, cold.

**FEB. 2022:** Temp. 50° (3° above avg.); precip. 7" (2" above avg.). 1–3 Sunny, turning mild. 4–14 Rain, then sunny, cold. 15–20 Rainy periods, warm. 21–22 Sunny. 23–28 Rain, then sunny, cool.

**MAR. 2022:** Temp. 61° (5° above avg.); precip. 6" (2" above avg. north, 2" below south). 1–3 Sunny, mild. 4–10 Rain, then sunny, warm. 11–19 Rainy periods, cool. 20–27 A few t-storms, warm. 28–31 Sunny, cool.

**APR. 2022:** Temp. 68° (7° above avg. north, 3° above south); precip. 4.5" (avg.). 1–9 Sunny, turning warm. 10–17 T-storms, warm. 18–23 Sunny, cool. 24–30 A few t-storms, warm.

**MAY 2022:** Temp. 74° (3° above avg.); precip. 2" (3" below avg.). 1–9 Sunny; cool, then warm. 10–17 Isolated t-storms, warm. 18–26 A few t-storms, hot. 27–31 Sunny, hot.

**JUNE 2022:** Temp. 81° (3° above avg.); precip. 5" (avg.). 1–4 Sunny, warm. 5–19 A few t-storms, warm. 20–30 Scattered t-storms, turning hot.

**JULY 2022:** Temp. 82° (1° above avg.); precip. 5.5" (1" below avg. north, 3" above south). 1–13 Scattered t-storms; hot north, warm south. 14–22 A few t-storms, warm. 23–25 Tropical storm threat. 26–31 Sunny north, t-storms south; warm.

**AUG. 2022:** Temp. 81.5° (3° above avg. north, avg. south); precip. 8.5" (4" above avg.). 1–9 A few t-storms, warm. 10–14 Sunny, cool north; t-storms south. 15–18 T-storms, cool. 19–28 Sunny, hot north; t-storms south. 29–31 T-storms, warm.

**SEPT. 2022:** Temp. 77° (1° above avg.); precip. 6.5" (2" above avg.). 1–5 Sunny north, t-storms south; warm. 6–12 A few t-storms, warm. 13–16 Sunny, warm. 17–24 Scattered t-storms; cool north, hot south. 25–30 Sunny, cool.

**OCT. 2022:** Temp. 64° (1° below avg.); precip. 4" (1" above avg.). 1–4 Rainy periods, cool. 5–16 Sunny, chilly. 17–24 Rain, then sunny, mild. 25–29 Showers, mild. 30–31 Tropical storm threat.

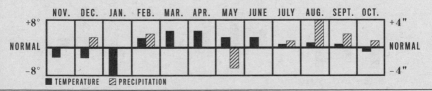

# UPPER MIDWEST

**SUMMARY: Winter** temperatures will be below normal, on average, with the coldest periods in early, mid-, and late December; early and late January; and mid-February. Precipitation will be above normal in the east and below normal in the west, while snowfall will be below normal in most areas. The snowiest periods will be in late November, mid- to late December, mid- and late January, mid- and late February, and late March. **April** and **May** will be warmer than normal, with near- to above-normal precipitation. **Summer** will have its hottest period in early to mid-July but otherwise be slightly cooler than normal and rainer. **September** and **October** will have above-normal temperatures and precipitation.

**NOV. 2021:** Temp. 22° (7° below avg.); precip. 1" (1" below avg.). 1–7 Snow showers, cold. 8–11 Sunny, mild. 12–19 Snow showers, cold. 20–25 Flurries, frigid. 26–30 Snowy periods, cold.

**DEC. 2021:** Temp. 12° (4° below avg.); precip. 0.5" (0.5" below avg.). 1–6 Snow showers, cold. 7–11 Sunny, mild. 12–16 Snow showers, cold. 17–20 Snowy periods, mild. 21–31 Snow showers, cold.

**JAN. 2022:** Temp. 5° (8° below avg.); precip. 0.5" (0.5" below avg.). 1–10 Snow showers, very cold. 11–17 Snowy periods, mild. 18–23 Snow showers, cold. 24–28 Snowy periods, mild. 29–31 Sunny, cold.

**FEB. 2022:** Temp. 17° (5° above avg.); precip. 1.5" (0.5" above avg.). 1–6 Sunny, mild. 7–16 Flurries; cold east, mild west. 17–22 Snow, then flurries, cold. 23–28 Snowy periods, mild.

**MAR. 2022:** Temp. 34° (6° above avg.); precip. 3" (3" above avg. east, 0.5" above west). 1–8 A few t-storms, warm. 9–16 Snow showers, cold. 17–21 Rainy periods, mild. 22–31 Snowy periods, cold.

**APR. 2022:** Temp. 51° (9° above avg.); precip. 3" (avg. east, 2" above west). 1–4 Sunny, turning warm. 5–12 A few t-storms, warm. 13–24 Scattered t-storms, mild. 25–30 T-storms, then sunny, cool.

**MAY 2022:** Temp. 64° (9° above avg.); precip. 3" (avg.). 1–6 Sunny, turning hot. 7–13 A few t-storms, warm. 14–23 Sunny east, a few t-storms west; warm. 24–31 Scattered t-storms, cool.

**JUNE 2022:** Temp. 65° (2° above avg.); precip. 5" (1" above avg.). 1–7 A few t-storms; cool east, warm west. 8–20 Scattered t-storms, warm. 21–30 A few t-storms; cool, then warm.

**JULY 2022:** Temp. 68° (avg.); precip. 4" (2" above avg. east, 1" below west). 1–9 Scattered t-storms, warm. 10–13 Sunny, hot. 14–20 Scattered t-storms, warm. 21–31 T-storms, cool.

**AUG. 2022:** Temp. 63° (3° below avg.); precip. 5.5" (2" above avg.). 1–9 A few t-storms, cool. 10–18 Scattered t-storms, cool. 19–22 T-storms, warm. 23–27 Severe t-storms, then showers, cool. 28–31 T-storms, cool.

**SEPT. 2022:** Temp. 57° (1° below avg.); precip. 5" (2" above avg.). 1–6 Showers, cool. 7–14 Sunny, turning mild. 15–23 Rainy periods, cool. 24–28 Sunny, cool. 29–30 Rainy, chilly.

**OCT. 2022:** Temp. 50° (3° above avg.); precip. 2.5" (1" above avg. east, 1" below west). 1–5 Rain and wet snow, cold. 6–15 Sunny, turning mild. 16–21 Showers, then sunny, warm. 22–31 Rainy periods, mild.

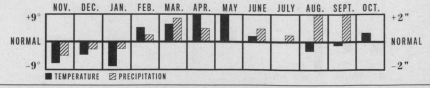

# HEARTLAND

**SUMMARY:** **Winter** will be colder and drier than normal, on average, with the coldest periods in mid- and late December, early and late January, and early to mid-February. Snowfall will be below normal in the north and above normal in central and southern areas. The snowiest periods will be in late December, early January, and mid-February. **April** and **May** will be warmer and drier than normal. **Summer** will be hotter and rainier than normal, with the hottest periods in early and late June and early to mid-July. **September** and **October** will be slightly warmer and rainier than normal.

WEATHER

**NOV. 2021:** Temp. 36° (7° below avg.); precip. 0.5" (2" below avg.). 1–3 Sunny, mild. 4–9 Rain to snow showers, then sunny, cold. 10–14 Sunny, mild. 15–17 Flurries, cold. 18–19 Showers, mild. 20–30 Snow showers, cold.

**DEC. 2021:** Temp. 29° (3° below avg.); precip. 0.5" (1" below avg.). 1–2 Snow showers, cold. 3–12 Sunny, turning warm. 13–21 Flurries, cold, then sunny, mild. 22–26 Flurries, frigid. 27–31 Snowy periods, cold.

**JAN. 2022:** Temp. 20° (9° below avg.); precip. 0.5" (0.5" below avg.). 1–12 Snowy periods, frigid. 13–20 Snow showers, milder. 21–28 Sunny; cold, then mild. 29–31 Snow showers, cold.

**FEB. 2022:** Temp. 35° (4° above avg.); precip. 0.5" (1" below avg.). 1–4 Sunny, quite mild. 5–10 Rain to snow, then sunny, cold. 11–16 Showers, turning warm. 17–23 Rain to snow, then flurries, cold. 24–28 Rain and snow showers, cool.

**MAR. 2022:** Temp. 49° (5° above avg.); precip. 3.5" (1" above avg.). 1–3 Sunny, warm. 4–11 Rainy periods, mild. 12–18 Snow north, rain south, then sunny, warmer. 19–22 T-storms, warm. 23–31 Periods of rain, then snow; turning chilly.

**APR. 2022:** Temp. 62° (8° above avg.); precip. 1.5" (2" below avg.). 1–10 Sunny, warm. 11–20 T-storms, then sunny, mild. 21–30 Scattered t-storms, warm.

**MAY 2022:** Temp. 69° (5° above avg.); precip. 1.5" (3" below avg.). 1–8 Sunny, turning warm. 9–16 A few t-storms, warm. 17–24 Isolated t-storms, warm. 25–31 Sunny, hot.

**JUNE 2022:** Temp. 75° (3° above avg.); precip. 5" (2" above avg. east, 1" below west). 1–5 Scattered t-storms, hot. 6–9 Sunny, warm. 10–17 A few t-storms, warm. 18–21 Sunny, hot north; t-storms south. 22–30 Scattered t-storms, hot.

**JULY 2022:** Temp. 78° (1° above avg.); precip. 3" (1" below avg.). 1–4 Sunny north, t-storms south. 5–11 Scattered t-storms, hot. 12–17 Sunny north, t-storms south. 18–28 Isolated t-storms; cool, then warm. 29–31 T-storms; cool north, hot south.

**AUG. 2022:** Temp. 75° (avg.); precip. 6.5" (3" above avg.). 1–6 A few t-storms, turning cool. 7–19 Scattered t-storms, cool. 20–31 A few t-storms, warm.

**SEPT. 2022:** Temp. 66° (1° below avg.); precip. 5.5" (2" above avg.). 1–8 Rainy periods, cool. 9–20 Scattered t-storms, warm. 21–27 Rain, then sunny, cool. 28–30 Sunny north, rain south; chilly.

**OCT. 2022:** Temp. 58° (2° above avg.); precip. 3.5" (2" above avg. north, 1" below south). 1–9 Rainy periods, cold. 10–14 Sunny, turning warm. 15–22 Rain, then sunny, warm. 23–31 Rainy periods, mild.

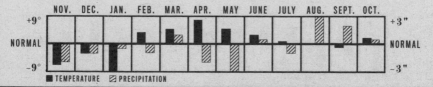

# TEXAS-OKLAHOMA

Oklahoma City
Dallas
San Antonio
Houston

**SUMMARY: Winter** will be colder than normal, especially in the south, with the coldest periods in mid- to late November, mid- and late December, and early and late January. Precipitation will be below normal in the north and above normal in the south. Snowfall will be near normal, with the best chances for snow in early and late January, mainly in the north. **April** and **May** will be warmer than normal, with rainfall below normal in the north and above normal in the south. **Summer** will be hotter than normal, with the hottest periods in late June and from mid-July into mid-August. Rainfall will be slightly above normal in the north and below normal in the south. Watch for a tropical storm in mid- to late June. **September** and **October** will be warmer and drier than normal.

**NOV. 2021:** Temp. 52° (5° below avg.); precip. 4" (1" below avg. north, 3" above south). 1–3 Sunny, warm. 4–10 Rainy periods, wet snow north; cold. 11–17 Sunny, cool. 18–25 Flurries north, rainy periods south; cold. 26–30 Rainy periods, cool.

**DEC. 2021:** Temp. 51° (1° below avg. north, 3° below south); precip. 3" (1" below avg. north, 2" above south). 1–7 Rainy periods, cool. 8–12 Sunny north, rain south; turning warm. 13–18 Sunny north, rain south; cold, then mild. 19–22 Sunny, mild. 23–31 Flurries OK, rainy periods TX; cold.

**JAN. 2022:** Temp. 45° (5° below avg.); precip. 2.5" (0.5" above avg.). 1–4 Snow showers north, rain south; cold. 5–8 Showers, mild. 9–14 Sunny, cold. 15–20 Rain, then sunny, mild. 21–27 Sunny OK, rain and snow north TX, rain south TX. 28–31 Sunny, cold.

**FEB. 2022:** Temp. 53° (3° above avg.); precip. 2" (avg.). 1–5 Rainy, turning warmer. 6–14 Sunny; cool, then warm. 15–23 Showers north, sunny south; turning cool. 24–28 Sunny, cool.

**MAR. 2022:** Temp. 62.5° (5° above avg. north, 2° above south); precip. 2.5" (avg.). 1–10 A few showers, turning warm. 11–16 Sunny, cool. 17–27 A few t-storms, warm. 28–31 Sunny; cool, then warm.

**APR. 2022:** Temp. 68.5° (4° above avg. north, 1° above south); precip. 6" (1" above avg. north, 5" above south). 1–5 Sunny, warm. 6–14 A few t-storms, warm. 15–21 Sunny; cool, then warm. 22–30 A few t-storms, warm.

**MAY 2022:** Temp. 75° (2° above avg.); precip. 3" (2" below avg.). 1–5 Sunny north, t-storms south. 6–13 T-storms north, sunny south; warm. 14–25 A few t-storms, warm. 26–31 Sunny, warm.

**JUNE 2022:** Temp. 82° (3° above avg.); precip. 3" (1" below avg.). 1–3 Sunny, warm. 4–14 Sunny north, a few t-storms south; warm. 15–18 T-storms, warm. 19–21 Tropical storm threat. 22–30 Isolated t-storms, hot.

**JULY 2022:** Temp. 83° (2° above avg.); precip. 2.5" (0.5" below avg.). 1–6 Sunny, warm. 7–13 Sunny north, a few t-storms south; hot. 14–18 Sunny, hot. 19–25 Scattered t-storms, warm. 26–31 Sunny north, t-storms south; hot.

**AUG. 2022:** Temp. 82° (1° above avg.); precip. 2.5" (2" above avg. north, 2" below south). 1–4 T-storms, hot. 5–11 Sunny, hot. 12–19 Isolated t-storms, hot. 20–31 A few t-storms, warm.

**SEPT. 2022:** Temp. 80° (4° above avg.); precip. 1.5" (2" below avg.). 1–5 Scattered t-storms, hot. 6–12 A few t-storms, warm. 13–17 Scattered t-storms, hot. 18–24 Sunny, hot. 25–30 Showers, cool.

**OCT. 2022:** Temp. 69° (2° above avg.); precip. 3" (1" below avg.). 1–4 Sunny, cool north; t-storms, hot south. 5–13 Sunny; cool, then warm. 14–24 A few t-storms, warm. 25–31 Showers, cool, then sunny, warm.

WEATHER

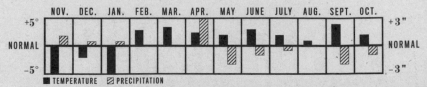

|  | NOV. | DEC. | JAN. | FEB. | MAR. | APR. | MAY | JUNE | JULY | AUG. | SEPT. | OCT. |

+5° / NORMAL / -5°   +3" / NORMAL / -3"

■ TEMPERATURE   ▨ PRECIPITATION

# HIGH PLAINS

**SUMMARY:** **Winter** will be milder than normal, with the coldest periods in mid- to late November, late December, and early and mid- to late January. Precipitation will be near to slightly above normal, with snowfall above normal in the north and below normal in the south. The snowiest periods will be in mid- to late November, late December, early to mid-January, and the last third of March. **April** and **May** will be warmer and drier than normal. **Summer** will be hotter than normal, with the hottest periods in mid-June and throughout the first half of July. The season will be drier than normal in the north and rainier than normal in the south. **September** and **October** will be warmer and slightly drier than normal.

**NOV. 2021:** Temp. 34° (2° below avg.); precip. 0.8" (0.2" below avg.). 1–3 Sunny, mild. 4–7 Snow showers, cold. 8–17 Sunny, mild. 18–22 Snowy periods, very cold. 23–26 Sunny, turning mild. 27–30 Snow showers, cold.

**DEC. 2021:** Temp. 33° (3° below avg.); precip. 0.45" (0.1" above avg. north, 0.2" below south). 1–5 Snow showers, mild. 6–12 Sunny, mild. 13–20 Snow showers; cold, then mild. 21–31 Snowy periods, cold.

**JAN. 2022:** Temp. 26.5° (4° below avg. east, 2° above west); precip. 0.7" (0.2" above avg.). 1–4 Snow showers, frigid. 5–11 Snowy periods, cold. 12–17 Sunny, mild. 18–23 Snow showers, cold. 24–31 Sunny, mild.

**FEB. 2022:** Temp. 35° (7° above avg.); precip. 0.3" (0.2" below avg.). 1–14 Sunny, mild. 15–24 Rain and snow showers, mild. 25–28 Sunny, turning warm.

**MAR. 2022:** Temp. 41° (2° above avg.); precip. 1.5" (0.5" above avg.). 1–6 Sunny, mild east; snowy west. 7–12 Snow showers, turning cold. 13–18 Sunny, mild. 19–22 Showers east, snowstorm west. 23–28 Snowy periods, cool. 29–31 Sunny, warm.

**APR. 2022:** Temp. 55° (7° above avg.); precip. 1.5" (0.5" below avg.). 1–3 Sunny, warm. 4–14 Rainy periods; mild, then cool. 15–19 Sunny, warm. 20–24 Showers, warm. 25–30 Rainy periods, turning cool.

**MAY 2022:** Temp. 63° (5° above avg.); precip. 1.5" (1" below avg.). 1–7 A few t-storms, warm. 8–13 Rainy, cool north; t-storms, warm south. 14–20 Scattered t-storms, warm. 21–31 Sunny north, a few t-storms south; turning hot.

**JUNE 2022:** Temp. 71° (4° above avg.); precip. 2.5" (avg.). 1–11 A few t-storms; turning cool north, hot south. 12–18 Scattered t-storms; hot north, turning cooler south. 19–26 A few t-storms, hot. 27–30 Sunny, cool north; t-storms, hot south.

**JULY 2022:** Temp. 71° (1° below avg.); precip. 2" (0.5" below avg. north, 0.5" above south). 1–16 A few t-storms, hot. 17–31 Scattered t-storms; cool north, hot south.

**AUG. 2022:** Temp. 70.5° (2° below avg. north, 1° above south); precip. 2" (avg.). 1–7 Scattered t-storms, turning cool. 8–17 Showers; cool north, warm south. 18–23 Rainy periods, cool. 24–31 Sunny, turning hot north; showers, warm south.

**SEPT. 2022:** Temp. 62° (2° below avg. north, 4° above south); precip. 1.5" (avg.). 1–8 Scattered showers, mild. 9–15 Showers, cool north; sunny, hot south. 16–23 A few t-storms; cool north, hot south. 24–30 Rainy periods; chilly north, mild south.

**OCT. 2022:** Temp. 53° (4° above avg.); precip. 0.5" (0.5" below avg.). 1–5 Snowy periods north, sunny south; cold. 6–13 Sunny, turning warm. 14–22 Isolated t-storms, warm. 23–31 Sunny, mild.

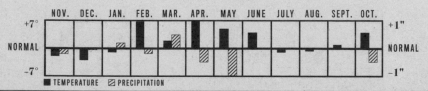

# INTERMOUNTAIN

Spokane
Pendleton
Boise
Reno
Salt Lake City
Grand Junction
Flagstaff

**WEATHER**

**SUMMARY: Winter** will be slightly colder than normal as well as drier, with below-normal snowfall in most areas. The coldest periods will be in late November, late December, and early and late January, with the snowiest periods in late December, late January, and early March. **April** and **May** will have above-normal temperatures, with slightly above-normal precipitation. **Summer** temperatures will be hotter than normal, with slightly above-normal rainfall. The hottest periods will be in mid-June, mid- and late July, and early to mid-August. **September** and **October** temperatures will be near normal in the north and above normal in the south, with near-normal precipitation.

**NOV. 2021:** Temp. 40° (avg.); precip. 0.5" (1" below avg.). 1–6 Sunny, turning cool. 7–17 A few showers; cold north, mild south. 18–25 Snow showers, then sunny, cold. 26–30 Snow showers.

**DEC. 2021:** Temp. 32° (1° below avg.); precip. 1" (0.5" below avg.). 1–4 Sunny, mild. 5–14 Showers, then sunny; mild north, cold south. 15–21 Snow showers north, sunny south; mild. 22–31 Snowy periods, turning very cold.

**JAN. 2022:** Temp. 30° (2° below avg.); precip. 0.5" (1" below avg.). 1–9 Snow showers, cold. 10–14 Sunny, mild. 15–21 Snow showers, then sunny, cold. 22–31 Snow showers, cold.

**FEB. 2022:** Temp. 37° (3° above avg.); precip. 2" (0.5" above avg.). 1–13 Showers, then sunny, mild. 14–23 Rain and snow showers, turning cold. 24–28 Sunny, mild.

**MAR. 2022:** Temp. 42° (1° below avg.); precip. 1" (0.5" below avg.). 1–12 Periods of rain and snow, cool. 13–16 Sunny, mild. 17–26 Sunny north, periods of rain and snow south; cool. 27–31 Sunny, warm.

**APR. 2022:** Temp. 53° (4° above avg.); precip. 0.5" (0.5" below avg.). 1–3 Sunny, turning cooler. 4–13 Showers, then sunny; cool north, warm south. 14–23 Sunny, warm. 24–30 Rainy periods, cool.

**MAY 2022:** Temp. 57° (avg.); precip. 2" (1" above avg.). 1–7 A few showers, cool. 8–12 Rainy periods, chilly. 13–19 Showers, cool. 20–25 Showers north; sunny, warm south. 26–31 Scattered t-storms, warm.

**JUNE 2022:** Temp. 69° (3° above avg.); precip. 0.5" (avg.). 1–5 Rainy periods, cool. 6–10 Sunny, warm. 11–20 Isolated t-storms, turning hot. 21–30 Scattered t-storms, turning cool.

**JULY 2022:** Temp. 75° (2° above avg.); precip. 0.5" (avg.). 1–9 Sunny, cool north; t-storms, warm south. 10–17 Scattered t-storms, hot. 18–27 Sunny north, t-storms south; hot. 28–31 Sunny, warm.

**AUG. 2022:** Temp. 74.5° (1° above avg. north, 4° above south); precip. 1.5" (0.5" above avg.). 1–6 Sunny, hot north; t-storms, warm south. 7–15 Isolated t-storms, hot. 16–25 Rainy periods, cool north; sunny, warm south. 26–31 Showers, then sunny, warm.

**SEPT. 2022:** Temp. 62° (3° below avg. north, 3° above south); precip. 1.5" (0.5" above avg.). 1–8 Sunny, warm north; rainy periods, warm south. 9–19 Rainy periods, cool north; sunny south. 20–30 Showers, then sunny, cool.

**OCT. 2022:** Temp. 54° (3° above avg.); precip. 0.5" (0.5" below avg.). 1–12 Sunny, warm. 13–18 Scattered showers, mild. 19–31 A few showers; mild, then cool.

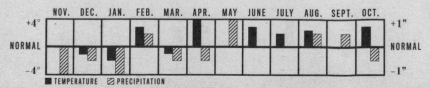

+4°   NOV.  DEC.  JAN.  FEB.  MAR.  APR.  MAY  JUNE  JULY  AUG.  SEPT.  OCT.   +1"
NORMAL                                                                      NORMAL
-4°                                                                          -1"
■ TEMPERATURE   ▨ PRECIPITATION

# DESERT SOUTHWEST

**SUMMARY: Winter** will be colder than normal in the east, with above-normal precipitation, while the west will be slightly warmer and drier than normal. The coldest periods will be in mid- to late November, from late December into early January, and in late February. Snowfall will be above normal in most areas that normally receive snow, with the snowiest periods in late November, early December, and early January. **April** and **May** will be slightly warmer than normal, with near-normal rainfall. **Summer** will be hotter than normal, with below-normal rainfall. The hottest periods will occur in mid-June, through much of July, and in mid-August. **September** and **October** will be warmer than normal, with near-normal precipitation.

**NOV. 2021:** Temp. 54.5° (6° below avg. east, 3° above west); precip. 1.2" (0.7" above avg. east, 0.3" below west). 1–3 Sunny, warm. 4–17 Showers, then sunny; cold east, warm west. 18–24 Snowy periods east, sunny west; cold. 25–30 Sunny, cool.

**DEC. 2021:** Temp. 47° (1° below avg.); precip. 0.5" (avg.). 1–3 Sunny, cool. 4–9 Snow east, then sunny, turning warmer. 10–21 Showers, then sunny, cool. 22–31 A few snow showers east, rain showers west; turning cold.

**JAN. 2022:** Temp. 47° (1° below avg.); precip. 0.4" (0.2" above avg. east, 0.4" below west). 1–6 Snowy periods east, sunny west; cold. 7–12 Sunny, turning warmer. 13–22 Showers, then sunny, cool. 23–31 Sunny; cool east, mild west.

**FEB. 2022:** Temp. 51° (3° below avg. east, 3° above west); precip. 0.2" (0.3" below avg.). 1–14 Sunny; cool east, mild west. 15–19 Rain and snow showers. 20–28 Sunny, cold.

**MAR. 2022:** Temp. 55° (3° below avg.); precip. 0.5" (avg.). 1–14 Sunny, cool. 15–19 Showers, cool. 20–27 Snow showers east, rain showers west; chilly. 28–31 Sunny, warm.

**APR. 2022:** Temp. 60° (3° above avg.); precip. 0.5" (avg.). 1–5 Sunny, warm. 6–13 A few showers east, sunny west; turning cooler. 14–20 Isolated showers east, cool; sunny, warm west. 21–25 Sunny, warm. 26–30 Scattered showers, turning cool.

**MAY 2022:** Temp. 72° (2° below avg.); precip. 0.5" (0.3" below avg. east, 0.3" above west). 1–6 Scattered showers, cool. 7–15 Sunny, cool. 16–19 T-storms, then sunny, cool. 20–31 Sunny, turning hot.

**JUNE 2022:** Temp. 84° (1° above avg.); precip. 0.3" (0.4" below avg. east, avg. west). 1–15 Showers, then sunny; hot east, warm west. 16–21 Isolated t-storms, hot. 22–30 Scattered t-storms, warm.

**JULY 2022:** Temp. 89° (2° above avg.); precip. 1" (0.5" below avg.). 1–14 Scattered t-storms, hot. 15–18 T-storms, warm east; sunny, hot west. 19–31 Isolated t-storms, hot.

**AUG. 2022:** Temp. 87° (2° above avg.); precip. 1.8" (0.3" above avg.). 1–12 A few t-storms, warm. 13–17 Scattered t-storms, hot. 18–21 Sunny, warm. 22–31 Scattered t-storms, warm east; sunny, hot west.

**SEPT. 2022:** Temp. 80° (3° above avg. east, 1° below west); precip. 1" (avg.). 1–5 Scattered t-storms, turning cooler. 6–14 Sunny; warm east, cool west. 15–30 Scattered t-storms, warm.

**OCT. 2022:** Temp. 71° (3° above avg.); precip. 1" (avg.). 1–2 Rain east, sunny west. 3–11 Sunny, warm. 12–24 Isolated showers, warm. 25–31 A few showers, cool.

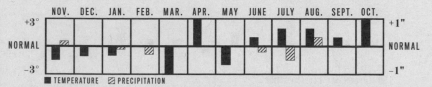

# PACIFIC NORTHWEST

Seattle
Portland
Eugene
Eureka

**SUMMARY: Winter** temperatures will be milder than normal, with below-normal precipitation and snowfall. The coldest periods will occur in early December, from late December into early January, and in mid-January and early March. The snowiest periods will occur in late December and early March. **April** and **May** will be slightly warmer and rainier than normal. **Summer** will have above-normal temperatures and rainfall. The hottest periods will be in late July and early August. **September** and **October** will be slightly cooler and rainier than normal.

**WEATHER**

**NOV. 2021:** Temp. 48° (1° above avg.); precip. 2.5" (4" below avg.). 1–5 Sprinkles, mild. 6–10 Rainy, mild. 11–18 Showers; cool, then mild. 19–27 Sunny, cold. 28–30 Rainy, mild.

**DEC. 2021:** Temp. 44° (1° above avg.); precip. 3.5" (3" below avg.). 1–5 Rain, then sunny, cold. 6–11 Occasional rain, mild. 12–14 Sunny, cool. 15–20 Rainy periods, mild. 21–28 Rainy periods, occasional wet snow; cold. 29–31 Sunny, cold.

**JAN. 2022:** Temp. 43° (avg.); precip. 3" (3" below avg.). 1–2 Sunny, cold. 3–11 Rainy periods, turning mild. 12–22 Sunny, cold. 23–25 Showers, milder. 26–31 Sunny, mild.

**FEB. 2022:** Temp. 48° (4° above avg.); precip. 5" (avg.). 1–5 Rainy periods, mild. 6–12 A few sprinkles, mild. 13–24 Rainy periods, cool. 25–26 Sunny, cool. 27–28 Rainy.

**MAR. 2022:** Temp. 47° (avg.); precip. 3" (1" below avg.). 1–7 Periods of rain and wet snow, cold. 8–14 Showers, turning mild. 15–24 Rainy periods, cool. 25–31 Sunny, turning warm.

**APR. 2022:** Temp. 52° (2° above avg.); precip. 3" (avg.). 1–9 Rainy periods, cool. 10–13 Sunny, cool. 14–25 Showers, turning warm. 26–30 Rainy periods, cool.

**MAY 2022:** Temp. 54° (1° below avg.); precip. 3" (1" above avg.). 1–6 Showers, cool. 7–15 Rainy periods, turning warm. 16–22 Showers, cool. 23–28 Rainy periods, turning warm. 29–31 Sunny, warm.

**JUNE 2022:** Temp. 61° (1° above avg.); precip. 1" (0.5" below avg.). 1–12 Sunny; cool, then warm. 13–23 Showers, then sunny, warm. 24–27 Rainy, cool. 28–30 Sunny, turning warm.

**JULY 2022:** Temp. 66° (1° above avg.); precip. 0.3" (0.2" below avg.). 1–4 Sunny, cool. 5–11 Isolated t-storms, cool. 12–22 Isolated showers, warm. 23–31 Sunny, hot.

**AUG. 2022:** Temp. 69 (3° above avg.); precip. 3" (2" above avg.). 1–10 Sunny, hot. 11–15 Showers, cool. 16–23 Rainy, cool. 24–25 Sunny, cool. 26–31 Rainy periods, mild.

**SEPT. 2022:** Temp. 59° (2° below avg.); precip. 3" (1.5" above avg.). 1–8 Sunny, cool. 9–22 Rainy periods, cool. 23–28 Sunny, cool. 29–30 Rainy.

**OCT. 2022:** Temp. 55° (1° above avg.); precip. 2" (1" below avg.). 1–13 A few showers, cool. 14–18 Rainy, mild. 19–20 Sunny, cool. 21–31 Rainy periods, cool.

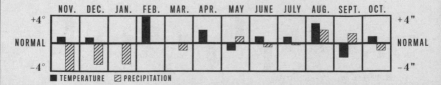

■ TEMPERATURE   ▨ PRECIPITATION

# PACIFIC SOUTHWEST

**SUMMARY: Winter** will be warmer and drier than normal, with below-normal mountain snows. The coldest temperatures will occur from mid-December into mid-January, in mid-February, and in early March. The stormiest period will be in late December. **April** and **May** will be slightly cooler than normal, with rainfall below normal in the north and above normal in the south. **Summer** temperatures will be hotter than normal, with generally above-normal rainfall. The hottest periods will be in mid-June, mid- to late July, and mid- to late August. **September** and **October** will bring temperatures close to normal and be a bit drier than usual.

San Francisco
• Fresno
Los Angeles
San Diego

WEATHER

**NOV. 2021:** Temp. 61° (1° above avg. north, 5° above south); precip. 0.8" (1" below avg. north, 0.5" below south). 1–3 Sunny, warm. 4–8 Rainy periods. 9–16 Isolated showers, warm. 17–30 Sunny, mild.

**DEC. 2021:** Temp. 56° (2° above avg.); precip. 3" (2" above avg. coast, avg. inland). 1–5 Scattered showers, warm. 6–14 Sunny; cool north, warm south. 15–21 Sunny, cool. 22–31 Rainy periods, some heavy; cool.

**JAN. 2022:** Temp. 55.5° (avg. north, 3° above south); precip. 1" (2" below avg.). 1–3 Sunny, cool. 4–13 Scattered showers, cool. 14–20 Sunny, mild. 21–26 Showers, then sunny, cool. 27–31 Sprinkles, mild.

**FEB. 2022:** Temp. 57° (2° above avg.); precip. 1" (1" below avg.). 1–11 Rain, then sunny, warm. 12–21 Rainy periods, turning cool. 22–28 Sunny, turning warm.

**MAR. 2022:** Temp. 56° (1° below avg.); precip. 1.5" (1" below avg.). 1–7 Rainy periods north, sunny south; cool. 8–15 Rain, then sunny, cool. 16–23 Rain, then sunny, cool. 24–31 Sunny, turning hot inland; a few sprinkles, cool coast.

**APR. 2022:** Temp. 60° (avg.); precip. 0.5" (0.5" below avg.). 1–11 Sunny; warm inland, cool coast. 12–19 Sunny, turning warm. 20–30 Occasional rain, turning cool.

**MAY 2022:** Temp. 62.5° (1° below avg.); precip. 1.5" (avg. north, 2" above south). 1–5 Rainy periods, cool. 6–10 Sunny, cool. 11–15 A.M. sprinkles, P.M. sun; cool. 16–23 Showers, then sunny, cool. 24–31 Sunny, hot inland; scattered showers, mild coast.

**JUNE 2022:** Temp. 68° (avg.); precip. 0.2" (0.2" above avg. north, avg. south). 1–2 Showers, cool. 3–13 A.M. sprinkles, P.M. sun; cool. 14–24 Sunny; hot inland, warm coast. 25–30 A few sprinkles, cool.

**JULY 2022:** Temp. 72° (1° above avg.); precip. 0" (avg.). 1–11 Sunny, turning warm. 12–17 Sunny inland; A.M. sprinkles, P.M. sun coast; warm. 18–27 Sunny, turning hot. 28–31 Sunny, cooler.

**AUG. 2022:** Temp. 71.5° (0.5° above avg.); precip. 1.1" (avg. north, 2" above south). 1–8 Sunny inland; A.M. sprinkles, P.M. sun coast; warm. 9–11 Sprinkles north, heavy rain south. 12–19 Sunny inland; A.M. sprinkles, P.M. sun coast; warm. 20–23 Sunny, hot. 24–31 Sunny, warm.

**SEPT. 2022:** Temp. 70° (1° below avg. north, 1° above south); precip. 0.2" (avg.). 1–7 Sunny, turning cool. 8–11 Sprinkles, mild. 12–22 Showers north, sunny south; warm. 23–27 Sunny, mild. 28–30 Showers; cool north, warm south.

**OCT. 2022:** Temp. 65° (avg.); precip. 0.2" (0.3" below avg.). 1–11 Sunny; hot, then cooler. 12–19 Showers, then sunny, warm. 20–26 Rain, then sunny, cool. 27–31 Showers, cool.

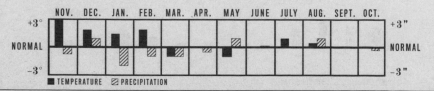

■ TEMPERATURE  ⧄ PRECIPITATION

# ALASKA

**SUMMARY: Winter** temperatures will be milder than normal, with the coldest periods in mid- to late January, late February, and early March. Precipitation will be near normal N and above normal S. Snowfall will be above normal in all areas but the south, with the snowiest periods in early November and mid- to late January. **April** and **May** will be warmer than normal, with near-normal precipitation. Watch for snow in late April. **Summer** will be warmer and drier than normal, with the hottest periods from mid-July into mid-August. **September** and **October** will be milder than normal, with precipitation below normal N and above normal S.

**Key:** north (N), central (C), south (S), panhandle (P), elsewhere (EW).

**NOV. 2021:** Temp. 7° N, 46° S (5° above avg. N, 10° above S); precip. 0.4" N, 8" S (avg. N, 3" above S). 1–4 Snowy, mild. 5–12 Showers P, flurries EW; mild. 13–17 Snow showers, mild. 18–30 Rain and snow, mild S; clear, cold EW.

**DEC. 2021:** Temp. 1° N, 39° S (8° above avg.); precip. 0.2" N, 4" S (avg. N, 1" below S). 1–12 Rainy P; snow showers, cold to mild C; clear, cold N. 13–19 Rainy P, flurries EW; mild. 20–31 Rain/snow S, snow showers EW; mild.

**JAN. 2022:** Temp. –5° N, 41° S (7° above avg. N, 12° above S); precip. 0.2" N, 6" S (avg. N, 1" above S). 1–13 Mainly dry, mild. 14–21 Flurries N, rain and snow EW; mild S. 22–27 Flurries, frigid N; snowy C; rain and snow, mild S. 28–31 Flurries N+C, showers S; mild.

**FEB. 2022:** Temp. –7° N, 38° S (7° above avg.); precip. 0.2" N, 4" S (avg.). 1–8 Flurries, turning cold N; flurries, mild C; rainy periods, mild S. 9–15 Snow showers N+C, clear S; quite mild. 16–23 Clear, cold N; snow showers, mild S. 24–28 Snow showers, very cold.

**MAR. 2022:** Temp. –12° N, 35° S (1° above avg.); precip. 0.5" N, 6" S (avg. N, 1" above S). 1–5 Snow showers, cold. 6–11 Clear, cold N; snow showers, mild S. 12–16 Clear, cold. 17–23 Snow showers, cold. 24–31 Flurries, cold N; periods of rain and snow, mild S.

**APR. 2022:** Temp. 2° N, 41° S (avg.); precip. 0.7" N, 3" S (avg.). 1–7 Snow showers, cold. 8–12 Flurries, cold N; sunny, milder C; rainy, mild S. 13–18 Flurries N, rainy S; mild. 19–22 Snow showers, cold. 23–30 Snowy N, showers S; mild.

**MAY 2022:** Temp. 23° N, 49° EW (2° above avg.); precip. 0.6" N, 3" S (avg.). 1–5 Snow showers, mild N; sunny, cooler S. 6–10 Flurries N, rainy periods, mild EW. 24–31 Snow showers, cold N; showers, mild S.

**JUNE 2022:** Temp. 34° N, 59° EW (1° below avg. N, 4° above S); precip. 0.7" N, 3" S (avg.). 1–10 Showers, turning mild. 11–17 A few showers, cool N; rainy periods, mild S. 18–26 Sunny, cool N; showers C; sunny, warm S. 27–30 Showers, cool.

**JULY 2022:** Temp. 46° N, 61° EW (4° above avg.); precip. 0.7" N, 3.5" S (0.5" below avg.). 1–5 Sunny, warm. 6–13 Sunny, mild N; a few showers, warm C+S. 14–22 Scattered showers, warm. 23–28 Sunny, hot N+C; showers, warm S. 29–31 Sunny, warm.

**AUG. 2022:** Temp. 45° N, 61° EW (5° above avg.); precip. 1.2" N, 4" S (avg. N, 1" below S). 1–6 Showers; cool N, hot C, warm S. 7–11 A few showers; cool S, warm EW. 12–16 Sunny, hot. 17–22 Rainy periods, cooler. 23–31 Rainy periods N, sunny S; warm.

**SEPT. 2022:** Temp. 36° N, 58° EW (4° above avg.); precip. 0.6" N, 9" S (0.5" below avg. N, 2" above S). 1–10 Rainy, mild. 11–15 Flurries N, showers S; colder. 16–22 Rainy, mild. 23–30 Rainy N, sunny S; mild.

**OCT. 2022:** Temp. 19° N, 44° S (2° above avg.); precip. 0.5" N, 7" S (avg.). 1–6 Snow showers N, showers S; mild. 7–12 Snowy periods, colder. 13–20 Snow showers, mild. 21–27 Snow, then sunny, cold. 28–31 Snow showers, cold.

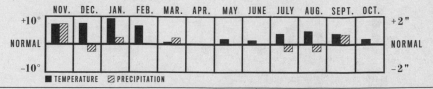

# HAWAII

**SUMMARY: Winter** temperatures will be warmer than normal, with the coolest periods in mid- to late December and mid- to late March. Rainfall will be below normal, with the stormiest periods in early December, late January, and early March. **April** and **May** will be warmer and rainier than normal. **Summer** will be warmer than normal, with the hottest periods from mid-July into early August and in late August. Rainfall will be below normal E and above normal W. **September** and **October** will be warmer than normal, with the hottest periods in early September and from late September into early October. Rainfall will be below normal despite a stormy period in mid-October.

**KEY:** east (E), central (C), west (W). Note: Temperature and precipitation are substantially based upon topography. The detailed forecast focuses on the Honolulu–Waikiki area and provides general trends elsewhere.

**WEATHER**

**NOV. 2021:** Temp. 76.8° (0.5° above avg. E, 2° below W); precip. 0.5" (5" below avg. E+W, 2" below C). 1–10 Rainy periods E, a few showers C+W; warm. 11–25 Daily showers E, scattered showers C+W; cool. 26–30 Rainy periods E+W, sunny C; warm.

**DEC. 2021:** Temp. 75° (1° above avg. E, 1° below W); precip. 1.3" (4" below avg. E+W, 2" below C). 1–5 Rainy periods E+W, sunny C; warm. 6–8 Showers, warm. 9–16 Showers E, sunny C+W; mild. 17–26 Rainy periods, cool E+W; sunny, warm C. 27–31 Showers E+W, sunny C.

**JAN. 2022:** Temp. 75° (2° above avg.); precip. 0.5" (4" below avg. E+W, 2" below C).). 1–9 Sunny E, showers C+W; warm. 10–20 Sunny E, a few showers C+W; warm. 21–31 Rainy periods, warm.

**FEB. 2022:** Temp. 75° (2° above avg.); precip. 2" (3" above avg. E, 3" below W). 1–9 Showers, warm. 10–15 Sunny, warm. 16–19 A few t-storms, warm. 20–28 Rainy periods E, showers C+W; warm.

**MAR. 2022:** Temp. 75.5° (2° above avg.); precip. 3" (1" below avg. E+W, 1" above C). 1–17 Rain, some heavy E; a few showers C; rainy periods W; warm. 18–25 Rainy periods, cool. 26–31 Rainy periods E, sunny C, showers W; warm.

**APR. 2022:** Temp. 76.5° (1° above avg.); precip. 1.7" (1" above avg. E+C, 2" below W). 1–7 Rainy periods E+W, a few showers C; warm. 8–13 Rainy periods, mild. 14–25 Rainy E, a few showers C+W; seasonable. 26–30 Rainy periods, warm.

**MAY 2022:** Temp. 77° (1° above avg. E, 0.5° below W); precip. 5.7" (2" above avg. E, 8" above W). 1–8 Rain and t-storms, some heavy. 9–13 Heavy rain E, sunny C+W; warm. 14–31 Rainy periods E+W, isolated showers C; warm.

**JUNE 2022:** Temp. 79.5° (1° above avg. E, 0.5° below W); precip. 0.4" (2" above avg. E, 2" below W). 1–7 Rainy periods E+W, scattered showers C; warm. 8–14 Rainy periods, mild E+W; isolated showers, warm C. 15–30 Rainy periods, warm E; showers, mild C+W.

**JULY 2022:** Temp. 82° (1° above avg.); precip. 0.5" (1" below avg. E, 1" above W). 1–5 Daily showers, warm. 6–14 Rainy periods E+W, isolated showers C; warm. 15–17 Sunny, hot. 18–31 Rain and t-storms E+W, a few showers C; hot.

**AUG. 2022:** Temp. 82.5° (1° above avg.); precip. 0.6" (3" below avg. E, 3" above W). 1–5 A few t-storms E+W, sunny C; hot. 6–9 Sunny, hot. 10–17 Rainy periods E, sunny C+W; warm. 18–31 Rainy periods E+W, a few showers C; hot.

**SEPT. 2022:** Temp. 82.5° (1° above avg.); precip. 0.2" (0.6" below avg.). 1–8 Showers E+W, sunny C; hot. 9–15 Showers E, sunny C+W; warm. 16–22 Showers E+W, sunny C; warm. 23–30 Rainy periods E, a few showers C+W; hot.

**OCT. 2022:** Temp. 81° (1° above avg.); precip. 1" (1" below avg.). 1–7 Showers, hot E; sunny, warm C+W. 8–17 Rainy periods, some heavy E, sunny C, showers W; hot. 18–31 Rainy periods E, a few showers C+W; warm.

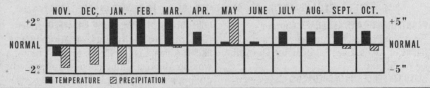

# SECRETS OF THE ZODIAC

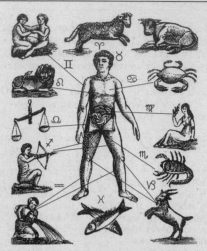

## The Man of the Signs

Ancient astrologers believed that each astrological sign influenced a specific part of the body. The first sign of the zodiac—Aries—was attributed to the head, with the rest of the signs moving down the body, ending with Pisces at the feet.

| ♈ Aries, head | ARI | *Mar. 21–Apr. 20* |
| ♉ Taurus, neck | TAU | *Apr. 21–May 20* |
| ♊ Gemini, arms | GEM | *May 21–June 20* |
| ♋ Cancer, breast | CAN | *June 21–July 22* |
| ♌ Leo, heart | LEO | *July 23–Aug. 22* |
| ♍ Virgo, belly | VIR | *Aug. 23–Sept. 22* |
| ♎ Libra, reins | LIB | *Sept. 23–Oct. 22* |
| ♏ Scorpio, secrets | SCO | *Oct. 23–Nov. 22* |
| ♐ Sagittarius, thighs | SAG | *Nov. 23–Dec. 21* |
| ♑ Capricorn, knees | CAP | *Dec. 22–Jan. 19* |
| ♒ Aquarius, legs | AQU | *Jan. 20–Feb. 19* |
| ♓ Pisces, feet | PSC | *Feb. 20–Mar. 20* |

## ASTROLOGY VS. ASTRONOMY

**Astrology** is a tool we use to plan events according to the placements of the Sun, the Moon, and the planets in the 12 signs of the zodiac. In astrology, the planetary movements do not cause events; rather, they explain the path, or "flow," that events tend to follow. *The Moon's astrological place is given on the next page.* **Astronomy** is the study of the actual placement of the known planets and constellations. The Moon's astronomical place is given in the **Left-Hand Calendar Pages, 120–146.** *(The placement of the planets in the signs of the zodiac is not the same astrologically and astronomically.)*

The dates in the **Best Days** table, **pages 226–227,** are based on the astrological passage of the Moon.

### WHEN MERCURY IS RETROGRADE

Sometimes the other planets appear to be traveling backward through the zodiac; this is an illusion. We call this illusion *retrograde motion.*

Mercury's retrograde periods can cause our plans to go awry. However, intuition is high during these periods and coincidences can be extraordinary.

When Mercury is retrograde, stay flexible, allow more time for travel, and don't sign contracts. Review projects and plans but wait until Mercury is direct again to make final decisions.

In 2022, Mercury will be retrograde during January 13–February 3, May 10–June 2, September 9–October 1, and December 28–(January 18, 2023).

*–Celeste Longacre*

## GARDENING BY THE MOON'S SIGN

USE CHART ON NEXT PAGE TO FIND THE BEST DATES FOR THE FOLLOWING GARDEN TASKS . . .

**PLANT, TRANSPLANT, AND GRAFT:** Cancer, Scorpio, Pisces, or Taurus
**HARVEST:** Aries, Leo, Sagittarius, Gemini, or Aquarius
**BUILD/FIX FENCES OR GARDEN BEDS:** Capricorn

**CONTROL INSECT PESTS, PLOW, AND WEED:** Aries, Gemini, Leo, Sagittarius, or Aquarius
**PRUNE:** Aries, Leo, or Sagittarius. During a waxing Moon, pruning encourages growth; during a waning Moon, it discourages it.

# SETTING EGGS BY THE MOON'S SIGN

Chicks take about 21 days to hatch. Those born under a waxing Moon in Cancer, Scorpio, or Pisces are healthier and mature faster. To ensure that chicks are born during these times, "set eggs" (place eggs in an incubator or under a hen) 21 days before the desired hatching dates.

**EXAMPLE:**
The Moon is new on April 30 and full on May 16 (EDT). Between these dates, the Moon is in the sign of Cancer on May 5 and 6. To have chicks born on May 5, count back 21 days; set eggs on April 14.

*Below are the best days to set eggs in 2022, using only the fruitful dates*
*between the new and full Moons, and counting back 21 days:*

| | | | |
|---|---|---|---|
| **JAN.:** 12, 13, 22, 23 | **APR.:** 14, 15, 23, 24 | **JULY:** 14, 15 | **OCT.:** 4, 5, 13, 14 |
| **FEB.:** 9, 10, 18–20 | **MAY:** 11–13, 21, 22 | **AUG.:** 10–12, 19, 20 | **NOV.:** 2, 9, 10 |
| **MAR.:** 17–19 | **JUNE:** 7–9, 17, 18 | **SEPT.:** 7, 8, 15, 16 | **DEC.:** 6, 7, 16 |

## The Moon's Astrological Place, 2021–22

| | NOV. | DEC. | JAN. | FEB. | MAR. | APR. | MAY | JUNE | JULY | AUG. | SEPT. | OCT. | NOV. | DEC. |
|---|---|---|---|---|---|---|---|---|---|---|---|---|---|---|
| 1 | VIR | SCO | SAG | AQU | AQU | ARI | TAU | CAN | LEO | VIR | SCO | SAG | AQU | PSC |
| 2 | LIB | SCO | CAP | PSC | PSC | TAU | GEM | CAN | LEO | LIB | SCO | CAP | AQU | ARI |
| 3 | LIB | SAG | CAP | PSC | PSC | TAU | GEM | CAN | VIR | LIB | SAG | CAP | PSC | ARI |
| 4 | SCO | SAG | AQU | ARI | ARI | TAU | GEM | LEO | VIR | SCO | SAG | AQU | PSC | TAU |
| 5 | SCO | CAP | AQU | ARI | ARI | GEM | CAN | LEO | VIR | SCO | CAP | AQU | ARI | TAU |
| 6 | SAG | CAP | PSC | ARI | TAU | GEM | CAN | VIR | LIB | SAG | CAP | PSC | ARI | TAU |
| 7 | SAG | AQU | PSC | TAU | TAU | CAN | LEO | VIR | LIB | SAG | AQU | PSC | TAU | GEM |
| 8 | CAP | AQU | ARI | TAU | TAU | CAN | LEO | LIB | SCO | SAG | AQU | ARI | TAU | GEM |
| 9 | CAP | PSC | ARI | GEM | GEM | CAN | LEO | LIB | SCO | CAP | PSC | ARI | GEM | CAN |
| 10 | AQU | PSC | TAU | GEM | GEM | LEO | VIR | LIB | SAG | CAP | PSC | ARI | GEM | CAN |
| 11 | AQU | PSC | TAU | GEM | CAN | LEO | VIR | SCO | SAG | AQU | ARI | TAU | GEM | CAN |
| 12 | PSC | ARI | TAU | CAN | CAN | VIR | LIB | SCO | CAP | AQU | ARI | TAU | CAN | LEO |
| 13 | PSC | ARI | GEM | CAN | CAN | VIR | LIB | SAG | CAP | PSC | TAU | GEM | CAN | LEO |
| 14 | ARI | TAU | GEM | LEO | LEO | VIR | SCO | SAG | AQU | PSC | TAU | GEM | LEO | VIR |
| 15 | ARI | TAU | CAN | LEO | LEO | LIB | SCO | CAP | AQU | ARI | TAU | CAN | LEO | VIR |
| 16 | ARI | TAU | CAN | LEO | VIR | LIB | SAG | CAP | PSC | ARI | GEM | CAN | LEO | VIR |
| 17 | TAU | GEM | CAN | VIR | VIR | SCO | SAG | AQU | PSC | TAU | GEM | CAN | VIR | LIB |
| 18 | TAU | GEM | LEO | VIR | LIB | SCO | CAP | AQU | ARI | TAU | CAN | LEO | VIR | LIB |
| 19 | GEM | CAN | LEO | LIB | LIB | SAG | CAP | PSC | ARI | GEM | CAN | LEO | LIB | SCO |
| 20 | GEM | CAN | VIR | LIB | SCO | SAG | AQU | PSC | ARI | GEM | CAN | VIR | LIB | SCO |
| 21 | GEM | CAN | VIR | SCO | SCO | CAP | AQU | ARI | TAU | GEM | LEO | VIR | LIB | SAG |
| 22 | CAN | LEO | VIR | SCO | SCO | CAP | PSC | ARI | TAU | CAN | LEO | VIR | SCO | SAG |
| 23 | CAN | LEO | LIB | SAG | SAG | AQU | PSC | TAU | GEM | CAN | VIR | LIB | SCO | CAP |
| 24 | LEO | VIR | LIB | SAG | SAG | AQU | PSC | TAU | GEM | LEO | VIR | LIB | SAG | CAP |
| 25 | LEO | VIR | SCO | CAP | CAP | PSC | ARI | TAU | CAN | LEO | LIB | SCO | SAG | AQU |
| 26 | LEO | LIB | SCO | CAP | CAP | PSC | ARI | GEM | CAN | LEO | LIB | SCO | CAP | AQU |
| 27 | VIR | LIB | SAG | CAP | AQU | ARI | TAU | GEM | CAN | VIR | LIB | SAG | CAP | PSC |
| 28 | VIR | LIB | SAG | AQU | AQU | ARI | TAU | CAN | LEO | VIR | SCO | SAG | AQU | PSC |
| 29 | LIB | SCO | CAP | — | PSC | ARI | GEM | CAN | LEO | LIB | SCO | CAP | AQU | ARI |
| 30 | LIB | SCO | CAP | — | PSC | TAU | GEM | CAN | LEO | LIB | SAG | CAP | PSC | ARI |
| 31 | — | SAG | AQU | — | ARI | — | GEM | — | VIR | SCO | — | AQU | — | TAU |

# BEST DAYS FOR 2022

This chart is based on the Moon's sign and shows the best days each month for certain activities. –*Celeste Longacre*

| | JAN. | FEB. | MAR. | APR. | MAY | JUNE | JULY | AUG. | SEPT. | OCT. | NOV. | DEC. |
|---|---|---|---|---|---|---|---|---|---|---|---|---|
| Quit smoking | 22, 26 | 18, 23 | 22, 30 | 18, 27 | 24, 29 | 20, 25 | 17, 22 | 14, 19 | 15, 25 | 12, 22 | 18, 23 | 15, 16 |
| Bake | 15–17 | 12, 13 | 11–13 | 7–9 | 5, 6 | 1–3, 28–30 | 25–27 | 22, 23 | 18–20 | 15–17 | 12, 13 | 9–11 |
| Brew | 25, 26 | 21, 22 | 20–22 | 17, 18 | 14, 15 | 11, 12 | 8, 9 | 4, 5, 31 | 1, 2, 28, 29 | 25, 26 | 22, 23 | 19, 20 |
| Dry fruit, vegetables, or meat | 27, 28 | 23, 24 | 23, 24 | 19, 20 | 25, 26 | 21, 22 | 18–20 | 15, 16 | 21, 22 | 18, 19 | 14–16 | 12, 13 |
| Make jams or jellies | 6, 7 | 2, 3 | 2, 3, 29, 30 | 25, 26 | 22–24 | 19, 20 | 16, 17 | 13, 14 | 9, 10 | 6, 7 | 3, 4, 30 | 1, 27, 28 |
| Can, pickle, or make sauerkraut | 25, 26 | 21, 22 | 20–22 | 25, 26 | 22–24 | 19, 20 | 16, 17 | 22, 23 | 18–20 | 15–17 | 12, 13 | 9–11 |
| Begin diet to lose weight | 22, 26 | 18, 23 | 22, 30 | 18, 27 | 24, 29 | 20, 25 | 17, 22 | 14, 19 | 15, 25 | 12, 22 | 18, 23 | 15, 16 |
| Begin diet to gain weight | 7, 12 | 4, 8 | 3, 8 | 4, 9 | 1, 11 | 8, 12 | 5, 31 | 1, 6 | 2, 10 | 8, 26 | 4, 30 | 1, 6, 28 |
| Cut hair to encourage growth | 10–12 | 7, 8 | 6–8 | 2–4 | 12, 13 | 9, 10 | 6, 7 | 2, 3 | 9, 10 | 6, 7 | 3, 4, 7 | 4–6 |
| Cut hair to discourage growth | 23, 24 | 19, 20 | 19, 29, 30 | 25, 26 | 27, 28 | 23–25 | 21, 22 | 17, 18 | 13–15 | 11, 12 | 19–21 | 17, 18 |
| Perm hair | 4, 5, 31 | 1, 28 | 1, 27, 28 | 23, 24 | 20, 21 | 17, 18 | 14, 15 | 11, 12 | 7, 8 | 4, 5, 31 | 1, 2, 28, 29 | 25, 26 |
| Color hair | 10–12 | 7, 8 | 6–8 | 2–4, 30 | 1, 27, 28 | 23–25 | 21, 22 | 17, 18 | 13–15 | 11, 12 | 7, 8 | 4–6, 31 |
| Straighten hair | 1, 27, 28 | 23, 24 | 23, 24 | 19, 20 | 16, 17 | 13, 14 | 10, 11 | 6–8 | 3, 4, 30 | 1, 27, 28 | 24, 25 | 21, 22 |
| Have dental care | 20–22 | 17, 18 | 16, 17 | 12–14 | 10, 11 | 6, 7 | 3–5, 31 | 1, 27, 28 | 23, 24 | 20–22 | 17, 18 | 14–16 |
| Start projects | 3 | 2 | 3 | 30 | 1 | 1 | 1 | 28 | 26 | 26 | 24 | 24 |
| End projects | 1 | 1 | 1 | 2 | 30 | 27 | 27 | 26 | 24 | 24 | 22 | 22 |
| Demolish | 25, 26 | 21, 22 | 20–22 | 17, 18 | 14, 15 | 11, 12 | 8, 9 | 4, 5, 31 | 1, 2, 28, 29 | 25, 26 | 22, 23 | 19, 20 |
| Lay shingles | 18, 19 | 14–16 | 14, 15 | 10, 11 | 7–9 | 4, 5 | 1, 2, 28–30 | 24–26 | 21, 22 | 18, 19 | 14–16 | 12, 13 |
| Paint | 23, 24 | 19, 20 | 18, 19 | 15, 16 | 12, 13 | 8–10 | 6, 7 | 2, 3, 29, 30 | 25–27 | 23, 24 | 19–21 | 17, 18 |
| Wash windows | 8, 9 | 4–6 | 4, 5, 31 | 1, 27–29 | 25, 26 | 21, 22 | 18–20 | 15, 16 | 11, 12 | 8–10 | 5, 6 | 2, 3, 29, 30 |
| Wash floors | 6, 7 | 2, 3 | 2, 3, 29, 30 | 25, 26 | 22–24 | 19, 20 | 16, 17 | 13, 14 | 9, 10 | 6, 7 | 3, 4, 30 | 1, 27, 28 |
| Go camping | 1, 27, 28 | 23, 24 | 23, 24 | 19, 20 | 16, 17 | 13, 14 | 10, 11 | 6–8 | 3, 4, 30 | 1, 27, 28 | 24, 25 | 21, 22 |

See what to do when via Almanac.com/2022.

| | JAN. | FEB. | MAR. | APR. | MAY | JUNE | JULY | AUG. | SEPT. | OCT. | NOV. | DEC. |
|---|---|---|---|---|---|---|---|---|---|---|---|---|
| Entertain | 18, 19 | 14–16 | 14, 15 | 10, 11 | 7–9 | 4, 5 | 1, 2, 28–30 | 24–26 | 21, 22 | 18, 19 | 14–16 | 12, 13 |
| Travel for pleasure | 18, 19 | 14–16 | 14, 15 | 10, 11 | 7–9 | 4, 5 | 1, 2, 28–30 | 24–26 | 21, 22 | 18, 19 | 14–16 | 12, 13 |
| Get married | 23, 24 | 19, 20 | 18, 19 | 15, 16 | 12, 13 | 8–10 | 6, 7 | 2, 3, 29, 30 | 25–27 | 23, 24 | 19–21 | 17, 18 |
| Ask for a loan | 25, 26 | 21, 22 | 20, 21 | 17, 18 | 27, 28 | 23–25 | 21, 22 | 17, 18 | 13, 14 | 11, 12 | 12, 13, 22 | 19, 20 |
| Buy a home | 10–12 | 7, 8 | 6–8 | 2–4 | 14, 15 | 11, 12 | 8, 9 | 4, 5 | 1, 2, 29 | 6, 7, 26 | 7, 8 | 4–6 |
| Move (house/household) | 13, 14 | 9–11 | 9, 10 | 5, 6 | 2–4, 29–31 | 26, 27 | 23, 24 | 19–21 | 16, 17 | 13, 14 | 9–11 | 7, 8 |
| Advertise to sell | 10–12 | 7, 8 | 6–8 | 2–4, 30 | 14, 15 | 11, 12 | 8, 9 | 4, 5 | 1, 2, 28, 29 | 2, 3, 26 | 7, 8 | 4–6 |
| Mow to promote growth | 8, 9 | 4–6 | 4, 5 | 1, 12–14 | 14, 15 | 11, 12 | 8, 9 | 4, 5 | 1, 2, 28, 29 | 8, 9 | 7, 8 | 2, 3, 29, 30 |
| Mow to slow growth | 25, 26 | 21, 22 | 20–22 | 17, 18 | 27, 28 | 21, 22 | 21, 22 | 17, 18 | 13–15 | 11, 12 | 15, 16 | 19, 20 |
| Plant aboveground crops | 6, 7 | 2, 3 | 2, 3 | 7–9 | 5, 6 | 1–3 | 8, 9 | 4, 5 | 1, 2, 28, 29 | 6, 7 | 3, 4, 30 | 1, 27, 28 |
| Plant belowground crops | 25, 26 | 21, 22 | 20–22 | 25, 26 | 22–24 | 19, 20 | 25–27 | 22, 23 | 18–20 | 15–17 | 12, 13 | 9–11 |
| Destroy pests and weeds | 8, 9 | 4–6 | 4, 5, 31 | 1, 27–29 | 25, 26 | 21, 22 | 18–20 | 15, 16 | 11, 12 | 8–10 | 5, 6 | 2, 3, 29, 30 |
| Graft or pollinate | 15–17 | 12, 13 | 11–13 | 7–9 | 5, 6 | 1–3, 28–30 | 25–27 | 22, 23 | 18–20 | 15–17 | 12, 13 | 9–11 |
| Prune to encourage growth | 8, 9 | 4–6 | 4, 5 | 10, 11 | 7–9 | 4, 5 | 10, 11 | 6–8 | 3, 4 | 27, 28 | 5, 6 | 2, 3, 29, 30 |
| Prune to discourage growth | 27, 28 | 23, 24 | 23, 24 | 19, 20 | 25, 26 | 21, 22 | 18–20 | 24–26 | 21, 22 | 18, 19 | 14–16 | 12, 13 |
| Pick fruit | 20–22 | 17, 18 | 16, 17 | 12–14 | 10, 11 | 6, 7 | 3–5 | 1, 27, 28 | 23, 24 | 20–22 | 17, 18 | 14–16 |
| Harvest aboveground crops | 10–12 | 7, 8 | 6–8 | 2–4 | 10, 11 | 6, 7 | 3–5 | 1, 4, 5 | 1, 2 | 2, 3 | 7, 8 | 4–6 |
| Harvest belowground crops | 20–22 | 17, 18 | 20–22 | 17, 18 | 27, 28 | 23–25 | 21, 22 | 17, 18 | 23, 24 | 20–22 | 17, 18 | 14–16 |
| Cut hay | 8, 9 | 4–6 | 4, 5 | 1, 27–29 | 25, 26 | 21, 22 | 18–20 | 15, 16 | 11, 12 | 8–10 | 5, 6 | 2, 3, 29, 30 |
| Begin logging, set posts, pour concrete | 2, 3, 29, 30 | 25–27 | 25, 26 | 21, 22 | 18, 19 | 15, 16 | 12, 13 | 9, 10 | 5, 6 | 2, 3, 29, 30 | 26, 27 | 23, 24 |
| Purchase animals | 15–17 | 12, 13 | 11–13 | 7–9 | 5, 6 | 1–3, 28–30 | 25–27 | 22, 23 | 18–20 | 15–17 | 12, 13 | 9–11 |
| Breed animals | 25, 26 | 21, 22 | 20–22 | 17, 18 | 14, 15 | 11, 12 | 8, 9 | 4, 5, 31 | 1, 2, 28, 29 | 25, 26 | 22, 23 | 19, 20 |
| Wean | 22, 26 | 18, 23 | 22, 30 | 18, 27 | 24, 29 | 20, 25 | 17, 22 | 14, 19 | 15, 25 | 12, 22 | 18, 23 | 15, 16 |
| Castrate animals | 4, 5, 31 | 1, 28 | 1, 27, 28 | 23, 24 | 20, 21 | 17, 18 | 14, 15 | 11, 12 | 7, 8 | 4, 5, 31 | 1, 2, 28, 29 | 25, 26 |
| Slaughter livestock | 25, 26 | 21, 22 | 20–22 | 17, 18 | 14, 15 | 11, 12 | 8, 9 | 4, 5, 31 | 1, 2, 28, 29 | 25, 26 | 22, 23 | 19, 20 |

# BEST FISHING DAYS AND TIMES

The best times to fish are when the fish are naturally most active. The Sun, Moon, tides, and weather all influence fish activity. For example, fish tend to feed more at sunrise and sunset, and also during a full Moon (when tides are higher than average). However, most of us go fishing simply when we can get the time off. But there are best times, according to fishing lore:

■ One hour before and one hour after high tides, and one hour before and one hour after low tides. The times of high tides for Boston are given on **pages 120–146**; also see **pages 236–237**. (Inland, the times for high tides correspond with the times when the Moon is due south. Low tides are halfway between high tides.)

**GET TIDE TIMES AND HEIGHTS NEAREST TO YOUR LOCATION VIA ALMANAC.COM/2022.**

■ During the "morning rise" (after sunup for a spell) and the "evening rise" (just before sundown and the hour or so after).

■ During the rise and set of the Moon.

■ When the barometer is steady or on the rise. (But even during stormy periods, the fish aren't going to give up feeding. The clever angler will find just the right bait.)

■ When there is a hatch of flies—caddis flies or mayflies, commonly.

■ When the breeze is from a westerly quarter, rather than from the north or east.

■ When the water is still or slightly rippled, rather than during a wind.

## THE BEST FISHING DAYS FOR 2022, WHEN THE MOON IS BETWEEN NEW AND FULL

January 2–17
February 1–16
March 2–18
April 1–16
April 30–May 16
May 30–June 14
June 28–July 13
July 28–August 11
August 27–September 10
September 25–October 9
October 25–November 8
November 23–December 7
December 23–31

*Dates based on Eastern Time.*

## HOW TO ESTIMATE THE WEIGHT OF A FISH

Measure the fish from the tip of its nose to the tip of its tail. Then measure its girth at the thickest portion of its midsection.

The weight of a fat-bodied fish (bass, salmon) = (length x girth x girth)/800

**SALMON**

The weight of a slender fish (trout, northern pike) = (length x girth x girth)/900

**TROUT**

**EXAMPLE:** If a trout is 20 inches long and has a 12-inch girth, its estimated weight is (20 x 12 x 12)/900 = 2,880/900 = 3.2 pounds

**CATFISH**

# GESTATION AND MATING TABLES

| | PROPER AGE OR WEIGHT FOR FIRST MATING | PERIOD OF FERTILITY (YRS.) | NUMBER OF FEMALES FOR ONE MALE | PERIOD OF GESTATION (DAYS) AVERAGE | RANGE |
|---|---|---|---|---|---|
| **CATTLE: Cow** | 15–18 mos.[1] | 10–14 | | 283 | 279–290[2] 262–300[3] |
| **Bull** | 1 yr., well matured | 10–12 | 50[4] / thousands[5] | | |
| **GOAT: Doe** | 10 mos. or 85–90 lbs. | 6 | | 150 | 145–155 |
| **Buck** | well matured | 5 | 30 | | |
| **HORSE: Mare** | 3 yrs. | 10–12 | | 336 | 310–370 |
| **Stallion** | 3 yrs. | 12–15 | 40–45[4] / record 252[5] | | |
| **PIG: Sow** | 5–6 mos. or 250 lbs. | 6 | | 115 | 110–120 |
| **Boar** | 250–300 lbs. | 6 | 50[6] / 35–40[7] | | |
| **RABBIT: Doe** | 6 mos. | 5–6 | | 31 | 30–32 |
| **Buck** | 6 mos. | 5–6 | 30 | | |
| **SHEEP: Ewe** | 1 yr. or 90 lbs. | 6 | | 147 / 151[8] | 142–154 |
| **Ram** | 12–14 mos., well matured | 7 | 50–75[6] / 35–40[7] | | |
| **CAT: Queen** | 12 mos. | 6 | | 63 | 60–68 |
| **Tom** | 12 mos. | 6 | 6–8 | | |
| **DOG: Bitch** | 16–18 mos. | 8 | | 63 | 58–67 |
| **Male** | 12–16 mos. | 8 | 8–10 | | |

[1]Holstein and beef: 750 lbs.; Jersey: 500 lbs. [2]Beef; 8–10 days shorter for Angus. [3]Dairy. [4]Natural. [5]Artificial. [6]Hand-mated. [7]Pasture. [8]For fine wool breeds.

## INCUBATION PERIOD OF POULTRY (DAYS)

| | |
|---|---|
| Chicken | 21 |
| Duck | 26–32 |
| Goose | 30–34 |
| Guinea | 26–28 |
| Turkey | 28 |

## AVERAGE LIFE SPAN OF ANIMALS IN CAPTIVITY (YEARS)

| | | | |
|---|---|---|---|
| Cat (domestic) | 14 | Goose (domestic) | 20 |
| Chicken (domestic) | 8 | Horse | 22 |
| Dog (domestic) | 13 | Pig | 12 |
| Duck (domestic) | 10 | Rabbit | 6 |
| Goat (domestic) | 14 | Turkey (domestic) | 10 |

| | ESTRAL/ESTROUS CYCLE (INCLUDING HEAT PERIOD) AVERAGE | RANGE | LENGTH OF ESTRUS (HEAT) AVERAGE | RANGE | USUAL TIME OF OVULATION | WHEN CYCLE RECURS IF NOT BRED |
|---|---|---|---|---|---|---|
| **Cow** | 21 days | 18–24 days | 18 hours | 10–24 hours | 10–12 hours after end of estrus | 21 days |
| **Doe goat** | 21 days | 18–24 days | 2–3 days | 1–4 days | Near end of estrus | 21 days |
| **Mare** | 21 days | 10–37 days | 5–6 days | 2–11 days | 24–48 hours before end of estrus | 21 days |
| **Sow** | 21 days | 18–24 days | 2–3 days | 1–5 days | 30–36 hours after start of estrus | 21 days |
| **Ewe** | 16½ days | 14–19 days | 30 hours | 24–32 hours | 12–24 hours before end of estrus | 16½ days |
| **Queen cat** | | 15–21 days | 3–4 days, if mated | 9–10 days, in absence of male | 24–56 hours after coitus | Pseudo-pregnancy |
| **Bitch** | 24 days | 16–30 days | 7 days | 5–9 days | 1–3 days after first acceptance | Pseudo-pregnancy |

# PLANTING BY THE MOON'S PHASE

## ACCORDING TO THIS AGE-OLD PRACTICE, CYCLES OF THE MOON AFFECT PLANT GROWTH.

Plant annual flowers and vegetables that bear crops above ground during the light, or waxing, of the Moon: from the day the Moon is new to the day it is full.

Plant flowering bulbs, biennial and perennial flowers, and vegetables that bear crops below ground during the dark, or waning, of the Moon: from the day after it is full to the day before it is new again.

The Planting Dates columns give the safe periods for planting in areas that receive frost. (See **page 232** for frost dates in your area.) The Moon Favorable columns give the best planting days within the Planting Dates based on the Moon's phases for 2022. (See **pages 120–146** for the exact days of the new and full Moons.)

*The dates listed in this table are meant as general guidelines only. For seed-sowing dates based on frost dates in your local area, go to* **Almanac.com/2022.**

Aboveground crops are marked *.
(E) means early; (L) means late.

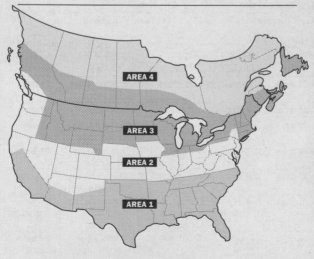

| | |
|---|---|
| * Barley | |
| * Beans | (E) |
| | (L) |
| Beets | (E) |
| | (L) |
| * Broccoli plants | (E) |
| | (L) |
| * Brussels sprouts | |
| * Cabbage plants | |
| Carrots | (E) |
| | (L) |
| * Cauliflower plants | (E) |
| | (L) |
| * Celery plants | (E) |
| | (L) |
| * Collards | (E) |
| | (L) |
| * Corn, sweet | (E) |
| | (L) |
| * Cucumbers | |
| * Eggplant plants | |
| * Endive | (E) |
| | (L) |
| * Kale | (E) |
| | (L) |
| Leek plants | |
| * Lettuce | |
| * Muskmelons | |
| * Okra | |
| Onion sets | |
| * Parsley | |
| Parsnips | |
| * Peas | (E) |
| | (L) |
| * Pepper plants | |
| Potatoes | |
| * Pumpkins | |
| Radishes | (E) |
| | (L) |
| * Spinach | (E) |
| | (L) |
| * Squashes | |
| Sweet potatoes | |
| * Swiss chard | |
| * Tomato plants | |
| Turnips | (E) |
| | (L) |
| * Watermelons | |
| * Wheat, spring | |
| * Wheat, winter | |

| AREA 1 | | AREA 2 | | AREA 3 | | AREA 4 | |
| PLANTING DATES | MOON FAVORABLE | PLANTING DATES | MOON FAVORABLE | PLANTING DATES | MOON FAVORABLE | PLANTING DATES | MOON FAVORABLE |
|---|---|---|---|---|---|---|---|
| 15-3/7 | 2/15-16, 3/2-7 | 3/15-4/7 | 3/15-18, 4/1-7 | 5/15-6/21 | 5/15-16, 5/30-6/14 | 6/1-30 | 6/1-14, 6/28-30 |
| 15-4/7 | 3/15-18, 4/1-7 | 4/15-30 | 4/15-16, 4/30 | 5/7-6/21 | 5/7-16, 5/30-6/14 | 5/30-6/15 | 5/30-6/14 |
| 7-31 | 8/7-11, 8/27-31 | 7/1-21 | 7/1-13 | 6/15-7/15 | 6/28-7/13 | — | — |
| 7-28 | 2/17-28 | 3/15-4/3 | 3/19-31 | 4/25-5/15 | 4/25-29 | 5/25-6/10 | 5/25-29 |
| 4-30 | 9/11-24 | 8/15-31 | 8/15-26 | 7/15-8/15 | 7/15-27, 8/12-15 | 6/15-7/8 | 6/15-27 |
| 15-3/15 | 2/15-16, 3/2-15 | 3/7-31 | 3/7-18 | 5/15-31 | 5/15-16, 5/30-31 | 6/1-25 | 6/1-14 |
| 7-30 | 9/7-10, 9/25-30 | 8/1-20 | 8/1-11 | 6/15-7/7 | 6/28-7/7 | — | — |
| 1-3/20 | 2/11-16, 3/2-18 | 3/7-4/15 | 3/7-18, 4/1-15 | 5/15-31 | 5/15-16, 5/30-31 | 6/1-25 | 6/1-14 |
| 1-3/20 | 2/11-16, 3/2-18 | 3/7-4/15 | 3/7-18, 4/1-15 | 5/15-31 | 5/15-16, 5/30-31 | 6/1-25 | 6/1-14 |
| 15-3/7 | 2/17-3/1 | 3/7-31 | 3/19-31 | 5/15-31 | 5/17-29 | 5/25-6/10 | 5/25-29 |
| 1-9/7 | 8/12-26 | 7/7-31 | 7/14-27 | 6/15-7/21 | 6/15-27, 7/14-21 | 6/15-7/8 | 6/15-27 |
| 15-3/7 | 2/15-16, 3/2-7 | 3/15-4/7 | 3/15-18, 4/1-7 | 5/15-31 | 5/15-16, 5/30-31 | 6/1-25 | 6/1-14 |
| 7-31 | 8/7-11, 8/27-31 | 7/1-8/7 | 7/1-13, 7/28-8/7 | 6/15-7/21 | 6/28-7/13 | — | — |
| 5-28 | 2/15-16 | 3/7-31 | 3/7-18 | 5/15-6/30 | 5/15-16, 5/30-6/14, 6/28-30 | 6/1-30 | 6/1-14, 6/28-30 |
| 15-30 | 9/25-30 | 8/15-9/7 | 8/27-9/7 | 7/15-8/15 | 7/28-8/11 | — | — |
| 1-3/20 | 2/11-16, 3/2-18 | 3/7-4/7 | 3/7-18, 4/1-7 | 5/15-31 | 5/15-16, 5/30-31 | 6/1-25 | 6/1-14 |
| 7-30 | 9/7-10, 9/25-30 | 8/15-31 | 8/27-31 | 7/1-8/7 | 7/1-13, 7/28-8/7 | — | — |
| 15-31 | 3/15-18 | 4/1-17 | 4/1-16 | 5/10-6/15 | 5/10-16, 5/30-6/14 | 5/30-6/20 | 5/30-6/14 |
| 7-31 | 8/7-11, 8/27-31 | 7/7-21 | 7/7-13 | 6/15-30 | 6/28-30 | — | — |
| 7-4/15 | 3/7-18, 4/1-15 | 4/7-5/15 | 4/7-16, 4/30-5/15 | 5/7-6/20 | 5/7-16, 5/30-6/14 | 5/30-6/15 | 5/30-6/14 |
| 7-4/15 | 3/7-18, 4/1-15 | 4/7-5/15 | 4/7-16, 4/30-5/15 | 6/1-30 | 6/1-14, 6/28-30 | 6/15-30 | 6/28-30 |
| 5-3/20 | 2/15-16, 3/2-18 | 4/7-5/15 | 4/7-16, 4/30-5/15 | 5/15-31 | 5/15-16, 5/30-31 | 6/1-25 | 6/1-14 |
| 5-9/7 | 8/27-9/7 | 7/15-8/15 | 7/28-8/11 | 6/7-30 | 6/7-14, 6/28-30 | — | — |
| 1-3/20 | 2/11-16, 3/2-18 | 3/7-4/7 | 3/7-18, 4/1-7 | 5/15-31 | 5/15-16, 5/30-31 | 6/1-15 | 6/1-14 |
| 7-30 | 9/7-10, 9/25-30 | 8/15-31 | 8/27-31 | 7/1-8/7 | 7/1-13, 7/28-8/7 | 6/25-7/15 | 6/28-7/13 |
| 5-4/15 | 2/17-3/1, 3/19-31 | 3/7-4/7 | 3/19-31 | 5/15-31 | 5/17-29 | 6/1-25 | 6/15-25 |
| 5-3/7 | 2/15-16, 3/2-7 | 3/1-31 | 3/2-18 | 5/15-6/30 | 5/15-16, 5/30-6/14, 6/28-30 | 6/1-30 | 6/1-14, 6/28-30 |
| 5-4/7 | 3/15-18, 4/1-7 | 4/15-5/7 | 4/15-16, 4/30-5/7 | 5/15-6/30 | 5/15-16, 5/30-6/14, 6/28-30 | 6/1-30 | 6/1-14, 6/28-30 |
| 5-6/1 | 4/15-16, 4/30-5/16, 5/30-6/1 | 5/25-6/15 | 5/30-6/14 | 6/15-7/10 | 6/28-7/10 | 6/15-7/7 | 6/28-7/7 |
| -28 | 2/17-28 | 3/1-31 | 3/1, 3/19-31 | 5/15-6/7 | 5/17-29 | 6/1-25 | 6/15-25 |
| 20-3/15 | 3/2-15 | 3/1-31 | 3/2-18 | 5/15-31 | 5/15-16, 5/30-31 | 6/1-15 | 6/1-14 |
| 5-2/4 | 1/18-31 | 3/7-31 | 3/19-31 | 4/1-30 | 4/17-29 | 5/10-31 | 5/17-29 |
| 5-2/7 | 1/15-17, 2/1-7 | 3/7-31 | 3/7-18 | 4/15-5/7 | 4/15-16, 4/30-5/7 | 5/15-31 | 5/15-16, 5/30-31 |
| 5-30 | 9/25-30 | 8/7-31 | 8/7-11, 8/27-31 | 7/15-31 | 7/28-31 | 7/10-25 | 7/10-13 |
| -20 | 3/2-18 | 4/1-30 | 4/1-16, 4/30 | 5/15-6/30 | 5/15-16, 5/30-6/14, 6/28-30 | 6/1-30 | 6/1-14, 6/28-30 |
| 0-28 | 2/17-28 | 4/1-30 | 4/17-29 | 5/1-31 | 5/17-29 | 6/1-25 | 6/15-25 |
| -20 | 3/7-18 | 4/23-5/15 | 4/30-5/15 | 5/15-31 | 5/15-16, 5/30-31 | 6/1-30 | 6/1-14, 6/28-30 |
| 1-3/1 | 1/21-31, 2/17-3/1 | 3/7-31 | 3/19-31 | 4/15-30 | 4/17-29 | 5/15-6/5 | 5/17-29 |
| 1-21 | 10/10-21 | 9/7-30 | 9/11-24 | 8/15-31 | 8/15-26 | 7/10-31 | 7/14-27 |
| -3/15 | 2/7-16, 3/2-15 | 3/15-4/20 | 3/15-18, 4/1-16 | 5/15-31 | 5/15-16, 5/30-31 | 6/1-25 | 6/1-14 |
| 1-21 | 10/1-9 | 8/1-9/15 | 8/1-11, 8/27-9/10 | 7/17-9/7 | 7/28-8/11, 8/27-9/7 | 7/20-8/5 | 7/28-8/5 |
| 5-4/15 | 3/15-18, 4/1-15 | 4/15-30 | 4/15-16, 4/30 | 5/15-6/15 | 5/15-16, 5/30-6/14 | 6/1-30 | 6/1-14, 6/28-30 |
| 3-4/6 | 3/23-31 | 4/21-5/9 | 4/21-29 | 5/15-6/15 | 5/29-6, 6/15 | 6/1-30 | 6/15-27 |
| -3/15 | 2/7-16, 3/2-15 | 3/15-4/15 | 3/15-18, 4/1-15 | 5/1-31 | 5/1-16, 5/30-31 | 5/15-31 | 5/15-16, 5/30-31 |
| -20 | 3/7-18 | 4/7-30 | 4/7-16, 4/30 | 5/15-31 | 5/15-16, 5/30-31 | 6/1-15 | 6/1-14 |
| 0-2/15 | 1/20-31 | 3/15-31 | 3/19-31 | 4/7-30 | 4/17-29 | 5/10-31 | 5/17-29 |
| -10/15 | 9/11-24, 10/10-15 | 8/1-20 | 8/12-20 | 7/1-8/15 | 7/14-27, 8/12-15 | — | — |
| 5-4/7 | 3/15-18, 4/1-7 | 4/15-5/7 | 4/15-16, 4/30-5/7 | 5/15-6/30 | 5/15-16, 5/30-6/14, 6/28-30 | 6/1-30 | 6/1-14, 6/28-30 |
| 5-28 | 2/15-16 | 3/1-20 | 3/2-18 | 4/7-30 | 4/7-16, 4/30 | 5/15-6/10 | 5/15-16, 5/30-6/10 |
| 15-12/7 | 10/25-11/8, 11/23-12/7 | 9/15-10/20 | 9/25-10/9 | 8/11-9/15 | 8/11, 8/27-9/10 | 8/5-30 | 8/5-11, 8/27-30 |

# FROSTS AND GROWING SEASONS

Dates given are normal averages for a light freeze; local weather and topography may cause considerable variations. The possibility of frost occurring after the spring dates and before the fall dates is 30 percent. The classification of freeze temperatures is usually based on their effect on plants. **Light freeze:** 29° to 32°F—tender plants killed. **Moderate freeze:** 25° to 28°F—widely destructive to most plants. **Severe freeze:** 24°F and colder—heavy damage to most plants. –dates courtesy of National Centers for Environmental Information

| STATE | CITY | GROWING SEASON (DAYS) | LAST SPRING FROST | FIRST FALL FROST | STATE | CITY | GROWING SEASON (DAYS) | LAST SPRING FROST | FIRST FALL FROST |
|---|---|---|---|---|---|---|---|---|---|
| AK | Juneau | 168 | Apr. 27 | Oct. 13 | NC | Fayetteville | 208 | Apr. 8 | Nov. 3 |
| AL | Mobile | 267 | Mar. 6 | Nov. 29 | ND | Bismarck | 122 | May 19 | Sept. 19 |
| AR | Pine Bluff | 226 | Mar. 26 | Nov. 8 | NE | Omaha | 160 | Apr. 27 | Oct. 5 |
| AZ | Phoenix | 340 | Jan. 20 | Dec. 27 | NE | North Platte | 146 | May 6 | Sept. 30 |
| AZ | Tucson | 304 | Feb. 5 | Dec. 7 | NH | Concord | 127 | May 19 | Sept. 24 |
| CA | Eureka | 276 | Mar. 2 | Dec. 4 | NJ | Newark | 209 | Apr. 8 | Nov. 4 |
| CA | Sacramento | 277 | Feb. 21 | Nov. 26 | NM | Carlsbad | 209 | Apr. 5 | Nov. 1 |
| CO | Denver | 153 | May 4 | Oct. 5 | NM | Los Alamos | 146 | May 10 | Oct. 4 |
| CO | Grand Junction | 162 | May 2 | Oct. 12 | NV | Las Vegas | 284 | Feb. 15 | Nov. 27 |
| CT | Hartford | 159 | May 1 | Oct. 8 | NY | Albany | 153 | May 4 | Oct. 5 |
| DE | Wilmington | 202 | Apr. 12 | Nov. 1 | NY | Syracuse | 156 | May 4 | Oct. 8 |
| FL | Orlando | 338 | Jan. 29 | Jan. 1 | OH | Akron | 165 | May 2 | Oct. 15 |
| FL | Tallahassee | 224 | Mar. 29 | Nov. 9 | OH | Cincinnati | 175 | Apr. 23 | Oct. 16 |
| GA | Athens | 214 | Apr. 3 | Nov. 4 | OK | Lawton | 211 | Apr. 3 | Nov. 1 |
| GA | Savannah | 249 | Mar. 15 | Nov. 20 | OK | Tulsa | 210 | Apr. 4 | Nov. 1 |
| IA | Atlantic | 136 | May 8 | Sept. 22 | OR | Pendleton | 152 | May 2 | Oct. 2 |
| IA | Cedar Rapids | 157 | Apr. 30 | Oct. 5 | OR | Portland | 255 | Mar. 11 | Nov. 22 |
| ID | Boise | 152 | May 7 | Oct. 7 | PA | Franklin | 156 | May 10 | Oct. 14 |
| IL | Chicago | 193 | Apr. 18 | Oct. 29 | PA | Williamsport | 164 | May 2 | Oct. 14 |
| IL | Springfield | 168 | Apr. 23 | Oct. 9 | RI | Kingston | 142 | May 12 | Oct. 2 |
| IN | Indianapolis | 171 | Apr. 25 | Oct. 14 | SC | Charleston | 298 | Feb. 19 | Dec. 15 |
| IN | South Bend | 162 | May 3 | Oct. 13 | SC | Columbia | 235 | Mar. 23 | Nov. 14 |
| KS | Topeka | 173 | Apr. 22 | Oct. 13 | SD | Rapid City | 146 | May 7 | Oct. 1 |
| KY | Lexington | 183 | Apr. 20 | Oct. 21 | TN | Memphis | 225 | Mar. 27 | Nov. 8 |
| LA | Monroe | 223 | Mar. 24 | Nov. 3 | TN | Nashville | 198 | Apr. 12 | Oct. 28 |
| LA | New Orleans | 297 | Feb. 17 | Dec. 12 | TX | Amarillo | 179 | Apr. 21 | Oct. 18 |
| MA | Boston | 206 | Apr. 10 | Nov. 3 | TX | Denton | 227 | Mar. 27 | Nov. 10 |
| MA | Worcester | 167 | Apr. 28 | Oct. 13 | TX | San Antonio | 262 | Mar. 5 | Nov. 23 |
| MD | Baltimore | 234 | Mar. 27 | Nov. 17 | UT | Cedar City | 122 | May 28 | Sept. 28 |
| ME | Portland | 152 | May 5 | Oct. 5 | UT | Spanish Fork | 158 | May 4 | Oct. 10 |
| MI | Lansing | 147 | May 9 | Oct. 4 | VA | Norfolk | 251 | Mar. 20 | Nov. 27 |
| MI | Marquette | 155 | May 11 | Oct. 14 | VA | Richmond | 202 | Apr. 10 | Oct. 30 |
| MN | Duluth | 119 | May 25 | Sept. 22 | VT | Burlington | 145 | May 10 | Oct. 3 |
| MN | Willmar | 146 | May 5 | Sept. 29 | WA | Seattle | 243 | Mar. 17 | Nov. 16 |
| MO | Jefferson City | 189 | Apr. 14 | Oct. 21 | WA | Spokane | 146 | May 10 | Oct. 4 |
| MS | Columbia | 234 | Mar. 20 | Nov. 10 | WI | Green Bay | 140 | May 11 | Sept. 29 |
| MS | Tupelo | 206 | Apr. 5 | Oct. 29 | WI | Sparta | 138 | May 12 | Sept. 28 |
| MT | Fort Peck | 129 | May 15 | Sept. 22 | WV | Parkersburg | 179 | Apr. 23 | Oct. 20 |
| MT | Helena | 123 | May 19 | Sept. 20 | WY | Casper | 107 | May 31 | Sept. 16 |

# PHENOLOGY: NATURE'S CALENDAR

*Study nature, love nature, stay close to nature. It will never fail you.*
–FRANK LLOYD WRIGHT, AMERICAN ARCHITECT (1867–1959)

For centuries, farmers and gardeners have looked to events in nature to tell them when to plant vegetables and flowers and when to expect insects. Making such observations is called "phenology," the study of phenomena. Specifically, this refers to the life cycles of plants and animals as they correlate to weather and temperature, or nature's calendar.

## VEGETABLES

- Plant peas when forsythias bloom.
- Plant potatoes when the first dandelion blooms.
- Plant beets, carrots, cole crops (broccoli, brussels sprouts, collards), lettuce, and spinach when lilacs are in first leaf or dandelions are in full bloom.
- Plant corn when oak leaves are the size of a squirrel's ear (about ½ inch in diameter). Or, plant corn when apple blossoms fade and fall.
- Plant bean, cucumber, and squash seeds when lilacs are in full bloom.
- Plant tomatoes when lilies-of-the-valley are in full bloom.
- Transplant eggplants and peppers when bearded irises bloom.
- Plant onions when red maples bloom.

## FLOWERS

- Plant morning glories when maple trees have full-size leaves.
- Plant zinnias and marigolds when black locusts are in full bloom.
- Plant pansies, snapdragons, and other hardy annuals when aspens and chokecherries have leafed out.

## INSECTS

- When purple lilacs bloom, grasshopper eggs hatch.
- When chicory blooms, beware of squash vine borers.
- When Canada thistles bloom, protect susceptible fruit; apple maggot flies are at peak.
- When foxglove flowers open, expect Mexican beetle larvae.
- When crabapple trees are in bud, eastern tent caterpillars are hatching.
- When morning glory vines begin to climb, Japanese beetles appear.
- When wild rocket blooms, cabbage root maggots appear.

If the signal plants are not growing in your area, notice other coincident events; record them and watch for them in ensuing seasons.

# TABLE OF MEASURES

## LINEAR

1 hand = 4 inches
1 link = 7.92 inches
1 span = 9 inches
1 foot = 12 inches
1 yard = 3 feet
1 rod = 5½ yards
1 mile = 320 rods = 1,760 yards = 5,280 feet
1 international nautical mile = 6,076.1155 feet
1 knot = 1 nautical mile per hour
1 fathom = 2 yards = 6 feet
1 furlong = ⅛ mile = 660 feet = 220 yards
1 league = 3 miles = 24 furlongs
1 chain = 100 links = 22 yards

## SQUARE

1 square foot = 144 square inches
1 square yard = 9 square feet
1 square rod = 30¼ square yards = 272¼ square feet = 625 square links

1 square chain = 16 square rods
1 acre = 10 square chains = 160 square rods = 43,560 square feet
1 square mile = 640 acres = 102,400 square rods

## CUBIC

1 cubic foot = 1,728 cubic inches
1 cubic yard = 27 cubic feet
1 cord = 128 cubic feet
1 U.S. liquid gallon = 4 quarts = 231 cubic inches
1 imperial gallon = 1.20 U.S. gallons = 0.16 cubic foot
1 board foot = 144 cubic inches

## DRY

2 pints = 1 quart
4 quarts = 1 gallon
2 gallons = 1 peck
4 pecks = 1 bushel

## LIQUID

4 gills = 1 pint
63 gallons = 1 hogshead
2 hogsheads = 1 pipe or butt
2 pipes = 1 tun

## KITCHEN

3 teaspoons = 1 tablespoon
16 tablespoons = 1 cup
1 cup = 8 ounces
2 cups = 1 pint
2 pints = 1 quart
4 quarts = 1 gallon

## AVOIRDUPOIS

(for general use)

1 ounce = 16 drams
1 pound = 16 ounces
1 short hundredweight = 100 pounds
1 ton = 2,000 pounds
1 long ton = 2,240 pounds

## APOTHECARIES'

(for pharmaceutical use)

1 scruple = 20 grains
1 dram = 3 scruples
1 ounce = 8 drams
1 pound = 12 ounces

## METRIC CONVERSIONS

### LINEAR

1 inch = 2.54 centimeters
1 centimeter = 0.39 inch
1 meter = 39.37 inches
1 yard = 0.914 meter
1 mile = 1.61 kilometers
1 kilometer = 0.62 mile

### SQUARE

1 square inch = 6.45 square centimeters
1 square yard = 0.84 square meter
1 square mile = 2.59 square kilometers

1 square kilometer = 0.386 square mile
1 acre = 0.40 hectare
1 hectare = 2.47 acres

### CUBIC

1 cubic yard = 0.76 cubic meter
1 cubic meter = 1.31 cubic yards

### HOUSEHOLD

½ teaspoon = 2.46 mL
1 teaspoon = 4.93 mL
1 tablespoon = 14.79 mL
¼ cup = 59.15 mL

⅓ cup = 78.86 mL
½ cup = 118.29 mL
¾ cup = 177.44 mL
1 cup = 236.59 mL
1 liter = 1.057 U.S. liquid quarts
1 U.S. liquid quart = 0.946 liter
1 U.S. liquid gallon = 3.78 liters
1 gram = 0.035 ounce
1 ounce = 28.349 grams
1 kilogram = 2.2 pounds
1 pound = 0.45 kilogram

TO CONVERT CELSIUS AND FAHRENHEIT: $°C = (°F - 32)/1.8$; $°F = (°C × 1.8) + 32$

# TIDAL GLOSSARY

**APOGEAN TIDE:** A monthly tide of decreased range that occurs when the Moon is at apogee (farthest from Earth).

**CURRENT:** Generally, a horizontal movement of water. Currents may be classified as tidal and nontidal. Tidal currents are caused by gravitational interactions between the Sun, Moon, and Earth and are part of the same general movement of the sea that is manifested in the vertical rise and fall, called tide. Nontidal currents include the permanent currents in the general circulatory systems of the sea as well as temporary currents arising from more pronounced meteorological variability.

**DIURNAL TIDE:** A tide with one high water and one low water in a tidal day of approximately 24 hours.

**MEAN LOWER LOW WATER:** The arithmetic mean of the lesser of a daily pair of low waters, observed over a specific 19-year cycle called the National Tidal Datum Epoch.

**NEAP TIDE:** A tide of decreased range that occurs twice a month, when the Moon is in quadrature (during its first and last quarters, when the Sun and the Moon are at right angles to each other relative to Earth).

**PERIGEAN TIDE:** A monthly tide of increased range that occurs when the Moon is at perigee (closest to Earth).

**RED TIDE:** Toxic algal blooms caused by several genera of dinoflagellates that usually turn the sea red or brown. These pose a serious threat to marine life and may be harmful to humans.

**RIP CURRENT:** A potentially dangerous, narrow, intense, surf-zone current flowing outward from shore.

**SEMIDIURNAL TIDE:** A tide with one high water and one low water every half-day. East Coast tides, for example, are semidiurnal, with two highs and two lows during a tidal day of approximately 24 hours.

**SLACK WATER (SLACK):** The state of a tidal current when its speed is near zero, especially the moment when a reversing current changes direction and its speed is zero.

**SPRING TIDE:** A tide of increased range that occurs at times of syzygy each month. Named not for the season of spring but from the German *springen* ("to leap up"), a spring tide also brings a lower low water.

**STORM SURGE:** The local change in the elevation of the ocean along a shore due to a storm, measured by subtracting the astronomic tidal elevation from the total elevation. It typically has a duration of a few hours and is potentially catastrophic, especially on low-lying coasts with gently sloping offshore topography.

**SYZYGY:** The nearly straight-line configuration that occurs twice a month, when the Sun and the Moon are in conjunction (on the same side of Earth, at the new Moon) and when they are in opposition (on opposite sides of Earth, at the full Moon). In both cases, the gravitational effects of the Sun and the Moon reinforce each other, and tidal range is increased.

**TIDAL BORE:** A tide-induced wave that propagates up a relatively shallow and sloping estuary or river with a steep wave front.

**TSUNAMI:** Commonly called a tidal wave, a tsunami is a series of long-period waves caused by an underwater earthquake or volcanic eruption. In open ocean, the waves are small and travel at high speed; as they near shore, some may build to more than 30 feet high, becoming a threat to life and property.

**VANISHING TIDE:** A mixed tide of considerable inequality in the two highs and two lows, so that the lower high (or higher low) may appear to vanish. ∎

# TIDE CORRECTIONS

Many factors affect tides, including the shoreline, time of the Moon's southing (crossing the meridian), and the Moon's phase. The High Tide Times column on the **Left-Hand Calendar Pages, 120–146,** lists the times of high tide at Commonwealth Pier in Boston (MA) Harbor. The heights of some of these tides, reckoned from Mean Lower Low Water, are given on the **Right-Hand Calendar Pages, 121–147.** Use the table below to calculate the approximate times and heights of high tide at the places shown. Apply the time difference to the times of high tide at Boston and the height difference to the heights at Boston. A more detailed and accurate tide calculator for the United States and Canada can be found via **Almanac.com/2022.**

**EXAMPLE:**

The conversion of the times and heights of the tides at Boston to those at Cape Fear, North Carolina, is given below:

| | |
|---|---|
| High tide at Boston | 11:45 A.M. |
| Correction for Cape Fear | - 3 55 |
| High tide at Cape Fear | 7:50 A.M. |
| | |
| Tide height at Boston | 11.6 ft. |
| Correction for Cape Fear | - 5.0 ft. |
| Tide height at Cape Fear | 6.6 ft. |

Estimations derived from this table are *not* meant to be used for navigation. *The Old Farmer's Almanac* accepts no responsibility for errors or any consequences ensuing from the use of this table.

| TIDAL SITE | TIME (H. M.) | HEIGHT (FT.) | TIDAL SITE | TIME (H. M.) | HEIGHT (FT.) |
|---|---|---|---|---|---|
| **CANADA** | | | Cape Cod Canal | | |
| Alberton, PE | *–5 45 | –7.5 | East Entrance | –0 01 | –0.8 |
| Charlottetown, PE | *–0 45 | –3.5 | West Entrance | –2 16 | –5.9 |
| Halifax, NS | –3 23 | –4.5 | Chatham Outer Coast | +0 30 | –2.8 |
| North Sydney, NS | –3 15 | –6.5 | Inside | +1 54 | **0.4 |
| Saint John, NB | +0 30 | +15.0 | Cohasset | +0 02 | –0.07 |
| St. John's, NL | –4 00 | –6.5 | Cotuit Highlands | +1 15 | **0.3 |
| Yarmouth, NS | –0 40 | +3.0 | Dennis Port | +1 01 | **0.4 |
| **MAINE** | | | Duxbury–Gurnet Point | +0 02 | –0.3 |
| Bar Harbor | –0 34 | +0.9 | Fall River | –3 03 | –5.0 |
| Belfast | –0 20 | +0.4 | Gloucester | –0 03 | –0.8 |
| Boothbay Harbor | –0 18 | –0.8 | Hingham | +0 07 | 0.0 |
| Chebeague Island | –0 16 | –0.6 | Hull | +0 03 | –0.2 |
| Eastport | –0 28 | +8.4 | Hyannis Port | +1 01 | **0.3 |
| Kennebunkport | +0 04 | –1.0 | Magnolia–Manchester | –0 02 | –0.7 |
| Machias | –0 28 | +2.8 | Marblehead | –0 02 | –0.4 |
| Monhegan Island | –0 25 | –0.8 | Marion | –3 22 | –5.4 |
| Old Orchard | 0 00 | –0.8 | Monument Beach | –3 08 | –5.4 |
| Portland | –0 12 | –0.6 | Nahant | –0 01 | –0.5 |
| Rockland | –0 28 | +0.1 | Nantasket | +0 04 | –0.1 |
| Stonington | –0 30 | +0.1 | Nantucket | +0 56 | **0.3 |
| York | –0 09 | –1.0 | Nauset Beach | +0 30 | **0.6 |
| **NEW HAMPSHIRE** | | | New Bedford | –3 24 | –5.7 |
| Hampton | +0 02 | –1.3 | Newburyport | +0 19 | –1.8 |
| Portsmouth | +0 11 | –1.5 | Oak Bluffs | +0 30 | **0.2 |
| Rye Beach | –0 09 | –0.9 | Onset–R.R. Bridge | –2 16 | –5.9 |
| **MASSACHUSETTS** | | | Plymouth | +0 05 | 0.0 |
| Annisquam | –0 02 | –1.1 | Provincetown | +0 14 | –0.4 |
| Beverly Farms | 0 00 | –0.5 | Revere Beach | –0 01 | –0.3 |

| TIDAL SITE | TIME (H. M.) | HEIGHT (FT.) | TIDAL SITE | TIME (H. M.) | HEIGHT (FT.) |
|---|---|---|---|---|---|
| Rockport | –0 08 | –1.0 | **PENNSYLVANIA** | | |
| Salem | 0 00 | –0.5 | Philadelphia | +2 40 | –3.5 |
| Scituate | –0 05 | –0.7 | **DELAWARE** | | |
| Wareham | –3 09 | –5.3 | Cape Henlopen | –2 48 | –5.3 |
| Wellfleet | +0 12 | +0.5 | Rehoboth Beach | –3 37 | –5.7 |
| West Falmouth | –3 10 | –5.4 | Wilmington | +1 56 | –3.8 |
| Westport Harbor | –3 22 | –6.4 | **MARYLAND** | | |
| Woods Hole | | | Annapolis | +6 23 | –8.5 |
|   Little Harbor | –2 50 | **0.2 | Baltimore | +7 59 | –8.3 |
|   Oceanographic | | | Cambridge | +5 05 | –7.8 |
|     Institute | –3 07 | **0.2 | Havre de Grace | +11 21 | –7.7 |
| **RHODE ISLAND** | | | Point No Point | +2 28 | –8.1 |
| Bristol | –3 24 | –5.3 | Prince Frederick– | | |
| Narragansett Pier | –3 42 | –6.2 |   Plum Point | +4 25 | –8.5 |
| Newport | –3 34 | –5.9 | **VIRGINIA** | | |
| Point Judith | –3 41 | –6.3 | Cape Charles | –2 20 | –7.0 |
| Providence | –3 20 | –4.8 | Hampton Roads | –2 02 | –6.9 |
| Sakonnet | –3 44 | –5.6 | Norfolk | –2 06 | –6.6 |
| Watch Hill | –2 50 | –6.8 | Virginia Beach | –4 00 | –6.0 |
| **CONNECTICUT** | | | Yorktown | –2 13 | –7.0 |
| Bridgeport | +0 01 | –2.6 | **NORTH CAROLINA** | | |
| Madison | –0 22 | –2.3 | Cape Fear | –3 55 | –5.0 |
| New Haven | –0 11 | –3.2 | Cape Lookout | –4 28 | –5.7 |
| New London | –1 54 | –6.7 | Currituck | –4 10 | –5.8 |
| Norwalk | +0 01 | –2.2 | Hatteras | | |
| Old Lyme– | | |   Inlet | –4 03 | –7.4 |
|   Highway Bridge | –0 30 | –6.2 |   Kitty Hawk | –4 14 | –6.2 |
| Stamford | +0 01 | –2.2 |   Ocean | –4 26 | –6.0 |
| Stonington | –2 27 | –6.6 | **SOUTH CAROLINA** | | |
| **NEW YORK** | | | Charleston | –3 22 | –4.3 |
| Coney Island | –3 33 | –4.9 | Georgetown | –1 48 | **0.36 |
| Fire Island Light | –2 43 | **0.1 | Hilton Head | –3 22 | –2.9 |
| Long Beach | –3 11 | –5.7 | Myrtle Beach | –3 49 | –4.4 |
| Montauk Harbor | –2 19 | –7.4 | St. Helena– | | |
| New York City–Battery | –2 43 | –5.0 |   Harbor Entrance | –3 15 | –3.4 |
| Oyster Bay | +0 04 | –1.8 | **GEORGIA** | | |
| Port Chester | –0 09 | –2.2 | Jekyll Island | –3 46 | –2.9 |
| Port Washington | –0 01 | –2.1 | St. Simon's Island | –2 50 | –2.9 |
| Sag Harbor | –0 55 | –6.8 | Savannah Beach | | |
| Southampton– | | |   River Entrance | –3 14 | –5.5 |
|   Shinnecock Inlet | –4 20 | **0.2 |   Tybee Light | –3 22 | –2.7 |
| Willets Point | 0 00 | –2.3 | **FLORIDA** | | |
| **NEW JERSEY** | | | Cape Canaveral | –3 59 | –6.0 |
| Asbury Park | –4 04 | –5.3 | Daytona Beach | –3 28 | –5.3 |
| Atlantic City | –3 56 | –5.5 | Fort Lauderdale | –2 50 | –7.2 |
| Bay Head–Sea Girt | –4 04 | –5.3 | Fort Pierce Inlet | –3 32 | –6.9 |
| Beach Haven | –1 43 | **0.24 | Jacksonville– | | |
| Cape May | –3 28 | –5.3 |   Railroad Bridge | –6 55 | **0.1 |
| Ocean City | –3 06 | –5.9 | Miami Harbor Entrance | –3 18 | –7.0 |
| Sandy Hook | –3 30 | –5.0 | St. Augustine | –2 55 | –4.9 |
| Seaside Park | –4 03 | –5.4 | | | |

*VARIES WIDELY; ACCURATE ONLY TO WITHIN 1½ HOURS. CONSULT LOCAL TIDE TABLES FOR PRECISE TIMES AND HEIGHTS.
**WHERE THE DIFFERENCE IN THE HEIGHT COLUMN IS SO MARKED, THE HEIGHT AT BOSTON SHOULD BE MULTIPLIED BY THIS RATIO.

# TIME CORRECTIONS

Astronomical data for Boston (42°22' N, 71°3' W) is given on **pages 104, 106, 108–109,** and **120–146.** Use the Key Letters shown on those pages with this table to find the number of minutes that you must add to or subtract from Boston time to get the correct time for your city. (Times are approximate.) For more information on the use of Key Letters, see **How to Use This Almanac, page 116.**

**GET TIMES SIMPLY AND SPECIFICALLY:** Download astronomical times calculated for your zip code and presented as Left-Hand Calendar Pages via **Almanac.com/2022.**

**TIME ZONES CODES** represent standard time. Atlantic is –1, Eastern is 0, Central is 1, Mountain is 2, Pacific is 3, Alaska is 4, and Hawaii-Aleutian is 5.

| STATE | CITY | NORTH LATITUDE ° | NORTH LATITUDE ' | WEST LONGITUDE ° | WEST LONGITUDE ' | TIME ZONE CODE | A | B | C | D | E |
|---|---|---|---|---|---|---|---|---|---|---|---|
| AK | Anchorage | 61 | 10 | 149 | 59 | 4 | –46 | +27 | +71 | +122 | +171 |
| AK | Cordova | 60 | 33 | 145 | 45 | 4 | –55 | +13 | +55 | +103 | +149 |
| AK | Fairbanks | 64 | 48 | 147 | 51 | 4 | –127 | +2 | +61 | +131 | +205 |
| AK | Juneau | 58 | 18 | 134 | 25 | 4 | –76 | –23 | +10 | +49 | +86 |
| AK | Ketchikan | 55 | 21 | 131 | 39 | 4 | –62 | –25 | 0 | +29 | +56 |
| AK | Kodiak | 57 | 47 | 152 | 24 | 4 | 0 | +49 | +82 | +120 | +154 |
| AL | Birmingham | 33 | 31 | 86 | 49 | 1 | +30 | +15 | +3 | –10 | –20 |
| AL | Decatur | 34 | 36 | 86 | 59 | 1 | +27 | +14 | +4 | –7 | –17 |
| AL | Mobile | 30 | 42 | 88 | 3 | 1 | +42 | +23 | +8 | –8 | –22 |
| AL | Montgomery | 32 | 23 | 86 | 19 | 1 | +31 | +14 | +1 | –13 | –25 |
| AR | Fort Smith | 35 | 23 | 94 | 25 | 1 | +55 | +43 | +33 | +22 | +14 |
| AR | Little Rock | 34 | 45 | 92 | 17 | 1 | +48 | +35 | +25 | +13 | +4 |
| AR | Texarkana | 33 | 26 | 94 | 3 | 1 | +59 | +44 | +32 | +18 | +8 |
| AZ | Flagstaff | 35 | 12 | 111 | 39 | 2 | +64 | +52 | +42 | +31 | +22 |
| AZ | Phoenix | 33 | 27 | 112 | 4 | 2 | +71 | +56 | +44 | +30 | +20 |
| AZ | Tucson | 32 | 13 | 110 | 58 | 2 | +70 | +53 | +40 | +24 | +12 |
| AZ | Yuma | 32 | 43 | 114 | 37 | 2 | +83 | +67 | +54 | +40 | +28 |
| CA | Bakersfield | 35 | 23 | 119 | 1 | 3 | +33 | +21 | +12 | +1 | –7 |
| CA | Barstow | 34 | 54 | 117 | 1 | 3 | +27 | +14 | +4 | –7 | –16 |
| CA | Fresno | 36 | 44 | 119 | 47 | 3 | +32 | +22 | +15 | +6 | 0 |
| CA | Los Angeles-Pasadena-Santa Monica | 34 | 3 | 118 | 14 | 3 | +34 | +20 | +9 | –3 | –13 |
| CA | Palm Springs | 33 | 49 | 116 | 32 | 3 | +28 | +13 | +1 | –12 | –22 |
| CA | Redding | 40 | 35 | 122 | 24 | 3 | +31 | +27 | +25 | +22 | +19 |
| CA | Sacramento | 38 | 35 | 121 | 30 | 3 | +34 | +27 | +21 | +15 | +10 |
| CA | San Diego | 32 | 43 | 117 | 9 | 3 | +33 | +17 | +4 | –9 | –21 |
| CA | San Francisco-Oakland-San Jose | 37 | 47 | 122 | 25 | 3 | +40 | +31 | +25 | +18 | +12 |
| CO | Craig | 40 | 31 | 107 | 33 | 2 | +32 | +28 | +25 | +22 | +20 |
| CO | Denver-Boulder | 39 | 44 | 104 | 59 | 2 | +24 | +19 | +15 | +11 | +7 |
| CO | Grand Junction | 39 | 4 | 108 | 33 | 2 | +40 | +34 | +29 | +24 | +20 |
| CO | Pueblo | 38 | 16 | 104 | 37 | 2 | +27 | +20 | +14 | +7 | +2 |
| CO | Trinidad | 37 | 10 | 104 | 31 | 2 | +30 | +21 | +13 | +5 | 0 |
| CT | Bridgeport | 41 | 11 | 73 | 11 | 0 | +12 | +10 | +8 | +6 | +4 |
| CT | Hartford-New Britain | 41 | 46 | 72 | 41 | 0 | +8 | +7 | +6 | +5 | +4 |
| CT | New Haven | 41 | 18 | 72 | 56 | 0 | +11 | +8 | +7 | +5 | +4 |
| CT | New London | 41 | 22 | 72 | 6 | 0 | +7 | +5 | +4 | +2 | +1 |
| CT | Norwalk-Stamford | 41 | 7 | 73 | 22 | 0 | +13 | +10 | +9 | +7 | +5 |
| CT | Waterbury-Meriden | 41 | 33 | 73 | 3 | 0 | +10 | +9 | +7 | +6 | +5 |
| DC | Washington | 38 | 54 | 77 | 1 | 0 | +35 | +28 | +23 | +18 | +13 |
| DE | Wilmington | 39 | 45 | 75 | 33 | 0 | +26 | +21 | +18 | +13 | +10 |

| STATE | CITY | NORTH LATITUDE | | WEST LONGITUDE | | TIME ZONE CODE | KEY LETTERS (MINUTES) | | | | |
|---|---|---|---|---|---|---|---|---|---|---|---|
| | | ° | ' | ° | ' | | A | B | C | D | E |
| FL | Fort Myers | 26 | 38 | 81 | 52 | 0 | +87 | +63 | +44 | +21 | +4 |
| FL | Jacksonville | 30 | 20 | 81 | 40 | 0 | +77 | +58 | +43 | +25 | +11 |
| FL | Miami | 25 | 47 | 80 | 12 | 0 | +88 | +57 | +37 | +14 | −3 |
| FL | Orlando | 28 | 32 | 81 | 22 | 0 | +80 | +59 | +42 | +22 | +6 |
| FL | Pensacola | 30 | 25 | 87 | 13 | 1 | +39 | +20 | +5 | −12 | −26 |
| FL | St. Petersburg | 27 | 46 | 82 | 39 | 0 | +87 | +65 | +47 | +26 | +10 |
| FL | Tallahassee | 30 | 27 | 84 | 17 | 0 | +87 | +68 | +53 | +35 | +22 |
| FL | Tampa | 27 | 57 | 82 | 27 | 0 | +86 | +64 | +46 | +25 | +9 |
| FL | West Palm Beach | 26 | 43 | 80 | 3 | 0 | +79 | +55 | +36 | +14 | −2 |
| GA | Atlanta | 33 | 45 | 84 | 24 | 0 | +79 | +65 | +53 | +40 | +30 |
| GA | Augusta | 33 | 28 | 81 | 58 | 0 | +70 | +55 | +44 | +30 | +19 |
| GA | Macon | 32 | 50 | 83 | 38 | 0 | +79 | +63 | +50 | +36 | +24 |
| GA | Savannah | 32 | 5 | 81 | 6 | 0 | +70 | +54 | +40 | +25 | +13 |
| HI | Hilo | 19 | 44 | 155 | 5 | 5 | +94 | +62 | +37 | +7 | −15 |
| HI | Honolulu | 21 | 18 | 157 | 52 | 5 | +102 | +72 | +48 | +19 | −1 |
| HI | Lanai City | 20 | 50 | 156 | 55 | 5 | +99 | +69 | +44 | +15 | −6 |
| HI | Lihue | 21 | 59 | 159 | 23 | 5 | +107 | +77 | +54 | +26 | +5 |
| IA | Davenport | 41 | 32 | 90 | 35 | 1 | +20 | +19 | +17 | +16 | +15 |
| IA | Des Moines | 41 | 35 | 93 | 37 | 1 | +32 | +31 | +30 | +28 | +27 |
| IA | Dubuque | 42 | 30 | 90 | 41 | 1 | +17 | +18 | +18 | +18 | +18 |
| IA | Waterloo | 42 | 30 | 92 | 20 | 1 | +24 | +24 | +24 | +25 | +25 |
| ID | Boise | 43 | 37 | 116 | 12 | 2 | +55 | +58 | +60 | +62 | +64 |
| ID | Lewiston | 46 | 25 | 117 | 1 | 3 | −12 | −3 | +2 | +10 | +17 |
| ID | Pocatello | 42 | 52 | 112 | 27 | 2 | +43 | +44 | +45 | +46 | +46 |
| IL | Cairo | 37 | 0 | 89 | 11 | 1 | +29 | +20 | +12 | +4 | −2 |
| IL | Chicago–Oak Park | 41 | 52 | 87 | 38 | 1 | +7 | +6 | +6 | +5 | +4 |
| IL | Danville | 40 | 8 | 87 | 37 | 1 | +13 | +9 | +6 | +2 | 0 |
| IL | Decatur | 39 | 51 | 88 | 57 | 1 | +19 | +15 | +11 | +7 | +4 |
| IL | Peoria | 40 | 42 | 89 | 36 | 1 | +19 | +16 | +14 | +11 | +9 |
| IL | Springfield | 39 | 48 | 89 | 39 | 1 | +22 | +18 | +14 | +10 | +6 |
| IN | Fort Wayne | 41 | 4 | 85 | 9 | 0 | +60 | +58 | +56 | +54 | +52 |
| IN | Gary | 41 | 36 | 87 | 20 | 1 | +7 | +6 | +4 | +3 | +2 |
| IN | Indianapolis | 39 | 46 | 86 | 10 | 0 | +69 | +64 | +60 | +56 | +52 |
| IN | Muncie | 40 | 12 | 85 | 23 | 0 | +64 | +60 | +57 | +53 | +50 |
| IN | South Bend | 41 | 41 | 86 | 15 | 0 | +62 | +61 | +60 | +59 | +58 |
| IN | Terre Haute | 39 | 28 | 87 | 24 | 0 | +74 | +69 | +65 | +60 | +56 |
| KS | Fort Scott | 37 | 50 | 94 | 42 | 1 | +49 | +41 | +34 | +27 | +21 |
| KS | Liberal | 37 | 3 | 100 | 55 | 1 | +76 | +66 | +59 | +51 | +44 |
| KS | Oakley | 39 | 8 | 100 | 51 | 1 | +69 | +63 | +59 | +53 | +49 |
| KS | Salina | 38 | 50 | 97 | 37 | 1 | +57 | +51 | +46 | +40 | +35 |
| KS | Topeka | 39 | 3 | 95 | 40 | 1 | +49 | +43 | +38 | +32 | +28 |
| KS | Wichita | 37 | 42 | 97 | 20 | 1 | +60 | +51 | +45 | +37 | +31 |
| KY | Lexington–Frankfort | 38 | 3 | 84 | 30 | 0 | +67 | +59 | +53 | +46 | +41 |
| KY | Louisville | 38 | 15 | 85 | 46 | 0 | +72 | +64 | +58 | +52 | +46 |
| LA | Alexandria | 31 | 18 | 92 | 27 | 1 | +58 | +40 | +26 | +9 | −3 |
| LA | Baton Rouge | 30 | 27 | 91 | 11 | 1 | +55 | +36 | +21 | +3 | −10 |
| LA | Lake Charles | 30 | 14 | 93 | 13 | 1 | +64 | +44 | +29 | +11 | −2 |
| LA | Monroe | 32 | 30 | 92 | 7 | 1 | +53 | +37 | +24 | +9 | −1 |
| LA | New Orleans | 29 | 57 | 90 | 4 | 1 | +52 | +32 | +16 | −1 | −15 |
| LA | Shreveport | 32 | 31 | 93 | 45 | 1 | +60 | +44 | +31 | +16 | +4 |
| MA | Brockton | 42 | 5 | 71 | 1 | 0 | 0 | 0 | 0 | 0 | −1 |
| MA | Fall River–New Bedford | 41 | 42 | 71 | 9 | 0 | +2 | +1 | 0 | 0 | −1 |
| MA | Lawrence–Lowell | 42 | 42 | 71 | 10 | 0 | 0 | 0 | 0 | 0 | +1 |
| MA | Pittsfield | 42 | 27 | 73 | 15 | 0 | +8 | +8 | +8 | +8 | +8 |
| MA | Springfield–Holyoke | 42 | 6 | 72 | 36 | 0 | +6 | +6 | +6 | +5 | +5 |
| MA | Worcester | 42 | 16 | 71 | 48 | 0 | +3 | +2 | +2 | +2 | +2 |

| STATE | CITY | NORTH LATITUDE ° | NORTH LATITUDE ' | WEST LONGITUDE ° | WEST LONGITUDE ' | TIME ZONE CODE | KEY LETTERS (MINUTES) A | B | C | D | E |
|---|---|---|---|---|---|---|---|---|---|---|---|
| MD | Baltimore | 39 | 17 | 76 | 37 | 0 | +32 | +26 | +22 | +17 | +13 |
| MD | Hagerstown | 39 | 39 | 77 | 43 | 0 | +35 | +30 | +26 | +22 | +18 |
| MD | Salisbury | 38 | 22 | 75 | 36 | 0 | +31 | +23 | +18 | +11 | +6 |
| ME | Augusta | 44 | 19 | 69 | 46 | 0 | −12 | −8 | −5 | −1 | 0 |
| ME | Bangor | 44 | 48 | 68 | 46 | 0 | −18 | −13 | −9 | −5 | −1 |
| ME | Eastport | 44 | 54 | 67 | 0 | 0 | −26 | −20 | −16 | −11 | −8 |
| ME | Ellsworth | 44 | 33 | 68 | 25 | 0 | −18 | −14 | −10 | −6 | −3 |
| ME | Portland | 43 | 40 | 70 | 15 | 0 | −8 | −5 | −3 | −1 | 0 |
| ME | Presque Isle | 46 | 41 | 68 | 1 | 0 | −29 | −19 | −12 | −4 | +2 |
| MI | Cheboygan | 45 | 39 | 84 | 29 | 0 | +40 | +47 | +53 | +59 | +64 |
| MI | Detroit-Dearborn | 42 | 20 | 83 | 3 | 0 | +47 | +47 | +47 | +47 | +47 |
| MI | Flint | 43 | 1 | 83 | 41 | 0 | +47 | +49 | +50 | +51 | +52 |
| MI | Ironwood | 46 | 27 | 90 | 9 | 1 | 0 | +9 | +15 | +23 | +29 |
| MI | Jackson | 42 | 15 | 84 | 24 | 0 | +53 | +53 | +53 | +52 | +52 |
| MI | Kalamazoo | 42 | 17 | 85 | 35 | 0 | +58 | +57 | +57 | +57 | +57 |
| MI | Lansing | 42 | 44 | 84 | 33 | 0 | +52 | +53 | +53 | +54 | +54 |
| MI | St. Joseph | 42 | 5 | 86 | 26 | 0 | +61 | +61 | +60 | +60 | +59 |
| MI | Traverse City | 44 | 46 | 85 | 38 | 0 | +49 | +54 | +57 | +62 | +65 |
| MN | Albert Lea | 43 | 39 | 93 | 22 | 1 | +24 | +26 | +28 | +31 | +33 |
| MN | Bemidji | 47 | 28 | 94 | 53 | 1 | +14 | +26 | +34 | +44 | +52 |
| MN | Duluth | 46 | 47 | 92 | 6 | 1 | +6 | +16 | +23 | +31 | +38 |
| MN | Minneapolis-St. Paul | 44 | 59 | 93 | 16 | 1 | +18 | +24 | +28 | +33 | +37 |
| MN | Ortonville | 45 | 19 | 96 | 27 | 1 | +30 | +36 | +40 | +46 | +51 |
| MO | Jefferson City | 38 | 34 | 92 | 10 | 1 | +36 | +29 | +24 | +18 | +13 |
| MO | Joplin | 37 | 6 | 94 | 30 | 1 | +50 | +41 | +33 | +25 | +18 |
| MO | Kansas City | 39 | 1 | 94 | 20 | 1 | +44 | +37 | +33 | +27 | +23 |
| MO | Poplar Bluff | 36 | 46 | 90 | 24 | 1 | +35 | +25 | +17 | +8 | +1 |
| MO | St. Joseph | 39 | 46 | 94 | 50 | 1 | +43 | +38 | +35 | +30 | +27 |
| MO | St. Louis | 38 | 37 | 90 | 12 | 1 | +28 | +21 | +16 | +10 | +5 |
| MO | Springfield | 37 | 13 | 93 | 18 | 1 | +45 | +36 | +29 | +20 | +14 |
| MS | Biloxi | 30 | 24 | 88 | 53 | 1 | +46 | +27 | +11 | −5 | −19 |
| MS | Jackson | 32 | 18 | 90 | 11 | 1 | +46 | +30 | +17 | +1 | −10 |
| MS | Meridian | 32 | 22 | 88 | 42 | 1 | +40 | +24 | +11 | −4 | −15 |
| MS | Tupelo | 34 | 16 | 88 | 34 | 1 | +35 | +21 | +10 | −2 | −11 |
| MT | Billings | 45 | 47 | 108 | 30 | 2 | +16 | +23 | +29 | +35 | +40 |
| MT | Butte | 46 | 1 | 112 | 32 | 2 | +31 | +39 | +45 | +52 | +57 |
| MT | Glasgow | 48 | 12 | 106 | 38 | 2 | −1 | +11 | +21 | +32 | +42 |
| MT | Great Falls | 47 | 30 | 111 | 17 | 2 | +20 | +31 | +39 | +49 | +58 |
| MT | Helena | 46 | 36 | 112 | 2 | 2 | +27 | +36 | +43 | +51 | +57 |
| MT | Miles City | 46 | 25 | 105 | 51 | 2 | +3 | +11 | +18 | +26 | +32 |
| NC | Asheville | 35 | 36 | 82 | 33 | 0 | +67 | +55 | +46 | +35 | +27 |
| NC | Charlotte | 35 | 14 | 80 | 51 | 0 | +61 | +49 | +39 | +28 | +19 |
| NC | Durham | 36 | 0 | 78 | 55 | 0 | +51 | +40 | +31 | +21 | +13 |
| NC | Greensboro | 36 | 4 | 79 | 47 | 0 | +54 | +43 | +35 | +25 | +17 |
| NC | Raleigh | 35 | 47 | 78 | 38 | 0 | +51 | +39 | +30 | +20 | +12 |
| NC | Wilmington | 34 | 14 | 77 | 55 | 0 | +52 | +38 | +27 | +15 | +5 |
| ND | Bismarck | 46 | 48 | 100 | 47 | 1 | +41 | +50 | +58 | +66 | +73 |
| ND | Fargo | 46 | 53 | 96 | 47 | 1 | +24 | +34 | +42 | +50 | +57 |
| ND | Grand Forks | 47 | 55 | 97 | 3 | 1 | +21 | +33 | +43 | +53 | +62 |
| ND | Minot | 48 | 14 | 101 | 18 | 1 | +36 | +50 | +59 | +71 | +81 |
| ND | Williston | 48 | 9 | 103 | 37 | 1 | +46 | +59 | +69 | +80 | +90 |
| NE | Grand Island | 40 | 55 | 98 | 21 | 1 | +53 | +51 | +49 | +46 | +44 |
| NE | Lincoln | 40 | 49 | 96 | 41 | 1 | +47 | +44 | +42 | +39 | +37 |
| NE | North Platte | 41 | 8 | 100 | 46 | 1 | +62 | +60 | +58 | +56 | +54 |
| NE | Omaha | 41 | 16 | 95 | 56 | 1 | +43 | +40 | +39 | +37 | +36 |
| NH | Berlin | 44 | 28 | 71 | 11 | 0 | −7 | −3 | 0 | +3 | +7 |
| NH | Keene | 42 | 56 | 72 | 17 | 0 | +2 | +3 | +4 | +5 | +6 |

| STATE | CITY | NORTH LATITUDE ° | NORTH LATITUDE ′ | WEST LONGITUDE ° | WEST LONGITUDE ′ | TIME ZONE CODE | KEY LETTERS (MINUTES) A | B | C | D | E |
|---|---|---|---|---|---|---|---|---|---|---|---|
| NH | Manchester-Concord | 42 | 59 | 71 | 28 | 0 | 0 | 0 | +1 | +2 | +3 |
| NH | Portsmouth | 43 | 5 | 70 | 45 | 0 | −4 | −2 | −1 | 0 | 0 |
| NJ | Atlantic City | 39 | 22 | 74 | 26 | 0 | +23 | +17 | +13 | +8 | +4 |
| NJ | Camden | 39 | 57 | 75 | 7 | 0 | +24 | +19 | +16 | +12 | +9 |
| NJ | Cape May | 38 | 56 | 74 | 56 | 0 | +26 | +20 | +15 | +9 | +5 |
| NJ | Newark-East Orange | 40 | 44 | 74 | 10 | 0 | +17 | +14 | +12 | +9 | +7 |
| NJ | Paterson | 40 | 55 | 74 | 10 | 0 | +17 | +14 | +12 | +9 | +7 |
| NJ | Trenton | 40 | 13 | 74 | 46 | 0 | +21 | +17 | +14 | +11 | +8 |
| NM | Albuquerque | 35 | 5 | 106 | 39 | 2 | +45 | +32 | +22 | +11 | +2 |
| NM | Gallup | 35 | 32 | 108 | 45 | 2 | +52 | +40 | +31 | +20 | +11 |
| NM | Las Cruces | 32 | 19 | 106 | 47 | 2 | +53 | +36 | +23 | +8 | −3 |
| NM | Roswell | 33 | 24 | 104 | 32 | 2 | +41 | +26 | +14 | 0 | −10 |
| NM | Santa Fe | 35 | 41 | 105 | 56 | 2 | +40 | +28 | +19 | +9 | 0 |
| NV | Carson City-Reno | 39 | 10 | 119 | 46 | 3 | +25 | +19 | +14 | +9 | +5 |
| NV | Elko | 40 | 50 | 115 | 46 | 3 | +3 | 0 | −1 | −3 | −5 |
| NV | Las Vegas | 36 | 10 | 115 | 9 | 3 | +16 | +4 | −3 | −13 | −20 |
| NY | Albany | 42 | 39 | 73 | 45 | 0 | +9 | +10 | +10 | +11 | +11 |
| NY | Binghamton | 42 | 6 | 75 | 55 | 0 | +20 | +19 | +19 | +18 | +18 |
| NY | Buffalo | 42 | 53 | 78 | 52 | 0 | +29 | +30 | +30 | +31 | +32 |
| NY | New York | 40 | 45 | 74 | 0 | 0 | +17 | +14 | +11 | +9 | +6 |
| NY | Ogdensburg | 44 | 42 | 75 | 30 | 0 | +8 | +13 | +17 | +21 | +25 |
| NY | Syracuse | 43 | 3 | 76 | 9 | 0 | +17 | +19 | +20 | +21 | +22 |
| OH | Akron | 41 | 5 | 81 | 31 | 0 | +46 | +43 | +41 | +39 | +37 |
| OH | Canton | 40 | 48 | 81 | 23 | 0 | +46 | +43 | +41 | +38 | +36 |
| OH | Cincinnati-Hamilton | 39 | 6 | 84 | 31 | 0 | +64 | +58 | +53 | +48 | +44 |
| OH | Cleveland-Lakewood | 41 | 30 | 81 | 42 | 0 | +45 | +43 | +42 | +40 | +39 |
| OH | Columbus | 39 | 57 | 83 | 1 | 0 | +55 | +51 | +47 | +43 | +40 |
| OH | Dayton | 39 | 45 | 84 | 10 | 0 | +61 | +56 | +52 | +48 | +44 |
| OH | Toledo | 41 | 39 | 83 | 33 | 0 | +52 | +50 | +49 | +48 | +47 |
| OH | Youngstown | 41 | 6 | 80 | 39 | 0 | +42 | +40 | +38 | +36 | +34 |
| OK | Oklahoma City | 35 | 28 | 97 | 31 | 1 | +67 | +55 | +46 | +35 | +26 |
| OK | Tulsa | 36 | 9 | 95 | 60 | 1 | +59 | +48 | +40 | +30 | +22 |
| OR | Eugene | 44 | 3 | 123 | 6 | 3 | +21 | +24 | +27 | +30 | +33 |
| OR | Pendleton | 45 | 40 | 118 | 47 | 3 | −1 | +4 | +10 | +16 | +21 |
| OR | Portland | 45 | 31 | 122 | 41 | 3 | +14 | +20 | +25 | +31 | +36 |
| OR | Salem | 44 | 57 | 123 | 1 | 3 | +17 | +23 | +27 | +31 | +35 |
| PA | Allentown-Bethlehem | 40 | 36 | 75 | 28 | 0 | +23 | +20 | +17 | +14 | +12 |
| PA | Erie | 42 | 7 | 80 | 5 | 0 | +36 | +36 | +35 | +35 | +35 |
| PA | Harrisburg | 40 | 16 | 76 | 53 | 0 | +30 | +26 | +23 | +19 | +16 |
| PA | Lancaster | 40 | 2 | 76 | 18 | 0 | +28 | +24 | +20 | +17 | +13 |
| PA | Philadelphia-Chester | 39 | 57 | 75 | 9 | 0 | +24 | +19 | +16 | +12 | +9 |
| PA | Pittsburgh-McKeesport | 40 | 26 | 80 | 0 | 0 | +42 | +38 | +35 | +32 | +29 |
| PA | Reading | 40 | 20 | 75 | 56 | 0 | +26 | +22 | +19 | +16 | +13 |
| PA | Scranton-Wilkes-Barre | 41 | 25 | 75 | 40 | 0 | +21 | +19 | +18 | +16 | +15 |
| PA | York | 39 | 58 | 76 | 43 | 0 | +30 | +26 | +22 | +18 | +15 |
| RI | Providence | 41 | 50 | 71 | 25 | 0 | +3 | +2 | +1 | 0 | 0 |
| SC | Charleston | 32 | 47 | 79 | 56 | 0 | +64 | +48 | +36 | +21 | +10 |
| SC | Columbia | 34 | 0 | 81 | 2 | 0 | +65 | +51 | +40 | +27 | +17 |
| SC | Spartanburg | 34 | 56 | 81 | 57 | 0 | +66 | +53 | +43 | +32 | +23 |
| SD | Aberdeen | 45 | 28 | 98 | 29 | 1 | +37 | +44 | +49 | +54 | +59 |
| SD | Pierre | 44 | 22 | 100 | 21 | 1 | +49 | +53 | +56 | +60 | +63 |
| SD | Rapid City | 44 | 5 | 103 | 14 | 2 | +2 | +5 | +8 | +11 | +13 |
| SD | Sioux Falls | 43 | 33 | 96 | 44 | 1 | +38 | +40 | +42 | +44 | +46 |
| TN | Chattanooga | 35 | 3 | 85 | 19 | 0 | +79 | +67 | +57 | +45 | +36 |
| TN | Knoxville | 35 | 58 | 83 | 55 | 0 | +71 | +60 | +51 | +41 | +33 |
| TN | Memphis | 35 | 9 | 90 | 3 | 1 | +38 | +26 | +16 | +5 | −3 |
| TN | Nashville | 36 | 10 | 86 | 47 | 1 | +22 | +11 | +3 | −6 | −14 |

| STATE/ PROVINCE | CITY | NORTH LATITUDE ° | NORTH LATITUDE ′ | WEST LONGITUDE ° | WEST LONGITUDE ′ | TIME ZONE CODE | KEY LETTERS (MINUTES) A | B | C | D | E |
|---|---|---|---|---|---|---|---|---|---|---|---|
| TX | Amarillo | 35 | 12 | 101 | 50 | 1 | +85 | +73 | +63 | +52 | +43 |
| TX | Austin | 30 | 16 | 97 | 45 | 1 | +82 | +62 | +47 | +29 | +15 |
| TX | Beaumont | 30 | 5 | 94 | 6 | 1 | +67 | +48 | +32 | +14 | 0 |
| TX | Brownsville | 25 | 54 | 97 | 30 | 1 | +91 | +66 | +46 | +23 | +5 |
| TX | Corpus Christi | 27 | 48 | 97 | 24 | 1 | +86 | +64 | +46 | +25 | +9 |
| TX | Dallas–Fort Worth | 32 | 47 | 96 | 48 | 1 | +71 | +55 | +43 | +28 | +17 |
| TX | El Paso | 31 | 45 | 106 | 29 | 2 | +53 | +35 | +22 | +6 | −6 |
| TX | Galveston | 29 | 18 | 94 | 48 | 1 | +72 | +52 | +35 | +16 | +1 |
| TX | Houston | 29 | 45 | 95 | 22 | 1 | +73 | +53 | +37 | +19 | +5 |
| TX | McAllen | 26 | 12 | 98 | 14 | 1 | +93 | +69 | +49 | +26 | +9 |
| TX | San Antonio | 29 | 25 | 98 | 30 | 1 | +87 | +66 | +50 | +31 | +16 |
| UT | Kanab | 37 | 3 | 112 | 32 | 2 | +62 | +53 | +46 | +37 | +30 |
| UT | Moab | 38 | 35 | 109 | 33 | 2 | +46 | +39 | +33 | +27 | +22 |
| UT | Ogden | 41 | 13 | 111 | 58 | 2 | +47 | +45 | +43 | +41 | +40 |
| UT | Salt Lake City | 40 | 45 | 111 | 53 | 2 | +48 | +45 | +43 | +40 | +38 |
| UT | Vernal | 40 | 27 | 109 | 32 | 2 | +40 | +36 | +33 | +30 | +28 |
| VA | Charlottesville | 38 | 2 | 78 | 30 | 0 | +43 | +35 | +29 | +22 | +17 |
| VA | Danville | 36 | 36 | 79 | 23 | 0 | +51 | +41 | +33 | +24 | +17 |
| VA | Norfolk | 36 | 51 | 76 | 17 | 0 | +38 | +28 | +21 | +12 | +5 |
| VA | Richmond | 37 | 32 | 77 | 26 | 0 | +41 | +32 | +25 | +17 | +11 |
| VA | Roanoke | 37 | 16 | 79 | 57 | 0 | +51 | +42 | +35 | +27 | +21 |
| VA | Winchester | 39 | 11 | 78 | 10 | 0 | +38 | +33 | +28 | +23 | +19 |
| VT | Brattleboro | 42 | 51 | 72 | 34 | 0 | +4 | +5 | +5 | +6 | +7 |
| VT | Burlington | 44 | 29 | 73 | 13 | 0 | 0 | +4 | +8 | +12 | +15 |
| VT | Rutland | 43 | 37 | 72 | 58 | 0 | +2 | +5 | +7 | +9 | +11 |
| VT | St. Johnsbury | 44 | 25 | 72 | 1 | 0 | −4 | 0 | +3 | +7 | +10 |
| WA | Bellingham | 48 | 45 | 122 | 29 | 3 | 0 | +13 | +24 | +37 | +47 |
| WA | Seattle–Tacoma–Olympia | 47 | 37 | 122 | 20 | 3 | +3 | +15 | +24 | +34 | +42 |
| WA | Spokane | 47 | 40 | 117 | 24 | 3 | −16 | −4 | +4 | +14 | +23 |
| WA | Walla Walla | 46 | 4 | 118 | 20 | 3 | −5 | +2 | +8 | +15 | +21 |
| WI | Eau Claire | 44 | 49 | 91 | 30 | 1 | +12 | +17 | +21 | +25 | +29 |
| WI | Green Bay | 44 | 31 | 88 | 0 | 1 | 0 | +3 | +7 | +11 | +14 |
| WI | La Crosse | 43 | 48 | 91 | 15 | 1 | +15 | +18 | +20 | +22 | +25 |
| WI | Madison | 43 | 4 | 89 | 23 | 1 | +10 | +11 | +12 | +14 | +15 |
| WI | Milwaukee | 43 | 2 | 87 | 54 | 1 | +4 | +6 | +7 | +8 | +9 |
| WI | Oshkosh | 44 | 1 | 88 | 33 | 1 | +3 | +6 | +9 | +12 | +15 |
| WI | Wausau | 44 | 58 | 89 | 38 | 1 | +4 | +9 | +13 | +18 | +22 |
| WV | Charleston | 38 | 21 | 81 | 38 | 0 | +55 | +48 | +42 | +35 | +30 |
| WV | Parkersburg | 39 | 16 | 81 | 34 | 0 | +52 | +46 | +42 | +36 | +32 |
| WY | Casper | 42 | 51 | 106 | 19 | 2 | +19 | +19 | +20 | +21 | +22 |
| WY | Cheyenne | 41 | 8 | 104 | 49 | 2 | +19 | +16 | +14 | +12 | +11 |
| WY | Sheridan | 44 | 48 | 106 | 58 | 2 | +14 | +19 | +23 | +27 | +31 |

## CANADA

| STATE/ PROVINCE | CITY | NORTH LATITUDE ° | NORTH LATITUDE ′ | WEST LONGITUDE ° | WEST LONGITUDE ′ | TIME ZONE CODE | A | B | C | D | E |
|---|---|---|---|---|---|---|---|---|---|---|---|
| AB | Calgary | 51 | 5 | 114 | 5 | 2 | +13 | +35 | +50 | +68 | +84 |
| AB | Edmonton | 53 | 34 | 113 | 25 | 2 | −3 | +26 | +47 | +72 | +93 |
| BC | Vancouver | 49 | 13 | 123 | 6 | 3 | 0 | +15 | +26 | +40 | +52 |
| MB | Winnipeg | 49 | 53 | 97 | 10 | 1 | +12 | +30 | +43 | +58 | +71 |
| NB | Saint John | 45 | 16 | 66 | 3 | −1 | +28 | +34 | +39 | +44 | +49 |
| NS | Halifax | 44 | 38 | 63 | 35 | −1 | +21 | +26 | +29 | +33 | +37 |
| NS | Sydney | 46 | 10 | 60 | 10 | −1 | +1 | +9 | +15 | +23 | +28 |
| ON | Ottawa | 45 | 25 | 75 | 43 | 0 | +6 | +13 | +18 | +23 | +28 |
| ON | Peterborough | 44 | 18 | 78 | 19 | 0 | +21 | +25 | +28 | +32 | +35 |
| ON | Thunder Bay | 48 | 27 | 89 | 12 | 0 | +47 | +61 | +71 | +83 | +93 |
| ON | Toronto | 43 | 39 | 79 | 23 | 0 | +28 | +30 | +32 | +35 | +37 |
| QC | Montreal | 45 | 28 | 73 | 39 | 0 | −1 | +4 | +9 | +15 | +20 |
| SK | Saskatoon | 52 | 10 | 106 | 40 | 1 | +37 | +63 | +80 | +101 | +119 |

# GLOSSARY OF TIME

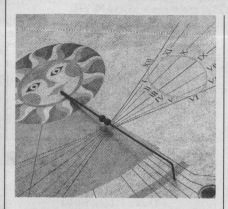

**ATOMIC TIME (TA) SCALE:** A time scale based on atomic or molecular resonance phenomena. Elapsed time is measured by counting cycles of a frequency locked to an atomic or molecular transition.

**DATE:** A unique instant defined in a specified time scale. NOTE: The date can be conventionally expressed in years, months, days, hours, minutes, seconds, and fractions.

**GREENWICH MEAN TIME (GMT):** A 24-hour system based on mean solar time plus 12 hours at Greenwich, England. Greenwich Mean Time can be considered approximately equivalent to Coordinated Universal Time (UTC), which is broadcast from all standard time and frequency radio stations. However, GMT is now obsolete and has been replaced by UTC.

**INTERNATIONAL ATOMIC TIME (TAI):** An atomic time scale based on data from a worldwide set of atomic clocks. It is the internationally agreed-upon time reference conforming to the definition of the second, the fundamental unit of atomic time in the International System of Units (SI).

**LEAP SECOND:** An intentional time step of one second used to adjust UTC. An inserted second is called a positive leap second, and an omitted second is called a negative leap second. We currently need to insert a leap second about once per year.

**MEAN SOLAR TIME:** Apparent solar time corrected for the effects of orbital eccentricity and the tilt of Earth's axis relative to the ecliptic plane; that is, corrected by the equation of time, which is defined as the hour angle of the true Sun minus the hour angle of the mean Sun.

**SECOND:** The basic unit of time or time interval in the International System of Units (SI), which is equal to 9,192,631,770 periods of radiation corresponding to the transition between the two hyperfine levels of the ground state of cesium-133 as defined at the 1967 Conférence Générale des Poids et Mesures.

**SIDEREAL TIME:** The measure of time defined by the apparent diurnal motion of the vernal equinox; hence, a measure of the rotation of Earth with respect to the reference frame that is related to the stars rather than the Sun. A mean solar day is about 4 minutes longer than a sidereal day.

*–(U.S.) National Institute of Standards and Technology (NIST)*

# GENERAL STORE CLASSIFIEDS

For advertising information and rates, go to Almanac.com/Advertising
or call RJ Media at 212-986-0016. The 2023 edition closes on April 30, 2022.

## ASTROLOGY

**REV. BROWN.** Removes bad luck, Sickness, Pain, Negativity. Specializing: Ritual Work, Spiritual Cleansing. Guaranteed! Call: 252-366-4078.

**SOPHIA GREEN.** Don't tell me, I'll tell you! Helps all problems—Reunites lovers. Guaranteed! Call: 956-878-7053.

**PSYCHIC SPIRITUALIST ROSELLA**
I don't judge, I solve all love problems.
Helps stop breakups & divorce.
Reunites loved ones.
Tells past, present, & future.
**Spiritual Soul Cleansing**
**Call: 586-215-3838**

**PSYCHIC HEALER LYNN**
Worried? Suffering?
Solves all problems!
Specializes: Love, Health, Finances
**Call today! 704-550-5975**

**ANN, SPIRITUALIST**
Relationship Specialist.
Solves Problems! Reunites Lovers.
Advice: Cheating, Marriage, Business.
Clears Negativity. Immediate Results.
**Call: 910-334-5137**

**ANGEL PSYCHIC**
**MEDIUM CLAIRVOYANT**
Spiritual ~ Positive Energy
*Accurate *Honest *Healing
**Call: 323-466-3684**
**www.TruePsychicReader.com**

**SEEKING LUCK, LOVE, MONEY?** With Spiritual Cleansing, achieve goals! FREE Tarot Reading! 811 Saluda Street, Rockville, SC 29730. Call: 803-371-7711.

**REV. JACKSON, VOODOO HEALER.** Guaranteed to remove Cross Conditions, Bad Luck, Sickness, Roots, Pain. Call: 252-469-6420.

## ASTROLOGY (continued)

**ATTENTION: SISTER LIGHT**
Spartanburg, South Carolina
One FREE READING when you call.
I will help you with all problems.
**Call: 864-576-9397**

## BOOKS, MAGAZINES, CATALOGS

Children's William Tell Drama, $10.00
Theory At Lyra, $10.00
7 Plate Armadillo Cloth Pattern, $30.00
Armadillo Astronomy Theory
3 Eastern Lane
West Gardiner, ME 04345

## BUSINESS OPPORTUNITIES

**$800 WEEKLY POTENTIAL!** Process HUD/FHA refunds from home. Free information available. Call: 860-357-1599.

## JEWELRY

**WWW.AZUREGREEN.NET** Jewelry, Amulets, Incense, Oils, Statuary, Gifts, Herbs, Candles, Gemstones. 8,000 Items. Wholesale inquiries welcome.

## PERSONALS

**ASIAN WOMEN!** Overseas Penpals. Romance! Free brochure (send SASE). P.I.C., Box 4601-OFA, Thousand Oaks, CA 91359. Call: 805-492-8040. www.pacisl.com

## PODCASTS

**THE NED NATTER SHOW**
*The funniest Podcast in America*
Everyday farm life and crazy antics of the folks
down on 2 Medicine Farm.
**www.NedNatter.com**

# 2021 ESSAY CONTEST WINNERS
### *"A Kindness I Will Always Remember"*

We received hundreds of entries for this contest—possibly the most ever! Thank you to all who entered and shared a heartfelt tribute.

## First Prize: $300

When I was in second grade in the late 1950s, the school principal's wife invited me to her home for an afternoon. My mother had passed away the year before, so I welcomed the extra attention. Soon after I stepped into her cheery kitchen, she suggested that we play "beauty shop." I stood on my tiptoes, my head bent over her gleaming sink, as she washed my hair with her very special shampoo. Then, while I sat perched on a stool with a fluffy towel wrapped around my head, she polished my fingernails and rubbed my hands and arms with a creamy lotion that smelled of lilacs. After she rinsed my hair one more time, we sat on her front porch swing enjoying cookies and milk, my feet dangling while my hair dried in the sun. I felt like a princess that afternoon as she carefully combed and styled my hair. Many years later, I found out that the very special shampoo was a treatment for head lice, but this kind and compassionate woman spared me the stigma and embarrassment by never letting on that I was anything but a princess in need of a little pampering.

–Susan Yarrington, Puposky, Minnesota

## Second Prize: $200

My youngest son died in a car accident on December 25, 1998. In the hospital, I made the decision to donate his organs so that others could be helped by our tragedy. It was my experience with the donor agency that the survivors were celebrated, not the donors. A few years later, I was sitting in an airport when I struck up a conversation with an attractive, much younger man. The conversation flowed easily between us as we were waiting for our flights. He mentioned that he was the recipient of a donor kidney. When I shared with him my son's story, he leaned in, stood me up, looked me in the eyes, and said, "I never thanked the person who donated their kidney to me, so I want to thank you and your son with all of my heart." He gave me the warmest, sweetest, hug that lasted long enough so that we were both in tears when we separated. It was one of the most magical moments in my life and replaced all of the negativity that I was feeling toward the organ donation agency. We then said "Good-bye" and boarded our flights.

–Monica Clark, New Orleans, Louisiana

# Third Prize: $100

When I was a young woman living in Miami, I walked to work. At one corner, there was a handicapped man who sat on a tattered blanket, trying to sell pencils. I was always in a hurry and never stopped to help him. One day, I was having coffee in a restaurant nearby. While I was there, the "pencil man" came in and sat two seats away from me at the counter. When I wanted to pay for the coffee, I found that I was penniless. I had left my wallet at home. Highly embarrassed, I told the waitress and just sat there. I saw the young man struggle to open the worn change purse in his hand. With great difficulty, he took out two quarters and slid them haltingly along the counter saying, "Take these." Even speech was a struggle for him. Thanking him profusely, I took them and paid . . . and then I left and cried.

The next morning, I rushed to the corner to buy all of the pencils and more. He wasn't there. He was never there again. It was as if an angel had come down to Earth to test my generosity. It changed my life. Since then, I've often been accused of being "too generous."

*–Sonja Karlsen, Tryon, North Carolina*

---

## Honorable Mention

I will never forget how when I was a child (probably around 7 or so) growing up in Virginia, I heard a tragic story on the news about a child who had accidentally drowned. They announced that the burial would be held later in Pennsylvania. A couple of days later, my dad and I were on the highway and ran out of gas. A gentleman stopped and offered to take us to get some gas and take it back to the car. While talking, we discovered that he was getting ready to head up to Pennsylvania for a funeral. It turned out that this stranger who stopped to help a man and his young daughter on the side of the road was the same man who had just lost his own child earlier that week. Even at what had to have been his lowest point, this kind man took the time out of all that he must have been going through to stop and help someone else in need. I am in my mid-50s now, and this extraordinary act of kindness can still bring tears to my eyes.

*–M. J. Dawley, Pewaukee, Wisconsin* ■

---

**ANNOUNCING THE 2022 ESSAY CONTEST TOPIC:
MY MOST MEMORABLE WILDLIFE EXPERIENCE**
SEE CONTEST RULES ON PAGE 251.

# MADDENING MIND-MANGLERS

## Tennessee Teasers for '22!

*Which one does not belong?*

**1.** Alligator • Cockroach • Crocodile • Hippopotamus • Iguana • Octopus

**2.** 1 • 7 • 11 • 13 • 14 • 17

**3.** Creek • Dam • Lake • Ocean • Pond • River • Snow

**4.** Chevrolet • Dodge • Ford • Nissan • Toyota • Volkswagen

*–Morris Bowles, Cane Ridge, Tennessee*

---

## Virginia Vexer

*One Devil of a Puzzle*

**5.** __ __ __ __ __ __ __ __
    1   2   3   4   5   6   7   8

*I am a word of eight letters.*

According to *The Devil's Dictionary* (1906) by Ambrose Bierce:

My 1, 7, 2, 4 is "a preparation that renders the hook more palatable."

My 5, 8, 6, 3, 7 is "a kind of animal that the ancients catalogued under many heads."

My 1, 7, 4, 5 is "a kind of mystic ceremony substituted for religious worship, with what spiritual efficacy has not been determined."

My 5, 8, 1, 3, 2, 6 is "a pooled issue."

My 6, 2, 7, 3, 8 is "a daily record of that part of one's life, which he can relate to himself without blushing."

My 5, 7, 1, 2, 4 is "a shackle for the free."

*–Monty Gilmer, Rosedale, Virginia*

---

## Types of Municipalities

What do the names of these six places have in common?

**6.** Asbury Park • Billings • Biloxi • Fresno • Louisville • Sitka

## The Farmer's Herd

**7.** A farmer in Arkansas passed away and left his 17 cows to his children, as follows: to his elder son, he left one-half; to his daughter, one-third; to his younger son, one-ninth. How did the children divide up the herd without killing or cutting up a cow?

## A Matter of Perspective

**8.** Here are top and side views of a solid object. What are two possible front views?

*Do you have a favorite puzzler for "Maddening Mind-Manglers" that you'd like to share? Send it to us at Mind-Manglers, The Old Farmer's Almanac, P.O. Box 520, Dublin, NH 03444, or via Almanac.com/ Feedback, Subject: Mind-Manglers.*

### ANSWERS

**1.** Iguana: only one with a repeating vowel pronounced in the same way, e.g., alligator has both short and long "a" sounds, while iguana has only the short "a" sound. **2.** 13: only one with a rounded digit. **3.** Ocean: only one not associated with fresh water. **4.** Nissan: only one with no letter "o". **5.** Bait, Hydra, Bath, Hybrid, Diary, Habit, BIRTHDAY. **6.** They are all names of typefaces (fonts). **7.** They borrowed a cow from a neighbor, making 18 in total. The elder son got nine; the daughter, six; the younger son, two. They then returned the extra cow. **8.**

# ESSAY AND RECIPE CONTEST RULES

Cash prizes (first, $300; second, $200; third, $100) will be awarded for the best essays in 200 words or less on the subject "My Most Memorable Wildlife Experience" and the best recipes in the category "Bananas." Entries must be yours, original, and unpublished. Amateur cooks only, please. One recipe per person. All entries become the property of Yankee Publishing, which reserves all rights to the material. The deadline for entries is Friday, January 28, 2022. Enter at Almanac.com/ EssayContest or at Almanac .com/RecipeContest or label "Essay Contest" or "Recipe Contest" and mail to The Old Farmer's Almanac, P.O. Box 520, Dublin, NH 03444. Include your name, mailing address, and email address. Winners will appear in *The 2023 Old Farmer's Almanac* and on Almanac.com. ∎

# ANECDOTES & PLEASANTRIES

*A sampling from the thousands of letters, clippings,
articles, and emails sent to us during the past year by our
Almanac family in the United States and Canada.*

ILLUSTRATIONS BY TIM ROBINSON

## THIS YEAR'S ANIMAL NEWS

A moment of silence, please, for Maurice, a raucous rooster in western France whose owners were once sued because of his "noise pollution." The crowing cockerel's case—which he won—became a cause célèbre that led to greater appreciation for and protection of that nation's countryside sounds. Alas, a respiratory infection recently claimed the cock-a-doodle-dooer, although laryngitis has been secretly suspected in some quarters. Maurice was survived by three hens and thousands of *omelettes françaises.* 　–*C. M. N., Sherbrooke, Quebec*

Satellite dishes have been sprouting atop beaver lodges across Canada. The work of pranksters or the sign of more fans for *Hockey Night in Canada?* As far as we know, no one has yet squeezed into a den to find out for sure, but come to think of it, who would better know "streaming" than the clever castors?

　–*J. W., Yellowknife, Northwest Territories*

Don't look now (especially if you're a cow, sheep, or pig!), but in a striking blow to animal privacy rights, facial recognition technology is now being used for livestock management through tracking individual animals' drinking, eating, and "other" habits. It also can ID suspects that are acting strangely, like kicking up their heels about being facially monitored.

　–*M. G., Ames, Iowa*

# Why Grandparents Play Silly Games With Grandchildren

On the first day, God created the dog and said, "Sit all day by the door of your house and bark at anyone who comes in or walks past. For this, I will give you a life span of 20 years." The dog replied, "That's a long time to be barking—how about only 10 years and I'll give you back the other 10?" And God saw that this was good.

On the second day, God created the monkey and said, "Entertain people, do tricks, and make them laugh. For this, I will give you a 20-year life span." The monkey replied, "Monkey tricks for 20 years? That's a pretty long time to perform. How about I give you back 10 like the dog did?" And again, God saw that this was good.

On the third day, God created the cow and said, "You must go into the field with the farmer all day long and suffer in the sun, have calves, and give milk to support the farmer's family. For this, I will give you a life span of 60 years." The cow replied, "That's kind of a tough life that you want me to live for 60 years. How about 20 and I'll give back the other 40?" And again, God agreed that this was good.

On the fourth day, God created the human and said, "Eat, sleep, play, marry, and enjoy your life. For this, I will give you 20 years." But the human replied, "Only 20 years? Could you possibly give me my 20, the 40 that the cow gave back, the 10 the monkey gave back, and the 10 the dog gave back—that would make 80, right?" And God said, "Okay, it shall be as you ask."

This is why for our first 20 years, we eat, sleep, play, and enjoy ourselves. For the next 40, we slave in the sun to support our family. For the next 10, we do monkey tricks to entertain the grandchildren. And for the last 10, we sit on the front porch and bark at everyone.

*–W. W., Taos, New Mexico*
*(continued)*

# Riddle Us These

Ever wonder why . . .

- the sun lightens our hair but darkens our skin?
- you never see the headline "Psychic Wins Lottery"?
- "abbreviated" is such a long word?
- doctors call what they do "practice"?
- you have to click "Start" to stop Windows?
- packaged lemon juice is made with artificial flavor, while dishwashing liquid is made with real lemon juice?
- the man who invests all your money is called a "broker"?
- there isn't mouse-flavor cat food?

- an airplane is not made from the same material as the indestructible black box?
- they are called apartments when they are all stuck together?

*–G. W. S., Marlborough, New Hampshire*

---

# How to De-Skunk a Dog

According to the Purdue University College of Medicine: For small to medium dogs (and other pets), use 2 ounces of Massengill douche with 1 gallon of water. For large dogs, double the amount of water and Massengill. Pour the mixture over the dog until it is thoroughly soaked, wait 15 minutes, and then rinse. Follow with a bath using the dog's regular shampoo.

*–A. B., Indianapolis, Indiana*

# WHY YOU SHOULD PAINT YOUR BATHROOM PURPLE*

As most people know, colors can impart or signify certain qualities.

**Black:** drama, formality, security

**Brown:** dependability, simplicity, trustworthiness

**Green:** freshness, healing, naturalness

**Orange:** bravery, confidence, sociability

**Pink:** compassion, sincerity, sweetness

**Purple:** luxury, royalty (*it's the "throne room," after all!), spirituality

**Red:** energy, love, strength

**Yellow:** creativity, happiness, warmth

*–M. B., Lorton, Virginia*

## When the Cat Doesn't Notice the Mouse

Pay attention to these old-time signs and omens around the house if you know what's good for you! (We think.) (Well, maybe.)

**Chairs back to back**—If chairs have accidentally been placed back to back, a stranger will arrive.

**Falling cup**—If a cup falls from your hand and does not break, you will be asked to witness a stranger's wedding.

**Last piece of pie**—The person who is asked to have the last piece of pie will have a handsome husband or wife.

**Mouse unnoticed by cat**—If a mouse should cross your room unnoticed by the cat, it is a sure sign of a visit from one you love.

**Overflowing water**—If a pail or tub overflows while you are filling it, you will be overrun with callers.

**Raising an empty glass**—This will bring unexpected news.

**Torn napkin**—This foretells a fortunate journey.

**Window blind rolls up askew**—This is a sign of impending disappointment.

–The Book of Signs and Omens: or How to Avoid Ill-Luck *(Toronto, 1905)*

## THANKS, BUT I'LL STICK WITH PEANUT BUTTER

I hope that I shall never see
A jellyfish as big as me.
The little ones are bad enough,
All filled with pulsing purple stuff;
A giant one might well deliver
Stings to make a strong man quiver.
I don't fear squids or octopuses–
Count me not among such wusses.
With equanimity I've viewed a
Toothsome tribe of barracuda,
Met with quiet heart the dreaded
Shark (both white and hammer-headed),
Mastered mantas without quail
And cowed the hulking killer whale.
But all my strength and skills desert me
When faced with squishy things that hurt me.

*–Tim Clark, Dublin, New Hampshire* ■

**Send your contribution for** *The 2023 Old Farmer's Almanac* **by January 28, 2022, to "A & P,"** The Old Farmer's Almanac, P.O. Box 520, Dublin, NH 03444, or email it to AlmanacEditors@yankeepub.com (subject: A & P).

*Now available in the U.S. without a prescription!*

# Pill Used in Germany For 53 Years Relieves Joint Pain In 7 Days Without Side Effects

**Approved by top doctors nationwide. Active ingredient numbs nerves that trigger pain. Relieves joint stiffness. Increases joint mobility and freedom.**

By J.K. Roberts
*Interactive News Media*

INM — A pill that relieves joint pain and stiffness in 7 days without side effects has been used safely in Germany for 53 years. It is now available in the United States.

This pill contains an active ingredient that not only relieves pain quickly, but also works to rebuild damaged cartilage between bones for greater range of motion.

It can cut your pain relief costs up to 82% less than using pain relief drugs and pain relief cream and heat products.

An improved version of this pill is now being offered in the United States under the brand name FlexJointPlus.

FlexJointPlus relieves joint pain, back pain, neck pain, carpal tunnel, sprains, strains, sports injuries, and more. With daily use, users can expect to feel 24-hour relief.

"Relief in pain and stiffness is felt in as quickly as 7 days," said Roger Lewis, Chief Researcher for FlexJointPlus.

"And with regular use, you can expect even more reduction in the following 30-60 days," added Lewis.

**WHAT SCIENTISTS DISCOVERED**

FlexJointPlus contains an amazing compound with a known ability to rebuild damaged cartilage and ligaments associated with joint pain.

This compound is not a drug. It is the active ingredient in FlexJointPlus.

Studies show it naturally reduces inflammation while repairing bone and cartilage in the joint.

Many joint pain sufferers see an increase in flexibility and mobility. Others are able to get back to doing the things they love.

With so much positive feedback, it's easy to see why sales for this newly approved joint pain pill continue to climb every day.

**IMPRESSIVE BENEFITS FOR JOINT PAIN SUFFERERS**

The 8 week clinical study was carried out by scientists across six different clinic sites in Germany. The results were published in the Journal of Arthritis in July 2014.

The study involved patients with a variety of joint pain conditions associated with osteoarthritis. They were not instructed to change their daily routines. They were only told to take FlexJointPlus's active ingredient every day.

The results were incredible.

Taking FlexJointPlus's active ingredient just once daily significantly reduced both joint pain and stiffness compared to placebo at 7, 30, and 60 days.

In fact, many patients experienced greater than 50% reduction in pain and stiffness at 60 days.

They also enjoyed an improvement in stiffness when first getting out of the bed in the morning, and an improvement in pain when doing light household chores.

The findings are impressive, no doubt, but results will vary.

But with results like these it's easy to see why thousands of callers are jamming the phone lines trying to get their hands on FlexJointPlus.

**HOW IT REBUILDS DAMAGED JOINTS**

Scientists have discovered that after the age of 40 the body is no longer able to efficiently repair bone and cartilage in the joint. This results in deterioration and inflammation in the joint, leading to pain.

The natural compound found in FlexJointPlus contains the necessary ingredients needed for the body to rebuild damaged bone and cartilage.

This compound is known as NEM®.

"Essentially, it contains the same elements found in your joints, which are needed to repair and rebuild cartilage and ligaments," explains chief researcher Roger Lewis.

There also have been no adverse side effects reported with the use of NEM®.

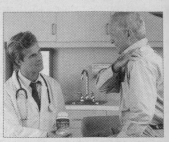

**Approved by U.S. Doctors:** U.S. medical doctors are now recommending the powerful new pill FlexJointPlus. Participants in clinical studies reported noticeable results in just days.

This seems to be another reason why FlexJointPlus's release has triggered such a frenzy of sales.

**RECOMMENDED BY U.S. MEDICAL DOCTORS**

"Based on my 20 years of experience treating people with osteoarthritis, FlexJointPlus receives my highest recommendation to any person suffering from joint pain and stiffness," said Dr. David Vallance, Rheumatologist from Ann Arbor, MI.

"I use FlexJointPlus every day for my stiff and aching joints. I also have my wife and daughter taking it regularly as well," said Dr. Oozer, G.P. from LaSalle, CA.

**OLD FARMER'S ALMANAC READERS GET SPECIAL DISCOUNT SUPPLY**

This is the official release of FlexJointPlus and so for a limited time, the company is offering a special discount supply to our readers. An Order Hotline has been set up for our readers to call, but don't wait. The special offer will not last forever. All you have to do is call TOLL FREE **1-800-540-7740**. The company will do the rest.

IMPORTANT: Due to FlexJoint's recent media exposure, phone lines are often busy. If you call, and do not immediately get through, please be patient and call back. Current supplies of FlexJoint are limited, so consumers that don't get through to the order hotline will have to wait until more inventory is available. Call **1-800-540-7740** today!

# A Reference Compendium

# CALENDAR

## PHASES OF THE MOON

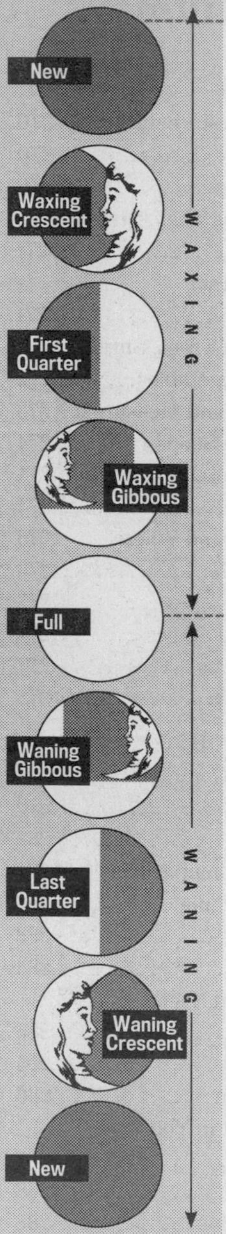

New

Waxing Crescent

First Quarter

Waxing Gibbous

Full

Waning Gibbous

Last Quarter

Waning Crescent

New

WAXING / WANING

## WHEN WILL THE MOON RISE?

Use the following saying to remember the time of moonrise on a day when a Moon phase occurs. Keep in mind that the phase itself may happen earlier or later that day, depending on location.

**The new Moon always rises near sunrise;**

**The first quarter, near noon;**

**The full Moon always rises near sunset;**

**The last quarter, near midnight.**

Moonrise occurs about 50 minutes later each day.

## FULL MOON NAMES

| NAME | MONTH | VARIATIONS |
|---|---|---|
| Full Wolf Moon | JANUARY | Full Greetings Moon |
| Full Snow Moon | FEBRUARY | Full Hungry Moon |
| Full Worm Moon | MARCH | Full Eagle Moon<br>Full Sore Eye Moon<br>Full Sugar Moon<br>Full Wind Strong Moon |
| Full Pink Moon | APRIL | Full Budding Moon<br>Moon When the Geese Lay Eggs |
| Full Flower Moon | MAY | Full Frog Moon<br>Full Planting Moon |
| Full Strawberry Moon | JUNE | Full Hoer Moon<br>Full Hot Moon |
| Full Buck Moon | JULY | Full Raspberry Moon<br>Full Salmon Moon |
| Full Sturgeon Moon | AUGUST | Full Black Cherries Moon<br>Full Flying Up Moon |
| Full Harvest Moon* | SEPTEMBER | Full Corn Moon<br>Full Yellow Leaf Moon |
| Full Hunter's Moon | OCTOBER | Full Falling Leaves Moon<br>Full Migrating Moon |
| Full Beaver Moon | NOVEMBER | Full Frost Moon |
| Full Cold Moon | DECEMBER | Full Long Night Moon |

*The Harvest Moon is always the full Moon closest to the autumnal equinox. If the Harvest Moon occurs in October, the September full Moon is usually called the Corn Moon.

REFERENCE

# THE ORIGIN OF FULL MOON NAMES

Historically, some Native Americans who lived in the area that is now the United States kept track of the seasons by giving a distinctive name to each recurring full Moon. (This name was applied to the entire month in which it occurred.) The names were used by various tribes and/or by colonial Americans, who also brought their own traditions.

## Meanings of Full Moon Names

**JANUARY'S** full Moon was called the **Wolf Moon** because wolves were more often heard at this time.

**FEBRUARY'S** full Moon was called the **Snow Moon** because it was a time of heavy snow. It was also called the **Hungry Moon** because hunting was difficult and hunger often resulted.

**MARCH'S** full Moon was called the **Worm Moon** because, as the weather warmed, wormlike insect larvae emerged from the bark of trees, and other winter homes.

**APRIL'S** full Moon was called the **Pink Moon** because it heralded the appearance of the moss pink, or wild ground phlox—one of the first spring flowers.

**MAY'S** full Moon was called the **Flower Moon** because blossoms were abundant everywhere at this time.

**JUNE'S** full Moon was called the **Strawberry Moon** because it appeared when the strawberry harvest took place.

**JULY'S** full Moon was called the **Buck Moon**; it arrived when a male deer's antlers were in full growth mode.

**AUGUST'S** full Moon was called the **Sturgeon Moon** because this large fish, which is found in the Great Lakes and Lake Champlain, was caught easily at this time.

**SEPTEMBER'S** full Moon was called the **Corn Moon** because this was the time to harvest corn.

The **Harvest Moon** is the full Moon that occurs closest to the autumnal equinox. It can occur in either September or October. Around this time, the Moon rises only about 30 minutes later each night, providing extra light after sunset for harvesting.

**OCTOBER'S** full Moon was called the **Hunter's Moon** because this was the time to hunt in preparation for winter.

**NOVEMBER'S** full Moon was called the **Beaver Moon** because it was the time when beavers finished preparations for winter and retreated to their lodges.

**DECEMBER'S** full Moon was called the **Cold Moon.** It was also called the **Long Night Moon** because nights at this time of year were the longest.

REFERENCE

## THE ORIGIN OF MONTH NAMES

**JANUARY.** For the Roman god Janus, protector of gates and doorways. Janus is depicted with two faces, one looking into the past, the other into the future.

**FEBRUARY.** From the Latin *februa*, "to cleanse." The Roman Februalia was a festival of purification and atonement that took place during this time of year.

**MARCH.** For the Roman god of war, Mars. This was the time of year to resume military campaigns that had been interrupted by winter.

**APRIL.** From the Latin *aperio*, "to open (bud)," because plants begin to grow now.

**MAY.** For the Roman goddess Maia, who oversaw the growth of plants. Also from the Latin *maiores*, "elders," who were celebrated now.

**JUNE.** For the Roman goddess Juno, patroness of marriage and the well-being of women. Also from the Latin *juvenis*, "young people."

**JULY.** To honor Roman dictator Julius Caesar (100 B.C.–44 B.C.). In 46 B.C., with the help of Sosigenes, he developed the Julian calendar.

**AUGUST.** To honor the first Roman emperor (and grandnephew of Julius Caesar), Augustus Caesar (63 B.C.–A.D. 14).

**SEPTEMBER.** From the Latin *septem*, "seven," because this was the seventh month of the early Roman calendar.

**OCTOBER.** From the Latin *octo*, "eight," because this was the eighth month of the early Roman calendar.

**NOVEMBER.** From the Latin *novem*, "nine," because this was the ninth month of the early Roman calendar.

**DECEMBER.** From the Latin *decem*, "ten," because this was the tenth month of the early Roman calendar.

## Easter Dates (2022–25)

Christian churches that follow the Gregorian calendar celebrate Easter on the first Sunday after the paschal full Moon on or just after the vernal equinox.

| YEAR | EASTER |
| --- | --- |
| 2022 | April 17 |
| 2023 | April 9 |
| 2024 | March 31 |
| 2025 | April 20 |

The Julian calendar is used by some churches, including many Eastern Orthodox. The dates below are Julian calendar dates for Easter converted to Gregorian dates.

| YEAR | EASTER |
| --- | --- |
| 2022 | April 24 |
| 2023 | April 16 |
| 2024 | May 5 |
| 2025 | April 20 |

## FRIGGATRISKAIDEKAPHOBIA TRIVIA

*Here are a few facts about Friday the 13th:*

In the 14 possible configurations for the annual calendar (see any perpetual calendar), the occurrence of Friday the 13th is this:

**6 of 14 years have one Friday the 13th.**
**6 of 14 years have two Fridays the 13th.**
**2 of 14 years have three Fridays the 13th.**

No year is without one Friday the 13th, and no year has more than three.

Months that have a Friday the 13th begin on a Sunday.

2022 has a Friday the 13th in May.

Love calendar lore? Find more via Almanac.com/2022.

REFERENCE

## THE ORIGIN OF DAY NAMES

The days of the week were named by ancient Romans with the Latin words for the Sun, the Moon, and the five known planets. These names have survived in European languages, but English names also reflect Anglo-Saxon and Norse influences.

| ENGLISH | LATIN | FRENCH | ITALIAN | SPANISH | ANGLO-SAXON AND NORSE |
|---|---|---|---|---|---|
| SUNDAY | dies Solis (Sol's day) | dimanche | domenica *from the Latin for "Lord's day"* | domingo | Sunnandaeg (Sun's day) |
| MONDAY | dies Lunae (Luna's day) | lundi | lunedì | lunes | Monandaeg (Moon's day) |
| TUESDAY | dies Martis (Mars's day) | mardi | martedì | martes | Tiwesdaeg (Tiw's day) |
| WEDNESDAY | dies Mercurii (Mercury's day) | mercredi | mercoledì | miércoles | Wodnesdaeg (Woden's day) |
| THURSDAY | dies Jovis (Jupiter's day) | jeudi | giovedì | jueves | Thursdaeg (Thor's day) |
| FRIDAY | dies Veneris (Venus's day) | vendredi | venerdì | viernes | Frigedaeg (Frigga's day) |
| SATURDAY | dies Saturni (Saturn's day) | samedi | sabato *from the Latin for "Sabbath"* | sábado | Saeterndaeg (Saturn's day) |

# How to Find the Day of the Week for Any Given Date

*To compute the day of the week for any given date as far back as the mid–18th century, proceed as follows:*

Add the last two digits of the year to one-quarter of the last two digits (discard any remainder), the day of the month, and the month key from the key box below. Divide the sum by 7; the remainder is the day of the week (1 is Sunday, 2 is Monday, and so on). If there is no remainder, the day is Saturday. If you're searching for a weekday prior to 1900, add 2 to the sum before dividing; prior to 1800, add 4. The formula doesn't work for days prior to 1753. From 2000 through 2099, subtract 1 from the sum before dividing.

### KEY
| | |
|---|---|
| JANUARY | 1 |
| LEAP YEAR | 0 |
| FEBRUARY | 4 |
| LEAP YEAR | 3 |
| MARCH | 4 |
| APRIL | 0 |
| MAY | 2 |
| JUNE | 5 |
| JULY | 0 |
| AUGUST | 3 |
| SEPTEMBER | 6 |
| OCTOBER | 1 |
| NOVEMBER | 4 |
| DECEMBER | 6 |

*Example:*

**THE DAYTON FLOOD WAS ON MARCH 25, 1913.**

| | |
|---|---|
| Last two digits of year: | 13 |
| One-quarter of these two digits: | 3 |
| Given day of month: | 25 |
| Key number for March: | 4 |
| **Sum:** | **45** |

*45 ÷ 7 = 6, with a remainder of 3. The flood took place on Tuesday, the third day of the week.*

REFERENCE

# ANIMAL SIGNS OF THE CHINESE ZODIAC

The animal designations of the Chinese zodiac follow a 12-year cycle and are always used in the same sequence. The Chinese year of 354 days begins 3 to 7 weeks into the western 365-day year, so the animal designation changes at that time, rather than on January 1. This year, the Lunar New Year in China starts on February 1.

## RAT

Ambitious and sincere, you can be generous with your money. Compatible with the dragon and the monkey. Your opposite is the horse.

| 1924 | 1936 | 1948 |
| 1960 | 1972 | 1984 |
| 1996 | 2008 | 2020 |

## DRAGON

Robust and passionate, your life is filled with complexity. Compatible with the monkey and the rat. Your opposite is the dog.

| 1928 | 1940 | 1952 |
| 1964 | 1976 | 1988 |
| 2000 | 2012 | 2024 |

## MONKEY

Persuasive, skillful, and intelligent, you strive to excel. Compatible with the dragon and the rat. Your opposite is the tiger.

| 1932 | 1944 | 1956 |
| 1968 | 1980 | 1992 |
| 2004 | 2016 | 2028 |

## OX OR BUFFALO

A leader, you are bright, patient, and cheerful. Compatible with the snake and the rooster. Your opposite is the sheep.

| 1925 | 1937 | 1949 |
| 1961 | 1973 | 1985 |
| 1997 | 2009 | 2021 |

## SNAKE

Strong-willed and intense, you display great wisdom. Compatible with the rooster and the ox. Your opposite is the pig.

| 1929 | 1941 | 1953 |
| 1965 | 1977 | 1989 |
| 2001 | 2013 | 2025 |

## ROOSTER OR COCK

Seeking wisdom and truth, you have a pioneering spirit. Compatible with the snake and the ox. Your opposite is the rabbit.

| 1933 | 1945 | 1957 |
| 1969 | 1981 | 1993 |
| 2005 | 2017 | 2029 |

## TIGER

Forthright and sensitive, you possess great courage. Compatible with the horse and the dog. Your opposite is the monkey.

| 1926 | 1938 | 1950 |
| 1962 | 1974 | 1986 |
| 1998 | 2010 | 2022 |

## HORSE

Physically attractive and popular, you like the company of others. Compatible with the tiger and the dog. Your opposite is the rat.

| 1930 | 1942 | 1954 |
| 1966 | 1978 | 1990 |
| 2002 | 2014 | 2026 |

## DOG

Generous and loyal, you have the ability to work well with others. Compatible with the horse and the tiger. Your opposite is the dragon.

| 1934 | 1946 | 1958 |
| 1970 | 1982 | 1994 |
| 2006 | 2018 | 2030 |

## RABBIT OR HARE

Talented and affectionate, you are a seeker of tranquility. Compatible with the sheep and the pig. Your opposite is the rooster.

| 1927 | 1939 | 1951 |
| 1963 | 1975 | 1987 |
| 1999 | 2011 | 2023 |

## SHEEP OR GOAT

Aesthetic and stylish, you enjoy being a private person. Compatible with the pig and the rabbit. Your opposite is the ox.

| 1931 | 1943 | 1955 |
| 1967 | 1979 | 1991 |
| 2003 | 2015 | 2027 |

## PIG OR BOAR

Gallant and noble, your friends will remain at your side. Compatible with the rabbit and the sheep. Your opposite is the snake.

| 1935 | 1947 | 1959 |
| 1971 | 1983 | 1995 |
| 2007 | 2019 | 2031 |

REFERENCE

## A Table Foretelling the Weather Through All the Lunations of Each Year, or Forever

This table is the result of many years of actual observation and shows what sort of weather will probably follow the Moon's entrance into any of its quarters. For example, the table shows that the week following January 9, 2022, will have snow or rain, because the Moon enters the first quarter on that day at 1:11 P.M. EST. (See the **Left-Hand Calendar Pages, 120-146,** for Moon phases.)

EDITOR'S NOTE: Although the data in this table is taken into consideration in the year-long process of compiling the annual long-range weather forecasts for *The Old Farmer's Almanac,* we rely far more on our projections of solar activity.

| TIME OF CHANGE | SUMMER | WINTER |
|---|---|---|
| Midnight to 2 A.M. | Fair | Hard frost, unless wind is south or west |
| 2 A.M. to 4 A.M. | Cold, with frequent showers | Snow and stormy |
| 4 A.M. to 6 A.M. | Rain | Rain |
| 6 A.M. to 8 A.M. | Wind and rain | Stormy |
| 8 A.M. to 10 A.M. | Changeable | Cold rain if wind is west; snow, if east |
| 10 A.M. to noon | Frequent showers | Cold with high winds |
| Noon to 2 P.M. | Very rainy | Snow or rain |
| 2 P.M. to 4 P.M. | Changeable | Fair and mild |
| 4 P.M. to 6 P.M. | Fair | Fair |
| 6 P.M. to 10 P.M. | Fair if wind is northwest; rain if wind is south or southwest | Fair and frosty if wind is north or northeast; rain or snow if wind is south or southwest |
| 10 P.M. to midnight | Fair | Fair and frosty |

*This table was created more than 180 years ago by Dr. Herschell for the* Boston Courier; *it first appeared in* The Old Farmer's Almanac *in 1834.*

## SAFE ICE THICKNESS*

| ICE THICKNESS | PERMISSIBLE LOAD | ICE THICKNESS | PERMISSIBLE LOAD |
|---|---|---|---|
| 3 inches | Single person on foot | 12 inches | Heavy truck (8-ton gross) |
| 4 inches | Group in single file | 15 inches | 10 tons |
| 7½ inches | Passenger car (2-ton gross) | 20 inches | 25 tons |
| 8 inches | Light truck (2½-ton gross) | 30 inches | 70 tons |
| 10 inches | Medium truck (3½-ton gross) | 36 inches | 110 tons |

**\*Solid, clear, blue/black pond and lake ice**

*The strength value of river ice is 15 percent less. Slush ice has only half the strength of blue ice.*

REFERENCE

## HEAT INDEX °F (°C)

| TEMP. °F (°C) | RELATIVE HUMIDITY (%) | | | | | | | | |
|---|---|---|---|---|---|---|---|---|---|
| | 40 | 45 | 50 | 55 | 60 | 65 | 70 | 75 | 80 |
| 100 (38) | 109 (43) | 114 (46) | 118 (48) | 124 (51) | 129 (54) | 136 (58) | | | |
| 98 (37) | 105 (41) | 109 (43) | 113 (45) | 117 (47) | 123 (51) | 128 (53) | 134 (57) | | |
| 96 (36) | 101 (38) | 104 (40) | 108 (42) | 112 (44) | 116 (47) | 121 (49) | 126 (52) | 132 (56) | |
| 94 (34) | 97 (36) | 100 (38) | 103 (39) | 106 (41) | 110 (43) | 114 (46) | 119 (48) | 124 (51) | 129 (54) |
| 92 (33) | 94 (34) | 96 (36) | 99 (37) | 101 (38) | 105 (41) | 108 (42) | 112 (44) | 116 (47) | 121 (49) |
| 90 (32) | 91 (33) | 93 (34) | 95 (35) | 97 (36) | 100 (38) | 103 (39) | 105 (41) | 109 (43) | 113 (45) |
| 88 (31) | 88 (31) | 89 (32) | 91 (33) | 93 (34) | 95 (35) | 98 (37) | 100 (38) | 103 (39) | 106 (41) |
| 86 (30) | 85 (29) | 87 (31) | 88 (31) | 89 (32) | 91 (33) | 93 (34) | 95 (35) | 97 (36) | 100 (38) |
| 84 (29) | 83 (28) | 84 (29) | 85 (29) | 86 (30) | 88 (31) | 89 (32) | 90 (32) | 92 (33) | 94 (34) |
| 82 (28) | 81 (27) | 82 (28) | 83 (28) | 84 (29) | 84 (29) | 85 (29) | 86 (30) | 88 (31) | 89 (32) |
| 80 (27) | 80 (27) | 80 (27) | 81 (27) | 81 (27) | 82 (28) | 82 (28) | 83 (28) | 84 (29) | 84 (29) |

RISK LEVEL FOR HEAT DISORDERS: CAUTION EXTREME CAUTION DANGER

EXAMPLE: *When the temperature is 88°F (31°C) and the relative humidity is 60 percent, the heat index, or how hot it feels, is 95°F (35°C).*

## THE UV INDEX FOR MEASURING ULTRAVIOLET RADIATION RISK

*The U.S. National Weather Service's daily forecasts of ultraviolet levels use these numbers for various exposure levels:*

| UV INDEX NUMBER | EXPOSURE LEVEL | ACTIONS TO TAKE |
|---|---|---|
| 0, 1, 2 | Low | Wear UV-blocking sunglasses on bright days. In winter, reflection off snow can nearly double UV strength. If you burn easily, cover up and apply SPF 30+ sunscreen. |
| 3, 4, 5 | Moderate | Apply SPF 30+ sunscreen; wear a hat and sunglasses. Stay in shade when sun is strongest. |
| 6, 7 | High | Apply SPF 30+ sunscreen; wear a hat, sunglasses, and protective clothing; limit midday exposure. |
| 8, 9, 10 | Very High | Apply SPF 30+ sunscreen; wear a hat, sunglasses, and protective clothing; limit midday exposure. Seek shade. Unprotected skin will be damaged and can burn quickly. |
| 11 or higher | Extreme | Apply SPF 30+ sunscreen; wear a hat, sunglasses, and protective clothing; avoid midday exposure; seek shade. Unprotected skin can burn in minutes. |

REFERENCE

| 85 | 90 | 95 | 100 |
|---|---|---|---|
| 135 (57) | | | |
| 126 (52) | 131 (55) | | |
| 117 (47) | 122 (50) | 127 (53) | 132 (56) |
| 110 (43) | 113 (45) | 117 (47) | 121 (49) |
| 102 (39) | 105 (41) | 108 (42) | 112 (44) |
| 96 (36) | 98 (37) | 100 (38) | 103 (39) |
| 90 (32) | 91 (33) | 93 (34) | 95 (35) |
| 85 (29) | 86 (30) | 86 (30) | 87 (31) |

# What Are Cooling/Heating Degree Days?

In an attempt to measure the need for air-conditioning, each degree of a day's mean temperature that is above a base temperature, such as 65°F (U.S.) or 18°C (Canada), is considered one cooling degree day. If the daily mean temperature is 75°F, for example, that's 10 cooling degree days.

Similarly, to measure the need for heating fuel consumption, each degree of a day's mean temperature that is below 65°F (18°C) is considered one heating degree. For example, a day with a high of 60°F and low of 40°F results in a mean of 50°, or 15 degrees less than 65°. Hence, that day had 15 heating degree days.

## HOW TO MEASURE HAIL

The **TORRO HAILSTORM INTENSITY SCALE** was introduced by Jonathan Webb of Oxford, England, in 1986 as a means of categorizing hailstorms. The name derives from the private and mostly British research body named the TORnado and storm Research Organisation.

| INTENSITY/DESCRIPTION OF HAIL DAMAGE | |
|---|---|
| H0 | True hail of pea size causes no damage |
| H1 | Leaves and flower petals are punctured and torn |
| H2 | Leaves are stripped from trees and plants |
| H3 | Panes of glass are broken; auto bodies are dented |
| H4 | Some house windows are broken; small tree branches are broken off; birds are killed |
| H5 | Many windows are smashed; small animals are injured; large tree branches are broken off |
| H6 | Shingle roofs are breached; metal roofs are scored; wooden window frames are broken away |
| H7 | Roofs are shattered to expose rafters; autos are seriously damaged |
| H8 | Shingle and tile roofs are destroyed; small tree trunks are split; people are seriously injured |
| H9 | Concrete roofs are broken; large tree trunks are split and knocked down; people are at risk of fatal injuries |
| H10 | Brick houses are damaged; people are at risk of fatal injuries |

## HOW TO MEASURE WIND SPEED

The **BEAUFORT WIND FORCE SCALE** is a common way of estimating wind speed. It was developed in 1805 by Admiral Sir Francis Beaufort of the British Navy to measure wind at sea. We can also use it to measure wind on land.

Admiral Beaufort arranged the numbers 0 to 12 to indicate the strength of the wind from calm, force 0, to hurricane, force 12. Here's a scale adapted to land.

*"Used Mostly at Sea but of Help to All Who Are Interested in the Weather"*

| BEAUFORT FORCE | DESCRIPTION | WHEN YOU SEE OR FEEL THIS EFFECT | WIND SPEED (mph) | (km/h) |
|---|---|---|---|---|
| 0 | CALM | Smoke goes straight up | less than 1 | less than 2 |
| 1 | LIGHT AIR | Wind direction is shown by smoke drift but not by wind vane | 1–3 | 2–5 |
| 2 | LIGHT BREEZE | Wind is felt on the face; leaves rustle; wind vanes move | 4–7 | 6–11 |
| 3 | GENTLE BREEZE | Leaves and small twigs move steadily; wind extends small flags straight out | 8–12 | 12–19 |
| 4 | MODERATE BREEZE | Wind raises dust and loose paper; small branches move | 13–18 | 20–29 |
| 5 | FRESH BREEZE | Small trees sway; waves form on lakes | 19–24 | 30–39 |
| 6 | STRONG BREEZE | Large branches move; wires whistle; umbrellas are difficult to use | 25–31 | 40–50 |
| 7 | NEAR GALE | Whole trees are in motion; walking against the wind is difficult | 32–38 | 51–61 |
| 8 | GALE | Twigs break from trees; walking against the wind is very difficult | 39–46 | 62–74 |
| 9 | STRONG GALE | Buildings suffer minimal damage; roof shingles are removed | 47–54 | 75–87 |
| 10 | STORM | Trees are uprooted | 55–63 | 88–101 |
| 11 | VIOLENT STORM | Widespread damage | 64–72 | 102–116 |
| 12 | HURRICANE | Widespread destruction | 73+ | 117+ |

## RETIRED ATLANTIC HURRICANE NAMES

*These storms have been some of the most destructive and costly.*

| NAME | YEAR | NAME | YEAR | NAME | YEAR | NAME | YEAR |
|---|---|---|---|---|---|---|---|
| Felix | 2007 | Tomas | 2010 | Matthew | 2016 | Florence | 2018 |
| Noel | 2007 | Irene | 2011 | Otto | 2016 | Michael | 2018 |
| Gustav | 2008 | Sandy | 2012 | Harvey | 2017 | Dorian | 2019 |
| Ike | 2008 | Ingrid | 2013 | Irma | 2017 | Eta | 2020 |
| Paloma | 2008 | Erika | 2015 | Maria | 2017 | Iota | 2020 |
| Igor | 2010 | Joaquin | 2015 | Nate | 2017 | Laura | 2020 |

**REFERENCE**

| ATLANTIC TROPICAL (AND SUBTROPICAL) STORM NAMES FOR 2022 | | | EASTERN NORTH-PACIFIC TROPICAL (AND SUBTROPICAL) STORM NAMES FOR 2022 | | |
|---|---|---|---|---|---|
| Alex | Hermine | Owen | Agatha | Ivette | Roslyn |
| Bonnie | Ian | Paula | Blas | Javier | Seymour |
| Colin | Julia | Richard | Celia | Kay | Tina |
| Danielle | Karl | Shary | Darby | Lester | Virgil |
| Earl | Lisa | Tobias | Estelle | Madeline | Winifred |
| Fiona | Martin | Virginie | Frank | Newton | Xavier |
| Gaston | Nicole | Walter | Georgette | Orlene | Yolanda |
| | | | Howard | Paine | Zeke |

The lists above are used in rotation and recycled every 6 years,
e.g., the 2022 list will be used again in 2028.

## How to Measure Hurricane Strength

The **SAFFIR-SIMPSON HURRICANE WIND SCALE** assigns a rating from 1 to 5 based on a hurricane's intensity. It is used to give an estimate of the potential property damage from a hurricane landfall. Wind speed is the determining factor in the scale, as storm surge values are highly dependent on the slope of the continental shelf in the landfall region. Wind speeds are measured at a height of 33 feet (10 meters) using a 1-minute average.

**CATEGORY ONE.** Average wind: 74–95 mph. Significant damage to mobile homes. Some damage to roofing and siding of well-built frame homes. Large tree branches snap and shallow-rooted trees may topple. Power outages may last a few to several days.

Frame homes may sustain major roof damage. Many trees snap or topple, blocking numerous roads. Electricity and water may be unavailable for several days to weeks.

**CATEGORY TWO.** Average wind: 96–110 mph. Mobile homes may be destroyed. Major roof and siding damage to frame homes. Many shallow-rooted trees snap or topple, blocking roads. Widespread power outages could last from several days to weeks. Potable water may be scarce.

**CATEGORY THREE.** Average wind: 111–129 mph. Most mobile homes destroyed.

**CATEGORY FOUR.** Average wind: 130–156 mph. Mobile homes destroyed. Frame homes severely damaged or destroyed. Windborne debris may penetrate protected windows. Most trees snap or topple. Residential areas isolated by fallen trees and power poles. Most of the area uninhabitable for weeks to months.

**CATEGORY FIVE.** Average wind: 157+ mph. Most homes destroyed. Nearly all windows blown out of high-rises. Most of the area uninhabitable for weeks to months.

REFERENCE

## HOW TO MEASURE A TORNADO

The original **FUJITA SCALE** (or F Scale) was developed by Dr. Theodore Fujita to classify tornadoes based on wind damage. All tornadoes, and other severe local windstorms, were assigned a number according to the most intense damage caused by the storm. An enhanced F (EF) scale was implemented in the United States on February 1, 2007. The EF scale uses 3-second gust estimates based on a more detailed system for assessing damage, taking into account different building materials.

| F SCALE | | EF SCALE (U.S.) |
|---|---|---|
| F0 · 40-72 mph (64-116 km/h) | LIGHT DAMAGE | EF0 · 65-85 mph (105-137 km/h) |
| F1 · 73-112 mph (117-180 km/h) | MODERATE DAMAGE | EF1 · 86-110 mph (138-178 km/h) |
| F2 · 113-157 mph (181-253 km/h) | CONSIDERABLE DAMAGE | EF2 · 111-135 mph (179-218 km/h) |
| F3 · 158-207 mph (254-332 km/h) | SEVERE DAMAGE | EF3 · 136-165 mph (219-266 km/h) |
| F4 · 208-260 mph (333-419 km/h) | DEVASTATING DAMAGE | EF4 · 166-200 mph (267-322 km/h) |
| F5 · 261-318 mph (420-512 km/h) | INCREDIBLE DAMAGE | EF5 · over 200 mph (over 322 km/h) |

## Wind/Barometer Table

| BAROMETER (REDUCED TO SEA LEVEL) | WIND DIRECTION | CHARACTER OF WEATHER INDICATED |
|---|---|---|
| 30.00 to 30.20, and steady | WESTERLY | Fair, with slight changes in temperature, for one to two days |
| 30.00 to 30.20, and rising rapidly | WESTERLY | Fair, followed within two days by warmer and rain |
| 30.00 to 30.20, and falling rapidly | SOUTH TO EAST | Warmer, and rain within 24 hours |
| 30.20 or above, and falling rapidly | SOUTH TO EAST | Warmer, and rain within 36 hours |
| 30.20 or above, and falling rapidly | WEST TO NORTH | Cold and clear, quickly followed by warmer and rain |
| 30.20 or above, and steady | VARIABLE | No early change |
| 30.00 or below, and falling slowly | SOUTH TO EAST | Rain within 18 hours that will continue a day or two |
| 30.00 or below, and falling rapidly | SOUTHEAST TO NORTHEAST | Rain, with high wind, followed within two days by clearing, colder |
| 30.00 or below, and rising | SOUTH TO WEST | Clearing and colder within 12 hours |
| 29.80 or below, and falling rapidly | SOUTH TO EAST | Severe storm of wind and rain imminent; in winter, snow or cold wave within 24 hours |
| 29.80 or below, and falling rapidly | EAST TO NORTH | Severe northeast gales and heavy rain or snow, followed in winter by cold wave |
| 29.80 or below, and rising rapidly | GOING TO WEST | Clearing and colder |

**NOTE:** *A barometer should be adjusted to show equivalent sea-level pressure for the altitude at which it is to be used. A change of 100 feet in elevation will cause a decrease of ¹⁄₁₀ inch in the reading.*

REFERENCE

## WINDCHILL TABLE

As wind speed increases, your body loses heat more rapidly, making the air feel colder than it really is. The combination of cold temperature and high wind can create a cooling effect so severe that exposed flesh can freeze.

| | **Calm** | **35** | **30** | **25** | **20** | **15** | **10** | **5** | **0** | **-5** | **-10** | **-15** | **-20** | **-25** | **-30** | **-35** |
|---|---|---|---|---|---|---|---|---|---|---|---|---|---|---|---|---|
| | **5** | 31 | 25 | 19 | 13 | 7 | 1 | -5 | -11 | -16 | -22 | -28 | -34 | -40 | -46 | -52 |
| | **10** | 27 | 21 | 15 | 9 | 3 | -4 | -10 | -16 | -22 | -28 | -35 | -41 | -47 | -53 | -59 |
| | **15** | 25 | 19 | 13 | 6 | 0 | -7 | -13 | -19 | -26 | -32 | -39 | -45 | -51 | -58 | -64 |
| | **20** | 24 | 17 | 11 | 4 | -2 | -9 | -15 | -22 | -29 | -35 | -42 | -48 | -55 | -61 | -68 |
| | **25** | 23 | 16 | 9 | 3 | -4 | -11 | -17 | -24 | -31 | -37 | -44 | -51 | -58 | -64 | -71 |
| | **30** | 22 | 15 | 8 | 1 | -5 | -12 | -19 | -26 | -33 | -39 | -46 | -53 | -60 | -67 | -73 |
| | **35** | 21 | 14 | 7 | 0 | -7 | -14 | -21 | -27 | -34 | -41 | -48 | -55 | -62 | -69 | -76 |
| | **40** | 20 | 13 | 6 | -1 | -8 | -15 | -22 | -29 | -36 | -43 | -50 | -57 | -64 | -71 | -78 |
| | **45** | 19 | 12 | 5 | -2 | -9 | -16 | -23 | -30 | -37 | -44 | -51 | -58 | -65 | -72 | -79 |
| | **50** | 19 | 12 | 4 | -3 | -10 | -17 | -24 | -31 | -38 | -45 | -52 | -60 | -67 | -74 | -81 |
| | **55** | 18 | 11 | 4 | -3 | -11 | -18 | -25 | -32 | -39 | -46 | -54 | -61 | -68 | -75 | -82 |
| | **60** | 17 | 10 | 3 | -4 | -11 | -19 | -26 | -33 | -40 | -48 | -55 | -62 | -69 | -76 | -84 |

*Column group header: TEMPERATURE (°F); Row group label: WIND SPEED (mph)*

**FROSTBITE OCCURS IN** ▨ 30 MINUTES ▨ 10 MINUTES ▨ 5 MINUTES

**EXAMPLE:** *When the temperature is 15°F and the wind speed is 30 miles per hour, the windchill, or how cold it feels, is -5°F. See a Celsius version of this table via Almanac.com/2022.*
–courtesy of National Weather Service

# HOW TO MEASURE EARTHQUAKES

In 1979, seismologists developed a measurement of earthquake size called **MOMENT MAGNITUDE.** It is more accurate than the previously used Richter scale, which is precise only for earthquakes of a certain size and at a certain distance from a seismometer. All earthquakes can now be compared on the same magnitude scale.

| MAGNITUDE | DESCRIPTION | EFFECT |
|---|---|---|
| LESS THAN 3 | MICRO | GENERALLY NOT FELT |
| 3-3.9 | MINOR | OFTEN FELT, LITTLE DAMAGE |
| 4-4.9 | LIGHT | SHAKING, SOME DAMAGE |
| 5-5.9 | MODERATE | SLIGHT TO MAJOR DAMAGE |
| 6-6.9 | STRONG | DESTRUCTIVE |
| 7-7.9 | MAJOR | SEVERE DAMAGE |
| 8 OR MORE | GREAT | SERIOUS DAMAGE |

## A GARDENER'S WORST PHOBIAS

| NAME OF FEAR | OBJECT FEARED |
|---|---|
| Alliumphobia | Garlic |
| Anthophobia | Flowers |
| Apiphobia | Bees |
| Arachnophobia | Spiders |
| Botanophobia | Plants |
| Bufonophobia | Toads |
| Dendrophobia | Trees |
| Entomophobia | Insects |
| Lachanophobia | Vegetables |
| Melissophobia | Bees |
| Mottephobia | Moths |
| Myrmecophobia | Ants |
| Ornithophobia | Birds |
| Ranidaphobia | Frogs |
| Rupophobia | Dirt |
| Scoleciphobia | Worms |
| Spheksophobia | Wasps |

## PLANTS FOR LAWNS

*Choose varieties that suit your soil and your climate. All of these can withstand mowing and considerable foot traffic.*

Ajuga or bugleweed (*Ajuga reptans*)
Corsican mint (*Mentha requienii*)
Dwarf cinquefoil (*Potentilla tabernaemontani*)
English pennyroyal (*Mentha pulegium*)
Green Irish moss (*Sagina subulata*)
Pearly everlasting (*Anaphalis margaritacea*)
Roman chamomile (*Chamaemelum nobile*)
Rupturewort (*Herniaria glabra*)
Speedwell (*Veronica officinalis*)
Stonecrop (*Sedum ternatum*)
Sweet violets (*Viola odorata* or *V. tricolor*)
Thyme (*Thymus serpyllum*)
White clover (*Trifolium repens*)
Wild strawberries (*Fragaria virginiana*)
Wintergreen or partridgeberry (*Mitchella repens*)

## Lawn-Growing Tips

• Test your soil: The pH balance should be 6.2 to 6.7; less than 6.0 puts your lawn at risk for fungal diseases. If the pH is too low, correct it with liming, best done in the fall.

• The best time to apply fertilizer is just before it rains.

• If you put lime and fertilizer on your lawn, spread half of it as you walk north to south, the other half as you walk east to west to cut down on missed areas.

• Any feeding of lawns in the fall should be done with a low-nitrogen, slow-acting fertilizer.

• In areas of your lawn where tree roots compete with the grass, apply some extra fertilizer to benefit both.

• Moss and sorrel in lawns usually means poor soil, poor aeration or drainage, or excessive acidity.

• Control weeds by promoting healthy lawn growth with natural fertilizers in spring and early fall.

• Raise the level of your lawn-mower blades during the hot summer days. Taller grass resists drought better than short.

• You can reduce mowing time by redesigning your lawn, reducing sharp corners and adding sweeping curves.

• During a drought, let the grass grow longer between mowings and reduce fertilizer.

• Water your lawn early in the morning or in the evening.

# Flowers and Herbs That Attract Butterflies

Allium . . . . . . . . . . . . . . . . . . . . . . . . *Alltum*
Aster . . . . . . . . . . . . . . . . . . . . . . . . *Aster*
Bee balm . . . . . . . . . . . . . . . . . . . *Monarda*
Butterfly bush . . . . . . . . . . . . . . . *Buddleia*
Catmint . . . . . . . . . . . . . . . . . . . . .*Nepeta*
Clove pink . . . . . . . . . . . . . . . . . .*Dianthus*
Cornflower . . . . . . . . . . . . . . . . . .*Centaurea*
Creeping thyme . . . . . . *Thymus serpyllum*
Daylily . . . . . . . . . . . . . . . . . .*Hemerocallis*
Dill . . . . . . . . . . . . . . *Anethum graveolens*
False indigo . . . . . . . . . . . . . . . . . *Baptisia*
Fleabane . . . . . . . . . . . . . . . . . . . . *Erigeron*
Floss flower . . . . . . . . . . . . . . . . *Ageratum*
Globe thistle . . . . . . . . . . . . . . . . *Echinops*
Goldenrod . . . . . . . . . . . . . . . . . . *Solidago*
Helen's flower . . . . . . . . . . . . . . .*Helenium*
Hollyhock . . . . . . . . . . . . . . . . . . . . . *Alcea*
Honeysuckle . . . . . . . . . . . . . . . . *Lonicera*
Lavender . . . . . . . . . . . . . . *Lavandula*
Lilac . . . . . . . . . . . . . . . . . . . . . *Syringa*
Lupine . . . . . . . . . . . . . . . . . . . . . . .*Lupinus*
Lychnis . . . . . . . . . . . . . . . . . . . . . . *Lychnis*

Mallow . . . . . . . . . . . . . . . . . . . . . *Malva*
Mealycup sage . . . . . . . . .*Salvia farinacea*
Milkweed . . . . . . . . . . . . . . . . . . *Asclepias*
Mint . . . . . . . . . . . . . . . . . . . . . . . . *Mentha*
Oregano . . . . . . . . . . . *Origanum vulgare*
Pansy . . . . . . . . . . . . . . . . . . . . . . . *Viola*
Parsley . . . . . . . . . . . . . . . *Petroselinum*
*crispum*
Phlox . . . . . . . . . . . . . . . . . . . . . . . .*Phlox*
Privet . . . . . . . . . . . . . . . . . . . . .*Ligustrum*
Purple coneflower . . *Echinacea purpurea*
Rock cress . . . . . . . . . . . . . . . . . . . .*Arabis*
Sea holly . . . . . . . . . . . . . . . . . . . *Eryngium*
Shasta daisy . . . . . . . . . . . *Leucanthemum*
Snapdragon . . . . . . . . . . . . . . . *Antirrhinum*
Stonecrop . . . . . . . . . . . . . . . . . . . .*Sedum*
Sweet alyssum . . . . . . . . . . . . .*Lobularia*
Sweet marjoram . . . . *Origanum majorana*
Sweet rocket . . . . . . . . . . . . . . . *Hesperis*
Tickseed . . . . . . . . . . . . . . . . . . . *Coreopsis*
Verbena . . . . . . . . . . . . . . . . . . . .*Verbena*
Zinnia . . . . . . . . . . . . . . . . . . . . . . . *Zinnia*

# FLOWERS* THAT ATTRACT HUMMINGBIRDS

Beard tongue . . . . . . . . . . . . . . . *Penstemon*
Bee balm . . . . . . . . . . . . . . . . . . .*Monarda*
Butterfly bush . . . . . . . . . . . . . . . *Buddleia*
Catmint . . . . . . . . . . . . . . . . . . . . .*Nepeta*
Clove pink . . . . . . . . . . . . . . . . . .*Dianthus*
Columbine . . . . . . . . . . . . . . . . *Aquilegia*
Coral bells . . . . . . . . . . . . . . . .*Heuchera*
Daylily . . . . . . . . . . . . . . . . . . *Hemerocallis*
Desert candle . . . . . . . . . . . . . . . . .*Yucca*
Flag iris . . . . . . . . . . . . . . . . . . . . . . . *Iris*
Flowering tobacco . . . . . . *Nicotiana alata*
Foxglove . . . . . . . . . . . . . . . . . . . *Digitalis*
Larkspur . . . . . . . . . . . . . . . .*Delphinium*
Lily . . . . . . . . . . . . . . . . . . . . . . . . . *Lilium*
Lupine . . . . . . . . . . . . . . . . . . . . . . .*Lupinus*
Petunia . . . . . . . . . . . . . . . . . . . . . *Petunia*
Pincushion flower . . . . . . . . . . . *Scabiosa*
Red-hot poker . . . . . . . . . . . . . *Kniphofia*
Scarlet sage . . . . . . . . . . *Salvia splendens*

Soapwort . . . . . . . . . . . . . . . . . .*Saponaria*
Summer phlox . . . . . . . .*Phlox paniculata*
Trumpet honeysuckle . . . . . . . . *Lonicera*
*sempervirens*
Verbena . . . . . . . . . . . . . . . . . . . .*Verbena*
Weigela . . . . . . . . . . . . . . . . . . . .*Weigela*

**\*NOTE:** *Choose varieties in red and orange shades, if available.*

# pH PREFERENCES OF TREES, SHRUBS, FLOWERS, AND VEGETABLES

An accurate soil test will indicate your soil pH and will specify the amount of lime or sulfur that is needed to bring it up or down to the appropriate level. A pH of 6.5 is just about right for most home gardens, since most plants thrive in the 6.0 to 7.0 (slightly acidic to neutral) range. Some plants (azaleas, blueberries) prefer more strongly acidic soil in the 4.0 to 6.0 range, while a few (asparagus, plums) do best in soil that is neutral to slightly alkaline. Acidic, or sour, soil (below 7.0) is counteracted by applying finely ground limestone, and alkaline, or sweet, soil (above 7.0) is treated with ground sulfur.

| COMMON NAME | OPTIMUM pH RANGE | COMMON NAME | OPTIMUM pH RANGE | COMMON NAME | OPTIMUM pH RANGE |
|---|---|---|---|---|---|
| **TREES AND SHRUBS** | | Bee balm | 6.0–7.5 | Snapdragon | 5.5–7.0 |
| Apple | 5.0–6.5 | Begonia | 5.5–7.0 | Sunflower | 6.0–7.5 |
| Azalea | 4.5–6.0 | Black-eyed Susan | 5.5–7.0 | Tulip | 6.0–7.0 |
| Beautybush | 6.0–7.5 | Bleeding heart | 6.0–7.5 | Zinnia | 5.5–7.0 |
| Birch | 5.0–6.5 | Canna | 6.0–8.0 | | |
| Blackberry | 5.0–6.0 | Carnation | 6.0–7.0 | **VEGETABLES** | |
| Blueberry | 4.0–5.0 | Chrysanthemum | 6.0–7.5 | Asparagus | 6.0–8.0 |
| Boxwood | 6.0–7.5 | Clematis | 5.5–7.0 | Bean | 6.0–7.5 |
| Cherry, sour | 6.0–7.0 | Coleus | 6.0–7.0 | Beet | 6.0–7.5 |
| Crab apple | 6.0–7.5 | Coneflower, purple | 5.0–7.5 | Broccoli | 6.0–7.0 |
| Dogwood | 5.0–7.0 | Cosmos | 5.0–8.0 | Brussels sprout | 6.0–7.5 |
| Fir, balsam | 5.0–6.0 | Crocus | 6.0–8.0 | Cabbage | 6.0–7.5 |
| Hemlock | 5.0–6.0 | Daffodil | 6.0–6.5 | Carrot | 5.5–7.0 |
| Hydrangea, blue-flowered | 4.0–5.0 | Dahlia | 6.0–7.5 | Cauliflower | 5.5–7.5 |
| Hydrangea, pink-flowered | 6.0–7.0 | Daisy, Shasta | 6.0–8.0 | Celery | 5.8–7.0 |
| | | Daylily | 6.0–8.0 | Chive | 6.0–7.0 |
| Juniper | 5.0–6.0 | Delphinium | 6.0–7.5 | Collard | 6.5–7.5 |
| Laurel, mountain | 4.5–6.0 | Foxglove | 6.0–7.5 | Corn | 5.5–7.0 |
| Lemon | 6.0–7.5 | Geranium | 6.0–8.0 | Cucumber | 5.5–7.0 |
| Lilac | 6.0–7.5 | Gladiolus | 5.0–7.0 | Eggplant | 6.0–7.0 |
| Maple, sugar | 6.0–7.5 | Hibiscus | 6.0–8.0 | Garlic | 5.5–8.0 |
| Oak, white | 5.0–6.5 | Hollyhock | 6.0–8.0 | Kale | 6.0–7.5 |
| Orange | 6.0–7.5 | Hyacinth | 6.5–7.5 | Leek | 6.0–8.0 |
| Peach | 6.0–7.0 | Iris, blue flag | 5.0–7.5 | Lettuce | 6.0–7.0 |
| Pear | 6.0–7.5 | Lily-of-the-valley | 4.5–6.0 | Okra | 6.0–7.0 |
| Pecan | 6.4–8.0 | Lupine | 5.0–6.5 | Onion | 6.0–7.0 |
| Plum | 6.0–8.0 | Marigold | 5.5–7.5 | Pea | 6.0–7.5 |
| Raspberry, red | 5.5–7.0 | Morning glory | 6.0–7.5 | Pepper, sweet | 5.5–7.0 |
| Rhododendron | 4.5–6.0 | Narcissus, trumpet | 5.5–6.5 | Potato | 4.8–6.5 |
| Willow | 6.0–8.0 | Nasturtium | 5.5–7.5 | Pumpkin | 5.5–7.5 |
| | | Pansy | 5.5–6.5 | Radish | 6.0–7.0 |
| **FLOWERS** | | Peony | 6.0–7.5 | Spinach | 6.0–7.5 |
| Alyssum | 6.0–7.5 | Petunia | 6.0–7.5 | Squash, crookneck | 6.0–7.5 |
| Aster, New England | 6.0–8.0 | Phlox, summer | 6.0–8.0 | Squash, Hubbard | 5.5–7.0 |
| Baby's breath | 6.0–7.0 | Poppy, oriental | 6.0–7.5 | Swiss chard | 6.0–7.0 |
| Bachelor's button | 6.0–7.5 | Rose, hybrid tea | 5.5–7.0 | Tomato | 5.5–7.5 |
| | | Rose, rugosa | 6.0–7.0 | Watermelon | 5.5–6.5 |

Get growing via Almanac.com/2022.

REFERENCE

## PRODUCE WEIGHTS AND MEASURES

### VEGETABLES

**ASPARAGUS:** 1 pound = 3 cups chopped

**BEANS (STRING):** 1 pound = 4 cups chopped

**BEETS:** 1 pound (5 medium) = 2½ cups chopped

**BROCCOLI:** 1 pound = 6 cups chopped

**CABBAGE:** 1 pound = 4½ cups shredded

**CARROTS:** 1 pound = 3½ cups sliced or grated

**CELERY:** 1 pound = 4 cups chopped

**CUCUMBERS:** 1 pound (2 medium) = 4 cups sliced

**EGGPLANT:** 1 pound = 4 cups chopped = 2 cups cooked

**GARLIC:** 1 clove = 1 teaspoon chopped

**LEEKS:** 1 pound = 4 cups chopped = 2 cups cooked

**MUSHROOMS:** 1 pound = 5 to 6 cups sliced = 2 cups cooked

**ONIONS:** 1 pound = 4 cups sliced = 2 cups cooked

**PARSNIPS:** 1 pound = 1½ cups cooked, puréed

**PEAS:** 1 pound whole = 1 to 1½ cups shelled

**POTATOES:** 1 pound (3 medium) sliced = 2 cups mashed

**PUMPKIN:** 1 pound = 4 cups chopped = 2 cups cooked and drained

**SPINACH:** 1 pound = ¾ to 1 cup cooked

**SQUASHES (SUMMER):** 1 pound = 4 cups grated = 2 cups sliced and cooked

**SQUASHES (WINTER):** 2 pounds = 2½ cups cooked, puréed

**SWEET POTATOES:** 1 pound = 4 cups grated = 1 cup cooked, puréed

**SWISS CHARD:** 1 pound = 5 to 6 cups packed leaves = 1 to 1½ cups cooked

**TOMATOES:** 1 pound (3 or 4 medium) = 1½ cups seeded pulp

**TURNIPS:** 1 pound = 4 cups chopped = 2 cups cooked, mashed

### FRUIT

**APPLES:** 1 pound (3 or 4 medium) = 3 cups sliced

**BANANAS:** 1 pound (3 or 4 medium) = 1¾ cups mashed

**BERRIES:** 1 quart = 3½ cups

**DATES:** 1 pound = 2½ cups pitted

**LEMON:** 1 whole = 1 to 3 tablespoons juice; 1 to 1½ teaspoons grated rind

**LIME:** 1 whole = 1½ to 2 tablespoons juice

**ORANGE:** 1 medium = 6 to 8 tablespoons juice; 2 to 3 tablespoons grated rind

**PEACHES:** 1 pound (4 medium) = 3 cups sliced

**PEARS:** 1 pound (4 medium) = 2 cups sliced

**RHUBARB:** 1 pound = 2 cups cooked

**STRAWBERRIES:** 1 quart = 4 cups sliced

REFERENCE

## SOWING VEGETABLE SEEDS

| | |
|---|---|
| **SOW OR PLANT IN COOL WEATHER** | Beets, broccoli, brussels sprouts, cabbage, lettuce, onions, parsley, peas, radishes, spinach, Swiss chard, turnips |
| **SOW OR PLANT IN WARM WEATHER** | Beans, carrots, corn, cucumbers, eggplant, melons, okra, peppers, squashes, tomatoes |
| **SOW OR PLANT FOR ONE CROP PER SEASON** | Corn, eggplant, leeks, melons, peppers, potatoes, spinach (New Zealand), squashes, tomatoes |
| **RESOW FOR ADDITIONAL CROPS** | Beans, beets, cabbage, carrots, kohlrabi, lettuce, radishes, rutabagas, spinach, turnips |

## A Beginner's Vegetable Garden

The vegetables suggested below are common, easy-to-grow crops. Make 11 rows, 10 feet long, with at least 18 inches between them. Ideally, the rows should run north and south to take full advantage of the sun. This garden, planted as suggested, can feed a family of four for one summer, with a little extra for canning and freezing or giving away.

**ROW**
1  Zucchini (4 plants)
2  Tomatoes (5 plants, staked)
3  Peppers (6 plants)
4  Cabbage

**ROW**
5   Bush beans
6   Lettuce
7   Beets
8   Carrots
9   Swiss chard
10  Radishes
11  Marigolds
    (to discourage rabbits!)

## SOIL FIXES

If you have **sandy** soil, amend with compost; humus; aged manure; sawdust with extra nitrogen; heavy, clay-rich soil.

If your soil contains a lot of **silt**, amend with coarse sand (not beach sand) or gravel and compost, or aged horse manure mixed with fresh straw.

If your soil is dense with **clay**, amend with coarse sand (not beach sand) and compost.

### TO IMPROVE YOUR SOIL, ADD THE PROPER AMENDMENT(S) . . .

**bark, ground:** made from various tree barks; improves soil structure

**compost:** an excellent conditioner

**leaf mold:** decomposed leaves, which add nutrients and structure to soil

**lime:** raises the pH of acidic soil and helps to loosen clay soil.

**manure:** best if composted; never add fresh ("hot") manure; is a good conditioner

**coarse sand (not beach sand):** improves drainage in clay soil

**topsoil:** usually used with another amendment; replaces existing soil

## IMPORTANT TIMES TO . . .

| | . . . FERTILIZE: | . . . WATER: |
|---|---|---|
| BEANS | After heavy bloom and set of pods | When flowers form and during pod-forming and picking |
| BEETS | At time of planting | Before soil gets bone dry |
| BROCCOLI | 3 weeks after transplanting | Continuously for 4 weeks after transplanting |
| BRUSSELS SPROUTS | 3 weeks after transplanting | Continuously for 4 weeks after transplanting |
| CABBAGE | 2 weeks after transplanting | Frequently in dry weather |
| CARROTS | 5 to 6 weeks after sowing | Before soil gets bone-dry |
| CAULIFLOWER | 3 to 4 weeks after transplanting | Frequently |
| CELERY | At time of transplanting, and after 2 months | Frequently |
| CORN | When 8 to 10 inches tall, and when first silk appears | When tassels form and when cobs swell |
| CUCUMBERS | 1 week after bloom, and every 3 weeks thereafter | Frequently |
| LETTUCE | 3 weeks after transplanting | Frequently |
| MELONS | 1 week after bloom, and again 3 weeks later | Once a week |
| ONION SETS | At time of planting, and then every 2 weeks until bulbing begins | In early stage to get plants going |
| PARSNIPS | 1 year before planting | Before soil gets bone-dry |
| PEAS | After heavy bloom and set of pods | When flowers form and during pod-forming and picking |
| PEPPERS | At time of planting, and after first fruit-set | Need a steady supply |
| POTATO TUBERS | At bloom time or time of second hilling | When the size of marbles |
| PUMPKINS | Just before vines start to run, when plants are about 1 foot tall | Only during drought conditions |
| RADISHES | Before spring planting | Need plentiful, consistent moisture |
| SPINACH | When plants are one-third grown | Frequently |
| SQUASHES, SUMMER & WINTER | When first blooms appear | Frequently |
| TOMATOES | When fruit are 1 inch in diameter, and then every 2 weeks | For 3 to 4 weeks after transplanting and when flowers and fruit form |

REFERENCE

## HOW TO GROW HERBS

| HERB | START SEEDS INDOORS (WEEKS BEFORE LAST SPRING FROST) | START SEEDS OUTDOORS (WEEKS BEFORE/AFTER LAST SPRING FROST) | HEIGHT/ SPREAD (INCHES) | SOIL | LIGHT** |
|---|---|---|---|---|---|
| BASIL* | 6–8 | Anytime after | 12–24/12 | Rich, moist | ○ |
| BORAGE* | Not recommended | Anytime after | 12–36/12 | Rich, well-drained, dry | ○ |
| CHERVIL | Not recommended | 3–4 before | 12–24/8 | Rich, moist | ◑ |
| CHIVES | 8–10 | 3–4 before | 12–18/18 | Rich, moist | ○ |
| CILANTRO/ CORIANDER | Not recommended | Anytime after | 12–36/6 | Light | ○◑ |
| DILL | Not recommended | 4–5 before | 36–48/12 | Rich | ○ |
| FENNEL | 4–6 | Anytime after | 48–80/18 | Rich | ○ |
| LAVENDER, ENGLISH* | 8–12 | 1–2 before | 18–36/24 | Moderately fertile, well-drained | ○ |
| LAVENDER, FRENCH | Not recommended | Not recommended | 18–36/24 | Moderately fertile, well-drained | ○ |
| LEMON BALM* | 6–10 | 2–3 before | 12–24/18 | Rich, well-drained | ○◑ |
| LOVAGE* | 6–8 | 2–3 before | 36–72/36 | Fertile, sandy | ○◑ |
| MINT | Not recommended | Not recommended | 12–24/18 | Rich, moist | ◑ |
| OREGANO* | 6–10 | Anytime after | 12–24/18 | Poor | ○ |
| PARSLEY* | 10–12 | 3–4 before | 18–24/6–8 | Medium-rich | ◑ |
| ROSEMARY* | 8–10 | Anytime after | 48–72/48 | Not too acidic | ○ |
| SAGE | 6–10 | 1–2 before | 12–48/30 | Well-drained | ○ |
| SORREL | 6–10 | 2–3 after | 20–48/12–14 | Rich, organic | ○ |
| SUMMER SAVORY | 4–6 | Anytime after | 4–15/6 | Medium-rich | ○ |
| SWEET CICELY | 6–8 | 2–3 after | 36–72/36 | Moderately fertile, well-drained | ○◑ |
| TARRAGON, FRENCH | Not recommended | Not recommended | 24–36/12 | Well-drained | ○◑ |
| THYME, COMMON* | 6–10 | 2–3 before | 2–12/7–12 | Fertile, well-drained | ○◑ |

*Recommend minimum soil temperature of 70°F to germinate

** ○ FULL SUN   ◑ PARTIAL SHADE

REFERENCE

## GROWTH TYPE

| |
|---|
| Annual |
| Annual, biennial |
| Annual, biennial |
| Perennial |
| Annual |
| Annual |
| Annual |
| Perennial |
| Tender perennial |
| Perennial |
| Perennial |
| Perennial |
| Tender perennial |
| Biennial |
| Tender perennial |
| Perennial |
| Perennial |
| Annual |
| Perennial |
| Perennial |
| Perennial |

## DRYING HERBS

Before drying, remove any dead or diseased leaves or stems. Wash under cool water, shake off excess water, and put on a towel to dry completely. Air drying preserves an herb's essential oils; use for sturdy herbs. A microwave dries herbs more quickly, so mold is less likely to develop; use for moist, tender herbs.

**HANGING METHOD:** Gather four to six stems of fresh herbs in a bunch and tie with string, leaving a loop for hanging. Or, use a rubber band with a paper clip attached to it. Hang the herbs in a warm, well-ventilated area, out of direct sunlight, until dry. For herbs that have full seed heads, such as dill or coriander, use a paper bag. Punch holes in the bag for ventilation, label it, and put the herb bunch into the bag before you tie a string around the top of the bag. The average drying time is 1 to 3 weeks.

**MICROWAVE METHOD:** This is better for small quantities, such as a cup or two at a time. Arrange a single layer of herbs between two paper towels and put them in the microwave for 1 to 2 minutes on high power. Let the leaves cool. If they are not dry, reheat for 30 seconds and check again. Repeat as needed. Let cool. Do not overcook, or the herbs will lose their flavor.

## STORING HERBS AND SPICES

**FRESH HERBS:** Dill and parsley will keep for about 2 weeks with stems immersed in a glass of water tented with a plastic bag. Most other fresh herbs (and greens) will keep for short periods unwashed and refrigerated in tightly sealed plastic bags with just enough moisture to prevent wilting. For longer storage, use moisture- and gas-permeable paper and cellophane. Plastic cuts off oxygen to the plants and promotes spoilage.

**SPICES AND DRIED HERBS:** Store in a cool, dry place.

## COOKING WITH HERBS

A **BOUQUET GARNI** is usually made with bay leaves, thyme, and parsley tied with string or wrapped in cheesecloth. Use to flavor casseroles and soups. Remove after cooking.

**FINES HERBES** use equal amounts of fresh parsley, tarragon, chives, and chervil chopped fine. Commonly used in French cooking, they make a fine omelet or add zest to soups and sauces. Add to salads and butter sauces or sprinkle on noodles, soups, and stews.

## HOW TO GROW BULBS

| | COMMON NAME | LATIN NAME | HARDINESS ZONE | SOIL | LIGHT* | SPACING (INCHES) |
|---|---|---|---|---|---|---|
| **SPRING-PLANTED BULBS** | ALLIUM | *Allium* | 3–10 | Well-drained/moist | ○ | 12 |
| | BEGONIA, TUBEROUS | *Begonia* | 10–11 | Well-drained/moist | ◐● | 12–15 |
| | BLAZING STAR/ GAYFEATHER | *Liatris* | 7–10 | Well-drained | ○ | 6 |
| | CALADIUM | *Caladium* | 10–11 | Well-drained/moist | ◐● | 8–12 |
| | CALLA LILY | *Zantedeschia* | 8–10 | Well-drained/moist | ○◐ | 8–24 |
| | CANNA | *Canna* | 8–11 | Well-drained/moist | ○ | 12–24 |
| | CYCLAMEN | *Cyclamen* | 7–9 | Well-drained/moist | ◐ | 4 |
| | DAHLIA | *Dahlia* | 9–11 | Well-drained/fertile | ○ | 12–36 |
| | DAYLILY | *Hemerocallis* | 3–10 | Adaptable to most soils | ○◐ | 12–24 |
| | FREESIA | *Freesia* | 9–11 | Well-drained/moist/sandy | ○◐ | 2–4 |
| | GARDEN GLOXINIA | *Incarvillea* | 4–8 | Well-drained/moist | ○ | 12 |
| | GLADIOLUS | *Gladiolus* | 4–11 | Well-drained/fertile | ○◐ | 4–9 |
| | IRIS | *Iris* | 3–10 | Well-drained/sandy | ○ | 3–6 |
| | LILY, ASIATIC/ORIENTAL | *Lilium* | 3–8 | Well-drained | ○◐ | 8–12 |
| | PEACOCK FLOWER | *Tigridia* | 8–10 | Well-drained | ○ | 5–6 |
| | SHAMROCK/SORREL | *Oxalis* | 5–9 | Well-drained | ○◐ | 4–6 |
| | WINDFLOWER | *Anemone* | 3–9 | Well-drained/moist | ○◐ | 3–6 |
| **FALL-PLANTED BULBS** | BLUEBELL | *Hyacinthoides* | 4–9 | Well-drained/fertile | ○◐ | 4 |
| | CHRISTMAS ROSE/ HELLEBORE | *Helleborus* | 4–8 | Neutral–alkaline | ○◐ | 18 |
| | CROCUS | *Crocus* | 3–8 | Well-drained/moist/fertile | ○◐ | 4 |
| | DAFFODIL | *Narcissus* | 3–10 | Well-drained/moist/fertile | ○◐ | 6 |
| | FRITILLARY | *Fritillaria* | 3–9 | Well-drained/sandy | ○◐ | 3 |
| | GLORY OF THE SNOW | *Chionodoxa* | 3–9 | Well-drained/moist | ○◐ | 3 |
| | GRAPE HYACINTH | *Muscari* | 4–10 | Well-drained/moist/fertile | ○◐ | 3–4 |
| | IRIS, BEARDED | *Iris* | 3–9 | Well-drained | ○◐ | 4 |
| | IRIS, SIBERIAN | *Iris* | 4–9 | Well-drained | ○◐ | 4 |
| | ORNAMENTAL ONION | *Allium* | 3–10 | Well-drained/moist/fertile | ○ | 12 |
| | SNOWDROP | *Galanthus* | 3–9 | Well-drained/moist/fertile | ○◐ | 3 |
| | SNOWFLAKE | *Leucojum* | 5–9 | Well-drained/moist/sandy | ○◐ | 4 |
| | SPRING STARFLOWER | *Ipheion uniflorum* | 6–9 | Well-drained loam | ○◐ | 3–6 |
| | STAR OF BETHLEHEM | *Ornithogalum* | 5–10 | Well-drained/moist | ○◐ | 2–5 |
| | STRIPED SQUILL | *Puschkinia scilloides* | 3–9 | Well-drained | ○◐ | 6 |
| | TULIP | *Tulipa* | 4–8 | Well-drained/fertile | ○◐ | 3–6 |
| | WINTER ACONITE | *Eranthis* | 4–9 | Well-drained/moist/fertile | ○◐ | 3 |

| DEPTH (INCHES) | BLOOMING SEASON | HEIGHT (INCHES) | NOTES |
|---|---|---|---|
| 3–4 | Spring to summer | 6–60 | Usually pest-free; a great cut flower |
| 1–2 | Summer to fall | 8–18 | North of Zone 10, lift in fall |
| 4 | Summer to fall | 8–20 | An excellent flower for drying; north of Zone 7, plant in spring, lift in fall |
| 2 | Summer | 8–24 | North of Zone 10, plant in spring, lift in fall |
| 1–4 | Summer | 24–36 | Fragrant; north of Zone 8, plant in spring, lift in fall |
| Level | Summer | 18–60 | North of Zone 8, plant in spring, lift in fall |
| 1–2 | Spring to fall | 3–12 | Naturalizes well in warm areas; north of Zone 7, lift in fall |
| 4–6 | Late summer | 12–60 | North of Zone 9, lift in fall |
| 2 | Summer | 12–36 | Mulch in winter in Zones 3 to 6 |
| 2 | Summer | 12–24 | Fragrant; can be grown outdoors in warm climates |
| 3–4 | Summer | 6–20 | Does well in woodland settings |
| 3–6 | Early summer to early fall | 12–80 | North of Zone 10, lift in fall |
| 4 | Spring to late summer | 3–72 | Divide and replant rhizomes every two to five years |
| 4–6 | Early summer | 36 | Fragrant; self-sows; requires excellent drainage |
| 4 | Summer | 18–24 | North of Zone 8, lift in fall |
| 2 | Summer | 2–12 | Plant in confined area to control |
| 2 | Early summer | 3–18 | North of Zone 6, lift in fall |
| 3–4 | Spring | 8–20 | Excellent for borders, rock gardens and naturalizing |
| 1–2 | Spring | 12 | Hardy, but requires shelter from strong, cold winds |
| 3 | Early spring | 5 | Naturalizes well in grass |
| 6 | Early spring | 14–24 | Plant under shrubs or in a border |
| 3 | Midspring | 6–30 | Different species can be planted in rock gardens, woodland gardens, or borders |
| 3 | Spring | 4–10 | Self-sows easily; plant in rock gardens, raised beds, or under shrubs |
| 2–3 | Late winter to spring | 6–12 | Use as a border plant or in wildflower and rock gardens; self-sows easily |
| 4 | Early spring to early summer | 3–48 | Naturalizes well; a good cut flower |
| 4 | Early spring to midsummer | 18–48 | An excellent cut flower |
| 3–4 | Late spring to early summer | 6–60 | Usually pest-free; a great cut flower |
| 3 | Spring | 6–12 | Best when clustered and planted in an area that will not dry out in summer |
| 4 | Spring | 6–18 | Naturalizes well |
| 3 | Spring | 4–6 | Fragrant; naturalizes easily |
| 4 | Spring to summer | 6–24 | North of Zone 5, plant in spring, lift in fall |
| 3 | Spring | 4–6 | Naturalizes easily; makes an attractive edging |
| 4–6 | Early to late spring | 8–30 | Excellent for borders, rock gardens, and naturalizing |
| 2–3 | Late winter to spring | 2–4 | Self-sows and naturalizes easily |

REFERENCE

## SUBSTITUTIONS FOR COMMON INGREDIENTS

| ITEM | QUANTITY | SUBSTITUTION |
|------|----------|--------------|
| BAKING POWDER | 1 teaspoon | ¼ teaspoon baking soda plus ¼ teaspoon cornstarch plus ½ teaspoon cream of tartar |
| BUTTERMILK | 1 cup | 1 tablespoon lemon juice or vinegar plus milk to equal 1 cup; or 1 cup plain yogurt |
| CHOCOLATE, UNSWEETENED | 1 ounce | 3 tablespoons cocoa plus 1 tablespoon unsalted butter, shortening, or vegetable oil |
| CRACKER CRUMBS | ¾ cup | 1 cup dry bread crumbs; or 1 tablespoon quick-cooking oats (for thickening) |
| CREAM, HEAVY | 1 cup | ¾ cup milk plus ⅓ cup melted unsalted butter (this will not whip) |
| CREAM, LIGHT | 1 cup | ⅞ cup milk plus 3 tablespoons melted, unsalted butter |
| CREAM, SOUR | 1 cup | ⅞ cup buttermilk or plain yogurt plus 3 tablespoons melted, unsalted butter |
| CREAM, WHIPPING | 1 cup | ⅔ cup well-chilled evaporated milk, whipped; or 1 cup nonfat dry milk powder whipped with 1 cup ice water |
| EGG | 1 whole | 2 yolks plus 1 tablespoon cold water; or 3 tablespoons vegetable oil plus 1 tablespoon water (for baking); or 2 to 3 tablespoons mayonnaise (for cakes) |
| EGG WHITE | 1 white | 2 teaspoons meringue powder plus 3 tablespoons water, combined |
| FLOUR, ALL-PURPOSE | 1 cup | 1 cup plus 3 tablespoons cake flour (not advised for cookies or quick breads); or 1 cup self-rising flour (omit baking powder and salt from recipe) |
| FLOUR, CAKE | 1 cup | 1 cup minus 3 tablespoons sifted all-purpose flour plus 3 tablespoons cornstarch |
| FLOUR, SELF-RISING | 1 cup | 1 cup all-purpose flour plus 1½ teaspoons baking powder plus ¼ teaspoon salt |
| HERBS, DRIED | 1 teaspoon | 1 tablespoon fresh, minced and packed |
| HONEY | 1 cup | 1¼ cups sugar plus ½ cup liquid called for in recipe (such as water or oil); or 1 cup pure maple syrup |
| KETCHUP | 1 cup | 1 cup tomato sauce plus ¼ cup sugar plus 3 tablespoons apple-cider vinegar plus ½ teaspoon salt plus pinch of ground cloves combined; or 1 cup chili sauce |
| LEMON JUICE | 1 teaspoon | ½ teaspoon vinegar |
| MAYONNAISE | 1 cup | 1 cup sour cream or plain yogurt; or 1 cup cottage cheese (puréed) |
| MILK, SKIM | 1 cup | ⅓ cup instant nonfat dry milk plus ¾ cup water |

REFERENCE

| ITEM | QUANTITY | SUBSTITUTION |
|---|---|---|
| MILK, TO SOUR | 1 cup | 1 tablespoon vinegar or lemon juice plus milk to equal 1 cup. Stir and let stand 5 minutes. |
| MILK, WHOLE | 1 cup | ½ cup evaporated whole milk plus ½ cup water; or ¾ cup 2 percent milk plus ¼ cup half-and-half |
| MOLASSES | 1 cup | 1 cup honey or dark corn syrup |
| MUSTARD, DRY | 1 teaspoon | 1 tablespoon prepared mustard less 1 teaspoon liquid from recipe |
| OAT BRAN | 1 cup | 1 cup wheat bran or rice bran or wheat germ |
| OATS, OLD-FASHIONED | 1 cup | 1 cup steel-cut Irish or Scotch oats |
| QUINOA | 1 cup | 1 cup millet or couscous (whole wheat cooks faster) or bulgur |
| SUGAR, DARK-BROWN | 1 cup | 1 cup light-brown sugar, packed; or 1 cup granulated sugar plus 2 to 3 tablespoons molasses |
| SUGAR, GRANULATED | 1 cup | 1 cup firmly packed brown sugar; or 1¾ cups confectioners' sugar (makes baked goods less crisp); or 1 cup superfine sugar |
| SUGAR, LIGHT-BROWN | 1 cup | 1 cup granulated sugar plus 1 to 2 tablespoons molasses; or ½ cup dark-brown sugar plus ½ cup granulated sugar |
| SWEETENED CONDENSED MILK | 1 can (14 oz.) | 1 cup evaporated milk plus 1¼ cups granulated sugar. Combine and heat until sugar dissolves. |
| VANILLA BEAN | 1-inch bean | 1 teaspoon vanilla extract |
| VINEGAR, APPLE-CIDER | — | malt, white-wine, or rice vinegar |
| VINEGAR, BALSAMIC | 1 tablespoon | 1 tablespoon red- or white-wine vinegar plus ½ teaspoon sugar |
| VINEGAR, RED-WINE | — | white-wine, sherry, champagne, or balsamic vinegar |
| VINEGAR, RICE | — | apple-cider, champagne, or white-wine vinegar |
| VINEGAR, WHITE-WINE | — | apple-cider, champagne, fruit (raspberry), rice, or red-wine vinegar |
| YEAST | 1 cake (⅗ oz.) | 1 package (¼ ounce) or 1 scant tablespoon active dried yeast |
| YOGURT, PLAIN | 1 cup | 1 cup sour cream (thicker; less tart) or buttermilk (thinner; use in baking, dressings, sauces) |

REFERENCE

## TYPES OF FAT

One way to minimize your total blood cholesterol is to manage the amount and types of fat in your diet. Aim for monounsaturated and polyunsaturated fats; avoid saturated and trans fats.

**MONOUNSATURATED FAT** lowers LDL (bad cholesterol) and may raise HDL (good cholesterol) or leave it unchanged; found in almonds, avocados, canola oil, cashews, olive oil, peanut oil, and peanuts.

**POLYUNSATURATED FAT** lowers LDL and may lower HDL; includes omega-3 and omega-6 fatty acids; found in corn oil, cottonseed oil, fish such as salmon and tuna, safflower oil, sesame seeds, soybeans, and sunflower oil.

**SATURATED FAT** raises both LDL and HDL; found in chocolate, cocoa butter, coconut oil, dairy products (milk, butter, cheese, ice cream), egg yolks, palm oil, and red meat.

**TRANS FAT** raises LDL and lowers HDL; a type of fat common in many processed foods, such as most margarines (especially stick), vegetable shortening, partially hydrogenated vegetable oil, many commercial fried foods (doughnuts, french fries), and commercial baked goods (cookies, crackers, cakes).

## Calorie-Burning Comparisons

If you hustle through your chores to get to the fitness center, relax. You're getting a great workout already. The left-hand column lists "chore" exercises, the middle column shows the number of calories burned per minute per pound of body weight, and the right-hand column lists comparable "recreational" exercises. For example, a 150-pound person forking straw bales burns 9.45 calories per minute, the same workout he or she would get playing basketball.

| | | |
|---|---|---|
| Chopping with an ax, fast | 0.135 | Skiing, cross country, uphill |
| Climbing hills, with 44-pound load | 0.066 | Swimming, crawl, fast |
| Digging trenches | 0.065 | Skiing, cross country, steady walk |
| Forking straw bales | 0.063 | Basketball |
| Chopping down trees | 0.060 | Football |
| Climbing hills, with 9-pound load | 0.058 | Swimming, crawl, slow |
| Sawing by hand | 0.055 | Skiing, cross country, moderate |
| Mowing lawns | 0.051 | Horseback riding, trotting |
| Scrubbing floors | 0.049 | Tennis |
| Shoveling coal | 0.049 | Aerobic dance, medium |
| Hoeing | 0.041 | Weight training, circuit training |
| Stacking firewood | 0.040 | Weight lifting, free weights |
| Shoveling grain | 0.038 | Golf |
| Painting houses | 0.035 | Walking, normal pace, asphalt road |
| Weeding | 0.033 | Table tennis |
| Shopping for food | 0.028 | Cycling, 5.5 mph |
| Mopping floors | 0.028 | Fishing |
| Washing windows | 0.026 | Croquet |
| Raking | 0.025 | Dancing, ballroom |
| Driving a tractor | 0.016 | Drawing, standing position |

REFERENCE

## FREEZER STORAGE TIME
*(freezer temperature 0°F or colder)*

| PRODUCT | MONTHS IN FREEZER |
|---|---|

**FRESH MEAT**
Beef . . . . . . . . . . . . . . . . . . . . . . . . . 6 to 12
Lamb . . . . . . . . . . . . . . . . . . . . . . . . . 6 to 9
Veal . . . . . . . . . . . . . . . . . . . . . . . . . . 6 to 9
Pork . . . . . . . . . . . . . . . . . . . . . . . . . . 4 to 6
Ground beef, veal, lamb, pork . . . . 3 to 4
Frankfurters . . . . . . . . . . . . . . . . . . . 1 to 2
Sausage, fresh pork . . . . . . . . . . . . . 1 to 2
Cold cuts . . . . . . . . . . Not recommended

**FRESH POULTRY**
Chicken, turkey (whole) . . . . . . . . . . . . 12
Chicken, turkey (pieces) . . . . . . . . 6 to 9
Cornish game hen, game birds . . . 6 to 9
Giblets . . . . . . . . . . . . . . . . . . . . . . . . 3 to 4

**COOKED POULTRY**
Breaded, fried . . . . . . . . . . . . . . . . . . . . . 4
Pieces, plain . . . . . . . . . . . . . . . . . . . . . . 4
Pieces covered with broth, gravy . . . . . 6

**FRESH FISH AND SEAFOOD**
Clams, mussels, oysters, scallops,
   shrimp . . . . . . . . . . . . . . . . . . . . . . . 3 to 6
Fatty fish (bluefish, mackerel, perch,
   salmon) . . . . . . . . . . . . . . . . . . . . . . 2 to 3
Lean fish (flounder, haddock, sole) . . . . 6

**FRESH FRUIT (PREPARED FOR FREEZING)**
All fruit except those
   listed below . . . . . . . . . . . . . . . . 10 to 12
Avocados, bananas, plantains . . . . . . . . 3
Lemons, limes, oranges . . . . . . . . . 4 to 6

**FRESH VEGETABLES (PREPARED FOR FREEZING)**
Beans, beets, bok choy, broccoli,
   brussels sprouts, cabbage, carrots,
   cauliflower, celery, corn, greens,
   kohlrabi, leeks, mushrooms, okra,
   onions, peas, peppers, soybeans,
   spinach, summer squashes . . . 10 to 12
Asparagus, rutabagas, turnips . . 8 to 10
Artichokes, eggplant . . . . . . . . . . . 6 to 8
Tomatoes (overripe or sliced) . . . . . . . 2
Bamboo shoots, cucumbers, endive,
   lettuce, radishes, watercress . . . . . . . .
   . . . . . . . . . . . . . . . . . Not recommended

| PRODUCT | MONTHS IN FREEZER |
|---|---|

**CHEESE** (except those listed below) . . . 6
Cottage cheese, cream cheese, feta,
   goat, fresh mozzarella, Neufchâtel,
   Parmesan, processed cheese (opened)
   . . . . . . . . . . . . . . . . . . Not recommended

**DAIRY PRODUCTS**
Margarine (not diet) . . . . . . . . . . . . . . 12
Butter . . . . . . . . . . . . . . . . . . . . . . . . 6 to 9
Cream, half-and-half . . . . . . . . . . . . . . . 4
Milk . . . . . . . . . . . . . . . . . . . . . . . . . . . . . 3
Ice cream . . . . . . . . . . . . . . . . . . . . . 1 to 2

## FREEZING HINTS

**FOR MEALS**, remember that a quart container holds four servings, and a pint container holds two servings.

**TO PREVENT STICKING**, spread the food to be frozen (berries, hamburgers, cookies, etc.) on a cookie sheet and freeze until solid. Then place in plastic bags and freeze.

**LABEL FOODS** for easy identification. Write the name of the food, number of servings, and date of freezing on containers or bags.

**FREEZE FOODS** as quickly as possible by placing them directly against the sides of the freezer.

**ARRANGE FREEZER** into sections for each food category.

**IF POWER IS INTERRUPTED**, or if the freezer is not operating normally, do not open the freezer door. Food in a loaded freezer will usually stay frozen for 2 days if the freezer door remains closed during that time period.

## PLASTICS

In your quest to go green, use this guide to use and sort plastic. The number, usually found with a triangle symbol on a container, indicates the type of resin used to produce the plastic. Visit **EARTH911.COM** for recycling information in your state.

**PETE**

**NUMBER 1** · *PETE or PET (polyethylene terephthalate)*
IS USED IN . . . . . . . . . . . . microwavable food trays; salad dressing, soft drink, water, and juice bottles
STATUS . . . . . . . . . . . . . . . hard to clean; absorbs bacteria and flavors; avoid reusing
IS RECYCLED TO MAKE . . . carpet, furniture, new containers, Polar fleece

**HDPE**

**NUMBER 2** · *HDPE (high-density polyethylene)*
IS USED IN . . . . . . . . . . . . household cleaner and shampoo bottles, milk jugs, yogurt tubs
STATUS . . . . . . . . . . . . . . transmits no known chemicals into food
IS RECYCLED TO MAKE . . . detergent bottles, fencing, floor tiles, pens

**V**

**NUMBER 3** · *V or PVC (vinyl)*
IS USED IN . . . . . . . . . . . . cooking oil bottles, clear food packaging, mouthwash bottles
STATUS . . . . . . . . . . . . . . . is believed to contain phalates that interfere with hormonal development; avoid
IS RECYCLED TO MAKE . . . cables, mudflaps, paneling, roadway gutters

**LDPE**

**NUMBER 4** · *LDPE (low-density polyethylene)*
IS USED IN . . . . . . . . . . . . bread and shopping bags, carpet, clothing, furniture
STATUS . . . . . . . . . . . . . . transmits no known chemicals into food
IS RECYCLED TO MAKE . . . envelopes, floor tiles, lumber, trash-can liners

**PP**

**NUMBER 5** · *PP (polypropylene)*
IS USED IN . . . . . . . . . . . . ketchup bottles, medicine and syrup bottles, drinking straws
STATUS . . . . . . . . . . . . . . transmits no known chemicals into food
IS RECYCLED TO MAKE . . . battery cables, brooms, ice scrapers, rakes

**PS**

**NUMBER 6** · *PS (polystyrene)*
IS USED IN . . . . . . . . . . . . disposable cups and plates, egg cartons, take-out containers
STATUS . . . . . . . . . . . . . . is believed to leach styrene, a possible human carcinogen, into food; avoid
IS RECYCLED TO MAKE . . . foam packaging, insulation, light switchplates, rulers

**OTHER**

**NUMBER 7** · *Other (miscellaneous)*
IS USED IN . . . . . . . . . . . . 3- and 5-gallon water jugs, nylon, some food containers
STATUS . . . . . . . . . . . . . . contains bisphenol A, which has been linked to heart disease and obesity; avoid
IS RECYCLED TO MAKE . . . . custom-made products

## HOW MUCH DO YOU NEED?

### WALLPAPER

Before choosing your wallpaper, keep in mind that wallpaper with little or no pattern to match at the seams and the ceiling will be the easiest to apply, thus resulting in the least amount of wasted wallpaper. If you choose a patterned wallpaper, a small repeating pattern will result in less waste than a large repeating pattern. And a pattern that is aligned horizontally (matching on each column of paper) will waste less than one that drops or alternates its pattern (matching on every other column).

#### TO DETERMINE THE AMOUNT OF WALL SPACE YOU'RE COVERING:

• Measure the length of each wall, add these figures together, and multiply by the height of the walls to get the area (square footage) of the room's walls.

• Calculate the square footage of each door, window, and other opening in the room. Add these figures together and subtract the total from the area of the room's walls.

• Take that figure and multiply by 1.15, to account for a waste rate of about 15 percent in your wallpaper project. You'll end up with a target amount to purchase when you shop.

• Wallpaper is sold in single, double, and triple rolls. Coverage can vary, so be sure to refer to the roll's label for the proper square footage. (The average coverage for a double roll, for example, is 56 square feet.) After choosing a paper, divide the coverage figure (from the label) into the total square footage of the walls of the room you're papering. Round the answer up to the nearest whole number. This is the number of rolls you need to buy.

• Save leftover wallpaper rolls, carefully wrapped to keep clean.

### INTERIOR PAINT

Estimate your room size and paint needs before you go to the store. Running out of a custom color halfway through the job could mean disaster. For the sake of the following exercise, assume that you have a 10x15-foot room with an 8-foot ceiling. The room has two doors and two windows.

#### FOR WALLS

Measure the total distance (perimeter) around the room:

 (10 ft. + 15 ft.) x 2 = 50 ft.

Multiply the perimeter by the ceiling height to get the total wall area:

 50 ft. x 8 ft. = 400 sq. ft.

Doors are usually 21 square feet (there are two in this exercise):

 21 sq. ft. x 2 = 42 sq. ft.

Windows average 15 square feet (there are two in this exercise):

 15 sq. ft. x 2 = 30 sq. ft.

Take the total wall area and subtract the area for the doors and windows to get the wall surface to be painted:

 400 sq. ft. (wall area)
 - 42 sq. ft. (doors)
 - 30 sq. ft. (windows)
 ───────────────
 328 sq. ft.

As a rule of thumb, one gallon of quality paint will usually cover 400 square feet. One quart will cover 100 square feet. Because you need to cover 328 square feet in this example, one gallon will be adequate to give one coat of paint to the walls. (Coverage will be affected by the porosity and texture of the surface. In addition, bright colors may require a minimum of two coats.)

## METRIC CONVERSION

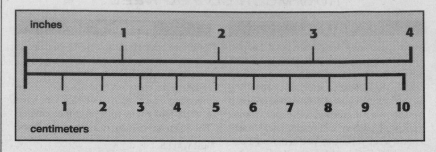

| U.S. MEASURE | X THIS = NUMBER | METRIC EQUIVALENT | METRIC MEASURE | X THIS = NUMBER | U.S. EQUIVALENT |
|---|---|---|---|---|---|
| inch | 2.54 | centimeter | | 0.39 | inch |
| foot | 30.48 | centimeter | | 0.033 | foot |
| yard | 0.91 | meter | | 1.09 | yard |
| mile | 1.61 | kilometer | | 0.62 | mile |
| square inch | 6.45 | square centimeter | | 0.15 | square inch |
| square foot | 0.09 | square meter | | 10.76 | square foot |
| square yard | 0.8 | square meter | | 1.2 | square yard |
| square mile | 2.59 | square kilometer | | 0.39 | square mile |
| acre | 0.4 | hectare | | 2.47 | acre |
| ounce | 28.0 | gram | | 0.035 | ounce |
| pound | 0.45 | kilogram | | 2.2 | pound |
| short ton (2,000 pounds) | 0.91 | metric ton | | 1.10 | short ton |
| ounce | 30.0 | milliliter | | 0.034 | ounce |
| pint | 0.47 | liter | | 2.1 | pint |
| quart | 0.95 | liter | | 1.06 | quart |
| gallon | 3.8 | liter | | 0.26 | gallon |

If you know the U.S. measurement and want to convert it to metric, multiply it by the number in the left shaded column (example: 1 inch equals 2.54 centimeters). If you know the metric measurement, multiply it by the number in the right shaded column (example: 2 meters equals 2.18 yards).

REFERENCE

# Where Do You Fit in Your Family Tree?

Technically it's known as consanguinity; that is, the quality or state of being related by blood or descended from a common ancestor. These relationships are shown below for the genealogy of six generations of one family. *–family tree information courtesy of Frederick H. Rohles*

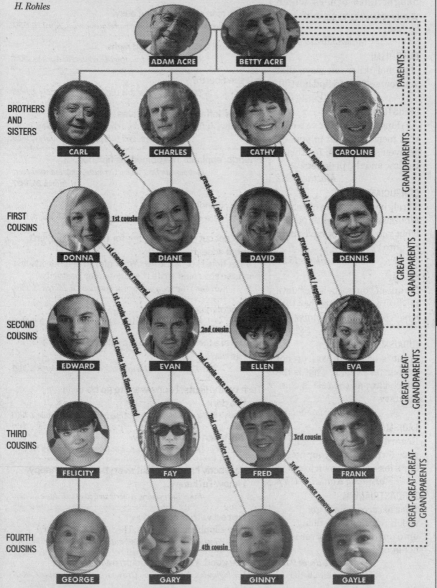

## The Golden Rule
*(It's true in all faiths.)*

**BRAHMANISM:**

This is the sum of duty: Do naught unto others which would cause you pain if done to you.

*Mahabharata 5:1517*

**BUDDHISM:**

Hurt not others in ways that you yourself would find hurtful.

*Udana-Varga 5:18*

**CHRISTIANITY:**

All things whatsoever ye would that men should do to you, do ye even so to them; for this is the law and the prophets.

*Matthew 7:12*

**CONFUCIANISM:**

Surely it is the maxim of loving-kindness: Do not unto others what you would not have them do unto you.

*Analects 15:23*

**ISLAM:**

No one of you is a believer until he desires for his brother that which he desires for himself.

*Sunnah*

**JUDAISM:**

What is hateful to you, do not to your fellow man. That is the entire Law; all the rest is commentary.

*Talmud, Shabbat 31a*

**TAOISM:**

Regard your neighbor's gain as your own gain and your neighbor's loss as your own loss.

*T'ai Shang Kan Ying P'ien*

**ZOROASTRIANISM:**

That nature alone is good which refrains from doing unto another whatsoever is not good for itself.

*Dadistan-i-dinik 94:5*
–courtesy of Elizabeth Pool

## FAMOUS LAST WORDS

**Waiting, are they? Waiting, are they? Well—let 'em wait.**
(To an attending doctor who attempted to comfort him by saying, "General, I fear the angels are waiting for you.")
*–Ethan Allen, American Revolutionary general, d. February 12, 1789*

**A dying man can do nothing easy.**
*–Benjamin Franklin, American statesman, d. April 17, 1790*

**Now I shall go to sleep. Good night.**
*–Lord George Byron, English writer, d. April 19, 1824*

**Is it the Fourth?**
*–Thomas Jefferson, 3rd U.S. president, d. July 4, 1826*

**Thomas Jefferson—still survives . . .**
(Actually, Jefferson had died earlier that same day.)
*–John Adams, 2nd U.S. president, d. July 4, 1826*

**Friends, applaud. The comedy is finished.**
*–Ludwig van Beethoven, German-Austrian composer, d. March 26, 1827*

**Moose . . . Indian . . .**
*–Henry David Thoreau, American writer, d. May 6, 1862*

**Go on, get out—last words are for fools who haven't said enough.**
(To his housekeeper, who urged him to tell her his last words so she could write them down for posterity.)
*–Karl Marx, German political philosopher, d. March 14, 1883*

**Is it not meningitis?**
*–Louisa M. Alcott, American writer, d. March 6, 1888*

**How were the receipts today at Madison Square Garden?**
*–P. T. Barnum, American entrepreneur, d. April 7, 1891*

**Turn up the lights, I don't want to go home in the dark.**
*–O. Henry (William Sidney Porter), American writer, d. June 4, 1910*

**Get my swan costume ready.**
*–Anna Pavlova, Russian ballerina, d. January 23, 1931*

**Is everybody happy? I want everybody to be happy. I know I'm happy.**
*–Ethel Barrymore, American actress, d. June 18, 1959*

**I'm bored with it all.**
(Before slipping into a coma. He died 9 days later.)
*–Winston Churchill, English statesman, d. January 24, 1965*

**You be good. You'll be in tomorrow. I love you.**
*–Alex, highly intelligent African Gray parrot, d. September 6, 2007*

REFERENCE